TRADE ASSOCIATIONS MONOGRAPHS

THE COMMERCIAL BANKING INDUSTRY
The American Bankers Association

THE CONSUMER FINANCE INDUSTRY
National Consumer Finance Association

LIFE INSURANCE COMPANIES AS
FINANCIAL INSTITUTIONS
Life Insurance Association of America

MANAGEMENT INVESTMENT COMPANIES
Investment Company Institute

MORTGAGE COMPANIES: THEIR PLACE
IN THE FINANCIAL STRUCTURE
*Miles L. Colean, for the
Mortgage Bankers Association of America*

MUTUAL SAVINGS BANKING: BASIC CHARACTERISTICS
AND ROLE IN THE NATIONAL ECONOMY
National Association of Mutual Savings Banks

PROPERTY AND CASUALTY INSURANCE COMPANIES:
THEIR ROLE AS FINANCIAL INTERMEDIARIES
*American Mutual Insurance Alliance
Association of Casualty and Surety Companies
National Board of Fire Underwriters*

THE SAVINGS AND LOAN BUSINESS: ITS PURPOSES,
FUNCTIONS, AND ECONOMIC JUSTIFICATION
*Leon T. Kendall, for the
United States Savings and Loan League*

In addition to the Trade Associations Monographs, the Committee for Economic Development is publishing for the Commission on Money and Credit

THE FEDERAL RESERVE AND THE TREASURY: ANSWERS TO QUESTIONS FROM THE COMMISSION ON MONEY AND CREDIT

and fifty-nine individual essays organized into nine separate volumes, each centered around a particular aspect of monetary and fiscal policy. Their titles and the contributing authors are as follows:

IMPACTS OF MONETARY POLICY

Daniel B. Suits; Robert Eisner and Robert H. Strotz, with a bibliography by G. R. Post; Edwin Kuh and John R. Meyer; Leo Grebler and Sherman J. Maisel; Charlotte DeMonte Phelps; Irwin Friend

STABILIZATION POLICIES

E. Cary Brown, Robert M. Solow, Albert Ando, and John Kareken; Milton Friedman and David Meiselman; Lawrence E. Thompson; Arthur M. Okun; Merton H. Miller; Allan H. Meltzer; Oswald Brownlee and Alfred Conrad

MONETARY MANAGEMENT

Frank M. Tamagna; Warren L. Smith; Clark Warburton; Michael D. Reagan; C. P. Kindleberger; Robert Z. Aliber

FISCAL AND DEBT MANAGEMENT POLICIES

William Fellner; Richard A. Musgrave; James Tobin; James R. Schlesinger; Paul H. Cootner; Irving Auerbach; Ralph K. Huitt; John Lindeman

FEDERAL CREDIT AGENCIES

George F. Break; Jack Guttentag; Ernest Bloch; D. Gale Johnson; Dale E. Hathaway; George S. Tolley; John McCroskey

FEDERAL CREDIT PROGRAMS

Stewart Johnson; Warren A. Law; James W. McKie; D. Gale Johnson; James Gillies; Robert C. Turner and Ross M. Robertson; J. Fred Weston

PRIVATE CAPITAL MARKETS

Irwin Friend; Hyman P. Minsky; Raymond W. Goldsmith

PRIVATE FINANCIAL INSTITUTIONS

Paul M. Horvitz; Deane Carson and Paul Cootner; Victor L. Andrews; Thomas G. Gies, Thomas Mayer, and Edward C. Ettin; Lawrence L. Werboff and Marvin E. Rozen; Fred H. Klopstock; E. Gordon Keith

INFLATION, GROWTH, AND EMPLOYMENT

Joseph E. Conard; Jesse W. Markham; Franklyn D. Holzman; John W. Kendrick; Daniel Creamer; Stanley Lebergott; Lawrence R. Klein and Ronald G. Bodkin; Tibor and Anne Scitovsky

THE COMMERCIAL BANKING INDUSTRY

PRENTICE-HALL INTERNATIONAL, INC.
London · Tokyo · Sydney · Paris
PRENTICE-HALL OF CANADA, LTD.
PRENTICE-HALL DE MEXICO, S.A.

The American Bankers Association

'THE COMMERCIAL
BANKING INDUSTRY

A MONOGRAPH
PREPARED FOR THE

Commission on Money and Credit

Prentice-Hall, Inc.

Englewood Cliffs, N.J. | *1962*

DR. NORMAN A. WIGGINS

© 1962 by Prentice-Hall, Inc., Englewood Cliffs, N.J.

All rights reserved. No part of this book may be repro-
duced in any form, by mimeograph or any other means,
without permission in writing from the publishers.

Library of Congress Catalog Card No.: 62-15503

Printed in the United States of America
15282-C

The Commission on Money and Credit was established in 1957 as an independent organization by the unanimous vote of the Board of Trustees of the Committee for Economic Development. The bylaws governing the Commission on Money and Credit state that "It shall be the responsibility of the Commission to initiate studies into the United States monetary and financial system."

This volume was especially prepared for the Commission on Money and Credit as part of its research program leading to the publication in June 1961 of its final report: *Money and Credit: Their Influence on Jobs, Prices, and Growth*. It is published by direction of the Commission according to its bylaws as a contribution to the understanding of the monetary and financial system of the United States. It is one of more than 100 research studies prepared for the Commission by trade organizations, individual scholars, the Federal Reserve System, and the Treasury of the United States.

A selected group of such papers will be published for the Commission by the Information Division of the Committee for Economic Development in accordance with commitments to The Ford Foundation and the Merrill Foundation which provided main financial support for the Commission.

Publication of this volume does not necessarily constitute endorsement of such study by the Commission, its Advisory Board, its Research Staff, or any member of any board or committee, or any officer of the Committee for Economic Development, The Ford Foundation, the Merrill Foundation, or any other organization participating in the work of the Commission.

882600

FOREWORD

One facet of the Commission on Money and Credit's investigation was an inquiry into the functioning of our financial system in order to arrive at a judgment of the adequacy of that system and its regulation to serve the needs of a growing economy.

In addition to examining other sources of information and having special studies prepared, the Commission also sought the advice, experience, and opinion of practitioners in the financial area. In this latter connection The American Bankers Association was invited to prepare a monograph on the commercial banking industry.

In soliciting the monograph, the Commission indicated the desirability of having it provide information on the following six topics:

1. The nature of government regulation of commercial banking, including tax treatment, and its impact upon the functioning of the industry.
2. The operations and practices of the industry, in terms of flow of funds, portfolio practices, liquidity requirements, and so forth.
3. The role of commercial banking in the economy, in terms of its influence upon economic growth, its contribution to economic stability, and its impact upon the allocation of resources.
4. The effects of monetary-debt management policy upon the industry and the role of commercial banking in transmitting these policies throughout the economy.
5. The structure and competitive position of commercial banking, both within itself and vis-à-vis other financial intermediaries.
6. The views of the commercial banking industry regarding possible changes in regulatory or tax provisions.

The American Bankers Association responded willingly to the invitation of the Commission and was most cooperative in working out with the staff of the Commission the scope and detailed outline of the planned monograph. The preparation of the monograph itself was a large task, and the finished product was a valuable contribution to the Commission.

In making its request to the ABA for a monograph on commercial banking, the Commission indicated its desire and expectation to publish important background and research materials which it used in the course of its work. We are pleased that the Association consented to the inclusion of the monograph among the supporting documents of the Commission and agreed to revise for publication the original paper in order to make this further contribution to the general fund of knowledge on the nature of commercial banking and its role in the economy.

On behalf of the Commission and its staff we would like to express our thanks to The American Bankers Association for the preparation of this study.

BERTRAND FOX
Research Director

ELI SHAPIRO
Deputy Research Director

December 1961

PREFACE

The American Bankers Association is pleased to respond to an invitation from the Commission on Money and Credit to prepare a monograph on commercial banking, which it hopes will be helpful to the Commission in its study of our monetary and credit system. The Association, aware of the need for a thoroughgoing objective study of the functioning of our financial mechanism, welcomes the opportunity to present the views of the commercial banking industry.

A special Banking Monograph Committee was appointed by the Association in the spring of 1959 to plan and to supervise the preparation of the monograph. Dr. Roy L. Reierson, Senior Vice President and Chief Economist, Bankers Trust Company, New York City, was designated as chairman and the following bankers were named to the Committee: S. Clark Beise, President, Bank of America N. T. & S. A., San Francisco; George Champion, Chairman, The Chase Manhattan Bank, New York; V. W. Johnson, President, The First National Bank, Cedar Falls, Iowa; David M. Kennedy, Chairman, Continental Illinois National Bank and Trust Company of Chicago; Homer J. Livingston, Chairman, The First National Bank of Chicago; George S. Moore, President, The First National City Bank of New York; Joseph C. Welman, President, Bank of Kennett, Missouri. Gordon A. McLean of The American Bankers Association staff was named Secretary of the Committee.

Preparation of the monograph was facilitated and followed closely by these officials of The American Bankers Association: John W. Remington, President 1959-60, and Chairman, Lincoln Rochester Trust Company, Rochester, New York; Carl Bimson, President 1960-61, and President, Valley National Bank of Arizona, Phoenix; Sam M. Fleming, Vice-President 1960-61, and President, Third National Bank in Nashville, Nashville, Tennessee; Dr. Charls E. Walker, Executive Vice President and Executive Manager, and his predecessor Merle E. Selecman.

In view of the magnitude of the task of describing adequately the role of commercial banking in our economy in the time available, the Committee enlisted the help of qualified academicians, bank officials, and bank economists. The Committee commissioned Dr. Jules I. Bogen and Dr. Marcus Nadler of the Graduate School of Business Administration, New York University, to exercise general editorial supervision over the preparation of drafts of the chapters.

The staff of the Department of Economics and Research of The American Bankers Association under Harold L. Cheadle, Deputy Manager and Director, reviewed and edited the several chapters and contributed a number of chapters to this monograph. Dr. Carter H. Golembe, Dr. Gordon A. McLean, Dr. Leslie C. Peacock, Dr. Seymour H. Miller, and Dr. Simon N. Whitney all made substantial contributions to the final product.

During the preparation of its published report, the Commission on Money and Credit had available to it the "Summary, Conclusions, and Recommendations" chapter in final form plus a preliminary version of the rest of the monograph. Several chapters have been revised and shortened somewhat for the present version.

CONTENTS

List of Charts

List of Tables

SUMMARY, CONCLUSIONS,
AND RECOMMENDATIONS

Among the financial institutions which serve the credit needs of our growing, dynamic economy the role of commercial banks is unique.

First, bank demand liabilities constitute much the larger portion of the nation's total money supply. Currency, the other component, enters the spending stream only through banking channels.

Second, credit and monetary policy, an essential part of any program for stable economic growth, is implemented initially through action on bank reserves. Changes in the supply, availability, and cost of bank reserves, as effected by monetary policy, set ultimate limits to the volume of bank lending and investing and hence to the volume of demand deposits. At appropriate times, such action acts as a damper on an excessive demand for credit and money; in other circumstances it may act as a stimulant to lagging demand. Commercial banks, then, are the primary vehicles through which the beneficial impact of credit and monetary policies are transmitted to the economy.

A third characteristic of commercial banks is the multifunctional nature of bank lending and investing. In contrast, savings banks and nonbank financial institutions are essentially specialized institutions, although a few lend to more than one category of borrower. Commercial banks, on the other hand, deal in a wide variety of debts and accommodate all types of borrowers.

This latter characteristic of bank lending is important to the well-being of the economy in two respects. First, as noted above, monetary policies affect the supply, availability, and cost of credit at banks. Since banks compete with all lenders, any change in the supply, availability, and cost of credit at the former can be expected to affect all lenders, though in varying degrees of magnitude and promptness. Thus, in ordinary circumstances the initial impact of monetary policies and actions is augmented as its influence spreads to nonbank lenders and to the economy generally.

1

Second, since banks provide facilities for financing all types of borrowers, their operations are highly flexible—much more so than those of other financial institutions. This flexibility is essential to the efficient operation of a market economy based on private enterprise and freedom of choice. What is produced, in what amounts, when, for and by whom, is determined largely by consumer demand. Experience demonstrates that consumer demands for final products change and that these changing demands require new and different alignments and combinations of resources—both human and otherwise. Moreover, a competitive economy —where success and failure are rewarded by profit and loss—generates change and progress as a normal consequence of the competitive process.

The stresses and strains to which a growing economy is always subject have been magnified in recent years by international tensions which have added significantly and unevenly to demands upon the economy.

If the economy is to respond smoothly and efficiently to the changing demands upon it—whether from consumers or resulting from innovation or developments abroad—it is axiomatic that resources must be free to move from one use to another. Unfortunately, it is not so well understood and appreciated that the funds to finance changing requirements must be free to move, too, if movements of resources are to take place smoothly and efficiently.

Well understood or not, it is primarily the commercial banking system which, by serving many types of users, provides the necessary flexibility to channel the funds from lesser into more urgent uses and in this way assist importantly in financing change and progress.

The role of commercial banking then has important implications for national policy. These will be highlighted in the following summary of the studies which comprise this monograph on *The Commercial Banking Industry.*

In this summary chapter we first examine the record in an effort to arrive at an objective evaluation of how well commercial banks have performed their multifunctional lending role. We have chosen to analyze the period 1930-59 because changes in credit demand were more drastic during this period than in any other in our history. This also permits us to concentrate on the period since the end of World War II and, hence, to evaluate better the near term future role of commercial banking in financing growth and progress.

Against this background, we then evaluate the relative position of commercial banking in our financial mechanism, giving attention to the competitive and other factors which have influenced the relative rates of growth of the several types of financial institutions. We discuss in this section the consequences of a continuation of postwar trends in the relative importance of commercial banks for the nation's borrowers, for an effective monetary and credit policy, and for the economy generally.

We comment on the degree of competition within commercial banking and appraise the earnings record of banks, emphasizing the bank capital problems resulting therefrom.

We pose the question of whether flexible credit and monetary policy are indispensable to national growth and stability. We discuss its limitations and some of the obstacles which have reduced its past contributions and may limit its usefulness in the future.

In this brief summary of the pages which comprise the studies, we must paint with a very broad brush indeed. For an elaboration of discussions here only briefly mentioned, the reader may have recourse to the fuller treatments in the several chapters.

With this admonition in mind, we proceed first to an evaluation of commercial banking performance over the past thirty years.

Commercial Banks—Multifunctional Lenders

The thirty-year period 1930-59, provided a number of unusual tests of the ability of the commercial banking system to serve the credit needs of its many and diverse borrowers in the face of unprecedented and unforeseen shifts in their requirements at various intervals.

From earliest times to 1930 commercial banks' principal customers were business firms of all sizes and types. In 1930 more than 50 percent of outstanding loans and investments of commercial banks had been made to accommodate businesses. Real estate loans were the next most important outlet for funds, primarily reflecting the investment of banks' time and savings deposits. Consumer instalment credit lending was at that time in its infancy. Commercial bank holdings of U.S. Treasury securities represented a large proportion of the total U.S. debt outstanding, but accounted for less than 10 percent of total bank loans and investments. Much the same can be said of bank holdings of obligations of state and local governments, except that they represented an even smaller percentage of total bank credit.

With the onslaught of the great depression, the demand for business credit contracted sharply. Throughout the long period of stagnation and halting recovery that followed, the dearth of credit demand from this sector persisted despite the ready availability of funds at historically low rates of interest. In an effort to put their funds to work and to stimulate business activity, banks offered a variety of new types of credit accommodation which were to prove of great importance in later years. Among these were consumer instalment credit loans and term loans to business. Both showed substantial growth during the late 1930's.

The principal new demands for credit in the 1930's were, of course, from the United States government and to a lesser degree from state and local governments. The reasons for the upsurge in government requirements are well known. When business failed to rebound from the depths of the depression, large-scale (for then) government expenditures were undertaken in order to get the economy on the road to recovery. Substantial annual budgetary deficits ensued.

A sizable proportion of the deficits was financed by commercial banks. Total bank holdings of Treasury securities rose in the ten years to 1940 from $5 billion to $17 billion. Holdings of state and local government securities over the same ten years rose from $2.1 billion to $3.7 billion. This combination of developments—the fall-off in credit demand from the private sector and the greatly augmented credit requirements of governments—had a startling impact on bank lending and investing. By 1940, investments in governments accounted for about 50 percent of commercial banks' earning assets; loans to business, on the other hand, had declined to less than 20 percent of total earning assets.

It would have been reasonable to suppose that businesses would require an enormous volume of credit in the hurried, all-out production associated with the military effort in World War II, as had been the case in World War I. However, the federal government by a variety of financing arrangements minimized the credit needs of business and, in effect, substituted its own credit. Bank loans to the private sector rose very slowly and by insignificant amounts during the war.

On the other hand, demands from the federal government rose to unprecedented heights. In the five years 1940-45 commercial bank holdings of Treasury securities rose from $17 billion to $84 billion. By the end of the period, such holdings accounted for almost three-quarters of total bank earning assets while loans to business had declined to a relatively insignificant 8 percent.

By war-end, banks were often characterized somewhat derisively as "depositaries of government securities." A word should be said about this. Once the decisions had been made to finance the war in large degree through incurring deficits and to substitute government for business credit, it was inevitable that banks, with the assistance of the Federal Reserve, would have to provide a large proportion of the required governmental financing. Certainly savings alone would have been woefully inadequate. Thus, banks found themselves heavily engaged in financing the war through the purchase of government securities, but the decisions which made this inevitable were not of the banks' making.

Regardless of the reason for bank investment in government securities, the point to be kept clearly in mind is that commercial banking met the test of the enormous wartime demands upon it and provided the nation with the bulk of the credit necessary to prosecute the war without financial fret or strain.

The special demands that had been made on commercial banks caused many of them to enter the post-World War period in a more uncertain mood than did most businesses. For more than a decade financing government had been their principal outlet for funds. From what sources would loan demand come?

Business Loans

With the conclusion of World War II, it was generally believed in bank and nonbank circles alike that there would be no substantial upsurge in the demand for business credit. Almost all businesses were unusually liquid because of a remarkably small amount of debt and large holdings of cash and liquid assets. Moreover, there had been extensive renovation of capital equipment during the war as well as substantial additions to capacity. While it was understood that there would be some expenditures involved in the shift from military to peacetime output, it was felt that most firms could accomplish this without substantial reliance on bank credit.

That these expectations, prevalent during the early postwar period, were not realized is, of course, now widely appreciated. Banks have again become very large suppliers of short-term credit to businesses of all industrial and financial classifications and important suppliers of intermediate credit. From war-end to 1959, business loans at banks increased fivefold from $9.3 billion to $46.7 billion, and these loans now represent about one-fourth of bank earning assets.

Loans to Agriculture

Banks have always, of course, been the principal institutional suppliers of credit for the nation's farmers, large and small, especially in the short and intermediate maturities.

The striking, upward surge in agricultural productivity over the past twenty years is well known. It is not always realized, however, that very substantial outlays of capital have been involved in the mechanization and the use of chemicals and other items necessary to raise productivity rapidly.

A very large proportion of these funds were obtained from commercial banks. Federal farm lending agencies have proliferated and expanded their activities during the past twenty-five years, yet in 1959 bank non-real estate farm loans were about three times the combined holdings of such loans by Production Credit Associations and the Farmers Home Administration. In mid-twentieth century America as in mid-nineteenth century America, farmers rely mainly on commercial banks for their credit requirements despite the intrusion of Federal lending agencies. No doubt some good has been realized from the activities of these agencies but it has involved substantial governmental competition with private financial institutions without solving the basic agricultural problems.

Consumer Credit

By the end of World War II the pent-up effective demand for consumer durables was enormous—mainly due to depression postponements, wartime deferments, and greatly expanded incomes. Although consumers had become very large holders of cash and liquid assets, these resources were inadequate to finance the desired purchases. Recourse to consumer credit was quick and grew rapidly in the postwar years.

Commercial bank participation in consumer instalment lending had been spotty prior to 1945; such loans accounted for only about 2 percent of bank earning assets in that year. In the years since, however, most banks have been eager lenders to consumers, and such loans now comprise about 12 percent of bank earning assets. Moreover, when loans to finance companies are considered along with bank-owned consumer paper, it is clear that banks today directly or indirectly account for much the larger share of consumer lending.

Bank participation in consumer lending has a highly beneficial effect, not only because more credit has been made available to consumers but also because they have been provided with an alternative source for funds at reasonable terms—an alternative not always available in the past. The amount of required down payments, the maturities of these loans and the relatively low "bank rate" have not only established general competitive standards but accounted in part for the excellent repayment record enjoyed by this type of loan.

Real Estate Credit

Commercial banks have always been a large factor in real estate lending.

Housing and construction generally have enjoyed near-boom conditions in the postwar period. Outstanding real estate loans of commercial banks increased about sixfold between 1945 and 1959—from $4.5 billion to $26.7 billion. In addition, a substantial amount of construction loans have been made as well as interim mortgage financing arranged for mortgage companies and insurance companies.

Investment in mortgages has been a major activity for many banks for many years. More recently the number of banks so involved has expanded significantly. In part this is explained by the relatively high yields but more importantly because savings deposits have expanded relative to demand deposits. It is clear that if commercial banks are allowed to compete on equitable terms for such funds more banks will invest larger sums to finance home ownership.

State and Local Government Securities

States and municipalities entered the postwar period with an unprecedented backlog of deferred services and improvements, including schools, roads, water and sewerage systems, and the like. Moreover, with a spurt in family formation and the heavy migration to the suburbs, it has been difficult for these governmental units to make up their backlog.

Fortunately, most of these governmental units entered the period with fairly light debt loads. However, the need for debt financing was evident early in the postwar period and has continued unabated since.

Commercial banks have provided a much larger share of total funds borrowed by state and local governments than have other financial institutions. Between 1945 and 1959 the obligations of state and local governments in bank portfolios rose from $3.8 billion to $17.0 billion.

Moreover, banks periodically provide local governmental units with essential short-term credit in anticipation of tax receipts or the proceeds from bond issues. Finally, banks are extensively engaged in the underwriting of the direct obligations of states and municipalities.

U.S. Government Securities

As noted above, since the conclusion of World War II, investments in U.S. government obligations have occupied a less important role in commercial bank lending and investing policies. This has been the result of several developments. First, for the period as a whole there has been only a modest net increase in demand for funds by the federal government and, second, the demands for credit from other sources have been much larger. Notwithstanding a substantial liquidation of Treasury securities in order to finance these other needs, bank holdings of these securities, totaling more than $60 billion, still dwarf those of other private financial institutions.

We may note at this point some special relationships between the Treasury and commercial banks. One is the Treasury's system of tax and loan accounts at banks through which flow the huge tax revenues of the U.S. Treasury as well as the proceeds of securities sold. This mechanism for handling Treasury funds tempers the disturbances which have resulted, and could again, when large sums are taken out of the hands of the public and later returned through government expenditures. This system was devised after many trial and error experiments by the Treasury aimed at eliminating or minimizing the unsettling effects upon the nation's economy of these huge and uneven transfers of funds. It has proved eminently satisfactory to the Treasury and the unsettling effects of these transfers have been reduced to tolerable minimums.

Furthermore, banks serve an important underwriting function in the marketing of Treasury issues. The Treasury benefits especially when it allows banks to buy its securities through credits to tax and loan accounts, for this device not only facilitates distribution of securities but induces the banks to bid correspondingly higher prices for new issues resulting in lower interest rates.

While banks do realize earnings on the Treasury balances in tax and loan accounts, the Treasury has found from a study of the data for 1959 that expenses incurred by the banks in rendering services to the Treasury for that year more than offset bank earnings, resulting in net costs to the banking system.

Financing Security Markets

The revival in security markets in the postwar period has provided another urgent need for bank financing. Credit plays a vital role in the underwriting of corporate securities for public distribution, and commercial banks are the most important and the most dependable source of such credit. Furthermore, bank credit contributes significantly to the effective day-to-day operation of security markets by enabling dealers to carry their inventories of securities and to finance margin accounts.

International Finance

International trade has expanded in a spectacular fashion in the postwar period. Like its domestic counterpart, international trade requires a large volume of credit and, in addition, such financing calls for special knowledge and technique. Commercial banks alone among financial institutions provide these comprehensive financial services. A number of large city banks have developed the skills and facilities required to service these specialized needs, both for their own customers and for those of their correspondents. Moreover, some banks assist in financing investment abroad, provide an international payment and collection service, facilitate tourist and other foreign travel, and participate actively in foreign exchange markets.

Conclusions

It is apparent that banks have performed a major role in finance as the nation's multifunctional lenders during the past twenty years, despite the variety and severity of lending problems which the period has produced. Money and credit were shifted from one use to another quickly and smoothly as the demands placed upon the economy and the financial community varied. In the period under review the bank credit mechanism participated heavily in financing the war and contributed much to the enormous growth in peacetime output that followed.

Relative Position of Commercial Banking

The volume of bank credit extended to private institutions and individuals, and the volume of bank deposits have grown considerably since World War II. This has been made possible by a reduction in reserve requirements, by some increase in total reserve funds, and by liquidation of government securities. However, bank assets have not grown as rapidly as the economy or the assets of nonbank financial institutions. This raises important questions. (1) Can monetary policy be expected to play its full role in promoting economic stability and in providing the funds essential to growth if the commercial banking system—the mechanism through which monetary policy operates almost exclusively—experiences a continued decline in its relative position as a source of funds? (2) In the future, can funds be channeled as quickly and as efficiently and in the right amounts to those sectors of the economy most in need of financing if those financial institutions possessing the greatest inherent flexibility necessary to the process are restricted in their rate of growth? The answers to these questions will determine whether the commercial banking system can be expected to continue to carry out its unique and highly essential role in financing stable economic growth in the years ahead.

Relative Growth of Demand Deposits

While total demand deposits adjusted held by U.S. commercial banks increased 38.5 percent between the end of 1946 and the end of 1959, gross national product rose by 128.8 percent. Thus, the main portion of the money supply did not keep pace with the increase in business activity. Furthermore, the total money supply, including hand-to-hand currency, increased by less than one-third during this period, although the amount of work for it to do more than doubled. To be sure, there was a very large build-up in bank deposits during World War II and such increases could not be expected to continue. Nevertheless the relative rate of growth in demand deposits has been dampened for a long time and there is legitimate ground for concern within the banking system as to whether such restraint will continue indefinitely and, if this is so, what the implications are for commercial banking.

Increase in Velocity

This relatively slow growth of the money supply was accompanied by a large increase in its velocity of circulation. The average annual turnover on demand deposits at more than 330 financial centers (other than the seven largest), one measurement of velocity, rose from fourteen in 1946 to twenty-five in 1959, an increase of 74 percent. Thus, by turning over more rapidly, a slowly growing money supply has made possible an increasing volume of payments in a rapidly growing economy.

There have been several reasons for this increase in velocity. As the excess liquidity prevailing throughout the economy at the end of the war was worked off, bank depositors in general found they could manage with smaller cash balances, used more intensively. Corporate managements became more sophisticated in the utilization and investment of cash in short-term money market instruments especially as interest rates tended to rise irregularly throughout the postwar period. Consumer balances, built to all-time highs in anticipation of the resumption of the production of consumer durables at war-end, were activated when these goods became available.

Another major factor contributing to the postwar increase in velocity has been the well-known rapid growth of nonbank savings-type financial institutions. The flow of funds from commercial banks to these institutions and back to the commercial banks results in increased activity of demand deposits—that is, increased lending and increased velocity.

Effects of Velocity on Banks

Whatever its causes, the prolonged increase in velocity necessarily has influenced monetary policy, in the direction of providing a smaller volume of reserves than would have been provided otherwise. A higher rate of money use has the same effect on total spending as an increase in the supply of money spent at a lesser rate. The economy has been subjected to inflationary pressures throughout most of the postwar period. Hence, the Federal Reserve has had to restrict the growth of demand deposits much more than would otherwise have been necessary had velocity remained constant or shown only moderate gains.

An inevitable short-run consequence of restraints on demand deposit growth during an inflationary period characterized by a strong demand for credit, is further economizing on the use of existing cash balances. Moreover, interest rates rise during such periods, which provides additional incentive to make more intensive use of cash balances both to avoid costs and to obtain returns.

These predictable developments have serious implications for commercial banks. Nonbank financial institutions, which for a number of reasons can pay higher rates of interest on their obligations than banks can on their deposits, are able to obtain additional funds and thereby continue to expand their loans. The monetary authorities then feel compelled to subject bank credit to still more severe restraint. The net effect, of course, in such periods is a slowing down of the growth of the commercial banking system without any necessarily equivalent dampening of inflationary pressures, which continue to be fed by credit expansion by other types of lenders.

For the future, it seems highly unlikely that velocity will continue to rise as rapidly as it has during the past fifteen years. Nevertheless, any further shrinking in the relative position of banks resulting from a rise in velocity could have serious implications for the over-all question of economic growth and stability.

Commercial Bank Savings Deposits

Although savings deposits are a much smaller source of funds to the commercial banks than demand deposits, they are, nevertheless, very important, especially for some banks and for most banks in some areas. Indeed, their importance has grown during the postwar period in part because the increase in demand deposits has been restricted in the face of a growing demand for bank loans. Yet the growth of savings deposits at the banks has been restricted, too, because of advantages enjoyed by competing nonbank institutions. For this reason, the advantages which competing thrift institutions have over commercial banks assume special significance.

Why Nonbank Lenders Have Grown Rapidly

To some extent, of course, the rapid growth of nonbank lenders has been a normal development. The great postwar demand for real estate credit naturally fostered the expansion of those lending institutions that specialize in such credit. It is undoubtedly true, too, that the conservatism of some bank managements has been responsible to some extent. Some bankers, because of the limited supply of funds available to them and a desire for liquidity, have been hesitant about expanding their holdings of real estate mortgages, whereas their competitors who are not required to pay out funds on demand and who have less experience and less conservative traditions have been less inhibited.

But in addition to these factors, the nonbank financial institutions, in competing for the savings dollar, have enjoyed a number of competitive advantages resulting from legislation or regulation. These add up to handicaps for commercial banks. Because of their advantages, competing institutions have been able to operate more freely and profitably than commercial banks and hence have been able to pay higher rates on funds entrusted to them. As a result, nonbank lenders have been more successful than banks in attracting funds.

Taxation

One very serious handicap under which the commercial banks operate arises from federal tax laws. Mutual savings banks and savings and loan associations, while nominally subject to the federal corporate income tax, are in effect virtually exempted from it by being permitted to build up tax-free capital accounts (undivided profits and reserves) in an amount equal to 12 percent of their total deposits or share accounts. Commercial banks, on the other hand, are allowed much smaller tax-free reserves for losses under a formula based on previous loss experiences, and not total assets. As a result, mutual savings institutions pay almost no corporate income taxes, while the commercial banks pay very large amounts. This is one of the factors which make it possible for the mutuals to pay their depositors or shareholders a much higher return than can the commercial banks.

Changed Nature of Mutuals

Savings banks and savings and loan associations have developed far beyond their original local character and their original objective of serving the specialized needs of groups of individuals banded together for mutual benefit. Today they are aggressive business enterprises, operating over large areas and across state lines and actively competing with commercial banks by offering many of the same services. Indeed, the differences between their liabilities and those of commercial banks appear to many to have narrowed to the point where a large part of the public mistakenly sees little difference between a savings deposit and a share account. Yet these mutual institutions continue to operate within the highly favorable tax, regulatory, and supervisory framework which was provided at a time when they were organized for limited and special purposes.

It is to be assumed that the mutual institutions will continue to be more successful than the commercial banks in attracting savings so long as they retain these competitive advantages, which up to now have been responsible in large part for the loss of relative position of commercial banks among financial institutions. Until legislators recognize the changes that have occurred in these so-called mutual institutions and equalize competitive conditions between them and commercial banks, the relative position of the latter seems likely to deteriorate further, thus making it increasingly difficult for the banks to perform their traditional function as multi-purpose lenders.

Rate Ceilings

A growing number of commercial banks have been limited in their ability to pay higher rates to holders of time and savings deposits by the ceiling imposed on such rates by regulation. No such rigid ceiling is applied to most nonbank institutions. Where their rates of return are limited by regulation, restrictions are more liberal. While bankers would differ now on the desirability of raising or completely removing the limits on rates commercial banks may pay on time and savings deposits, they would agree that maximum rates should be adjusted in accordance with cyclical developments. Further, although foreign time deposits do not enter into the competition between commercial banks and savings institutions, in periods of rising interest rates the rate ceiling on these deposits makes them relatively unattractive to depositors as compared to short-term investments in the United States and abroad. Thus, the ability of the banks to compete for or to hold these deposits is weakened. This is a particularly severe hardship to banks in the large financial centers.

Reserve Requirements

Another obvious handicap under which commercial banks operate is the current requirement (for those banks which are members of the Federal Reserve System) that a 5 percent reserve be held at Federal Reserve Banks against time deposits. No such reserve requirement of this type is imposed generally upon other savings institutions. This forced immobilization of a portion of savings funds in a nonearning asset (legal reserves) reduces the earning capacity and thus the interest paying capacity of the banks. While economic as well as equity considerations are involved, considerations of fairness in the treatment of competing institutions would suggest that there is no more reason to retain reserve requirements on commercial bank time deposits than there would be to impose such requirements on competing nonbank financial institutions.

Lending Operations

In addition, the lending operations of commercial banks are subject to many restrictions which curtail their ability to compete with nonbank financial institutions, and this impairs the earning capacity of banks. Some of these restrictions are imposed by legislation, others by the supervisory authorities. They include, for example, limitations on the amount of real estate credit the banks can extend and the proportion of risk assets to nonrisk assets they can maintain. Many of these restrictions have been imposed in order to ensure the continued safety and liquidity of depositors' funds and the soundness of the banking system, and are, therefore, not opposed by most bankers. But it seems legitimate to inquire why competing institutions should not be held to comparable standards, where applicable, for the protection of their depositors or shareholders. Laxity in this respect, although permitting these institutions to pay higher returns for the present, could have seriously adverse effects in the event of another major depression. On the other hand, if public policy is to be based on the supposition that a major depression is improbable, then regulations and standards imposed upon banks should be relaxed.

Branch Limitations

The statutes in several states that limit a commercial bank to one office constitute an impediment to some commercial banks in their competition with nonbank financial institutions. However, The American Bankers Association has long felt that whether branching privileges should be permitted is a matter for the individual state to decide. The establishment of branch systems on a national scale has been opposed by the Association.

Economic Consequences of a Lag in the Growth of Commercial Banking

Deterioration in the relative position of the commercial banks can have adverse effects on the economy as a whole. It may already have had this effect in some measure. For one thing, it has become increasingly difficult for the banks to perform their economic functions, particularly that of providing credit to all parts of the economy, as their relative position has diminished. There is a loss of flexibility in our financial system—that is, a diminution of the ability of that system to channel available credit rapidly from one sector of the economy to another in response to changing credit demands. The commercial banks alone provide this kind of flexibility. Other lending institutions can substitute for them only in the specialized areas in which these institutions operate.

For another thing, it may be more difficult to implement monetary policy effectively because the size of the medium through which it operates—the commercial banking system—shrinks relative to the size of the economy which monetary management serves. Nonbank financial institutions are affected by changes in monetary policy but less directly and effectively and with some time lags. The continuing enlargement, then, of the nonbank sector of the financial community means that to achieve any given result, the Federal Reserve System may find itself compelled to take somewhat stronger actions affecting commercial bank reserves, thus further dampening the growth of the commercial banking system and increasing the danger of producing unsettling side effects.

Another adverse consequence of the commercial banks' loss of relative position in the nation's financial structure is that restrictive credit measures may come to have more discriminatory effects upon borrowers. Those who borrow from commercial banks may be restricted more sharply, while those who borrow from other lending institutions are less affected. Since these two broad classes of borrowers are likely to use the funds they obtain for different purposes, the effects upon economic activity are also discriminatory—and not necessarily in desirable ways.

To the extent that the rapid growth of nonbank lenders represents the development of specialized institutions that are better able to provide some services or that can operate more efficiently in some areas than the commercial banks, this is a normal and desirable development. But when such growth springs mainly from legislative, regulatory, or tax advantages, it tends to prevent the nation's financial system from allocating credit—and the real resources that credit can command—in an optimum manner. In a perfectly competitive credit market in which all financial intermediaries could be assumed to operate on an equal footing, funds would be channeled from savers to investors in accordance with their economic needs. But when certain lending institutions are accorded a favored status, in whatever manner, then the particular types of loans and investments they make are also favored at the expense of other users of credit.

Commercial banking is the central and indispensable part of our financial system. As such, it closely touches the activities of virtually all sectors of the economy. If its operations are unduly hampered and its relative position is forcibly restricted by legislation, regulation, or tax disadvantages, neither the banks themselves, nor the financial system in general, nor the economy as a whole will be able to function with maximum efficiency in the promotion of vigorous growth.

This is a development which, if permitted to continue, could have economy-wide repercussions. Monetary policy has been the mainstay in our efforts to maintain a satisfactory rate of stable economic growth despite this and other untimely developments. We ought, therefore, to be seeking ways and means to enhance its effectiveness rather than to tolerate those developments which tend to hamper it and which are onerous on other grounds as well. It is important, therefore, to reiterate that it is not the restrictive monetary policy of the Federal Reserve System which is at fault, even though it forms a part of the chain of events which has hampered the growth of commercial banking. Such a policy is essential wherever the demand for credit is excessive relative to the available real resources. While there is room for argument as to just how monetary policies should be carried out and how much they can accomplish, there can be little question about the desirability of pursuing a generally countercyclical monetary policy which both restricts the use of credit during inflationary booms and encourages its use during business recessions.

Rather, the fault lies in developments in the field of finance discussed above that penalize growth in commercial banking by artificially stimulating the growth of competing financial institutions. Techniques of monetary management based on control over bank credit are relatively more effective at a time when banks are free to compete on equal terms with other financial institutions, but they become relatively less effective if other institutions are permitted to compete on a favored basis.

Competition, Earnings, and Capital

Competition between commercial banks and other financial institutions has been discussed in an earlier section. The importance of this kind of competition should not be permitted to obscure the fact that the banking industry is itself intensively competitive—certainly among the most competitive industries in the nation. The reasons for this and their implications are discussed here.

Competition

The importance of healthy competition as a means of assuring the most beneficial and efficient allocation of resources is so apparent as to preclude the need for its discussion. Because of the commercial banks' unique function of supplying the nation's circulating medium, public policy guards against the destructive effects of unlimited competition among these institutions. Nevertheless, intensive, healthy competition is clearly in the public interest and the degree to which it exists today is one of the distinguishing characteristics of commercial banking.

Perhaps the most noteworthy indication of the difference between commercial banking and many other industries is the fact that banking is an industry in which those seeking to analyze financial trends resort to discussing the "one hundred largest" or the "fifty largest" commercial banks. In any other industry the mere existence of this many "giants" would be considered *prima facie* evidence of the existence of intense competition.

There are, of course, considerably fewer banks today than there were forty years ago, and even during recent years there has been a slow decline in the number of banks, although not in the total number of banking offices.

Recently some concern has been expressed over this development, and data has been compiled to indicate that in many areas there has been an increase in banking concentration. It is not generally recognized, however, that almost any standard indicator of bank concentration will show that concentration is, generally speaking, less prevalent today than during the 1930's.

Quite apart from changes in the number of banks, it is clear that the transportation and communications revolution which has been developing during the past several decades has been instrumental in greatly increasing competition among commercial banks. Many banks which formerly dominated a local market must now meet the competition of banks in neighboring towns or counties, or even in neighboring states. Some localities in which there is a single bank are now within metropolitan areas and, for the first time, the bank finds itself competing with downtown institutions. In still other localities, particularly where mergers have taken place involving smaller-sized banks, customers now find that their business is eagerly sought by two or three strong, aggressive banks, whereas formerly there might have been one large bank and a number of very small banks.

The increase in number of banking offices in states permitting branch banking is one of the consequences of the intensive competitive situation prevailing within the commercial banking industry. It is true that in some population centers in such states unit banks have virtually disappeared, to be replaced by branches of one or several of the larger banks. There is every reason to believe, however, that branches of competing banks in such localities compete as intensively among themselves as did the unit banks which they replaced.

It is worthy of note in this connection that the increase in number of commercial banking offices within recent years has proceeded at a faster rate than population growth, and at such a pace as to ensure that there are few persons who do not have ready access to one or more such offices. With a total of more than 14,000 banks and 24,000 commercial bank offices (or one for every 7,500 persons), the commercial banking system provides a density of coverage of the domestic market for financial services that is unique.

Not only has competition been largely responsible for an increase in the accessibility of commercial banking facilities, but it has also been responsible for the marked change in their character. Many banks have provided such specialized types of facilities as drive-in windows, instalment loan offices and, in a few cases, even mobile offices. Some of these changes, of course, reflect in part the movement of population from urban centers to the suburbs, with the consequent enlargement of metropolitan areas.

Parenthetically, it should be noted that the availability of commercial bank facilities has not increased as rapidly in some states as in others, due largely to the wide differences in statutes relating to branch banking. In those states in which branching is prohibited or severely limited, it will be found that more new banks have been organized than in states which permit relatively unrestricted branch banking.

However, since the requirements for the organization of a new bank are frequently stricter or more difficult to meet than for the establishment of a branch, those states which permit branch banking have had a more rapid growth in commercial banking facilities than others. However, it does not necessarily follow that additional facilities can be attributed solely to the branching privilege. In some branch banking states population has grown faster than the national average. Many individual banks in unit banking states have aggressively promoted and diversified their services and are fully satisfying the banking needs of their respective communities.

The relatively large number of bank mergers during recent years is also a reflection of stronger competition within the commercial banking industry. The overriding consideration in most mergers, so far as the continuing bank is concerned, has been to extend services into contiguous areas through the acquisition of branches, or else to compete more effectively with other unit banks by increasing its loan limit, diversifying its operations, or realizing economies in operations which larger size makes possible.

Competition and New Services

Still another consequence of the degree of competition among commercial banks, as well as between commercial banks and other financial institutions, is the continued development of new and improved financial services offered by commercial banking. For example, there has been a general trend in commercial banking toward meeting the needs of customers of modest means by providing special checking accounts, more convenient money remittance methods, and special types of consumer credit plans.

Both domestically and internationally, commercial banks provide credit information which is invaluable to businessmen. In agricultural credit, banks have trained specialized personnel who counsel farmers on farm operations and farm programs. Moreover, banks have developed correspondent relationships through which credit available from larger banks and insurance companies can be made available in rural areas.

To a far greater extent than is generally realized, the nation's business depends upon commercial banking for the rapid and efficient transmission of funds. Commercial banks have under constant study means by which clearance and collections and remittances may be speeded. Many new operating procedures designed to accomplish this result have been devised and more are announced with each passing year.

Progressive commercial banking is characterized, too, by the widespread development of trust services. Particularly notable are growing common trust funds, designed to make fiduciary services useful to individuals with moderate amounts of funds, and the increased services available to pension and welfare funds.

To list all of the developments in recent years which reflect the adaptability of commercial banking to new and varied demands would require more space than is available. Nevertheless, it should be evident that the commercial banking system is not only a remarkably flexible instrument serving the needs of the American economy but is also an industry which, under the spur of competition, has constantly devised new ways of serving its customers.

Bank Earnings

The degree of competition within the commercial banking industry, as well as between commercial banks and other financial institutions, is clearly reflected in the rate of net profits earned by commercial banks on their capital funds. This rate has been averaging about 8.5 percent per year during recent years, and is substantially below that of the great majority of other industries and below that earned by public utilities on their equity capital.

It is sometimes alleged that banks profiteer, especially in periods of rising interest rates. It should be noted, however, that bank earnings, even of 8.5 percent, have made possible during the past decade only by a combination of special factors which cannot be expected to continue indefinitely. These have been (1) a very sharp rise in business, consumer, and real estate credit demands which have resulted in a substantial decline in capital-risk asset ratios and thus raised the earning power of each dollar of capital funds; (2) a decline in reserve requirements; (3) a rising secular trend of interest rates from abnormally low levels.

It may be noted that while bank earnings rates have been relatively low, they have been rather stable. In periods of strong loan demand, rising interest rates, and increased velocity, bank earnings on capital have tended to decline rather than to increase, as is commonly believed to be the case. One of the reasons for this is that restrictive credit policy, highly essential for the health of the economy, slows the rate of growth of earning assets of the banks. Another important factor is that increased interest rates represent increased costs to banks in the form of higher rates on time and savings deposits, as well as increased income, and the former is generally overlooked by the public. Still another potent factor causing bank earnings on capital to decline in such periods is that banks, in fulfilling their obligations to meet the needs of customers, have to sell securities at relatively low prices and take losses in order to have more funds available for lending. These sales, resulting in considerable losses to the banks, have reduced the rate of earnings on capital when interest rates have risen.

Conversely, in periods of easier credit characterized by falling interest rates, banks have been able to expand their earning assets through the purchase of securities. Sales of securities in such periods are usually made at rising prices, so that profits are realized at such times. It should be noted too that bank lending rates are highly flexible as contrasted with certain other costs common to banks and all business.

The net effect of lower rates of return in boom periods and relatively higher rates of return when business activity declines or slows its rate of growth has been to produce relatively stable earnings for the banks, albeit at an average level below that realized on capital by the great majority of industries.

Consequently, banks on the whole have been able to pay only modest dividends after making necessary additions to surplus and reserves. This has a bearing on the bank capital problem.

Bank Capital

Bank capital serves as a cushion to protect depositors against losses and thereby enables a bank safely to meet the expanding credit needs of its community.

When capital is measured simply in relation to total assets or total deposits, it is clear that banks today have far less capital, relatively, than they had twenty or thirty years ago. A very rapid decline in capital margins occurred during World War II, when the expansion of total assets and deposits far outstripped the rise in capital accounts. Moreover, in recent years, despite substantial additions to capital accomplished largely through the retention of earnings, capital-risk asset ratios have continued to decline. Commercial banks have not yet been able to rebuild capital margins to the levels which prevailed in the late 1930's.

It is clear that no particular ratio will indicate whether capital is adequate for an individual bank, or for the banking system. The amount of capital needed is dependent on a wide variety of factors, including the types and relative amounts of different assets held by a bank, the liquidity requirements arising from deposit volatility, and the character of the bank's management. In addition, broader changes in the economy affect capital adequacy standards, so that capital margins which may have been judged adequate in one period can become more than adequate or quite inadequate in another period when the economic circumstances change.

There is no intention here to suggest that present capital margins are inadequate. Very possibly lower capital ratios, however computed, are acceptable now in view of the important environmental changes which have taken place both in the economy and within the banking system since 1933. Nevertheless, it is clear that if banking is to meet the financial needs of an expanding economy during the years to come, it will have to acquire substantial amounts of new capital to keep pace with the inevitable growth in demand for bank credit, and hence in earning assets. These additions must come either from retained earnings or from the sales of capital stock, and both of these depend upon the earning capacity of banks. In the past twenty-five years the largest part of these additions has been obtained through the retention of earnings.

The foregoing factors and trends make the modest earnings record of commercial banks a matter of concern from the standpoint of public policy. Commercial banks in the future must be able to operate under conditions which will enable them to obtain the necessary additional capital. This is essential if commercial banking is to serve the needs of a growing economy adequately.

Monetary and Credit Policies

Bankers are understandably aware, perhaps more than most persons, that money must be managed, and that monetary management, if it is to serve the public interest, must be flexible. This is one of the oldest and most widely-accepted lessons of economic history, both here and abroad. It is disturbing that the need for it should be challenged by some in mid-twentieth century America.

The techniques of management should be continuously reviewed as to their adequacy, as should the policy decisions of the monetary authorities. "Times change" in a dynamic, private enterprise economy, and "changing times" can be expected in the future, as in the past, to call for the discarding of some techniques of monetary management, the modernization of others, and the addition of new ones. No doubt the Federal Reserve discount rate will play a different role in the years ahead than it now does, just as it now performs a somewhat different function than in the past. There is little doubt, either, that new tools will be added when the need arises, just as open-market operations, flexible reserve requirements, and others have been added to the instruments of monetary management in the years since the establishment of the Federal Reserve System. But the need for flexible monetary management remains as urgent now as ever in our history. For one thing the dollar is the world's leading currency. It can remain so only as long as the world has faith in its strength and integrity. Its stability is one of the aims of monetary management.

Bankers are agreed, too, that monetary management is best entrusted to an organization of experts created and guided as to ultimate objectives by the Congress, but free of any partisan political domination or responsibilities. History is replete with examples of economic disasters which have resulted when monetary policies have been subordinated to political convenience. The consequences of divorcing monetary authority completely from governmental direction have been equally harmful. The present system, which provides for a monetary authority which is independent within the framework of government, was developed with great care. It deserves and has the full support of bankers.

During periods of monetary restraint in recent years, monetary management and the banks have been subjected to criticism, mainly from political sources, on the grounds that small businesses have been discriminated against in obtaining credit accommodation. It is perhaps enough to say in rebuttal that the great majority of commercial banks are small banks whose resources are inadequate to deal with other than small businesses. As an industry, it is impractical and virtually impossible for banking to discriminate in the manner charged. It is worth noting, in addition, that many larger banks maintain small business divisions, for an obvious reason: all large businesses began as small businesses and it is in the larger banks' best interests to make the necessary association as soon as possible. Finally, every study of the allegation by disinterested observers, including governmental agencies, has shown no evidence of unfair discrimination.

Much of the additional criticism aimed at the performance of monetary policy in recent years stems from a miscalculation of the limitations of the role which monetary policy can play in attaining the national objectives of growth and stability. Monetary policy is an essential part of any program to promote progress and a stable dollar, but it is only a part. Sound fiscal and debt management policies also are at all times essential to the attainment of these goals; frequently they can make an even more important contribution than can monetary policy. Much of the inflationary pressure prevalent since the war can be attributed to inadequate and inappropriate fiscal and debt management policies. Much of the time these policies have, in fact, been procyclical in character.

In any examination, therefore, of the economy's performance and the role of monetary policy and our financial institutions therein—whether for a short or a long period, whether it is the past being evaluated or history in the making—it would be a grievous error to attribute success or failure to any single policy without also examining the impact of other related policies.

It is widely recognized that the successful operation of monetary policy —and of fiscal policy, too, for that matter—has been threatened in recent years by the development of a new inflationary factor, the so-called "cost push" pressure on prices. This is not the place to discuss this problem or to suggest solutions, but it is a more or less elementary conclusion that monetary policy is significantly limited in the performance of its indispensable function when the wage-price practices of unions and management exert a continuing upward pressure on the general price level. This is a problem, moreover, which blurs analysis of the performance of the financial sector of our economy, especially as to its ability to finance future growth. In a real sense, current wage-price practices constitute a major stumbling block to the attainment of the rate of stable economic progress which it is reasonable to expect the nation to achieve.

The special impact of monetary and credit policies on commercial banks has given rise to many schools of thought within the banking community as to how such policies should be implemented.

There are those who favor the use of one monetary technique over another in any given set of circumstances. For example, some would prefer to see the discount rate utilized as a penalty rate. Others would have the monetary authority abandon the "bills only" policy in order that it might act more directly and quickly on a broader spectrum of interest rates.

Still others, hopeful for a quicker and more direct impact of monetary policy on nonbank financial institutions, would favor the imposition of reserve requirements on the latter. A number of well-informed observers have long been intrigued by the possibility of devising monetary techniques which would influence not only the magnitude of the money supply but its use (velocity) as well. Some persons would replace or supplement general monetary controls with selective credit controls.

Bank Reserve Requirements

One aspect of monetary policy that concerns the commercial banks especially is the practice of requiring banks to hold a certain proportion of their assets in balances with the Federal Reserve. Such balances or reserves are the fulcrum upon which monetary controls operate, but at the same time they tend to reduce bank earning capacities, since such balances are nonearning assets. Consequently, many bankers as well as economists and others, have given thought to the possibilities of improving our system of required bank reserves.

A fractional reserve system provides a flexible means of influencing the size of the money supply and the total volume of bank credit. The present system could be improved in several ways. One would be the adoption of uniform requirements for all banks throughout the country. The present geographical breakdown was based on historical grounds that have long since ceased to be significant.

While other types of variable reserve requirements have occasionally been suggested, careful study indicates that such plans rest on assumptions of doubtful validity or introduce needless complexities. Uniform reserve requirements have the important advantage that shifts of deposits between banks will not change the over-all reserve position of the banking system. A uniform reserve requirement is the simplest, most equitable, and most effective system that has yet been devised.

If our economy is to continue growing in the future, the banking system will have to provide a growing money supply. This can be facilitated through gradual reductions in the required reserve ratios over the years ahead, so that a given volume of reserves will suffice for a larger volume of deposits. Moreover, present reserve requirements are so high that they immobilize unduly credit granting resources of the banks, reduce earnings to a level that hampers the banks' ability to attract needed capital, and discourage membership in the Federal Reserve System. Reducing the required reserve ratios from their present high levels would moderate these difficulties, provide for continued expansion of the money supply, and still permit bank reserves to play effectively their key role in monetary management.

The present reserve requirement of 5 percent against time deposits serves no useful purpose and discriminates unfairly against commercial banks as compared to other savings institutions that are not required to maintain such reserves. Reduction or elimination of this requirement would leave the reserve mechanism free to perform its essential function, that of regulating the active money supply.

Selective Credit Controls

Some persons would replace or supplement general monetary controls with selective credit controls, which limit the extension of credit to specific sectors of the economy. At present, the only such controls in effect are those on security credit, although at times in the past, consumer instalment and housing credit have also been subject to direct controls.

While selective credit controls can be useful during wartime or other periods of emergency—particularly if pressures for undue credit expansion are concentrated in certain sectors of the economy—they have serious drawbacks which militate against their general adoption under more normal circumstances. Experience has shown that consumer and housing credit controls are difficult to administer and of doubtful effectiveness. Even more serious, they involve considerable government interference with free market forces. The collective judgment of buyers and sellers is usually more reliable than the views of a few administrators, no matter how well informed and well intentioned the latter may be.

Consequently, while selective credit controls may be useful under certain circumstances or in special cases, such as restraining undue expansion of credit to finance speculation in securities, the drawbacks generally far outweigh possible advantages.

The American Bankers Association has several recommendations to make for the improvement of the techniques of monetary policy and other aspects of monetary management for which there would be near-universal agreement within the banking community. These would have the beneficial effects of making monetary policy more effective and of removing certain inequities from which banks now suffer in competing with other financial institutions, and which prevent banking from performing its unique and historic role in the financing of growth as well as it might. They may be found in the section on Recommendations.

Although bankers may differ among themselves as to the details of the implementation of monetary policy, it would be a mistake to exaggerate these differences. It would be especially unfortunate if they should be interpreted, as seems to have been the case on occasion, as an attack on the need for a flexible monetary policy directed toward economic growth and stability.

Bankers are unanimously agreed, too, that there is an urgent need for a more widespread understanding and demand for appropriate fiscal and debt management action in order that monetary and credit policy not be overworked. Such action would reduce the severity of monetary policies and hence their burden on commercial banking. Moreover, and most important, appropriate fiscal and debt management policies can provide a healthy atmosphere in which economic growth and stability can flourish.

Recommendations

I. Credit and Monetary Policy

A. We wholeheartedly and without reservation endorse the use of countercyclical monetary policy as an indispensable part of any program designed to achieve the maximum sustainable rate of economic growth and a minimum of cyclical fluctuations; however, there has been overreliance on monetary policy alone for the achievement of national economic goals. We believe that fiscal and debt management policies can and should be utilized more effectively to help in attaining growth and stability. Avoidance of inflation is not only consistent with these goals but is indispensable to their achievement and should, therefore, be a primary objective of monetary, fiscal, and debt management policies.

B. To be countercyclical, monetary and credit policy must be flexibly administered. Such flexibility is possible only if interest rates are free to fluctuate. We therefore conclude that any policy aimed at maintaining interest rates at artificial, inflexible levels, whether high or low, is inconsistent with and inimical to the achievement of broader objectives of national economic policies.

C. Movements in interest rates which fully reflect the conditions prevailing in the markets for loanable funds are also essential to the maintenance of the pre-eminent position of the dollar as the world's leading currency and of the United States as an international financial center.

D. The rapid relative postwar growth of nonbank financial institutions combined with the absence of a more effective fiscal and debt management program, has progressively limited the effectiveness of Federal Reserve policies in influencing spending based on credit expansion. We recommend that a study be made to devise ways and means whereby monetary policy can be made to bear more immediately, more directly, and more effectively upon the nonbank financial institutions.

E. It is our opinion that a convincing case has not been made in support of the broader use of selective credit controls in peacetime, either as a substitute for or as an adjunct to general credit policy. Selective credit controls are extremely difficult to administer equitably and without undue and costly interference with the most desirable allocation of resources from the national viewpoint.

II. Organization of the Federal Reserve System

A. We strongly recommend the maintenance of the present district organization of the Federal Reserve System, coordinated and governed nationally by the Board of Governors and the Federal Open Market Committee. We believe the existing allocation of authority among the components of the System should be retained, and that the present ownership of stock of the Federal Reserve banks be maintained.

B. We recommend without reservation the continuance of the present independent status of the Federal Reserve System within the federal government. The proposals which have been advanced for changes in its independent status would be viewed both here and abroad, and properly so, as evidence of a lack of real intent on the part of the nation to combat inflation, to pursue sound fiscal policies, and to promote sustainable real economic growth.

III. Reserve Requirements

A. We recommend that steps be taken, as soon as appropriate—
   1) To reduce the reserves required to be held by commercial banks against demand deposits in order to enable them to play their necessary role in financing economic growth in years ahead.
   2) To eliminate the outmoded geographic differentials in reserve requirements of commercial banks and to establish a uniform percentage reserve requirement for all demand deposits.
   3) To eliminate or to reduce to nominal levels the reserves required to be held against member bank time and savings deposits. It is manifestly unfair to impose reserve requirements on the time and savings deposits of commercial banks so long as no such requirement is imposed upon other financial institutions which compete for this type of savings.

IV. Government Credit Operations

We recommend that the following principles be followed in the operation of government lending agencies:

A. Credit should not be provided by government lending agencies where adequate private credit is already available. When made available, such credit should not have the effect of perpetuating or inducing maladjustments in the economy, but rather of facilitating and hastening the adjustment process.

B. The lending operations and policies of these agencies should be more effectively coordinated with the nation's economic stabilization policies. In lending and credit guarantees and insurance operations the principle should be followed of adjusting rates to changes in market rates and to the cost of money to the Treasury. In order to reduce the subsidy element in such operations, rates should not be rigidly fixed by statute.

C. The operations of these lending agencies should be subject to a periodic review and examination by appropriate committees of the Congress at intervals of four years or less.

D. The progressive relaxation of lending, guarantee, or insurance standards and terms should be stopped.

V. Competitive Situation

A. Banking is subjected to manifold and complex regulations, instituted in large part in periods of financial crisis, but retained, in some instances, long after the need for them has disappeared. Failure to remove antiquated and unnecessary regulations interferes with the ability of banks to serve the economy as they should. While banking is over-regulated in many ways, other types of financial institutions are under-regulated. The public interest will be served best when financial institutions can compete on a fair basis.

B. Consistency and assurance of competitive equality should be the standard for government policies affecting commercial banks and competing financial institutions. These could be achieved in the following respects:

1) Requirements for charters. We believe that the same considerations of managerial ability, and the need for new facilities from the standpoint of public convenience should be applied in chartering financial institutions in all areas of the United States as are now applied in chartering commercial banks.

2) Examination practices. We recommend the adoption for non-bank financial institutions in all areas of the United States of examination standards comparable to those applied to commercial banks.

3) Regulation of lending and investment. We recommend a thorough study by the Banking and Currency Committees of the Congress of the laws and regulations on bank lending and investing in order to determine whether some of them are unduly restrictive or have outlived their usefulness. In any case, we strongly urge that where applicable the same or comparable laws and regulations should govern for all financial institutions doing a comparable kind of business.

4) Provisions for reserves against possible future losses on assets. While the bad debt reserves now permitted have been adequate in recent years, it should be emphasized that, in order to make their full contribution to our economy, banks must take risks, not only at home but also in some cases abroad, where a number of banks have become involved in lending, because of their desire to assist industry in meeting foreign banking competition in accordance with governmental policies and approval. It is impossible to determine what the ultimate loss experience on such foreign lending will be. Further, our economy has not been subjected to the strains of a major recession for decades, and the rate of losses experienced over the past two decades may be considerably lower than those which banks may have to bear in coming decades if they are to pursue dynamic policies. We recommend, as a precautionary measure, the liberalization of current regulations on the accumulation of bad debt reserves.

5) Reserve Requirements. See III.A.3 above.

6) Borrowing from the central bank or its equivalent. We believe that a discount mechanism such as is now provided in the Federal Reserve System is an absolute essential for the proper functioning of commercial banking and of central banking. We recommend that the same aims of Federal Reserve discount policies be adopted by the Home Loan Banks in the advances which they may make to member savings and loan associations and that they should be guided by the over-all monetary policy of the Federal Reserve System. That is to say, the Home Loan Banks should lend on shorter term, make fewer commitments in times of monetary restraint than in times of monetary ease, and should be lenders of last resort and not suppliers of funds for the expansion of mortgage portfolios of member savings and loan associations.

7) Taxation. The tax burden of the nation should be distributed

in a way which is most conducive to the optimum allocation of the country's resources and to the equitable sharing of the burden. The present tax structure, as it relates to the several categories of financial institutions, violates these principles: it grants most types of financial institutions tax advantages which are denied to commercial banks, thereby artificially stimulating the growth of such institutions at the expense of banks and handicapping the effective use of monetary policy in combatting inflation. The resultant distortions in the allocation of credit produce similar distortions in the use of the nation's physical resources.

VI. Dual System of Regulation

A. We favor the dual system of banking. Great strides have been made by supervisory bodies but we stress the need for active continued efforts to achieve greater uniformity of regulatory and examination practices in the various jurisdictions.

B. We believe there is a demonstrated need for greater conformity between state and federal jurisdictions in the chartering, branching, and other regulatory policies followed with respect to other financial institutions, especially the savings and loan associations and credit unions. In the case of savings and loan associations, policies of the federal agencies need to be brought up to the standards that are being followed in those states which have established sound supervisory policies and procedures.

C. In the case of savings and loan associations, especially, there is an obvious need in the public interest for the application of those standards of liquidity and adequacy of capital funds and reserves that are applied to commercial banks, as well as for coordination of Federal Home Loan Bank lending with Federal Reserve credit policy, as noted earlier.

VII. Branch Banking

Bankers have strongly held divergent views as to whether unit or branch banking is the more desirable for the community and for the banking industry.

A. We believe that the statutes in several states that limit a commercial bank to one office constitute an impediment to some commercial banks in their competition with nonbank financial institutions.

B. We endorse the principle and practice now in effect that branching privileges of national banks and of competing nonbank financial institutions conform to the standards established by the individual states, and we oppose the establishment of branch systems on a national scale.

VIII. Payment of Interest on Time Deposits

A. Bankers have diverse opinions with reference to the regulation of the maximum rate permitted to be paid on time and savings deposits. Therefore, we make no recommendations for change in the present system. A sizable number of bankers, however, would prefer that supervisory authorities respond more quickly to cyclical developments in adjusting maximum rates of interest that may be paid on such deposits.

B. We favor freeing foreign time deposits from this regulation. If we hope to maintain and strengthen our position as a world financial center, banks must be free to compete on an equal rate basis with competition abroad.

IX. Trust Functions

We believe statutes and regulations governing the trust functions of commercial banks and trust companies should be modernized so as to permit greater flexibility in trust investment policy and greater efficiency in trust operations in the interests of the beneficiaries.

Chapter 1

THE STRUCTURE OF
COMMERCIAL BANKING

For generations, the unique characteristics—particularly the structure—and the performance of commercial banking in the United States have attracted the attention of scholars and other observers both here and abroad. There are many aspects of banking structure which have no counterpart in other countries. The most striking probably has been the existence of a very large number of unit, individually-owned banks, typically of small size, and the multiplicity of laws, rules, and regulations which shape their activities.

The over-all performance of the banking system in this country has similarly attracted extensive study and discussion. At times in the past, the system has shown an amazing flexibility and capacity to finance the rapidly growing economy of which it is an integral part. At other times it has contributed to extreme fluctuations in business activity.

This uneven performance has, of course, called for corrective measures and these have been largely successful. For more than two decades the banking system has been remarkably stable but at the same time flexible enough to accommodate the large and uneven demands placed upon it.

Nevertheless, now as in the past, the structure of commercial banking is subject to many criticisms, some of them serious. For example: "There are too many commercial banks, particularly when compared with other Western nations." "There are too few banks." "Bank chartering methods are archaic." "Supervisory jurisdictions overlap and are both burdensome and confusing to the banks." "Branch banking laws are inconsistent from state to state."

None of these, or other, criticisms can be dealt with simply by reviewing federal or state statutes, or through a general description of various structural arrangements. Such an approach emphasizes form, rather than substance. Accordingly, this chapter seeks to view the commercial banking system as it operates within its present structure, in order to provide a realistic framework against which bank performance can be measured and appraised. Only in this way is it possible to distinguish between real and imaginary drawbacks of the banking structure.

Before proceeding to an examination of the commercial banking structure, consideration must be given to the standards against which banking's performance should be measured. It is true that the performance of the economy itself is a measure of the success or failure of the banking system, since the two, in a money economy, are inextricably tied together. Yet this measure is scarcely sufficient for the purposes of this chapter.

That the commercial banking system has worked well in the past—with several notable and overemphasized exceptions—is evident from the fact that the American economy has developed into the strongest and most productive in the world. But it is also evident, if only because of these exceptions, that performance could have been still better. Relatively little space will be given here to chronicling the difficulties of the past, however, and attention will be focused instead on the present. But how can the performance of the banking system be evaluated?

Without attempting to set forth a rigorous set of standards, it would appear that there are at least three areas in which important questions should be asked:

1) Is the system reasonably cohesive and stable, free from the kind of sudden and drastic change which is unsettling to the economy?

2) Are the number and distribution of commercial bank facilities adequate to meet the requirements of the public? [1]

3) Is the banking system sufficiently flexible and competitive?

In the sections to follow, banking structure is discussed in terms of each of these questions. It is hoped thereby to provide not only a gauge of the present situation, but also, and more important, an indication of the ability of the banking system to meet the challenges of the future.

Banking Stability

The story of commercial banking in the United States is replete with illustrations of instability in the banking structure. Although historians are properly subject to criticism for their insistence on dwelling on these occurrences—and neglecting the much longer periods of stability—the record is nevertheless clear. Mushroom growth in number of banks during certain periods, for example, the mid-1830's and the years just prior to 1920, contrast with other occasions, characterized by numerous bank suspensions, the most notable of which were probably 1839-42 and 1932-33. At still other times the inability of the banking system to

---

[1] The adequacy with which banks are serving the credit needs of the economy is one of several important measures of performance which are dealt with in later chapters of this monograph. The focus of this chapter is on standards having a special relevance to bank structure.

mobilize its resources smoothly and efficiently, as well as the absence of a mechanism for providing needed reserves, magnified minor problems into what came to be known as financial "panics."

In the face of these occurrences it was often predicted—if not urged—that the American system of thousands of independent banks could not survive. Indeed, it was frequently said that the system itself was the root cause of these problems. Yet today commercial banking is as vigorous as it has ever been, and the independent system still flourishes. Moreover, the difficulties which were once so serious have largely faded into insignificance. This section describes how this has come about.

Number of Banks

Of the many unique characteristics of American banking, perhaps the most striking is the large number of commercial banks as noted above. At the end of 1960 there were 13,484 active commercial banks in the United States. This may be contrasted with Canada's nine chartered banks, with about 4,000 branches, and England's eleven banks which are members of the London Clearing House, with about 9,700 branches in England and Wales.

In the United States, commercial banks embrace a wide variety of institutions regularly engaged in the business of receiving demand or time deposits from the public, including national banks, incorporated state banks, trust companies, and bank and trust companies. Also included (though of minor importance) are private banks, industrial banks operating under general banking codes or specifically authorized to accept deposits, and special types of banks of deposit, such as cash depositaries in South Carolina and cooperative exchanges in Arkansas. Trust companies not regularly engaged in deposit banking, of which there were fifty-four at the end of 1960, are usually included within the commercial bank category. However, mutual savings banks and savings and loan associations, a number of whose activities overlap those of commercial banks, are not included under the classification of commercial banking.

Table 1-1 shows the number of commercial banks at five-year intervals from 1900 to 1960. It will be noted that the number reached an all-time high in 1920, exceeding 30,000 in that year. By 1935, following the severe depression of the early 1930's, the number had been halved. Since that time the banking system has been relatively stable, with only a slow downward drift in the number of commercial banks.

The forces instrumental in bringing stability to the banking system did not all originate after 1933. Yet in the period since that year their combined influence has been of major significance. Among the more important of these factors have been: (1) the Federal Reserve System;

TABLE 1-1
Commercial Banks, by Class
Selected Years, 1900-1960

Year[a]	Total	National	State and Private
1900	12,427	3,731	8,696
1905	18,152	5,664	12,488
1910	24,514	7,138	17,376
1915	27,390	7,597	19,793
1920	30,291	8,024	22,267
1925	28,442	8,066	20,376
1930	23,679	7,247	16,432
1935	15,488	5,425	10,063
1940	14,534	5,164	9,370
1945	14,126	5,015	9,111
1950	14,146	4,971	9,175
1955	13,780	4,743	9,037
1960	13,503	4,542	8,961

[a]June 30 or nearest available date.

Source: Federal Deposit Insurance Corporation.

(2) deposit insurance; (3) bank supervision; (4) cooperative arrangements among individual banks.

Federal Reserve System

Established in 1913 after more than a century of experiment and debate, the Federal Reserve System serves as the capstone of the commercial banking system. Although its original function was viewed as the limited one of pooling bank reserves to avoid "panics," it has since developed—along with much expanded authority—into a full central banking system, with major responsibility for the formulation and implementation of monetary policy.

It should be observed that the Federal Reserve System was superimposed on the existing banking structure and thus made no essential change in that structure, except with respect to the supervision of a portion of the banks. Nevertheless, operations of the Federal Reserve have had considerable influence on the commercial banking structure. Of particular importance has been the System's operations in recent years, conducted in the light of much greater understanding of the business cycle and appreciation of the role of monetary policy. This aspect of Federal Reserve operations is treated in a later chapter; at this point it is sufficient to note that the System's contribution to general economic stability has been a key factor in helping to account for relative stability in the banking structure during recent years.

One can, in a sense, trace the shortcomings of the banking system in the history of Federal Reserve legislation. There was widespread agreement that the principal weakness in the banking system prior to 1913 stemmed from the absence of a central bank which, in periods of stress stemming from seasonal, cyclical, or growth factors, would provide commercial banks with the necessary liquidity.

However, the provisions in the original act which limited the types of credit instruments which commercial banks could use for discounting at the Federal Reserve proved to be woefully inadequate when put to the test in the late 1920's and the early 1930's. Subsequent legislation greatly broadened the authority of the Federal Reserve to grant credit to banks in emergency periods and it seems reasonable to conclude that the banking system as a whole will never again be subject to a nationwide liquidity squeeze.

Despite its position as the nation's central banking organization, the System numbers less than half the commercial banks among its members; yet these banks account for almost 85 percent of total commercial banking assets. At the end of 1960 there were 6,174 banks members of the Federal Reserve System, consisting of 4,530 national banks—for whom membership is required by law—and 1,644 state-chartered banks. The System includes twelve Federal Reserve Banks, each operating in a separate district, and a central coordinating and policy-making body known as the Board of Governors.

Efforts to encourage greater participation by state banks in the Federal Reserve System have been largely unsuccessful. In addition to those banks which cannot meet Federal Reserve capital requirements, most smaller country banks have been unwilling to sacrifice certain privileges enjoyed under state law, particularly since they can obtain some of the benefits of membership in the System without joining either through their correspondent banks or by maintaining a check clearing deposit with the Reserve Bank. In 1933 an attempt was made to bring more state banks into the System by making membership a requirement for retaining deposit insurance; however, before the effective date was reached this statutory requirement was repealed by the Congress (1939). Recent legislation authorizing the inclusion of vault cash in the computation of required reserves removes one advantage enjoyed by many state nonmember banks and thus may encourage increased membership.

Deposit Insurance

Like central banking, nationwide deposit insurance was adopted in the Banking Act of 1933 after a long history of experimentation and controversy. Fourteen states had instituted insurance or guaranty systems prior to 1933, the earliest in 1829. At the federal level, insurance or guaranty of bank deposits had been sought by 150 bills introduced in the Congress, the first of which appeared in 1886.

By providing insurance for each depositor in the case of bank failure—

originally to a maximum of $2,500 but subsequently raised to $5,000 and then to $10,000—the Federal Deposit Insurance Corporation contributes significantly to the underlying confidence among depositors which is essential to bank stability.

At the end of 1960 there were 13,126 commercial banks participating in Federal deposit insurance. These represented 97 percent of all commercial banks and held 99 percent of commercial bank deposits. Membership is obligatory for all commercial banks members of the Federal Reserve System, and is optional for state banks not members of that System. Depositors in the 440 insured banks which have closed since the end of 1933 have recovered more than 99 percent of their deposits. Most of the closings occurred in the first decade of deposit insurance.

Although the deposit insurance system, like the Federal Reserve, was superimposed upon the existing banking structure, its adoption in 1933 played a crucial part in preserving that structure. Among the strongest supporters of deposit insurance were advocates of independent, unit banking, who saw in deposit insurance an alternative to—and a means of combatting—regional or nationwide branch banking. At the same time deposit insurance received support from opponents of fundamental reorganization of the banking system under federal government authority. In short: the unprecedented banking crisis of 1933 had created one of those rare moments in history when far-reaching change in the banking structure was feasible; deposit insurance was advocated and accepted as a means of minimizing the economic consequences of bank failure and removing one of the causes without altering the basic structure of the banking system.

Bank Supervision

Perhaps the most complex area in the field of bank structure is the existing supervisory arrangement. In form it would appear to have little logic. Critics never tire of commenting, for example, on the number of examinations to which an individual bank could be subjected. In practice, however, the supervisory structure is far less complex than would appear. Moreover, there are no services overlapping at the federal level. And most important, it has worked reasonably well during the past quarter century.

The key fact of bank supervision today—particularly when compared with supervision prior to 1935—is that virtually all commercial banks are subject to some degree of federal regulation. The result has been imposition of a uniformity which was lacking prior to 1935 and, in addition, a marked improvement in the quality of the supervision given banks in those states where supervisory standards had been weak. Banks chartered by the federal government (national banks) are supervised by the Comptroller of the Currency. In addition to supervision by state author-

PUBLISHED BY PRENTICE-HALL

THE FINANCIAL INSTITUTION MONOGRAPHS FROM THE LIBRARY OF MONEY AND CREDIT

Order now the volumes on institutions allied to yours. You will want to be aware of the growth and potentials of the competition.

Douglas Dillon, Secretary of the Treasury, says, "Here is a valuable library of pertinent information about fiscal, monetary, debt management and other topics of vital interest in the financial community."

ACT NOW — LIMITED PRINTING AVAILABLE

ORDER FROM YOUR BOOKSTORE OR USE THIS HANDY ORDER CARD

	PRICE
☐ The Commercial Banking Industry	$7.50
☐ The Consumer Finance Industry	5.75
☐ Life Insurance Companies as Financial Institutions	7.50
☐ Management Investment Companies	5.00
☐ Mortgage Companies	2.95
☐ Mutual Savings Banking	7.50
☐ Property and Casualty Insurance Companies	3.95
☐ The Savings and Loan Business	6.00
☐ Federal Reserve and the U.S. Treasury	5.00
☐ 9-Volume Supporting Research Studies prepared by 125 leading economists...each 6.50, total $58.50	

☐ **Send complete 18-Volume Money and Credit Library at a special subscription price of $87.72 (regular price $109.65).**

NAME_____

ADDRESS_____

CITY & STATE_____

☐ Payment enclosed   ☐ Bill me
☐ Send for free descriptive brochure on the complete Library of Money and Credit (18 Volumes) — Final volume available approximately April, 1963.

DM862

No
Postage Stamp
Necessary
If Mailed in the
United States

BUSINESS REPLY MAIL
FIRST CLASS PERMIT NO. 365, ENGLEWOOD CLIFFS, N. J.

Prentice-Hall, Inc.

ENGLEWOOD CLIFFS, NEW JERSEY

Postage
Will be Paid
by
Addressee

ATTENTION: DWIGHT MYERS

ities, state banks which are members of the Federal Reserve System are supervised by the Federal Reserve Bank of their district and insured state banks not members of the Federal Reserve System are supervised by the Federal Deposit Insurance Corporation. Only those state commercial banks not insured by the FDIC—numbering only 304 at the end of 1960—are regularly supervised by state authorities alone.

Table 1-2 contains a distribution of banks according to supervisory status. It will be noted that of the three federal agencies, the FDIC regularly supervises by far the largest number of banks; indeed, more than the Comptroller of the Currency and the Federal Reserve Banks combined. On the other hand, the largest part of banking assets is held

TABLE 1-2
Number and Assets of Commercial Banks
by Supervisory Status
December 31, 1960

Supervisory Agent[b]	Number[a]		Assets	
	Total	Percent	Amount (Millions)	Percent
Total	13,430	100.0%	$258,143	100.0%
Comptroller of the Currency	4,537	33.8	139,996	54.2
Federal Reserve Bank and State	1,637	12.2	76,740	29.7
Federal Deposit Insurance Corporation and State	6,952	51.8	39,587	15.3
State only	304	2.2	1,820	0.7

Detail may not add to totals because of rounding.
[a]Excludes trust companies not regularly engaged in deposit banking.
[b]Classification relates to regular examination and periodic submission of reports of condition.

Source: Federal Deposit Insurance Corporation.

by those banks regularly supervised by the Comptroller of the Currency, i.e., national banks plus several nonnational banks in the District of Columbia. State banks members of the Federal Reserve System, while much smaller in number than either national banks or state banks not members of the Federal Reserve System, nevertheless held 30 percent of total commercial bank assets at the end of 1960. The commercial banks regularly examined by the FDIC held only 15 percent of total commercial bank assets.

Apparent duplication or overlapping of supervisory effort stems essentially from two facts. First, all banks members of the FDIC are subject to examination by that Corporation. Since membership in the insurance system is obligatory for all banks members of the Federal Reserve System, both national and state, this means that national banks and state banks members of the Federal Reserve System could, in theory, be examined both by the FDIC and by either the Comptroller or by a

Federal Reserve Bank. As a matter of practice, however, the FDIC regularly examines only those insured state banks which are not members of the Federal Reserve System, and would utilize its powers with respect to Federal Reserve member banks only in very unusual circumstances. The Corporation does, however, receive for purposes of review all examination reports of national and state bank members of the Federal Reserve System.

A second possible area of duplication arises from the fact that state banking authorities supervise banks chartered by their respective states. Thus a state bank, member of the Federal Reserve System, is supervised both by its own state banking authority and by the Federal Reserve Bank of its district; an insured state bank not a member of the Federal Reserve System is supervised by state authorities and by the FDIC. In most cases this is far less of a problem to the bank than would appear at first glance, since the state and federal agencies have devised various methods of cooperating. For example, examinations are usually conducted jointly or concurrently by federal and state examiners, thus minimizing the hardship for the banks concerned.

The fundamental objective of supervision is the maintenance of sound and solvent banks. It includes not only periodic examination of a bank's operations, but also control over organization and liquidation, issuance and enforcement of regulations, measures to correct unsatisfactory situations, and collection and review of reports of condition and of earnings and dividends. The issuance of new stock, the establishment of a branch, merger with another bank, and many other actions of banks require prior approval of the supervisory agency or agencies under which it operates. The scope of a bank examination embraces every phase of bank activity to determine whether or not the bank is operating soundly and in conformity with applicable laws. Special attention is given to an appraisal of the quality of its management as evidenced by the bank's lending and investing policies, the soundness of its assets, and its earnings record.

Among the many aspects of bank supervision, three have particular relevance to maintenance of stability in number of banks: (1) quality of bank assets; (2) organization of new banks; (3) capital adequacy standards. Of course, each of these factors also plays an important role in such matters as availability of banking facilities and the nature of bank competition. Their influence in these connections is discussed later in this chapter.

First, the importance attached since 1933 to an improvement in the quality of bank assets has led supervisory authorities to attack the problem from several angles. Numerous specific limitations on the acquisition of earning assets by commercial banks are found in federal and state statutes. A comprehensive summary is impractical, but the listing of a few which apply to national banks will help indicate their character and scope.

With respect to loans: A national bank generally may not lend to any one borrower an amount greater than 10 percent of its capital and unimpaired surplus. It may not lend on the security of its own stock; nor may it lend to any of its own officers, except with the approval of a majority of the entire board of directors and in an amount not exceeding $2,500. In real-estate lending, a national bank may lend only on the security of first liens on improved real estate; no such real-estate loans shall exceed twenty years in term nor two-thirds of the appraised value of the mortgaged property in amount. With respect to investments: A national bank may not purchase for investment purposes any equity securities, or any nonmarketable debt issues of any private corporate issuer. It may purchase only (1) obligations of the United States government; (2) general obligations of states and political subdivisions thereof; (3) obligations of certain federal government agencies and instrumentalities; (4) the marketable "bonds, notes, and/or debentures, commonly known as investment securities" of private corporate issuers.

Another approach to the asset quality problem has been through interest regulation. The practice prior to 1933 of paying interest on demand deposits was believed to have reached unsound proportions, leading banks to acquire high-yield, high-risk assets. Unrestricted competition for savings deposits was similarly criticized. Accordingly, the Banking Acts of 1933 and 1935 prohibited the payment of interest on demand deposits by all Federal Reserve member banks and FDIC insured nonmembers banks and limited the payment of interest on savings and time deposits to maximum rates specified by the Board of Governors and the Federal Deposit Insurance Corporation.

Still another influence on the quality of bank assets has been the concerted effort by supervisory authorities, through their examining force, to remove high-risk assets from bank portfolios and to restrict the proportion of various types of earning assets in each bank's portfolio to some "desirable" level, typically that suggested by national or regional averages. The importance of this particular development can scarcely be exaggerated—yet neither can it be measured.

The combined effect of these, and other, supervisory operations has been the maintenance of a much higher quality of assets in bank portfolios and, as a consequence, has helped to minimize the problem of bank failure. Although supervisors have been aided in this regard by the generally favorable economic climate in recent decades, it should be remembered that during similar prosperous periods in the past, for example the 1920's, hundreds of bank failures in each year were typical, and even minor economic downturns, no more severe than those since 1945, precipitated additional hundreds of failures.

Second, a basic cause of instability in the banking structure prior to 1933 was virtually unrestricted entry into the banking system. The philosophy underlying this situation had a long history, dating back to the early part of the nineteenth century when strong opposition developed to the then prevailing practice of permitting banks to organize only through special legislative chartering. In an attempt to rectify this situation, which was not only cumbersome but also subject to abuse, New York and Michigan in 1837-38 adopted "free banking" laws, throwing open the business of banking to all persons able to meet specified requirements. A number of other states soon followed their lead, as did the federal government in 1863 through the National Bank Act.

With the passage of the latter Act, "dual banking" made its appearance on the banking scene to remain to the present day. The advantages of a dual banking system are many. Perhaps the most important gain to the nation is the fact that entry into the banking system cannot be foreclosed by reason of favoritism or special or unusual legislation at the individual state or federal level. The existence of two chartering agencies goes a long way toward assuring flexibility and competition in the banking system. However, early experience with dual chartering gave rise to several problems. Perhaps the most important was the fact that in many states it was possible to organize a bank with inadequate capital and, perhaps even more serious, in the absence of any clear need for a new banking facility. Loose chartering standards largely account for the rapid rise in the number of banks, both state and national, prior to 1920, and must also share the blame for the shakeout which followed.

By the mid-1930's this chartering problem had been largely solved. Legislative steps against overbanking took the form of restrictions on freedom of entry into the banking business. Although the free banking principle remained nominally in effect, the conditions that had to be met before a new bank charter could be granted were substantially stiffened as well as increased in number. For example, at the federal level, and with respect to the chartering of national banks, the Banking Act of 1933 doubled the minimum capital requirement. Also, the Banking Act of 1935 instructed the Comptroller of the Currency to give consideration to each of the following factors:

> The financial history and condition of the bank, the adequacy of its capital structure, its future earnings prospects, the general character of its management, the convenience and needs of the community to be served by the bank, and whether or not its corporate powers are consistent with the purposes of this section.

Although the federal government could not establish similar standards for state banks directly, it did so indirectly by requiring the Federal Deposit Insurance Corporation to give consideration to the same factors.

Since it is extremely difficult, if not impossible, for a new bank to operate without deposit insurance the effect has been to impose on newly organized state banks the same requirements with respect to capital, earnings prospects, character of management, and convenience and needs of the community as were applied to national banks by the Banking Act of 1935. Indeed, in many states authorities cooperate by refusing to grant permission to operate a new bank unless the bank can obtain deposit insurance. Also, many state legislatures have surrounded the chartering of new banks with restrictions and conditions similar to those applicable to new national banks.

Thus the advantages of dual chartering have been retained and the disadvantages which characterized the period prior to 1933 have been largely eliminated. Indeed, it may well be questioned whether the pendulum has swung too far in the conservative direction. Further discussion of the organization of new banks will be found later in this chapter.

Third, insistence by supervisory authorities on adequate capital margins has affected both the organization of new banks and the quality of assets. Organizers of a proposed new bank can no longer count on having to meet only minimum statutory requirements if those requirements provide for an amount of capital less than that which appears necessary in view of the anticipated volume of deposits which the new bank will attract. Also, supervisory pressure on operating banks to maintain or improve capital margins has frequently had the effect—at times when new capital is difficult to acquire—of causing banks to cut down on the proportion of risk assets in their portfolios. Thus, in two ways, focusing on capital margins has promoted sound banking and contributed to banking stability.

Bank Cooperation

As indicated earlier, a banking system composed of thousands of independent banks can scarcely operate effectively in the absence of certain unifying forces. The Federal Reserve System provides one such unifying force, particularly through its check clearing system, as well as the other services it renders commercial banks. With respect to check clearance, mention should be made of the fact that the Federal Reserve has been reasonably successful in enforcing clearance at par, i.e., without payment of exchange charges, except in certain of the southern and western plains states. At mid-1961 all but 1,652 commercial banks were on the par clearance list.

Within the banking system itself, cooperative arrangements have been developed and play a crucial role in providing the kind of coordinated and unified financial service demanded by a complex economic system. Particularly worthy of mention in this connection are correspondent relations and clearing houses.

The need for a system to collect checks drawn on banks located in other parts of the country very early gave rise to the use of city correspondent banks in which country banks maintained deposit accounts. City banks competed for such deposits by paying interest and providing free services. Although payment of interest is no longer permitted, a variety of services are performed by correspondents for bank depositors. Although relatively less important than they were at the beginning of the century and during the 1930's, the ratio of interbank deposits to total deposits is only slightly less than during the 1920's.

Among the services provided by correspondent banks, one of the most important is the collection of checks and other out-of-town items. Correspondent banks also participate in loans; provide advice on credit and appraisals; handle investments, including buying and selling securities and their safekeeping; render important assistance of an advisory nature with respect to bank operations, systems, and personnel; and provide many other services. A survey of country banks (with assets under $7.5 million) conducted in 1959 indicated the following percentage of banks availing themselves of the more important services of correspondents: [2]

	Percent of Banks Using
Collections	95
Safekeeping of securities	90
Buying and selling securities	87
Loan participation	67
Portfolio analysis	65
Credit information	60
Foreign department service	62
Bank wire service	55

There has been competition among city banks for these correspondent relationships. While they generally do not charge for the services rendered and recover only out-of-pocket expenses, most city banks find their correspondent accounts profitable. Compensating balances are, of course, required and the accounts are analyzed to determine profitability.

The banking system has been further integrated by the establishment of city and regional clearing houses. There are about 235 clearing houses in the United States. City clearing houses are associations of banks in the same city (and sometimes adjoining cities) formed for the principal purpose of clearing and collecting checks drawn on the participating banks. They also frequently serve as an agency for establishing uniform standards within a community with respect to such things as business hours and holidays.

In recent years regional clearing houses have been established to serve wider trading areas. They do not clear checks but conduct such activities as improving public relations and solving banking problems in the area.

---

[2] *Banking,* September 1959.

Conclusion

A commercial banking system comprised of thousands of banks of various types and sizes can be both unwieldy and unstable. Indeed, this was a characteristic of commercial banking in certain early periods. Today, however, a complex (and not always entirely logical) structure has achieved reasonable stability through a combination of governmental and private efforts. But the achievement of stability is not the sole measure of performance, for it is important that banking facilities be adequate and that the system be reasonably competitive. Thus it is necessary to turn next to a review of the number and distribution of banking facilities, and the forces influencing their change.

Adequacy of Banking Facilities

In the case of an ordinary business the judgment as to whether the public is being provided with a sufficient number of facilities is made in the market place. That number which can be profitably supported is the desirable number; competition will bring in additional units if there is a shortage and will ruthlessly eliminate outlets if there is an over-supply.

The case of commercial bank facilities is different. Because the failure of a commercial bank with its attendant destruction of circulating medium is a more serious matter than the failure of an ordinary business, the determination of the number of banking facilities is not left solely to the impersonal workings of the market. Rather, entry is closely supervised as noted above and, in addition, differs in ease or difficulty depending on the type of banking (unit or branch, for example) permitted in the various states. Thus to determine whether the public is adequately served with banking facilities requires that the number and distribution of offices at any given time be compared with an "ideal" situation—and standards for the latter do not exist.

Recognition of the basic difficulty of measuring the adequacy or availability of commercial bank facilities does not mean that no judgment can be passed—only that no judgment can be definitive. Actually, considerable insight into the subject can be obtained from an examination of changes in the number of banking offices, both in absolute terms and relative to population, as well as of the factors responsible for these changes.

Change in Number of Banking Offices

In 1920 the number of commercial banking offices reached an all-time peak, totaling almost 31,600 in that year, or about one office for every 3,400 persons; at the end of 1960 there were close to 24,000 offices, or about one for every 7,500 persons. Which, if either, of these extremes represented a desirable level of banking facilities can only be determined by examining more closely the magnitude and character of the changes which occurred. Table 1-3 shows the number of banking offices, by type of office, since 1920.

TABLE 1-3
Commercial Banking Offices,[a] by Type
Selected Years, 1920-1960

Year[b]	Total Offices	Banks	Branches
1920	31,572	30,291	1,281
1925	30,967	28,442	2,525
1930	27,201	23,679	3,522
1933	16,991	14,207	2,784
1935	18,643	15,488	3,155
1940	18,059	14,534	3,525
1945	18,070	14,123	3,947
1950	18,964	14,121	4,843
1955	20,639	13,716	6,923
1960	23,955	13,472	10,483

[a]Commercial bank offices in the states and District of Columbia.
[b]End of year except 1920-40 bank data as of June 30 and 1930 branch data as of June 30.

Source: Board of Governors of the Federal Reserve System.

The major part of the decline in total number of banking offices occurred between 1920 and the end of 1933, during which time the number fell from 31,600 to less than 17,000. All of the decline is attributable to banks, since the number of branches, although falling somewhat during the depression, was still larger in 1933 than in 1920. In all, there was a net decline of about 16,000 commercial banks during the period, whereas the number of branches of commercial banks rose from 1,281 in 1920 to 2,784 at the end of 1933.

After 1933 the number of commercial banking offices remained relatively stable until the end of World War II. During this period the number of banks continued to decline but at a slow rate and one which was offset by a steady increase in number of branches. At the end of 1945 there were 18,070 offices of commercial banks, only 1,079 more than in 1933.

Following World War II the number of banking offices began to move sharply upward, due entirely to an acceleration in the opening of new branches. In recent years this growth has been at an annual rate of 8 or 9 percent, compared with about 4 percent per year in the immediate postwar years. The number of banks continued its slow decline, as in almost every year mergers and voluntary liquidations exceeded somewhat the number of newly organized banks. At the end of 1960 total banking offices consisted of 13,472 banks and 10,483 branches.

Because the number of banking offices was declining in the 1920's and 1930's, the number of persons per banking office necessarily rose, from 3,400 in 1920 to 7,400 at the end of 1933. After the decline in number of banking offices had leveled off, and even after a noticeable upward trend appeared, the number of persons per banking office continued to increase, as population growth outstripped growth in commercial banking offices. However, by the early 1950's the reverse became true and since then the number of persons per office has declined.

Changes in the number of commercial banking offices in individual states varied greatly. In general, most states showed a declined in the total number of offices between 1920 and the end of 1933 and an increase since that time. Interestingly, the increase since 1933 occurred in many of the states prohibiting branch banking, reflecting the fact that newly organized banks are more likely to be found in unit banking states, while mergers occur more frequently in states permitting branch banking.

As already suggested, changes in the number of commercial bank offices reflect four factors: (1) bank suspensions, (2) newly organized banks, (3) bank mergers, (4) the opening of branches.

Bank Suspensions

The net decline of 16,000 commercial banks between 1920 and the end of 1933 is even more impressive when viewed by type of change. Actually, almost 22,000 commercial banks ceased operations during that period, about two-thirds by failure and most of the remainder through absorption or merger. New banks and reopenings of suspended banks during the same periods numbered about 7,500.

Failures during the nine years 1921-29—usually identified as a prosperous period—were 5,400, or about 600 per year. For the most part, such failures occurred in farm areas, where banks had been particularly hard hit by the agricultural difficulties of the 1920's.

Beginning in 1930 there was a catastrophic rise in bank failures, due to the nationwide depression. In all, approximately 9,000 commercial banks suspended operations in the four years 1930-33.

Since 1933 bank failures have been negligible. In the twenty-seven years beginning with 1934 there have been only 548 failures, or less than the average for any single year during the prosperous 1920's. Most of these failures occurred during the first years following the depression and typically involved banks already seriously weakened by the depression. The relatively few failures in recent years, since 1945 for example, have been almost entirely attributable to financial irregularities on the part of officers or employees of the banks concerned.

New Banks

Despite the large number of bank closings in the 1920's the number of new banks organized was substantial, typically numbering 300 to 400 per year. This rate far exceeds the annual average since 1934 of seventy-seven new banks per year.[3] In recent years there has been a slight upward movement, with the number of new banks averaging 110 per year since 1955.

A number of reasons have been advanced for the relatively small number of new bank organizations since 1934. The stricter requirements imposed by statute and by supervisory authorities, discussed earlier in this chapter, are a factor. On the other hand, it should be pointed out that, at least until 1952, supervisory officials (except in states in the Southwest) reported few applications for new banks, due to the adequacy of existing facilities and to the unfavorable bank earnings record when compared with other industries.[4] Finally, the fact that more states have permitted some form of branch banking since 1934 (as compared with the 1920's) means that the demand for new banks in those states is correspondingly reduced.

Bank Mergers

Mergers were an important cause of the decline in number of banks prior to 1934, accounting for approximately three out of every ten banks closed. For the most part mergers during this period, which totaled 6,500, stemmed from the same causes as bank failures and seem to have had little relationship to the relatively modest increase in branching. In other words, most mergers prior to 1934 appear to have been alternatives to either suspension or voluntary liquidation; in many cases whether a bank was classified as suspended or merged depended on whether it was able to find a purchaser before or after it closed its doors because of financial difficulty.

Since 1933 bank mergers have been the primary cause of the slow decline in number of banks. However, the number of mergers has been considerably less than in the 1920's and early 1930's. The causes also differ from the 1920's. In general, mergers today reflect, from the point of view of absorbing banks, attempts to obtain additional branch locations, as illustrated by the fact that 85 percent of merged banks are retained as branches. From the point of view of the absorbed banks the

---

[3] Average excludes reopenings of suspended banks, which were numerous in 1934-35.

[4] *Monetary Policy and Management of the Public Debt,* Joint Committee on the Economic Report (1952), Part 2, pp. 995-97.

primary motivation typically stems from one or more of the following: inability to replace retiring management, the attractive price frequently offered, or a poor earnings record.

Branch Banking

Except for several years in the depression of the early 1930's, the number of commercial bank branches has grown in every year since 1920. At the end of 1960 the 10,483 branches of commercial banks probably exceeded in number the total number of branches in any country in the world.

Various factors account for this growth. Perhaps the most important was the fact that, after the debacle of the early 1930's, many areas were underbanked and, as a consequence, branch banking authority was permitted or enlarged in many states which had previously prohibited or severely restricted branches.

In this connection, however, it should be cautioned against assuming that the growth in number of branches since 1933 directly offset the decline in number of banks in the areas in which the decline occurred. Actually, many of the states suffering the most serious bank failure problems in the 1920's and 1930's remain unit banking states today. It will be recalled from discussion earlier in this chapter that these were the states which most strongly supported deposit insurance in 1933—rather than branch banking—as a solution to their problem of instability.

It is beyond the scope of this chapter to appraise the relative merits of unit and branch banking. Probably there is no older or deeper banking controversy than that between the proponents of unit banking, who believe that such a system is essential to the maintenance of competition and the preservation of small banks, and the proponents of branch banks, who insist that efficiency and stability require multi-office institutions. The gap between these two philosophies is reflected in the wide variety of state laws on branching, ranging from outright prohibition of branching to statewide branch banking. Table 1-4 summarizes the present status of state laws.

Clearly, the record of branch banking has been influenced by the different state laws. It might be noted that one result has been that the nation's banks remain primarily unit banks; at the end of 1960 only 2,400 commercial banks, of a total of 13,471, were operating the 10,483 branch offices.

It should be noted that no definite statistical case has ever been made which clearly demonstrates the superiority of the one type of banking over the other, although there has been no dearth of effort to do so. For this reason The American Bankers Association has taken the view that that choice of type of banking should be left to the several states.

TABLE 1-4
Commercial Banking Offices and Population Per Office,
by State and by Branch Banking Status
December 31, 1960

	Population Per Office [a]	Commercial Banks Total	Banks	Branches
Statewide Branching				
Vermont	4,381	89	56	33
Alaska	4,917	46	13	33
Delaware	6,031	74	20	54
Idaho	5,802	115	32	83
Rhode Island	8,595	100	9	91
Connecticut	9,460	268	70	198
Hawaii	6,457	98	12	86
Nevada	6,484	44	7	37
North Carolina	6,594	691	183	508
Arizona	6,890	189	10	179
Oregon	7,190	246	51	195
Utah	7,182	124	50	74
Washington	7,548	378	87	291
Maryland	8,075	384	133	251
South Carolina	8,160	292	145	147
California	8,766	1,793	117	1,676
Limited Area Branching				
Maine	5,385	180	47	133
Massachusetts	9,447	545	171	374
Kentucky	6,064	501	355	146
Indiana	6,184	754	443	311
Mississippi	6,620	329	193	136
Virginia	6,735	589	305	284
Tennessee	6,953	513	297	216
Pennsylvania	7,566	1,496	703	793
Georgia	7,482	527	421	106
Ohio	7,937	1,223	585	638
New York	9,396	1,786	402	1,384
Michigan	8,166	958	380	578
New Jersey	8,805	689	253	436
New Mexico	8,568	111	55	56
Louisiana	8,899	366	190	176
Alabama	9,960	328	238	90
Unit Banking				
South Dakota	2,921	233	174	59
Iowa	3,221	856	673	183
Nebraska	3,222	438	426	12
North Dakota	3,419	185	156	29
Kansas	3,560	612	587	25
Minnesota	4,912	695	689	6
New Hampshire	7,781	78	74	4
Wisconsin	5,512	717	559	158
Montana	5,531	122	121	1
Oklahoma	5,651	412	389	23
Wyoming	5,894	56	55	1
Arkansas	6,312	283	237	46
Missouri	6,636	651	626	25
Colorado	8,814	199	192	7
Texas	9,220	1,039	1,011	28
West Virginia	10,222	182	182	-
Illinois	10,393	970	966	4
Florida	15,330	323	309	14
Average: 50 States and D.C.:	7,486			

[a] April 1, 1960, population data.

Source: Federal Deposit Insurance Corporation.

48

Distribution of Banking Offices

Revealing as aggregate data can be with respect to number of banking offices, they conceal wide variation in various measures of the distribution of offices. Several of the more significant measures are distribution by state, by population of center, and by localities with various numbers of banking offices.

Table 1-4 also shows the number of commercial banks and branches by state at the end of 1960, along with the number of persons per banking office in each state. It should again be cautioned, however, that states vary so widely in such important matters as stage of economic development, distribution of population between urban and rural areas, and transportation and communication facilities that comparisons must be made cautiously.

Perhaps the most interesting feature of Table 1-4 is the demonstration that most states appear to have adjusted reasonably well to the presence or absence of branch banking. As examples: Texas, which prohibits all branching, had 1,011 banks at the end of 1960, or one office for every 9,220 persons. California, which permits statewide branch banking, had about the same number of persons per office (8,766), but in its case the large majority of offices consisted of branches.

Generally it is true that states permitting branch banking have more offices relative to population than do unit banking states. Nevertheless, the pattern is far from consistent. Some states with liberal branching laws, such as Maryland, California, and South Carolina, have more persons per office than the national average. By way of contrast, unit banking states such as Minnesota and Montana rank among the states with the smallest number of persons per banking office.

Table 1-5 shows commercial banking offices distributed by population of center and by the number of offices in the respective centers as of June 1958. It should be noted that this distribution includes metropolitan areas, so that a center of, say, 2,500 persons located within the New York metropolitan area is included within that area. This branch of distribution is not available for years subsequent to 1958.

Approximately one-third of all banking offices were located within centers (as defined above) with only one banking office. Put another way, there were approximately 8,000 population centers with only one commercial banking office (main office or a branch). However, it can also be seen from Table 1-5 that three-fifths of these one-office towns had a population of less than 1,000 persons.

Most centers having from 5,000 to 25,000 population had two or more banking offices; indeed, there were many with five or more offices. No center with 25,000 to 100,000 population had less than two offices and the majority had four or more offices. When population exceeded 100,000

TABLE 1-5
Commercial Banking Offices
by Population of Center or Metropolitan Area
June 30, 1958

Population of Center or Metropolitan Area	Total Banking Offices	Banking Offices in Centers or Metropolitan Areas with:							
		1 Office	2 Offices	3 Offices	4 Offices	5 Offices	6-8 Offices	9-19 Offices	20 or more Offices
Total[a]	21,736	7,703	3,412	921	472	220	421	872	7,715
Less than 250	644	642	2						
250 to 1,000	4,116	3,950	160	6					
1,000 to 5,000	4,843	2,919	1,788	120	16				
5,000 to 25,000	2,848	192	1,422	675	308	135	116		
25,000 to 100,000	860		40	120	148	80	264	208	
100,000 to 500,000	3,024					5	41	664	2,314
500,000 to 2,500,000	2,723								2,723
2,500,000 or more	2,678								2,678

[a]Excludes trust companies not regularly engaged in deposit banking and facilities at military or other federal government establishments.

Source: Federal Deposit Insurance Corporation.

only one center had as few as five offices, with the other centers having from six to more than twenty offices.

Summary and Conclusions

The present number and distribution of commercial bank facilities is a result of the combined effects of cyclical changes, population and economic growth, statutory and supervisory regulations, and the availability of facilities provided by competing nonbank financial institutions. To disentangle these influences in order to determine with precision the present adequacy of banking facilities is as impractical as attempting to apply some ideal standard. Nevertheless, the following conclusions seem warranted:

1) The number and distribution of banking facilities in 1920 should not be used—as some desire—as a standard applicable to today's economy. Quite apart from the revolutionary changes in transportation and mechanization since that date, the record after 1920, particularly with

respect to bank failures, reveals the essential instability of the banking system at that time.

2) It is likely that the nation was seriously underbanked by the late 1930's and until well into the 1940's. The drastic shakeout attributable to the depression almost certainly left many areas without a sufficient number of banking facilities. The growth of nonbank financial institutions probably reflects, in part, this situation.

3) The spurt in number of banking offices during recent years is another indication of the failure to keep pace during the 1930's and 1940's. The fact that offices have been growing faster than population would suggest that part of the explanation is the need to make up for inadequate growth in earlier years. However, this recent growth also reflects prosperity and economic growth in the postwar years, as well as the movement of the population to the suburbs.

4) Unlike the 1920's, bank mergers have had relatively little effect on the availability of banking facilities, since most banks merged are replaced by branches.

5) The need for new banking offices is, of course, most evident in the rapidly growing areas of the country, for example, the west and southwest, and it is in these areas, generally speaking, that branch banking laws are particularly liberal and helpful in meeting the need. In certain rapidly growing states, such as Texas and Florida, which prohibit branching, the number of new banks organized has been impressive. Indeed, in the past three years, these two states account for about 30 percent of all newly organized banks.

6) Supervisory officials have been alert to prevent a reappearance of the overbanking problem of the 1920's and have been successful, both because of their own efforts and the force of events. At present there does not appear to be any serious problem with respect to overbanking or underbanking, although individual areas may require attention from time to time.

Interbank Competition

One of the most important tests of the adequacy of the structure of the commercial banking system is whether it permits a sufficient amount of competition. That competition is desirable is generally recognized, yet it is also well settled that it should proceed within a framework designed, in part at least, to restrain destructive interbank competition. Here, again, the difficulty stems from the dual role of commercial banking: on the one hand to serve the financial and credit needs of individuals and business; on the other hand to provide circulating medium (i.e., deposits) for the banks' respective localities and, collectively, for the nation.

It might be observed that there is no heaven-sent requirement that there be such a dual role. The monetary and credit functions could be served by entirely separate institutions. However, for more than a century and a half the Congress has permitted the bulk of circulating medium to be provided by commercial banks, first in the form of circulating notes and later in the form of deposits. And on balance the arrangement has worked well, as is perhaps indicated by the remarkable development of the American economy over the same century and a half.

Nevertheless, combining the two functions of providing money and credit within the same institutions has brought (and continues to bring) into conflict two differing philosophies, and in the process each has been blunted. Free competition requires acceptance of the proposition that weaker, uneconomic units, unable to meet the tests of the market, should be permitted to fail. But since a bank failure means destruction (or, at best, temporary unavailability) of circulating medium, those aspects of competition which weaken (or are thought to weaken) banks and make them susceptible to failure are restricted or severely regulated.

From the earliest days of commercial banking, public policy has veered between encouraging competition at some times and limiting it at others. Two fairly recent illustrations will suffice. Commercial banks are prevented from engaging in price competition for demand deposits (payment of interest) and severely restricted in engaging in such competition for savings deposits. On the other hand, the 1960 Act giving federal supervisory authorities more control over bank mergers, had as a major objective the prevention of those mergers which might unduly diminish competition among and between commercial banks.

It is against this background that interbank competition must be appraised. The sections to follow deal with the following topics: (1) the nature of present-day interbank competition; (2) nationwide or regional competition; (3) local competition; (4) the relationship between bank concentration and competition; (5) the changes which have taken place in bank concentration.

Forms of Interbank Competition

American commercial banks are privately owned, profit-seeking institutions; hence they must have adequate earnings in order to survive and prosper. For earnings they must acquire earning assets. But to be able to acquire earning assets, they must attract deposits. Thus acquisition of both deposits and earning assets is essential to the success of each bank, and in principle both are equally important.

The competitive chances for deposits and for assets are frequently part of the same process and cannot easily be distinguished. Nevertheless, at some times bank managements direct their competitive efforts primarily toward the acquisition of earning assets (mainly loans), while at other times the major competitive effort will be aimed at acquiring additional deposits. In less formal language, sometimes bankers are more interested in securing loans than in attracting deposits; at other times, they would rather attract deposits than make more loans.

This ambivalent attitude is easy to explain. Since both are essential to banking success, whether a banker would rather have loans or deposits at a given time depends on which is the harder to get at the time. They are never equally easy or difficult to obtain. Rather, depending on the cyclical level of business activity (hence loan demand) and counter-cyclical variations in the central bank's monetary policy of "ease" of commercial bank deposit creation or "restraint," one—sometimes loans, sometimes deposits—is always harder to get than the other.

Both in seeking deposits and in seeking loans commercial banks often compete on the basis of "quality of product" more than price. This is so because banks are faced with a narrow range of possible price variation in their three main functional areas of competition: time deposits, demand deposits, and loans. Hence price competition alone is an inadequate channel for expressing the full range and intensity of interbank competitive action. Price competition between banks therefore must be and is substantially supplemented by nonprice, or quality, competition.

Bankers turn to quality competition to compete with each other more effectively than price competition alone permits in this field. For example, in competing for time deposits, the maximum rate of interest that banks may offer is set and regulated by federal bank-supervisory authorities, acting under Congressional mandate. This maximum rate has never been higher than 3 percent; for the years 1936-56, in fact, it was only $2\frac{1}{2}$ percent. In that earlier period, however, both customer-loan rates of interest and open-market yields available to the banks on investment assets were historically low, so that banks could not earn enough on their funds to be able to afford to pay even $2\frac{1}{2}$ percent for time deposits. For most of the period, the banks' effective ceiling rate, reflecting earnings opportunities available to banks for funds acquired through time deposits, was closer to 1 percent than to $2\frac{1}{2}$ percent.

A range of possible variation in the rate paid on time deposits of from 0.0 percent to 1 percent is obviously not very wide. It sufficed in the 1930's and 1940's only because, as has been indicated, bankers were not urgently interested then in acquiring additional time deposits anyhow; they were much more concerned about acquiring earning assets. Subsequently—especially since 1955—interbank competitive efforts have shifted in emphasis away from loans and toward deposits.

This situation has emerged as general monetary conditions have tightened appreciably and as bank loan rates and the rates of return available to banks on open-market investment assets have both risen responsively. Now, bankers are quite eager to secure additional savings and other time deposits because they can earn more from having them and because they are both able and willing to pay more to get them. Yet the maximum rate banks are permitted to offer for time deposits has been raised only 0.5 percent, and this maximum rate has been widely adopted. Since they may legally pay no more, commercial banks are forced to compete for time deposits primarily on a nonprice, or quality basis.

In competing among themselves for demand deposits, commercial banks are entirely prohibited by law from offering any positive price inducements. In this area of interbank competition, therefore, commercial banks stress the inducement of more and better service to the depositor. Cutting of service charges is not a common form of competition. For one thing, a reduction in the level of service charges sufficiently large to have any effect in attracting new deposits would apply not only to new deposits attracted by the reduction but also to all existing demand deposits. A substantial reduction in service-charge income to the bank would thus result. Secondly, service-charge income is too important for many banks willingly to make a sharp reduction in its amount. Finally, there is no element of profit in service-charge pricing to begin with. As typically (in fact, practically universally) imposed by American commercial banks, service charges on demand deposit accounts aim only to recover the banks' costs of servicing these accounts.

Finally, in interbank competition for loans, the banks' ability to make use of measures of price competition is likewise severely limited. Price competition is a more significant element in interbank competition for loans than it is in interbank competition for either time deposits or demand deposits. But the banks' range of price-competitive action is usually limited as a factual matter to the area between the floor under loan rates provided by the prime loan rate and the ceiling over them resulting from state-imposed "usury laws," setting maximum legal rates of interest on loans.[5]

The very character of bank lending explains why so much emphasis is placed on quality competition in bank lending. At first glance, bank credit may seem to be the most homogeneous of commodities. Actually, though, no two prospective borrowers offer the bank quite the same package of credit quality and other assurances of repayment, and of compensating balances and other commensurate advantages of making the loan. Thus each customer loan, and especially each business loan, in a separately negotiated transaction, is a custom-made product with its own special costs and must be separately priced. In a market with such

---

[5] The prime loan rate is the rate that the nations' biggest banks charge their biggest and "best" (in terms of credit quality) corporate borrowing customers for short-term, unsecured credit accommodation.

wide product variation and limited range of price difference, buyers generally recognize that (within limits) quality is more important than price.

National or Regional Competition

There are about 13,500 separate commercial banks in the United States, but they do not all compete with each other. Most of them compete directly for most types of business with the relatively small number of banks and other financial institutions that operate in the same geographically limited market area; and compete indirectly only with banks and other financial institutions that operate in contiguous market areas. There is, however, one significant exception to this generalization.

A moderate number of the nation's banks—the largest ones—do compete actively with each other for two classes of deposit and loan business in markets that (for these classes of business) are regional or national rather than local, in geographic scope.

The two kinds of business for which large banks compete on a regional and national basis are (1) the deposit accounts and borrowings of large regional and national business corporations; (2) the deposit accounts (correspondent balances) of "country" banks. It is difficult to be precise about the number of large banks actively engaged in competing for these kinds of business in a regional or national market. Probably no more than several hundred compete on the regional level; and the number competing on a national basis is much smaller—probably no more than 100. While these numbers are small in relation to the total number of banks in the country, they are large in relation to the usual number of bank competitors in a given market area. Also, the large banks engaged in regional and national competition for corporate deposits and loans, and for interbank deposits, are alert and aggressive competitors, and they are competing for the business of a sophisticated and well-informed group of customers—the financial officers of large corporations and the money position managers of other banks. The competition between these banks is intense, and involves a substantial element of price competition. However, for the general reasons noted earlier, quality competition predominates over price competition in this area also.

The fact that there are probably 100 commercial banks competing nationally is significant in appraising the degree of competition. Few, if any, major industries can point to that number of competitors. Whether it be steel, automobiles, or electric equipment, to name a few, the number of "giants" is exceedingly small, certainly less than ten. If any of these industries were to include 100 major competitors it would probably be considered *prima facie* evidence of substantial competition, yet commercial banking is frequently charged with being insufficiently competitive. Whether this criticism is valid at the local level is yet to be considered, but it would appear to have little relevance to the national picture.

Local Competition

As already indicated, most interbank competition takes place within individual trade areas. The extent to which it is present cannot be measured precisely, but it is at least possible to examine the conditions necessary to the existence of sufficient competition.

Ideally, a community or trade area would need two or more offices of commercial banks to meet the minimum requirement for the existence of competition. It has already been pointed out that about 8,000 communities have only one banking office. Possibly an additional 1,000 have two or more offices but of the same bank. Standing alone, these data would imply a large area in which interbank competition does not exist. However, the data are subject to several important qualifications.

First, communities with one office are seldom isolated, and interbank competition may exist within the community even though one or more of the competitors is located in nearby communities. Second, it can be roughly estimated from the data that not more than one-fourth of the population (on a 1950 census base) lives within single-office communities, whereas at least three-fourths of the population lives in centers or trade areas with less than 50,000 persons, with the number of banking offices typically two, three, or four.

Another condition for workable competition is that there be no marked disparity in size of competing units. Generally, size disparity (i.e., concentration of bank assets) increases with the size of the community, so that there is likely to be noticeable concentration in the largest cities. This is due to the fact that the larger cities contain some banks which compete both locally and nationally.

Offsetting the fact of greater concentration in larger cities is the typically larger size of all banks in such cities, as well as the larger number of banks. Accordingly, it would appear that in smaller communities with two or more banks there is less apt to be size disparity inimical to the workings of competition; in larger cities such disparity does exist but the number and size of banks suggests that even smaller banks in such places are sufficiently large to offer a full range of banking services and thus to enforce workable competition within the city or trade area.

Concentration and Interbank Competition

In the absence of traditional characteristics of competition, such as unrestricted entry into the industry or most forms of price competition, attention is frequently centered for commercial banking on bank concentration and changes therein. There is no question that concentration and competition may be related, but the relationship may be quite different under various circumstances.

It should be noted first that the presence or absence of a certain degree of concentration, however measured, may tell nothing about the competitive picture. As already noted, a one-bank town—where concentration is 100 percent, by definition—may experience more intensive interbank competition than another town with more ·than one bank. As another example, two banks competing vigorously in a particular town may hold the overwhelming proportion of the community's banking assets. Nevertheless, competition may be much more effective in this town than in a town in which three or four banks hold the major portion of bank assets.

Changes in concentration can be similarly misleading. An increase in concentration over a period of time can reflect either decreased or increased competition. The latter would be the case, for example, where two or three banks compete strenuously and, in so doing, attract an increasing share of the banking business in the city. Also, of course, a decline in concentration may be accompanied by a decline in competition.

The answers to questions posed by situations such as those described above are important, and of more than academic interest. Under legislation enacted in 1960 each of the federal supervisory agencies is required to approve each bank merger coming within its jurisdiction, i.e., depending on the continuing bank, the Comptroller of the Currency if it is a national bank; the Board of Governors if a state member bank; the FDIC if an insured nonmember bank. The legislation further specifies that "the effect of the transaction on competition" be taken into consideration. Each merger automatically increases the degree of bank concentration in a given geographic area—always within the state and usually within the community unless the absorbed bank is acquired as a branch by a bank not previously operating a branch in the community. Thus, the relationship between increased concentration and competition is almost always in the forefront of the consideration of any such transaction.

Because of the interest in concentration and competition, as well as because of the impact of changes in concentration on the banking structure, it is important to note the extent to which banking is or is not becoming more concentrated. In this connection it should be observed that most measures understate to some degree the extent of concentration because of the existence of two types of multi-office banking not previously discussed: group banking and chain banking.

Group banking refers to control of banks through holding companies. At the beginning of 1960, there were forty-eight such companies subject to regulation by the Board of Governors of the Federal Reserve System under the Bank Holding Company Act of 1956. These companies had

413 banks with total deposits of $17.3 billion. Chain banking commonly refers to ownership of (or controlling interest in) two or more banks by an individual or family. Information on the number of banks included in chains is not available but it is believed that chain banking is less extensive than group banking.

Changes in Bank Concentration

There are probably as many measures of bank concentration as there are writers on the subject. Table 1-6 shows changes in concentration since 1920, measured in various ways, for the nation as a whole. It will

TABLE 1-6
Concentration of Commercial Bank Deposits
Selected Years 1920-1960

(Dollar amounts in millions)

Commercial Bank Group	1920	1934	1940	1949	1960
Total					
Number of banks	30,444	15,518	14,477	14,156	13,471
Deposits	$35,947	$40,060	$65,431	$145,174	$229,824
Largest 100 banks					
Percent of total number	.33%	.64%	.69%	.71%	.74%
Deposits	n.a.	$21,462	$37,081	$ 64,611	$105,838
Percent of total deposits	n.a.	53.6%	56.7%	44.5%	46.1%
Largest 10 banks					
Deposits	$ 3,481	$ 9,169	$17,244	$ 27,505	$ 46,436
Percent of total deposits	9.7%	22.9%	26.4%	18.9%	20.2%
Largest bank					
Deposits	$ 699	$ 1,629	$ 3,466	$ 5,656	$ 10,285
Percent of total deposits	1.9%	4.1%	5.3%	3.9%	4.5%
Largest ½ of 1 percent of banks					
Number of banks	152	78	72	71	67
Deposits	n.a.	$20,135	$34,159	$ 58,519	$ 93,522
Percent of total deposits	n.a.	50.3%	52.2%	40.3%	40.7%
Largest 1/10 of 1 percent of banks					
Number of banks	30	16	14	14	13
Deposits	n.a.	$11,897	$20,360	$ 32,607	$ 52,783
Percent of total deposits		29.7%	31.1%	22.5%	22.9%

n.a. - Not available.
Data are for states and District of Columbia.

Source: Federal Deposit Insurance Corporation.

be noted that these measures include the proportion of commercial bank deposits held by the largest 100 banks, largest ten banks, largest single bank, largest 0.5 percent of all commercial banks, and largest 0.1 percent of all commercial banks.

It is a striking fact that the general pattern of change since 1920 is the same, regardless of the measure used. Between 1920 and 1934 there was a substantial increase in bank concentration, and then a further increase during the six years 1934 to 1940. Since 1940, however, bank concentration has declined, usually to a significant extent. Thus the 100 largest commercial banks held 46 percent of commercial bank deposits in 1960, compared with 57 percent in 1940; the largest bank held 4.5 percent of deposits in 1960, compared with 5.3 percent in 1940. It is also interesting that in all but one of the measures shown in Table 1-6 concentration in 1960 was less than in 1934. When data are adjusted for holding companies (adjustment cannot be made for chains) the same general pattern prevails, although the various percentages are one to several percentage points higher.

Changes in concentration by state are shown in Table 1-7. These data reflect the same general trend as described earlier; in the majority of the states the percentage of deposits held by the largest bank and by the five largest banks declined between 1940 and 1960, after increasing between 1920 and 1940.

The data in Table 1-7 also reveal that bank concentration is more pronounced in states permitting branch banking than in unit banking states. However, the disparity is reduced if group banking is taken into account since this type of banking is particularly prevalent in unit banking areas.

The pattern of change in bank concentration in various cities reveals more diversity than do the state data, but the main outlines remain the same. Unfortunately, city data are not as complete as state or national; however, several studies support the foregoing conclusion. The 1956 *Annual Report of the Comptroller of the Currency* contains data for all cities with more than 50,000 persons, which indicate that there was practically no change in concentration during the ten years 1946-56. A study of fifty-three leading cities by the FDIC shows a decline in concentration, when measured by the proportion of assets held by the largest bank in each city, for three-fifths of the cities between 1936 and 1956. Two-fifths of the cities showed a decline in the proportion of assets held during the same period by the largest bank and by the five largest banks.

A tabulation of bank concentration in metropolitan areas by the FDIC in its *1960 Annual Report* for three dates only (1920, 1934, and 1958) shows a general increase in concentration, particularly between 1920 and 1934. However, in about half the metropolitan areas there was a decline in bank concentration (measured by the proportion of deposits held by the largest and by the five largest banks) between 1934 and 1958. It seems likely that if 1940 data had been available the changes between that date and 1958 would have been similar in nature to those previously described for the nation and for the majority of the states.

TABLE 1-7
Concentration of Commercial Bank Deposits in the Largest and in the Five Largest Banks in Each State[a]
December 31 of Selected Years 1920-1960

	Deposits as a Percent of Total Commercial Bank Deposits in[b]—							
	Largest Bank				Five Largest Banks			
State	1920	1934	1940	1960	1920	1934	1940	1960
Statewide Branching								
Nevada	12.5	52.9	80.8	63.1	49.4	83.7	94.8	97.2
Rhode Island	30.7	41.6	38.0	52.6	71.9	84.1	81.9	95.9
Arizona	6.4	25.8	46.1	47.2	26.7	68.2	89.2	96.9
Delaware	23.6	35.2	52.0	44.8	63.4	73.3	81.3	91.5
Oregon	11.9	40.6	45.6	43.7	42.0	73.2	87.7	88.4
Hawaii	-	-	-	43.0	-	-	-	95.7
California	6.9	30.6	35.5	42.3	23.4	63.9	66.4	77.7
Idaho	4.9	29.7	27.5	36.0	18.7	60.2	68.0	83.8
Washington	5.5	24.9	35.2	33.4	22.4	55.6	69.1	72.2
Utah	8.3	26.1	25.6	30.3	32.6	79.3	77.8	76.5
Alaska	-	-	-	29.4	-	-	-	79.1
South Carolina	5.0	14.2	25.2	24.7	12.6	46.0	51.3	51.3
North Carolina	5.8	19.2	20.5	23.3	13.9	43.9	48.4	56.1
Connecticut	4.6	11.8	12.6	18.0	21.7	37.3	38.7	55.6
Maryland	4.9	30.7	29.5	16.2	20.3	52.5	55.3	55.1
Vermont	4.7	5.8	6.2	9.4	18.8	21.9	22.6	35.2
Limited Area Branching								
Massachusetts	11.2	37.4	38.6	27.5	35.5	61.4	63.5	53.4
Michigan	8.5	30.2	30.6	21.5	26.2	55.1	57.7	50.1
Alabama	13.5	21.1	21.4	17.8	34.4	51.9	54.5	40.6
Georgia	10.2	26.7	24.1	17.2	26.4	67.3	67.6	48.2
New York	8.6	13.4	16.0	16.6	28.5	46.0	51.7	54.8
New Mexico	10.6	14.4	17.4	16.5	27.3	55.8	54.3	45.4
Louisiana	16.3	30.2	26.1	14.3	47.1	63.2	59.1	38.7
Maine	6.3	7.4	8.4	13.2	23.1	30.4	29.9	46.5
Pennsylvania	3.1	17.7	18.5	12.9	12.4	39.0	42.0	38.7
Ohio	12.0	16.0	15.8	11.8	25.5	39.2	38.9	30.9
Mississippi	3.2	4.5	6.9	11.7	13.8	19.7	22.2	28.7
Tennessee	6.0	15.9	14.5	11.5	24.7	56.1	55.4	40.8
Kentucky	9.8	13.3	14.7	11.2	21.9	35.8	39.6	33.5
Indiana	3.6	12.6	14.2	9.8	11.8	27.3	29.5	29.3
Virginia	6.3	11.9	12.1	7.7	20.0	34.4	35.2	27.7
New Jersey	4.9	8.7	8.8	6.3	16.3	21.8	21.9	23.5
Unit Banking								
Illinois	10.5	27.5	28.0	15.9	25.9	70.1	66.5	42.1
Colorado	9.8	19.0	18.2	15.8	33.4	57.7	54.7	47.0
Wisconsin	10.7	34.5	31.4	15.4	20.6	46.9	44.0	28.6
Nebraska	4.5	15.9	14.4	14.8	15.2	47.6	45.6	37.6
North Dakota	5.9	28.0	21.5	14.0	11.7	67.2	58.5	27.4
Oklahoma	5.7	12.9	13.7	12.3	15.4	42.1	44.5	42.1
Minnesota	6.6	38.4	35.9	12.0	30.0	70.4	67.8	35.6
Wyoming	8.1	9.6	12.3	11.2	25.0	38.1	40.6	38.8
Missouri	9.4	16.5	16.9	9.5	25.4	56.1	53.4	35.7
South Dakota	2.1	29.4	28.6	8.8	6.9	49.5	48.7	31.2
Texas	2.7	8.6	7.7	8.2	11.0	26.8	24.6	27.8
Florida	9.7	18.9	17.9	7.0	28.0	59.4	58.3	20.3
Arkansas	4.1	8.1	10.7	6.8	14.0	31.8	36.7	23.3
Kansas	1.5	6.5	7.3	6.8	5.8	21.6	22.2	18.7
West Virginia	3.2	8.5	7.7	6.1	12.7	31.0	30.0	22.6
Montana	4.1	38.0	37.0	5.7	15.4	69.3	63.9	24.4
New Hampshire	7.5	7.6	8.5	5.7	23.9	31.4	29.3	25.5
Iowa	1.6	10.7	8.7	4.7	6.0	26.6	25.0	17.4

[a] States ranked within branch states by percent in largest bank in 1960.
[b] Includes branches.

Source: Federal Deposit Insurance Corporation.

60

Summary and Conclusions

Interbank competition largely takes the form of quality, rather than price, competition because of the nature of the statutory and supervisory restrictions placed on commercial banking.

Interbank competition for deposits and loans most frequently takes place in a geographically limited local market area and characteristically involves but a small number of competing banks. The regional and national competition between several hundred of the nation's largest banks, for large corporate balances and borrowings and for correspondent-bank accounts, occurs on a national scale. But otherwise, although most American people reside in communities served by at least one bank, at least 20 percent of the people live in one-bank towns; and almost half the people live in towns with only a few banks.

Interbank competition is not absent in a one-bank town in view of modern transportation and communication facilities, but it is less prevalent there than in a two-bank town. Unless the one-bank-town local market area is judged big enough to support an additional bank profitably, however, nonbank financial institutions and other partial substitutes for another local bank as may be available must of necessity be deemed to constitute workable competition, since the local market can sustain no greater amount of interbank competition.

Local interbank competition tends to be keen in towns with only a few banks, provided the competing banks are not so unequal in size as to bring about a significant differential in the quality, quantity, and variety of banking services that each is equipped to offer in the local market. Thus the degree of interbank competition in such towns is best evaluated by reference to the degree of banking concentration that exists in local markets for banking services.

Apart from the situation in one-bank communities, it is generally the rule that banking concentration increases as the size of the local market area increases. It is greater in cities than it is in towns, and significantly greater in large cities than in small ones, becoming greatest in the very largest cities. There are two reasons for this pattern of bank-asset concentration. As communities grow, the borrowing needs of the market area's bigger borrowers ordinarily grow more rapidly than the market does; and some of the area's banks must also grow more rapidly than the market does, to facilitate the economic growth of the community. Also, the largest cities with the highest degree of relative banking concentration are the locations of the several hundred large banks that engage in regional and national, as well as local, interbank competition.

And even the smaller banks in these larger local market areas are generally large enough to offer the full range and quality of banking services that the local markets demand.

Concentration in banking is substantially less today than twenty years ago on a national basis, and the same is true of most states and individual localities. To the extent that less concentration may mean more competition the system is probably more competitive today than in the 1930's and early 1940's.

Conclusion

By the tests posed at the beginning of the chapter, the commercial banking structure receives good to excellent grades. Stability, in the sense of avoidance of erratic fluctuation in the number of banks, has been achieved; bank facilities are sufficient in most areas, and where there is a shortage the banking system itself seems to be on the way toward solving the difficulty; interbank competition—or at least the necessary framework for competition—appears to be at a desirable level.

There is no question that in each of these areas improvement is still possible. Even the handful of bank failures each year may be too many; the procedures for providing new bank facilities could be eased in some places; interbank competition could be intensified. The difficulty in each instance is that something essential must be sacrificed. To eliminate the possibility of bank failure except under the most extraordinary circumstances would require a highly concentrated system, little or no interbank competition, and particular emphasis on bank soundness. To assure a banking facility at every possible location would necessitate relaxation of standards for the opening of new banks or branches. To obtain still more interbank competition than already prevails would also mean a relaxation of standards for new banks or branches and, in addition, would probably require more restrictions on branch banking in some localities.

Thus it is apparent that perfection is impossible, if only because it would involve contradictory approaches. On the other hand, the history of the commercial banking structure indicates that where improvement is genuinely needed the appropriate steps will be taken, either by the banks or by governmental authorities. In the meantime the present structure seems peculiarly well adapted to an economy of the size and complexity of the United States.

Chapter 2

COMMERCIAL BANKS AS DEPOSIT INSTITUTIONS

Commercial banking can be said to perform two basic functions: a credit function and a deposit function. The former involves commercial bank financing of the needs of individuals, business, and government, but aside from the wide variety of customers and loans there is nothing extraordinary about this function, which is shared with many other financial institutions. The unique character of commercial banking lies in the fact that its obligations to the public consist of highly liquid claims, the major part of which (demand deposits) comprise most of the nation's money supply.

This chapter focuses attention on the deposit function of commercial banking, first with respect to demand deposits and second with respect to those deposits which are only technically less liquid than demand deposits, i.e., savings and time deposits. In each instance two questions underlie the analysis: (1) What are the functions of deposits? (2) What factors are important in determining the volume of deposits held by the commercial banking system?

Later in this monograph, individual chapters will analyze commercial banks in terms of their role as multifunctional lenders. But the ability of the banking system to perform this important function adequately depends to a large extent upon the way in which the banks serve—or are permitted to serve—as deposit institutions.

Demand Deposits

Demand deposits account for approximately two-thirds of the total deposits of commercial banks. They differ from other claims on banks or on other financial institutions because they are the chief medium of payments used by the American economy. They constitute the bulk of the nation's active money supply.

It is well to recall that commercial banks from the beginning have exercised the responsibility of providing circulating medium, although not always in the form of demand deposits. Early in our history the proceeds of most bank loans took the form, from the borrower's standpoint, of banknotes issued by the individual bank and payable to the bearer on demand. Prior to 1860 these notes constituted an important part of the money supply. However, their use gradually declined as commercial banks, particularly in the larger financial centers, substituted the creation of demand balances (checking accounts) for the issuance of notes in the case of loans. From a bank's standpoint there was no essential difference between the two procedures—in both cases an obligation was acquired from a borrower and the bank's liabilities were increased by an equivalent amount (deposits or banknotes). Deposit banking, although firmly established and growing before 1860, was further stimulated by the *de facto* prohibition in 1865 (through a special federal tax) of the issuance of banknotes by any but national banks. By the end of the nineteenth century circulating banknotes were a minor portion of the money supply and demand deposits had achieved the dominant position which they continue to occupy.

Special Functions of Demand Deposits

The specific ways in which demand deposits play their unique part in the economy are best illustrated by briefly discussing the manner in which they serve as (1) a payments medium; (2) a collection service; (3) a liquidity medium.

1) Checks drawn on commercial banks constitute by far the chief payments medium of the American economy. The only other payments media of significance are circulating currency and coins, and bank demand deposits are about four times as large in volume. Other media of payment such as money orders and travelers' checks sold by other than banks are quite small by comparison. Specialized devices like credit cards and drafts drawn on corporate treasurers involve payment by check or direct debit to bank deposit accounts, and so have the same ultimate effect as payment by check.

Commercial banks have developed a wide variety of specialized payment services to fit the requirements of particular classes of depositors. For businesses, banks provide such services as the handling of payrolls, telegraphic transfers of funds and payments by drafts drawn on corporate treasurers instead of banks. For individuals, checking accounts without minimum deposit balances have achieved popularity.

There is no known mechanism in this country that can take the place of commercial banks in providing the payments services required by a highly developed economy like that of the United States. However, there is constant effort, especially in periods of credit stringency, for individuals and businesses to reduce demand deposit balances relative to increased expenditures. There are no statistics of the volume of "transactions balances" maintained by depositors, but the widespread efforts to reduce such balances to absolute minimums are a matter of common knowledge. These efforts have made it increasingly necessary for individual commercial banks to measure the cost of providing service to depositors and to weigh this cost against the revenue derived from balances maintained.

2) Commercial banks receive for collection not only virtually all checks drawn, but also bond coupons, notes and drafts, and other credit instruments. In a few cities where branch banking is prohibited or large foreign-born populations live, check collection agencies handle a relatively small volume of collections. But the collection function, like the payments function, is almost entirely conducted by the commercial banks.

Commercial banks constantly are seeking to speed collections and to reduce their cost. Great strides have been made towards the achievement of this objective, particularly for business deposits. Apart from maintaining round-the-clock service and utilizing elaborate equipment to hasten the flow of collection items, specialized arrangements have been evolved for businesses. The Post Office lock box collection system, under which remittances due a concern are sent to a Post Office lock box which the bank's representative empties at frequent intervals, typifies efforts to speed cash realization on remittances received by depositors. "Remittance banking" is sometimes used as a term to describe the speedier flow of remittances to collecting banks to reduce the "mail float," and the faster collection of these items by banks to reduce the "bank float."

Another major advance towards increasing the efficiency and reducing the cost of bank collection service is being achieved by the use of numerals printed with magnetic ink on checks to make possible automation in check handling.

As in the case of payments service, the commercial banking system is the only mechanism available to process the vast and ever-expanding volume of payment and credit media that now flow to it for prompt, efficient collection.

3) Demand deposits in commercial banks constitute the most widely used liquidity medium in the economy.

All classes of depositors utilize checking accounts for the triple purpose of making payments, effecting collections and providing liquidity, so that the distinct character of these three services is often overlooked. As payment and collection services are elaborated, particularly for business depositors, and liquid balances are held down because of heavy spending to acquire needed assets, it has become increasingly important to set minimum deposit requirements related to services performed for the depositor. The elaboration and rapidly growing cost of the payment and collection services rendered by commercial banks make it unrealistic to assume without close comparisons between all prorated costs and estimated earnings from each deposit account that balances maintained are adequately compensatory.

A variety of other liquidity media compete aggressively with bank demand deposits. Because the payment of interest on demand deposit balances has been prohibited for member banks since 1933 and for insured nonmember banks since 1935, such competition has been particularly keen in periods of rising interest rates when competing liquidity media have offered increased yields. Liquidity media that compete with bank demand deposits include time deposits in commercial and savings banks, savings capital in savings and loan associations and credit unions, short-term government securities, commercial paper, and bankers' acceptances. While financial institutions receiving time deposits or savings represented by shares have the legal right to specified advance notice before funds need to be paid out, as a practical matter they pay out funds on demand. As a result, moneys placed in such accounts are regarded by the owners as a source of liquidity comparable with demand deposit accounts in banks.

The same holds true of short-term government obligations, commercial paper and bankers' acceptances, which are readily marketable at prices that can fluctuate only within a narrow range of par value due to the nearness of maturity, regardless of changes in the level of interest rates. All such media can be designated as "near money" or "money substitutes" so far as their use as a substitute for demand deposit balances in banks as a source of liquidity is concerned. But since funds placed in these alternative liquidity media are as a rule first shifted by the owners into bank checking accounts before being used to make payments through the drawing of checks, only bank demand deposits among liquidity media are in active use as money.

This special character of demand deposits is made clear by available data on velocity. Demand deposits in banks were turned over on the average of sixty times in New York City banks, thirty-five times in banks of six other reporting centers and twenty-six times in banks in 337 other reporting centers during 1960. In savings and loan associations and mutual savings banks, withdrawals have averaged about one-fourth of funds held, so that deposits or savings capital are turned over once in four years.

Generation of Demand Deposits

Basic to the creation of demand deposits is the fractional reserve system, which necessitates the keeping by each bank of a reserve balance which is equal to only a portion of total deposits. Thus, Bank A may receive on deposit $100 in currency and, if its required reserve is 10 percent, can make a loan of $90 to a new borrower. The borrower will generally spend his new deposit of $90 immediately so that, perhaps after passing through several hands, it may be checked out of Bank A and be placed in Bank B. Bank B, in turn, can lend this out—except for keeping 10 percent or $9 on reserve—and the $81 balance, after being spent by the second borrower, may eventually lodge in Bank C.

The process can go through many additional steps but the simple fact of the creation of demand deposits can be demonstrated by stopping the process at this point and reviewing the situations of Bank A and B. Bank A has a new deposit of $100, for which it holds $10 on reserve and a borrower's note for $90. Bank B has a new deposit of $90, for which it holds $9 in reserve and a borrower's note for $81. Neither bank has created a deposit out of thin air—each in fact first received additional deposit funds before it made a new loan, and even then did not loan out as much as it received since it kept a portion on reserve. Nevertheless, in the two banks there is now a total of $190 in demand deposits—available to serve as a means of payment—whereas only $100 of new money entered the banking system. Thus, $90 of additional money—in the form of a demand balance—has been created, and if the process were followed through Banks C, D, E, etc. the total which could be created—assuming a 10 percent reserve requirement for all banks—is $900.

Commercial banks, because of the unique character of demand deposits, differ from all other financial institutions in the forces on which they must depend to obtain growth in demand deposits. All other financial institutions are free to attract additional funds for lending and investing by offering higher rates of return, better service or actively soliciting funds. Commercial banks, on the other hand, may compete vigorously with one another for demand balances, but the maximum total which the banking system can hold is determined by the volume of reserves and the level of reserve requirements—both of which are controlled by monetary authorities. Thus, the dominant influence on deposit behavior is the Federal Reserve System, which numbers among its members commercial banks with about 85 percent of all commercial bank deposits.

Reserves of members of the Federal Reserve System must be kept on deposit with the Federal Reserve Banks (except for relatively small holdings of vault cash, which also are counted as legal reserves). Thus, unless there is a change in reserve requirements, the extent to which the banking system may expand (or be forced to contract) the volume of its demand deposits depends upon the volume of reserve funds held with the Federal Reserve or as vault cash, and this in turn depends primarily on the extent to which the Federal Reserve Banks acquire (or relinquish) assets.

Whether at any one time the Federal Reserve Banks acquire or relinquish assets, and the extent to which they do either, is determined by the monetary policy decisions made by Federal Reserve authorities. The various tools used for this purpose, and the impact on the credit function of the banking system, are discussed in detail in a later chapter of this monograph. Thus for the purposes of this chapter it is sufficient to note that it is the Federal Reserve which determines, for all practical purposes, the extent to which commercial banks may expand the volume of their demand deposits. It is against this background that the trend of demand deposits during the past thirty years is best understood.

The Trend of Demand Deposits, 1920-1960

For the whole period since 1929 demand deposits in commercial banks have more than kept pace with economic growth as measured by the gross national product. Demand deposits adjusted [1] increased from $22.8 billion at the end of 1929 to $115.1 billion at the end of 1960, an expansion of 405 percent. The gross national product increased from $104.4 billion in 1929 to $504.4 billion in 1960, a growth of 383 percent.

While bank demand deposits have increased more than gross national product over the whole period, the more significant fact is that the trend of these deposits has varied greatly from time to time over the period. The year-to-year change in demand deposits adjusted is shown in Table 2-1.

The volume of bank demand deposits paralleled the decline and recovery in gross national product during the 1930's. It rose much more rapidly than the output of the economy during the World War II period, when commercial banks expanded their holdings of U.S. Government securities almost fivefold to finance the huge wartime needs of the Treasury and so produced an enormous expansion of demand deposits. Federal Reserve policy at that time was devoted to insuring the success of Treasury financings. Reserves not only were provided abundantly, but the policy of pegging interest rates also enabled member banks to secure additional reserve balances at will.

During the decade of the 1950's, a very different trend of bank demand deposits developed. From the end of 1949 to the end of 1960, demand deposits adjusted increased by only 33 percent, whereas gross national product grew by 95 percent. The rate of increase in demand deposits for the decade was less than two-fifths that of the gross national product. The "income velocity" [2] of demand deposits rose sharply, as the volume

---

[1] The statistical series of "demand deposits adjusted" excludes interbank deposits and cash items in process of collection, since they involve a counting of deposits twice so far as the commercial banking system is concerned. It also excludes U.S. Government deposits, a questionable omission from the viewpoint of this chapter.

[2] This ratio, usually computed by dividing gross national product by demand deposits, relates the "work" performed by the money supply to the value of goods and services produced by the economy.

TABLE 2-1
Annual Change in Demand Deposits and Gross National Product
1929-1960

(Dollars in billions)

End of Year	Demand Deposits Adjusted			Percentage Change in Gross National Product
	Total	Annual Change		
1929	$ 22.8			
1930	21.0	-$ 1.8	- 7.1%	-12.8%
1931	17.4	- 3.6	-17.1	-16.3
1932	15.7	- 1.7	- 9.8	-23.3
1933	15.0	- 0.7	- 4.5	- 4.3
1934	18.5	+ 3.5	+23.3	+16.1
1935	22.1	+ 3.6	+19.5	+11.6
1936	25.5	+ 3.4	+15.4	+14.1
1937	24.0	- 1.5	- 5.9	+ 9.7
1938	26.0	+ 2.0	+ 8.3	- 6.1
1939	29.8	+ 3.8	+14.6	+ 6.9
1940	34.9	+ 5.1	+17.1	+10.5
1941	39.0	+ 4.1	+11.7	+25.0
1942	48.9	+ 9.9	+25.4	+26.5
1943	60.8	+ 11.9	+24.3	+21.0
1944	66.9	+ 6.1	+10.0	+ 9.8
1945	75.9	+ 9.0	+13.5	+ 1.0
1946	83.3	+ 7.4	+ 9.7	- 1.4
1947	87.1	+ 3.8	+ 4.6	+11.2
1948	85.8	- 1.3	- 1.5	+10.7
1949	86.7	+ 0.9	+ 1.0	- 0.5
1950	92.3	+ 5.6	+ 6.5	+10.3
1951	98.1	+ 5.8	+ 6.3	+15.6
1952	101.5	+ 3.4	+ 3.5	+ 5.5
1953	103.3	+ 1.8	+ 1.8	+ 5.3
1954	106.7	+ 3.4	+ 3.3	- 0.6
1955	109.9	+ 3.2	+ 3.0	+ 9.5
1956	111.4	+ 1.5	+ 1.4	+ 5.5
1957	110.3	- 1.1	- 1.0	+ 5.6
1958	115.5	+ 5.2	+ 4.7	+ 0.3
1959	115.4	- 0.1	- 0.1	+ 8.5
1960	115.1	- 0.3	- 0.3	+ 4.6

Source: Board of Governors of the Federal Reserve System and Department of Commerce.

of deposits lagged far behind the growth of gross national product and national income. The great expansion of demand deposits during the World War II years had given rise to excess liquidity in the economy that lessened the need for additional deposits to keep pace with the growth of the economy in the early postwar years.

Equally significant with the marked slowing up in the rise of demand deposits was the pronounced countercyclical pattern they assumed. In a recession year such as 1954, when the gross national product declined, bank demand deposits increased by $3.4 billion. By contrast, in 1957, when the gross national product increased by $23.3 billion, demand deposits actually declined by $1.1 billion. The recession year 1958 witnessed a rise in demand deposits of $5.2 billion, the largest since 1951, while the recovery year 1959 saw another slight decline in the adjusted total for demand deposits in a year when the gross national product increased by $37.8 billion.

The pursuit of a flexible monetary policy since the early 1950's has been responsible for this countercyclical pattern. The monetary authorities have attempted to accelerate the growth of the money supply in recession years and to slow or halt its growth in years of inflationary pressures in order to combat cyclical swings of economic activity.

This brief survey of the past behavior of demand deposits provides a basis for an appraisal of the probable future trend of such deposits.

The Outlook for Demand Deposits

Whether demand-deposit growth will continue in the pattern and at the rates observable during the past ten years depends in large part upon monetary policy. A particularly important factor in this connection as noted above, is the rate of turnover of demand deposits. Each of these factors is discussed below.

It would seem reasonable to anticipate that monetary management in the future will continue to place primary emphasis on controlling the volume of demand deposits to promote economic stability. Accordingly, Federal Reserve authorities can be expected to pursue a restrictive credit policy in a period of high-level economic activity and heavy credit demands, when disproportionate growth in the money supply relative to advances in the economy's physical output would contribute to inflationary pressures. A policy of active credit restraint, implemented chiefly through open market operations that produce pressures on bank reserve positions, will slow up or halt the rise in bank deposits.

Conversely, a credit policy of active ease will almost certainly be pursued in a recession in order to provide the credit environment conducive to recovery. True, the demand for loans is sluggish at such times, but expansion in bank investments will then become the means through which deposit expansion is achieved.

It should be noted that some aspects of fiscal policy, like monetary policy, have assumed a marked countercyclical character. In a recession, the sharp contraction of tax receipts combined with automatically expanded federal expenditures result frequently in large-scale deficit financing. In a period of prosperity, tax collections increase while some types of spending automatically decline, so that deficit financing becomes less of a likelihood. Accordingly, fiscal policy will tend to promote countercyclical movements in the volume of demand deposits.

The prospects for continued countercyclical variation in demand deposits seem good. By itself, such a pattern need not prevent the growth of demand deposits from keeping pace with economic growth. Expansion of deposits during recession periods can compensate for the absence of significant deposit growth during periods of credit restraint. However, the rate of demand deposit growth may lag behind other measures of economic expansion if, because of continued advances in the rate of deposit turnover, monetary authorities are compelled to take more restrictive action than would otherwise be necessary. It is thus important to review changes in velocity and to examine the cause of these changes.

The change in velocity for each year since 1945 is traced in Table 2-2. That year, when World War II ended, was marked by the end of the

TABLE 2-2
Demand Deposit Annual Turnover Rate,[a] 1945-1960

Year	New York Turnover	New York Annual Change	Other Leading Centers[b] Turnover	Other Leading Centers[b] Annual Change	337 Other Reporting Centers[c] Turnover	337 Other Reporting Centers[c] Annual Change
1945	24.1		17.5		13.5	
1946	25.1	+1.0	18.3	+0.8	14.1	+0.6
1947	23.8	-1.3	19.7	+1.4	15.5	+1.4
1948	26.9	+3.1	21.6	+1.9	16.6	+1.1
1949	27.9	+1.0	20.9	-0.7	15.9	-0.7
1950	31.1	+3.2	22.6	+1.7	17.2	+1.3
1951	31.9	+0.8	24.0	+1.4	18.4	+1.2
1952	34.4	+2.5	24.1	+0.1	18.4	0
1953	36.7	+2.3	25.6	+1.5	18.9	+0.5
1954	42.3	+5.6	25.8	+0.2	19.2	+0.3
1955	42.7	+0.4	27.3	+1.5	20.4	+1.2
1956	45.8	+3.1	28.8	+1.5	21.8	+1.4
1957	49.5	+3.7	30.4	+1.6	23.0	+1.2
1958	53.6	+4.1	30.0	-0.4	22.9	-0.1
1959	56.4	+2.8	32.5	+2.5	24.5	+1.6
1960	60.0	+3.6	34.8	+2.3	25.7	+1.2

[a] Excludes interbank and U.S. Government deposits.
[b] Boston, Philadelphia, Chicago, Detroit, San Francisco, and Los Angeles.
[c] Prior to April 1955, 338 centers.

Source: Board of Governors of the Federal Reserve System.

rapid expansion of demand deposits based on large-scale purchases of Government securities by the commercial banks. The wartime decline in deposit velocity, resulting from the imposition of selective economic controls against a background of large year-to-year deposit gains, was halted.

As would be expected, years of economic prosperity and credit restraint under a flexible monetary policy such as has been pursued in the United States since 1951 have been characterized by an acceleration of the rise in velocity. In 1959, the year of most acute credit stringency of the decade, demand deposit turnover increased by fully 7 percent for the year. This increase was equalled only in 1951, when the full impact of the Korean War, accompanying rearmament and accelerated purchasing in anticipation of scarcities of a renewal of controls, were reflected in a similar sharp velocity increase.

The velocity of turnover of bank demand deposits increases in a period of prosperity as a rise in total expenditure swells the volume of checks drawn on demand deposit accounts. But this is by no means the whole story. In addition, velocity rises because higher interest rates attract relatively inactive liquid balances into interest-earning liquidity media or other outlets, with the result that such deposits are activated to a greater or lesser extent. When borrowing becomes more costly and more difficult, there is strong incentive to reduce both liquid and transactions balances more intensively.

Business corporations, as is to be expected, have been most aggressive in reducing their demand deposit balances relative to their expenditures and investments as the need for funds and favorable opportunities for short-term investments have expanded and as the cost of borrowing has risen. Nonfinancial corporations owned close to 40 percent of demand deposits in 1939, 37 percent in 1959. Since business deposit accounts involve far higher turnover than individual accounts, it is evident that business corporations account for a large part of the rise in velocity.[3]

But individuals have also been responsible to a large extent for speeding deposit turnover. This is particularly true when they shift funds to thrift institutions to obtain higher rates of return.

It is through their impact on velocity that thrift institutions have a major effect upon monetary policy in a period of credit restraint. By attracting funds out of demand deposit accounts with the high yields they offer on savings balances, savings and loan associations in particular have played an important role in contributing to the rise in deposit velocity. True, as the funds placed in savings and loan associations are loaned out, they are returned to the total of demand deposits by those who receive the borrowed funds. But these funds are usually shifted to active deposit accounts, so that they continue to accelerate deposit turnover.

Payment of higher interest rates on short-term obligations has attracted a substantial volume of previously idle balances into Government obliga-

---

[3] See George Garvy, *Deposit Velocity and Its Significance,* Federal Reserve Bank of New York, 1959, pp. 38-39.

tions and other liquidity media and such balances generally are shifted to active deposit accounts in the process. The Securities and Exchange Commission estimated net individual purchases of bonds and other obligations at $11 billion for 1959. U.S. Government securities accounted for the larger part of this huge total. This figure is the more significant when compared with estimated net sales of $0.7 billion of obligations by individuals in 1958, when low interest rates stimulated sales of such securities and the placing of the proceeds in demand deposits or savings accounts.

The *Federal Reserve Bulletin* recognized the close relation that exists between the velocity of demand deposits and money market interest rates when it stated: [4]

As interest yields on short-term Treasury securities and other substitutes for cash rose in 1959, the holding of noninterest-bearing assets such as demand deposits became increasingly disadvantageous. Businesses and individuals had an increased incentive to invest idle cash balances and to carry smaller balances in relation to the volume of their check payments. The volume of deposits grew more slowly than spending and the rate of turnover of demand deposits, a measure of the velocity of money, rose.

Chart 1, based on the *Federal Reserve Bulletin*, illustrates the parallel movement of demand-deposit turnover and Treasury bill rates, the rise of which led to "a large increase in nonbank holdings of money substitutes, particularly short-term government securities." [5]

A rise in interest rates may lead to the emergence of newer liquidity instruments that offer additional competition to deposit accounts in commercial banks, since banks are barred from paying interest on demand deposits and may not pay interest on savings and other time deposits in excess of the maximum rates set by the Board of Governors of the Federal Reserve System. In 1959, a substantial shift of foreign dollar balances took place from American to Canadian and other foreign banks. More than $2.25 billion of U.S. dollar deposits had accumulated in Canadian banks by the end of 1959 and perhaps another $1 billion in European banks, because higher rates of return were offered there than United States banks were permitted to pay.[6] Such deposits were then reloaned in the United States by the banks receiving such deposits, to avoid exchange risk.

Time deposit balances have been particularly vulnerable to such competition because of the interest rate ceiling to which commercial banks are subject.

The effect of all such shifts in deposits is to step up the turnover of

---

[4] *Federal Reserve Bulletin* (February 1960), p. 123.
[5] *Ibid.*
[6] See *A Study of Regulation Q as It Applies to Foreign Time Deposits,* The New York Clearing House Association, July 20, 1960.

CHART 1

DEMAND DEPOSIT TURNOVER RATE AND TREASURY BILL RATE
1954–1959

Three-month moving average based on the following: Treasury bill rate, averages of monthly market yields on three-month bills. Demand deposit turnover, seasonally adjusted monthly rates of turnover except interbank and U.S. Government deposits at 337 reporting centers outside New York and six other financial centers.

Source: Board of Governors of the Federal Reserve System.

the funds involved, especially since these foreign dollar balances tend to have a very low rate of turnover in their original form.

Summarizing the causes of an increase in velocity of demand deposits, George Garvy states: [7]

> The activation of balances is a complex process, involving an increased use of balances owned by the *same* economic unit, shifts of deposit balances *among* units which rearrange their holdings of liquidity instruments, and loan expansion. It would appear that the influence of rising interest rates on velocity operates primarily not through a reduction of idle funds, but through the considerable volume of debits generated by the endeavor of corporate treasurers . . . to earn income on the last dollar of temporarily redundant funds. To a considerable extent, statistical data showing rising turnover velocity reflect the churning-over of funds rather than the cyclical reduction of hazards.

Garvy stressed the highly developed character of the money market in the United States as a basic factor lessening the uniqueness of bank demand deposits as a liquidity medium, both for business and individuals and for other financial institutions.

---

[7] George Garvy, *op. cit.*, p. 37.

Thus, increasing velocity over the past decade has been due to a variety of factors, not all of them cyclical. Should there be a continuation of this secular upward trend, the outlook for demand deposits—given a countercyclical monetary policy—is not favorable, since the need for payments media by a growing economy can be supplied by an increase in the money supply, a more rapid turnover of the money supply, or both. At present, monetary authorities are restricted in their operations to measures affecting the volume of commercial bank demand deposits. Therefore the question of the extent to which the financial requirements of economic growth will be provided by an increased rate of deposit turnover, as contrasted with demand deposit expansion, has far-reaching implications for the future place of commercial banking in the nation's financial system. The nature of the problem thus posed is explored more fully in the following chapter on monetary policy.

Savings and Time Deposits

From their inception commercial banks have provided the public with facilities for the deposit of savings, and within recent decades savings deposits have become increasingly important to commercial banks. Accordingly, this section directs attention to the commercial banks' role as savings institutions.[8]

Function of Savings

From the viewpoint of the economy as a whole, savings have both a "real" aspect and a financial aspect. In their real aspect, they represent the financial counterpart of economic resources that are available for investment in productive assets. The saving process thus involves a diversion of some real resources (labor, materials, and equipment) from the production of consumer goods to the production of capital goods. Such savings and investment are essential if an economy is to grow and to provide higher living standards for its people.

This "real" saving process has a financial counterpart. In its simplest form, individuals refrain voluntarily from spending their entire incomes for purposes of current consumption. The funds not so spent may be invested directly in capital goods (such as farm equipment), or they may be invested in the securities of a corporation which uses them to buy productive equipment, or they may be entrusted to a financial institution which relends them for investment purposes. One way or another, the funds that individuals save out of their incomes will normally end

---

[8] In this section the terms "savings," "savings deposits," or "savings and time deposits" when used with reference to commercial banks refers to the savings and time deposits of individuals, partnerships, and corporations. Time deposits held by banks or governmental units are excluded.

up paying for productive equipment (and housing, which is also a "capital" or "investment" good) somewhere in the economy. Businesses, by retaining a portion of current income which is used to buy plant and equipment, also contribute substantially to the savings-investment process. Thus, this financial savings process is actually the means by which real economic resources are diverted from current consumption to the creation of plant and equipment for future production.

Thrift institutions play an essential and increasingly important part in this savings process. In our modern, complex society, savers and investors are not usually the same persons. Hence, facilities are necessary for channeling funds from savers to investors and, when required, back again. Savings institutions perform this function in addition to stimulating the total flow of savings by providing ready savings outlets.

To accomplish these purposes, a variety of thrift institutions have developed in the United States. Commercial banks, of course, are one of the most important of these. Other such institutions are the mutual savings banks, savings and loan associations, credit unions, and the Postal Savings System. In addition, savings are channeled through a variety of other outlets for idle funds such as life insurance companies, pension funds, savings bonds and other Government obligations, investment companies, and corporate securities.

Role of Savings in Commercial Banks

To most commercial banks, savings are of great importance. Next to demand deposits, they are the largest single source of funds. At present, savings deposits make up about one-third of total commercial bank deposits (excluding interbank deposits and items in process of collection). This proportion has been rising during the postwar period, as savings deposits have increased more rapidly than demand deposits. Without this increase in savings deposits, it seems likely commercial banks would not have been able to keep pace with the growth of the economy and would not be able today to serve adequately the nation's credit needs. During the postwar period, savings deposits at commercial banks have grown almost continually, irrespective of business conditions, changes in credit policy, or other economic changes.

Savings deposits are important to the commercial banks not only by virtue of the large amounts involved but also because they are different in nature from demand deposits. The former are much more stable than the latter, having an average annual turnover rate of only about one-half, compared with roughly thirty for demand deposits. As a result, savings deposits enable banks to make mortgage loans, term business loans, and other long-term investments which they might not be able to make if all their deposits were volatile and subject to withdrawal on demand. Hence, the growth of savings deposits at commercial banks has been essential to the modern development of the latter from institutions specializing in short-term business loans to their present status as "department stores of finance."

Aside from the advantages they offer savers, commercial banks have a unique and vital role to play in our financial system by virtue of the fact that they are general credit institutions. Whereas other thrift institutions specialize in granting credit of certain types or for certain purposes, commercial banks make it available in various forms, to nearly all classes of borrowers, and for most legitimate credit needs. Consequently, they are able to direct savings into any channel to meet the demand, and can shift them easily and quickly from one use to another as conditions change. Commercial banks thus give our financial system the flexibility necessary to insure that loan funds can always be directed into the most important uses, as reflected in changes in the demand for funds. Specialized lending agencies do not always provide this kind of flexibility.

To the extent that savings deposits make it possible for commercial banks to engage in a broad range of credit operations, such deposits contribute significantly to the flexibility of our financial system. Hence, while there is certainly a place in our financial system for specialized thrift and lending institutions, it is essential that commercial banks, too, continue to receive a large share of the public's savings.

Extent of Commercial Bank Holdings of Savings Deposits

Since the end of World War II, the volume of savings deposits at commercial banks has more than doubled, as can be seen in Table 2-3. This increase has been about twice as great as for demand deposits. To be more exact, savings deposits rose 112 percent, as compared with 53 percent for demand deposits adjusted between the end of 1945 and the end of 1959.

This large increase in savings deposits reflects, first of all, the tremendous growth in total savings that has occurred as a result of rising incomes, a growing labor force, and perhaps higher interest rates. It also reflects the fact that savings deposits have become increasingly important to commercial banks and the latter have made greater efforts to attract such deposits.

A number of factors have been responsible for this changed attitude. One is the development of more profitable outlets for bank funds than existed during the depression of the 1930's or during World War II. In particular, the growing demand for mortgage loans and the insurance or guarantee by the government of a large part of such loans has provided banks with a profitable and relatively safe outlet for savings funds. Another important factor has been the restraints which the Federal Reserve System has imposed on the growth of demand deposits since 1951 in order to prevent an excessive expansion of the money supply from adding

TABLE 2-3
Savings and Time Deposits and Shares, Selected
Financial Institutions, 1945-1960

(Millions)

Year	Total	All Commercial Banks [a]	Mutual Savings Banks [a]	Savings and Loan Associations
1945	$ 52,885	$30,135	$15,385	$ 7,365
1946	59,025	33,808	16,869	8,548
1947	62,748	35,249	17,746	9,753
1948	65,155	35,804	18,387	10,964
1949	67,890	36,146	19,273	12,471
1950	70,315	36,314	20,009	13,992
1951	74,853	37,859	20,887	16,107
1952	82,447	40,666	22,586	19,195
1953	90,863	43,659	24,358	22,846
1954	100,398	46,844	26,302	27,252
1955	108,630	48,359	28,129	32,142
1956	117,725	50,577	30,000	37,148
1957	129,711	56,139	31,662	41,912
1958	145,148	63,166	34,006	47,976
1959	155,414	65,884	34,947	54,583
1960	169,852	71,380	36,318	62,154

[a] Excludes interbank time deposits, U.S. Treasurer's time deposits, open accounts, and deposits of Postal Savings System in banks.

Source: Board of Governors of the Federal Reserve System and United States Savings and Loan League.

to existing inflationary pressures. Faced with heavy demands for loans while their chief source of funds was being limited, the commercial banks naturally have turned increasingly to savings deposits as an alternative source. A third factor has been a change in the bankers' concept of their proper role in the financial system. At one time, many commercial bankers regarded savings deposits as an incidental or even unwelcome adjunct to their demand deposit business, just as many of them looked with disfavor on lending other than for short-term business purposes. In recent years, however, commercial banking has come to realize that its proper function in our financial system is to act as a general, multiple-type credit institution rather than a specialized one, and that therefore savings deposits have an essential part to play in the banking operation.

Some idea of the importance of savings deposits to commercial banks may be obtained from Table 2-4, which classifies Federal Reserve member banks into four size groups and, within each of these, into three classes according to the proportion of each bank's total deposits that are in the form of time deposits.

At the end of 1959, time deposits made up more than one-half of total deposits for about 25 percent of these banks and more than one-fourth

TABLE 2-4
Member Banks
by Size of Bank and by Ratio of Time to Total Deposits
1959

Banks with Deposits of (Millions)	Ratio of Time Deposits to Total Deposits			
	Total	Under 25%	25-50%	50% & over
(Number of Banks)				
Total	6,184	1,857	2,804	1,523
Less than $2	939	429	329	181
$2 - 5	2,027	639	846	542
$5 - 25	2,422	518	1,241	663
Over $25	796	271	388	137
(Percentage Distribution)				
Total	100.0%	30.0%	45.3%	24.6%
Less than $2	100.0	45.7	35.0	19.3
$2 - 5	100.0	31.5	41.7	26.7
$5 - 25	100.0	21.4	51.2	27.4
Over $25	100.0	34.0	48.7	17.2

Detail may not add to totals because of rounding.

Source: Board of Governors of the Federal Reserve System.

of total deposits for 70 percent of them. Thus, time deposits are an important source of funds for the great majority of Federal Reserve member banks (of which all but three are commercial banks). Savings deposits, as defined here, make up the great bulk of time deposits except at a few of the larger banks which hold substantial amounts of interbank time deposits.

In general, savings deposits appear to be more important to the medium-sized and small banks (except for the very smallest—those with total deposits of one million dollars or less) than to the large banks. Thus, Table 2-5 reveals that the ratio of time to total deposits is about 39 percent for banks with total deposits of $5-25 million, but less than 28 percent for those with total deposits of over $100 million. Moreover, time deposits made up 37.3 percent of the total at country banks, 31.1 percent at reserve city banks, and only 17.5 percent at the central reserve city (New York and Chicago) banks.

The greater relative importance of savings deposits at most small and medium-sized banks is easily explained. In major metropolitan areas, where the largest banks are located, other types of thrift institutions are to be found also. These generally offer higher returns than the commercial banks and compete aggressively for the saver's dollar. Small towns and rural areas, on the other hands, often do not provide a sufficient

TABLE 2-5
Member Banks Ratio of Time Deposits to Total Deposits
by Size of Bank and by Reserve Classification
1959

Banks with Deposits of (Millions)	Ratio of Time Deposits to Total Deposits
Less than $1	22.3%
$1 - 2	31.3
$2 - 5	35.5
$5 - 10	39.1
$10 - 25	38.9
$25 - 50	37.6
$50 - 100	32.9
Over $100	27.8
Reserve Classification	
Central reserve city banks	17.5%
Reserve city banks	31.1
Country banks	37.3

Source: Board of Governors of the Federal Reserve System.

volume of savings to warrant the opening of these other types of institutions, which normally cannot operate profitably on a very small scale. In thousands of localities, the commercial banks are the only convenient outlet for savings. In such localities, therefore, the holding of savings deposits is necessarily a major function of the commercial banks.

Factors Influencing Placement of Savings in Commercial Banks

In deciding how and where to hold his savings, an individual will normally be governed by the following five considerations: (1) the safety of his funds, (2) the readiness with which the savings can be converted back into cash, (3) the ease and convenience of making the necessary transactions, (4) other services offered in conjunction with the savings facilities, (5) the rate of interest or other return received. Each of these factors is examined below, with special reference to the position of commercial banks.

With respect to safety of funds, the commercial banks have much to offer savers. For one thing, funds deposited with them enjoy virtually complete insurance protection. Except in a few banks, savings deposits are insured by the Federal Deposit Insurance Corporation up to a maximum of $10,000 per depositor. Equally important is the fact that banks are held by tradition, by legislation and by supervision to very high standards of prudence in their handling of funds entrusted to them—standards which are much stricter than those applied to some competing thrift institutions. As a result, losses to savings depositors have been negligible during the past twenty-five years. And, of course, savings deposits are not subject to the risk of market price fluctuations, as are corporate securities and marketable Government bonds.

Bank deposits also have the advantage of being a highly liquid form of savings, despite the fact that banks can legally require time depositors to give advance notice before withdrawing their funds. In practice, such notice is never required except under extraordinary circumstances, and then usually only for brief periods. For practical purposes, savings deposits in banks have been withdrawable on demand with no penalty or loss attached to such withdrawal.

Convenience is another important reason why millions of Americans keep their savings at commercial banks. With 24,000 commercial banking offices in the nation, few towns or neighborhoods are without such an office. Indeed, thousands of American communities have no other local savings institution (except the nearly defunct Postal Savings System). Many people, if not most, prefer to do their saving at a local institution where it is convenient to make deposits and withdrawals.

Commercial banks also offer their customers a variety of other important services. These include the use of checking accounts, a wide range of credit facilities, trust services, the sale and redemption of Treasury securities, financial information and counseling, contacts with other financial centers through correspondent banks, etc. Commercial banks, in other words, offer "one-stop" banking facilities. Many persons find it convenient to save where they conduct their other banking transactions.

With respect to the fifth factor usually taken into consideration by savers—the rate of return earned by their funds—commercial banks are at a definite disadvantage. It is true that the average return paid on savings deposits at commercial banks has increased steadily and substantially since the end of World War II. In general, however, they are not able to provide as generous rates of return on savings as do most of their competitors. This is due in large part to various supervisory and regulatory restrictions, which not only limit the amount which can be paid but also prevent commercial banks from investing savings deposits as profitably as their main competitors. The tax laws applicable to banks as opposed to certain competing financial institutions are also a significant factor.

These disadvantages under which commercial banks operate have been sufficiently serious so that their relative position in the thrift field has worsened markedly since World War II. The extent of this change, and its causes and consequences are discussed next.

Competition for Savings

As indicated previously, savings may be placed in a variety of institutions or media, not all of which are directly competitive with one another. For all practical purposes, commercial banks may be considered as competing for savings in most areas with one or more of the following institutions: savings and loan associations, mutual savings banks, credit unions, and the Postal Savings System. In this competition commercial banks have been steadily losing ground.

At the end of World War II commercial banks held 53 percent of the total savings in the five groups of institutions. Five years later the proportion had dropped to 48 percent and during the past decade it has continued to decline until at the end of 1960 only 41 percent of financial savings were in commercial banks.

This continuing loss of position in the competition for savings is quite serious to commercial banks, and, as will be pointed out in the next section, can have serious repercussions in the economy. Nevertheless, if it had been due largely or entirely to the workings of free and unrestricted competition for savings among the principal financial institutions involved, the public interest would have been served. This has not been the case, however, for the simple fact is that commercial banks do not have an equal opportunity to compete for savings under present laws or regulations.

The present situation, under which commercial banks are hampered in their attempts to obtain a reasonable share of the savings dollar, reflects the existence of legislation and regulations adopted at an earlier time and no longer applicable to present-day circumstances. This applies both to commercial banks and to the mutual thrift institutions (the Postal Savings System is now of minor importance) but is particularly true with respect to the latter institutions.

To a significant degree legislative and regulatory provisions treat the mutual thrift institutions as if they were still organized and run by groups of individuals with modest means and common interests who had banded together to obtain savings facilities or create savings "pools" from which each member may borrow. That this was the case many years ago is beyond question, but today this industry, with assets of about $120 billion, business oriented, aggressively competing for the public's funds, and numbering among its members many firms with assets in excess of $100 million (and several with more than $1 billion) continues to operate under rules which give it a decided advantage over commercial banks.

Perhaps the single most important competitive advantage enjoyed by the mutual institutions is freedom from all or substantially all federal income tax. The tax advantage of the savings and loan and mutual savings banks—presently commercial banks' principal competitors for savings—stems from two unique provisions of the tax laws, applicable only to these mutual concerns. These permit deduction from income of (1) all interest and dividend payments; (2) virtually all additions to reserves. Commercial banks, along with other businesses, can deduct only interest payments and cannot deduct any return paid on invested funds and, further, can deduct only such additions to reserves as are permitted by the Treasury, based on the actual loss experience of the banks.

The competitive advantage attributable to the tax difference goes a long way towards explaining the ability of the mutual institutions to pay such attractive rates on savings. From 1955 through 1960, insured commercial banks paid federal income taxes equal to 35 percent of net income; FHLB member savings and loan associations paid federal income taxes equal to 1.1 percent of net income; and insured mutual savings banks paid taxes equal to only .49 percent of net income. Credit unions, as noted, pay no federal income tax at all.

In addition to the tax handicap, commercial banks are subject to a variety of restrictions which prevent them from investing savings deposits in as profitable a manner as their competitors. For example, only commercial banks are required to maintain a legal reserve against savings deposits, even though the purpose of such reserves is to implement monetary policy and should thus apply only to demand deposits; only commercial banks are restricted in the amount of savings deposits which can be invested in mortgages, a relatively high-yielding asset.

Still another competitive handicap arises from the decision of the Congress, following the 1930-33 depression, that interest-rate competition was harmful and, accordingly, limited the rate of interest payable on savings deposits. Presently this limit is 3 percent; and it applies only to commercial banks. Whether such a regulation is in fact necessary to prevent excessive interest payments and attendant weakening of institutions is not at issue. If it is needed it should apply to all institutions competing for savings; if it is not needed it should be removed for commercial banks.

Summarizing: commercial banks are gradually losing the competitive struggle for savings deposits, due largely to the fact that existing laws and regulations prevent them from competing on an equal footing with the mutual thrift institutions. The implications for public policy of this development are discussed next.

Public Interest Considerations in the Declining Position of Commercial Banks

The increasing inability of commercial banks to compete effectively for savings is, of course, a matter of grave concern to the thousands of commercial banks to whom savings deposits are essential for successful operation. But it is also a matter of public concern, in four areas: (1) monetary management, (2) allocation of credit, (3) incentive to save, (4) maintenance of competition.

Increasing concern has been expressed in monetary and credit circles that the proliferation of financial intermediaries outside the commercial banking industry seriously weakens the effectiveness of traditional monetary controls. These controls are impaired, they point out, because the Federal Reserve has direct control over neither the ability of intermediaries to extend credit nor over the increased velocity of money which results from expansion of such credit. For example, new credit provided by financial intermediaries appeared to be little affected during "tight money" periods such as 1952, 1956, and 1957, and the entire dampening of the total flow of credit during these periods was accomplished through the commercial banking system.

It is true that actions taken by the Federal Reserve affect the entire economy through changes in credit availability and resultant changes in interest rates and that these, in turn, influence economic activity. Here again, however, the effect on nonbank financial intermediaries may be much less than is commonly assumed. Higher interest rates attract additional funds into these unhampered intermediaries as they gear the incentive they offer the saver to the higher returns they can obtain in the mortgage market.

In order to achieve the results desired, Federal Reserve authorities must operate directly in the only area under its control—commercial banking. This means that, as the proportion of total credit granted by intermediaries increases with its consequent stimulation of the velocity of money, the monetary authorities must further restrain bank lending by adding to pressures on their reserve positions.

A continuing increase in the extent of financial "intermediation" by nonbank institutions, with a concurrent decrease in the relative importance of the banking system, may weaken the efficiency of monetary controls by reducing the proportion of total credit affected by them. As this occurs, more drastic action on commercial bank reserves may be required to achieve the desired economic results. The result might be, at the minimum, a greater delay in adequate response to these controls and greater inability of banks to provide credit to their customers when it is most needed.

Chapter 3

MONETARY POLICY
AND THE COMMERCIAL BANKS

It is generally agreed that among the basic functions of government (which includes the monetary authorities) are the fostering of a sustainable rate of economic growth, the maintenance of a reasonably stable price level, the maximizing of job opportunities, and the moderating of cyclical fluctuations in economic activity. It is further generally agreed that monetary control measures can contribute to the attainment of these objectives, although opinions differ as to precisely what their role should be and how much they can accomplish.

The commercial banks obviously play an essential part in carrying out monetary policy, since they serve as the primary medium through which monetary measures are effected. Through its power to regulate the reserve position of member banks, the Federal Reserve System is able to regulate fairly closely the volume of demand deposits, which constitute the bulk of our money supply. It is possible to envisage different types of control measures, of course, but in our financial system the commercial banks are the media through which monetary and credit influences are transferred from the Federal Reserve to the economy as a whole.

For this reason the commercial banks are themselves subject, more directly than any other sector of the economy, to the effects of monetary control measures. In regulating the volume of their reserves, the Federal Reserve necessarily influences the banks' lending and investing activities, and hence their earnings and capital positions as well.

The commercial banks thus occupy a unique position in the nation's financial system. In seeking to satisfy the needs of a growing economy for credit and financial services, they are necessarily in competition with a variety of other financial institutions. But alone among such institutions, the commercial banks are subject to direct influence by the Federal Reserve of the total volume of their lending and investing. As a result, they sometimes operate under handicaps vis-à-vis their competitors—

handicaps which affect their rate of growth, their earning capacity, and their ability to serve the nation's credit needs.

The large and complex subject of monetary policy, and the question of its proper role in our economy and its effectiveness, cannot be discussed in great detail here. Nevertheless, the subject is too intimately related to the commercial banks to be ignored. What needs to be stressed particularly—since it is overlooked in many discussions—is the nature of the two-way relationship between the banks and monetary policy: the contribution that the banks make to the effective implementation of monetary control measures, and the effects that these measures have upon the banks themselves.

It should be noted, in passing, that for the most part the terms "monetary policy" and "general credit policy" will be used here interchangeably. Under our present financial setup these terms are nearly synonymous, since measures taken by the central bank will simultaneously affect both bank deposits and bank credit. The distinction between monetary control and general credit control is important mainly in considering alternative types of institutional setups, in which central bank measures might affect the volume of credit more directly than the money supply or vice versa.

The following sections will discuss, first, the tools of monetary policy; second, the impact of monetary policy upon the commercial banks; and, third, its impact upon the economy as a whole.

The Tools of Monetary Management

As noted above, the impact of monetary policy is transmitted to the commercial banking system primarily through the Federal Reserve System's control over member bank reserve positions. Such control is exercised by means of three financial tools: (1) open-market operations, (2) the discount mechanism, (3) reserve requirements. Together, these enable the Federal Reserve System to regulate fairly closely the total volume of reserves available to member banks and the maximum amount of bank deposits and bank credit that a given volume of reserves can support.

In addition to these tools of general credit control, the System has at times had authority to regulate certain specific types of credit, such as mortgage, consumer instalment and stock market credit. At present, however, only stock market credit is subject to direct control.

Open-Market Operations

Because the instruments of general credit control must be used in a complementary manner—each reinforcing the other—it is not possible to single out one instrument as being more important than another. Nevertheless, open-market policy is inherently the most versatile of the three instruments of general credit control, and it is the instrument which is used most frequently to effectuate credit policy on a day-to-day basis. For this reason, open-market operations commonly receive priority in general discussions of monetary policy.

Open-market operations, or the purchase and sale of Government securities and bankers' acceptances by the Federal Reserve, lend a high degree of flexibility to the implementation of monetary policy. With respect to both the timing and the amount of System transactions in the market, purchases and sales can be attuned to money market requirements on virtually an hour-to-hour basis. In large part, System purchases and sales are made to offset the effects of nonmanaged factors that affect bank reserves, such as gold movements, currency flows, or fluctuations in Federal Reserve float. But, in addition, open-market operations are employed to bring about net changes in bank reserve positions and thereby influence the volume of bank credit and demand deposits.

While there is general agreement that open-market operations are a highly useful tool of monetary control, there is considerable disagreement as to precisely how they should be conducted. Specifically, the disagreement centers mainly about the question of whether the System should confine its transactions to short-term securities. In 1953, the Federal Open-Market Committee announced that thereafter it would follow a policy—the so-called "bills only" policy—of dealing exclusively in short-term Government securities except to the extent that "disorderly conditions" required intervention in the market for longer issues. This policy has been severely criticized, and it has been argued that the System should try to influence directly the prices and yields of long-term securities by operating in all maturity ranges. The System view stressed that open-market operations are aimed directly at regulating the volume of bank reserves rather than influencing security prices and yields in any predetermined fashion and that, moreover, Federal Reserve intervention in the bond market would be an unsettling influence which would impair the proper functioning of the market. The System also has argued that changes in security prices and yields would no longer provide useful guides to basic demand and supply forces in the capital market if those prices and yield were directly subject to Federal Reserve pressures. Finally, and the most important, is the System's view that the central bank should limit its objective to governing the over-all supply of credit while leaving the allocation of this credit, as between the various maturity sectors, to free-market processes.

A great deal of discussion has failed to resolve this problem, and it seems likely that only experience will do so. Meanwhile, it must be borne in mind that the System's preferred policy of dealing in short-term issues exclusively is not a rigid one, but a policy which is under frequent review and subject to adaptations as credit-policy considerations warrant. The System's departure from the "bills only" policy in early 1961, when international financial considerations suggested the need for exerting upward pressure on short-term interest rates while preserving an over-all policy of credit ease, provided ample assurance that the System will not remain irrevocably wedded to the "bills only" technique when circumstances clearly warrant a different approach. Indeed, it would seem that the "bills only" issue is essentially a technical problem rather than a theoretical one, and as such its solution may properly be left to the technicians concerned with it.

Discount Operations

The discount rate is the cost to member banks of borrowing from the Federal Reserve Banks. Such borrowing is undertaken when banks are threatened with temporary reserve deficiencies, usually resulting from unexpected deposit withdrawals or loan requests or from seasonal factors. It is always understood that such borrowing is temporary and is to be repaid within a reasonable time.

Changes in the discount rate affect member banks primarily in two ways. First, they influence the cost and hence the attractiveness of borrowing from the Federal Reserve. Second, discount rate changes afford concrete evidence of the intentions of Federal Reserve authorities, and therefore influence the expectations of investors, including banks, with respect to the trend of interest rates. Changes in discount rates sometimes signal a reversal of monetary policy, as in the fall of 1957, and on such occasions are usually reflected rather quickly in other interest rates. Often, however, changes in discount rates are simply confirmations of changes which already have taken place in money-market rates.

The ability to borrow from the Federal Reserve represents a "safety valve" by means of which individual member banks can temporarily adjust their reserve positions to changed conditions, thus providing sufficient time, if necessary, for more fundamental adjustments. When pressure develops on the banking system, such pressure is likely to fall unevenly upon individual banks. Some may feel it very heavily for a time, and the discount window offers them a means of temporarily restoring their reserve positions until they can make the necessary adjustments to the new conditions. There are, of course, other ways of obtaining additional reserves quickly, such as by borrowing in the federal funds market or by selling securities. However, the first of these ways is generally convenient only to larger banks, and the second is often impractical for short-term adjustment purposes. In addition, through the discount window the central bank can also serve as a "lender of last resort" in case of emergency, such as a run on the banks.

It is sometimes argued that discounting tends to frustrate monetary control measures by permitting the banks to evade System pressures on their reserve positions. However, this would be true only if the banks could borrow unlimited amounts, and at favorable rates, from the Federal Reserve. Actually, such borrowings are limited by four factors: (1) there is a cost involved, which is under the control of the Federal Reserve Banks; (2) discounting is a privilege which may be denied if it is used excessively or for improper purposes; (3) discounting tends to impair a bank's liquidity position; (4) most banks have a long-standing tradition against remaining continuously in debt to the Federal Reserve. Discounting offers banks temporary and partial relief from monetary control pressures, but it does not offer escape. Because of the requirement for repayment, reserve funds extended through the discount window have a much different impact than reserve funds created through System open-market purchases. Banks indebted to the Federal Reserve generally are under pressure to adopt more conservative lending and investing policies, and it is for this reason that the volume of member bank discounting is frequently a good indicator of the degree of tightness or ease in the banking system.

It has also been argued that changes in discount rates often have unfavorable or perverse psychological effects. A decrease in the rate, for instance, may announce the System's belief that a recession is under way and thereby cause a deterioration of business sentiment that might serve to intensify the recession. To prevent this, it has been suggested that the discount rate should be tied directly to the Treasury bill rate, as is done in Canada, so that changes in it will be automatic rather than deliberate expressions of Federal Reserve policy.

Criticisms of present discount rate practices are very probably exaggerated. There are today so many sources of economic information and predictions, including pronouncements and open-market actions by the Federal Reserve System, that the public does not have to wait for changes in the discount rate to know that a turn in business conditions has taken place. On the other hand, such changes may have favorable psychological effects by announcing shifts in Federal Reserve policy and thereby prompting changes in credit markets which will be in accord with the new policy. For instance, the reduction of discount rates in November 1957 was followed by a sharp decline in other interest rates as the credit markets adjusted quickly to the prospects of an easier credit policy, as well as to declining credit demands. Thus the "announcement" effect of discount rate changes are probably useful at times and harmless at other times.

At the opposite extreme from those who favor abolishing the discount window altogether are those who argue that it should be kept open at all times. Every member bank, assert the latter, should have the right to borrow from the Federal Reserve at any time provided it has eligible paper to pledge as collateral and is willing to pay the discount rate. The System would then rely solely on changes in the discount rate to regulate the volume of member bank borrowing instead of approving or rejecting particular loan requests, as at present, on the basis of criteria set forth in Regulation A. Such a policy would effect far-reaching changes in the manner in which the discount mechanism now functions. Among other points to be mentioned is that unlimited access to the discount window probably would require the establishment of discount rates substantially in excess of market rates, and these penalty rates would impose a heavy burden on those banks, especially agricultural banks, which find it necessary to borrow fairly heavily on a seasonal basis.

Bank Reserve Requirements

The third important tool of general credit policy is the authority of the Board of Governors to vary the reserve requirement ratios of member banks. While such variations do not affect the banks' actual reserves, they limit the volume of earning assets, and hence of deposits, that can be held with any given volume of reserves.

As an instrument of monetary control, authority to vary reserve requirement ratios dates only from the banking legislation of 1933 and 1935. Prior to that time, legal reserve requirements had been imposed upon commercial banks solely in order to insure their liquidity and to provide for the safety of depositors. Today, however, these functions are performed in other ways, such as by secondary reserves, access to the Federal Reserve Banks, and deposit insurance. It is now generally recognized that the primary function of required reserves is to provide an additional instrument for regulating credit and the money supply.

However, changes in required reserve ratios are not an efficient means of effecting day-to-day or other short-run shifts in monetary policy. Such changes may have temporary but serious unsettling effects because even small changes in the ratios have relatively large effects upon the banks' reserve positions—effects, moreover, that are felt abruptly rather than over a period of time. In general, therefore, day-to-day fluctuations in member banks' reserve positions can be effected much more precisely and delicately through open-market operations than by frequent manipulation of the legal reserve requirements.

Nevertheless, the authority to vary reserve requirement within a limited range has been useful on occasion and is likely to prove so in the future. For example, the device can be employed to give strong added emphasis to Federal Reserve policy when open-market operations and discount rate changes appear insufficient to achieve a desired result. Situations of this sort are likely to occur infrequently, but the possibility should be provided for. Indeed, changes in reserve requirements were made for this purpose a number of times during the 1930's and 1940's. Also, reductions in the reserve ratios can be employed—at least, up to a point—to permit commercial bank accommodation of the secular deposit expansion that long-run growth of the economy will require. It is perhaps significant, in this connection, that only downward changes in the reserve requirement ratios have been made since the Federal Reserve–Treasury Accord of 1951.

The present system of reserve requirements has several serious defects. First, the level of reserve ratios now prescribed is higher than necessary and perhaps too high for the long-run welfare of the financial structure or of the economy. Second, the present system of basing reserve requirements on geographic location is unsatisfactory. Third, member banks are discriminated against by the fact that reserves must be held against their savings and other time deposits, while savings accounts at some competing financial institutions are not subject to comparable requirements. These three points require some elaboration.

Since the function of legal reserve requirements today is to serve as part of the mechanism through which monetary controls operate, the prescribed reserve ratios should neither be higher nor lower than is needed to make such controls effective. To set the reserve ratios any higher than necessary is not only to discriminate against the commercial banks, which almost alone are subject to reserve requirements, but also to limit their ability to serve the credit needs of a growing economy and, by reducing the earnings of the banks, to make it more difficult for them to raise needed new capital.

The question of how high the reserve ratios need be cannot be answered precisely, but it seems clear that there is ample room for reduction without impairing the effectiveness of reserve requirements as an instrument of credit control. The reserves required to be held against demand deposits have ranged since 1917 from 13 to 26 percent at central reserve city banks, from 10 to 22 percent at reserve city banks, and from 7 to 16 percent at country banks. Although changes in the level of reserve requirements have been an important instrument of credit control, the effectiveness of monetary policy does not appear to have been related to the absolute levels prevailing at any particular time. In England and Canada reserve ratios have been considerably lower in recent years than in the United States without appearing to handicap the monetary authorities in those countries.

From the standpoint of credit control, the principal effect of a reduction in reserve ratios is to increase the multiple by which a given change in the volume of available reserves can be translated into a change in the volume of deposits. For instance, a reduction of average reserve requirements from 20 percent to 16⅔ percent increases the multiple expansion ratio from 5:1 to 6:1.

A higher expansion multiple than now exists would have mixed implications for open-market operations. Under a lower set of reserve requirements, net changes in the size of System holdings of Government securities to promote a desired change in the money supply and credit conditions would be smaller than at present. In contrast with the reduction in the size of net changes in System holdings, however, the frequency of the System's entry into the market probably would be increased. This is true because movements in the so-called "operating" factors influencing bank reserves (factors including float, currency in circulation, and gold stock) would have greater significance under a system of lower reserve requirements, and greater efforts to offset these random fluctuations might therefore be in order. More sophisticated arguments related to the interest-rate effect, as distinguished from the reserve effect, of open-market operations under a system of lower reserve requirements also could be advanced, but they do not point conclusively either to the desirability or undesirability of lowering the reserve requirement percentages. On balance, it does not appear that the achievement of lower reserve requirements would interfere with the flexible conduct of open-market operations.

Admittedly, if the expansion multiple were very large the System would have difficulty in regulating the money supply with adequate precision, because there is always some uncertainty as to the exact effects of monetary measures and this uncertainty would increase as the expansion multiple rose. However, experience suggests that the reserve ratios could be reduced and the expansion multiple increased considerably before this would become a serious difficulty.

A strong case can be made for gradually reducing the reserve requirement ratio over the long term. If our economy is to continue expanding, the money supply will also have to continue growing. This can be provided for in two principal ways: (1) by increasing bank reserves through open-market purchases, or (2) by lowering the level of reserve requirements against demand deposits.

Providing for the secular growth of the money supply through open-market purchases would have one important advantage to the government, it is alleged. The income from the securities purchased would accrue to the Federal Reserve Banks rather than to private holders and most of it would be turned back to the Treasury. However, this consideration is not of great significance. Even when securities are privately owned, the Treasury recovers a large part of the interest payments through income taxes. For example, if they are held by commercial banks or other corporations, roughly half of the interest payments eventually flow back to the Treasury in the form of corporate income tax receipts. More important, is the fact that profits earned by the Federal Reserve Banks are not relevant to credit-policy considerations. The basic function of the Federal Reserve System is to manage the nation's monetary system in the way most conducive to efficient functioning of the economy as a whole, and it should not be distracted from this aim by profit-making considerations.

In the light of this basic objective, there are a number of reasons for preferring reductions in the reserve requirements to open-market purchases as a means of providing for the long-run growth of the money supply. Some of these reasons apply directly to the commercial banks. Excessive reserve requirements reduce bank earnings, which are already modest by comparison with most other industries, and thereby make it difficult for the banks to attract needed capital. This could in time hamper the growth of the banking system and seriously curtail its ability to serve the economy. Since banking is one of the most strategic of industries, providing essential services for the entire nation, it must be able to compete with other industries for capital on favorable terms.

There are still other reasons why reducing the reserve ratios would be preferable to open-market purchases as a means of providing for the long-run growth of the money supply. For one thing, high legal reserve requirements place a penalty upon membership in the Federal Reserve System. Lowering these requirements, by encouraging more banks to join the System, might tend to enhance the effectiveness of monetary policy. For another, open-market purchases, unlike reductions in reserve requirements, have the effect of expanding the note-and-deposit liabilities of the Reserve Banks and thereby reducing their gold coverage ratios. These ratios recently have become less comfortable as a result of the outflow of gold from the country. So long as the prescribed minimum of 25 percent remains in effect, further reductions in the gold coverage ratio could serve to undermine confidence in the ability of the United States to continue paying out gold on demand, thereby rendering our gold supply vulnerable to speculative drains. Finally, it should be pointed out that the Federal Reserve System already has in its portfolio a substantial part of the outstanding volume of short- and intermediate-term Government securities, which constitute the principal liquidity medium in our economy today. Further concentration of the government debt in the Reserve Banks could make it difficult for banks and other private investors to meet their liquidity needs.

All of these factors taken together would seem to outweigh by far the relatively minor loss of revenue to the Treasury that would result from providing for the secular growth of the money supply through reductions in reserve requirements rather than through open-market purchases.

Another unsatisfactory feature of the present reserve requirement system is the basing of reserve ratios on the geographic location of banks. It is true that the recent elimination of the central reserve city classification and the narrowing of the differential between the reserve ratios of the two remaining classes has somewhat reduced the seriousness of the problem. Nevertheless, the difference between the 16½ percent minimum required of reserve city banks and the 12 percent ratio applied to country banks is still considerable.

The present reserve classification system is inequitable in its requirements on individual banks. All reserve city banks are subject to the same reserve ratios, yet many of these are small banks that do little or no correspondent business and more nearly resemble country banks. On the other hand, some country banks more nearly resemble those in large cities. Banks that are very similar may be subject to different reserve requirements merely because of their location.

Moreover, careful analysis of the various arguments that have been advanced to justify differential reserve ratios leaves doubt as to whether any of these are valid or whether, indeed, there are any logical grounds for distinguishing between different banks or different types of deposits insofar as reserve requirements are concerned.

A tripartite geographic classification of national banks existed before the passage of the Federal Reserve Act in 1914. The justification for it at that time was that many banks located in large cities held interbank balances representing redeposited reserves of other banks, and it was felt that these large city banks should carry extra large reserves because such balances were liable to sudden withdrawal and were of peculiarly strategic importance. Establishment of the Federal Reserve System in 1914 largely eliminated this justification for the geographic classification of banks, since member banks were thereafter required to hold their reserves at the Reserve Banks and hence only a relatively small amount of nonmember reserves continued to be held in the form of interbank balances. Despite this, the tripartite geographic classification was carried over into the Federal Reserve System.

The argument has also been made that *all* interbank balances, not merely those representing legal reserves of other banks, should be backed by additional reserves at the holding banks. The reason advanced is that such balances tend to be more volatile than most other types of deposits, and hence banks that hold large amounts of them require more liquidity. While the latter statement may readily be granted, the notion that legal reserves are an effective means of providing liquidity is largely mistaken. Such reserves usually cannot be called upon when needed precisely because the law requires them to be held. It is now widely recognized, therefore, that individual banks obtain liquidity primarily through secondary reserves (backed up, if needed, by access to the Federal Reserve discount window) rather than through their legal reserves.

It has been proposed at times that reserve requirements be based not on the location of banks but on the turnover rates of their deposits. A deposit that turns over rapidly contributes more to economic activity than one that turns over slowly, it is argued, and hence should be backed by more reserves in periods of booming economic activity. Although a case can be made for this proposal in theory, it is doubtful that in practice it would be feasible. For one thing, the computation of each bank's turnover rate would be difficult and costly. For another, it would unfairly penalize some banks whose turnover rates are greatly inflated by purely financial transactions, such as the sale of securities or real estate. Transactions of this sort are not likely to have as immediate or direct an effect on economic activity as those associated with the purchase of final products.

One version of the preceding plan would have reserve requirements vary with variations in the turnover rates. This would tend to keep required reserves automatically adjusted to changing economic conditions, so that aggregate expenditures would be held more or less constant. The possibility of having an automatic governor in our monetary mechanism is certainly an intriguing one. However, besides the difficulties mentioned in the preceding paragraph, this scheme might be dangerously inflexible. Under our present reserve system, changes in velocity can moderate the effects of changes in reserve positions, so that sudden or sharp changes in credit conditions are avoided. If reserve requirements were based on velocity, the sacrifice of this cushioning effect might expose the economy to unsettling influences and moreover the effects of errors and miscalculations in monetary management would tend to be more serious.

A system of uniform reserve requirements, applying equally to all member banks and to all demand deposits, would eliminate defects in the present system while still preserving the usefulness of bank reserve requirements as an instrument of credit control. Of course, equalization of reserve requirements would have to be approached gradually so as not to disturb monetary conditions unduly during the transition. But once this had been accomplished, the uniformity of reserve requirements would provide a system that would be simple, efficient, and more equitable than the present system of differential requirements.

The present system of reserve requirements also is unsatisfactory in its applicability to commercial bank time deposits. Federal Reserve member banks (all but three of which are commercial banks) are required to hold reserves against their savings and other time deposits. At present the prescribed reserve ratio is 5 percent. Most other banks, including nearly all of the savings banks, generally need hold only smaller reserves or none at all, and such competing institutions as savings and loan associations are not required to hold cash reserves against their savings accounts. Since such reserves tie up funds in nonearning assets, member banks operate under a serious handicap vis-à-vis their competitors.

Reserve requirements against time deposits serve no useful purpose in view of the fact that monetary control is the one significant function of reserve requirements. Time deposits are not part of the active money supply, since they are not actually used for making payments. Consequently, legal reserves against time deposits do not serve as an essential part of the monetary control mechanism and there is no justification for requiring commercial banks to hold large reserves against their time deposits when competing savings institutions are not compelled to do so.

Selective Credit Controls

The foregoing pages have discussed the instruments of general monetary or credit control—that is, those that are designed to affect the overall volume of credit and the money supply. Numerous proposals have also been made—and a few adopted—for regulating particular uses of credit. Some of these have involved the provision by the government of special credit-granting facilities in order to channel resources into certain favored industries, such as agriculture, residential construction, defense-related industries, etc. Others have been designed to curb the flow of credit into certain economic activities when the flow threatens to become excessive. It is this latter type of measure which is usually meant when one refers to "selective" or "qualitative" credit controls and which will be discussed in the present section.

The basic argument for the imposition of selective credit controls (except during periods of war or similar emergency) reflects the fact that the speculative or unsound use of credit in some areas of economic activity may lead to excesses and imbalances capable of threatening the stability of the economy in general. Regulation of security credit is the only type of selective credit control now exercised by the monetary authorities. However, at times in the past, consumer instalment credit and housing credit have also been subject to specific regulation. (These three types of selective credit control are discussed in Chapters 8, 5, and 7, respectively.) In addition, suggestions have been made from time to time for regulating credit used for inventory purchases, plant and equipment expenditures, or other purposes.

The present authority of the Federal Reserve System to regulate security credit was an outgrowth of the 1929 debacle. At that time, the Federal Reserve Board attempted to curb excessive speculation in the stock market by restricting the over-all supply of credit. It succeeded only in hampering legitimate business activity without significantly reducing speculative excesses. Despite some complaints, the present system of fixing margin requirements on security purchases appears to have worked well. It has not prevented sharp fluctuations in stock prices (nor is it meant to), but it has eliminated instability associated with the unbridled use of speculative credit in securities transactions.

However, the fact that selective controls have worked reasonably well in the field of stock market credit does not prove that they will work equally well in other credit areas. There are important differences between stock market credit and consumer, housing, or other types of credit. Most loans have to be repaid either at a fixed date or in periodic instalments, and the fact that provision has to be made for such repayment tends to limit the amount borrowed. With respect to stock market credit, repayment provisions are generally not rigid; indeed, speculators commonly increase their indebtedness by pyramiding when the prices of their securities rise. Moreover, the collateral behind loans to stock purchasers is subject to sharp price fluctuations, which may at times compel widespread selling of the collateral by lenders. There is less danger of this with other types of credit, since the collateral used in these cases is usually more stable in value, and in addition the borrowers (unlike security buyers) are usually required to give some evidence of their credit-worthiness. Furthermore, stock market credit is relatively insensitive to interest rate changes—and hence to quantitative credit controls—because the interest cost usually seems unimportant relative to the possible speculative gains. For these reasons, stock market credit is in a class by itself and requires specific controls which may not be needed for other types of credit.

Selective credit controls involve governmental interference with the freedom to borrow and spend in accordance with personal preferences. Even if such controls resulted in a more efficient operation of the economy —and this is far from certain—the gain in efficiency might still be outweighed by the loss of freedom and by the annoyance of greater governmental interference in economic activities. Selective credit controls are therefore objectionable because they interfere with free market forces. They substitute the dictates of government administrators for the decisions of millions of private firms and individuals. No matter how capable and well-meaning these administrators may be, they cannot be familiar with every corner of the economy, as they must be if they are to direct credit into or out of particular industries. Also, it is difficult to know what is a "normal" level of activity in any particular sector of the economy and therefore to know whether credit facilities there should be increased or decreased. If the monetary authorities guess wrong about the need for credit in particular areas, their policies might well contribute to greater economic instability. Another drawback to selective credit controls is that certain types, notably the regulation of consumer instalment credit, have proved very difficult to administer.

Under certain circumstances, such as wartime or serious inflationary situations, selective credit controls of some types may prove useful or even necessary, and we may then be willing temporarily to pay the price of increased direction of our economy for the sake of preventing dis-. astrous inflation. But in more normal times, the burden of proof would seem to be on those who favor greater resort to such controls.

The Impact of Monetary Policy Upon the Banks

Effects on Bank Deposits

It is obvious that Federal Reserve policy closely affects the volume of demand deposits of commercial banks. By operating directly on the banks' reserve positions, it induces them to increase or decrease their earning assets and, as a result, their deposits. The ability of the monetary authorities to regulate the volume of bank reserves is somewhat limited by practical considerations, such as the avoidance of policy changes during periods of Treasury financings, the unexpected behavior of operating factors affecting reserves, and other considerations. But aside from such limitations, the Federal Reserve can closely regulate the volume of the banking system's basic raw material—reserve funds. As a result, the commercial banks are compelled to operate within the limits set by monetary policy.

In analyzing the effects of monetary policy on the banking system, we need to consider first the short-run effects of countercyclical measures and second, the long-run effects.

In the absence of a central monetary authority, the volume of bank deposits would show a procyclical movement, increasing during expansion periods in response to rising credit demand and decreasing during contraction periods as the demand for credit contracted. But the volume of deposits shows almost the reverse behavior when the central bank attempts to reduce cyclical fluctuations in economic activity through the use of monetary and credit controls. Deposits then increase rapidly during the contraction phase of the cycle (at least, after the first few months) as the monetary authorities attempt to cushion the economic contraction by making more reserves available and, conversely, increase less rapidly or even decrease during most of the expansion phase. Thus the volume of demand deposits behaves countercyclically, with perhaps a lag of a few months, under the influence of stabilizing monetary policies.

The necessity for such countercyclical fluctuations in the volume of deposits results from short-run variability in the rate of turnover or velocity of circulation of the money supply. During the expansion phase of the cycle, when growth in the supply of credit is restrained, velocity rises both because the difficulty of obtaining desired credit encourages the fullest use of cash balances and because the rise in interest rates makes it more profitable to utilize idle funds. Conversely, the turnover rate tends to decline during the contraction phase as interest rates decline and the demand for funds eases.

Such fluctuations in velocity tend to frustrate to some extent the aims of the monetary authorities. In order, then, to offset or outweigh these velocity changes, the Federal Reserve finds it necessary to take more drastic action on the reserve position of banks. Deposit growth generally must be restrained during booms and promoted during recessions more than would otherwise be necessary. As a result, the volume of deposits at commercial banks does not grow steadily but rather increases in spurts.

This is naturally of some concern to the banks, particularly as they are provided with additional funds precisely at the times when they have least need for them (that is, during recessions when the demand for loans falls off) and, conversely, find it difficult to acquire additional funds precisely at the times when they could make best use of them (that is, during periods of high prosperity when the loan demand is strong). Banks have adapted to this situation mainly by buying government securities when provided with additional reserves during recession periods and by selling off these investments during periods of rising business activity in order to meet the larger loan demands. This behavior has proved costly to the banks, since it has resulted in their buying securities when prices were high (during recessions, interest rates tend to be low and bond prices high) and selling them when prices were low. As a result, during the past decade commercial banks have taken net losses of roughly one billion dollars on their security transactions, not counting unrealized losses they currently may have in their bond portfolios.

In addition to cyclical changes, the secular increase in velocity since World War II has been highly significant to the commercial banking system. The fact that the average turnover rate of demand deposits roughly doubled between 1945 and 1960 (see Table 2-2), compelled the monetary authorities to slow down the growth of the money supply in order to combat price inflation. During the same period, the volume of demand deposits increased only 52 percent while the gross national product was rising 136 percent. Thus, the increase in velocity and the exigencies of monetary policy have tended to slow the growth of the banking system during the postwar period.

While there is presumably some limit to how high velocity can rise, there is no convincing evidence that this limit has already been reached or will be reached soon. Velocity may well continue to rise for a period, especially if the rapid expansion of other savings institutions continues. If so, the commercial banks may face a further period of restrictive monetary policies, during which their growth will continue to be affected.

The issue raised by these trends is not whether quantitative credit controls should continue to be utilized as a device for stabilizing the economy and for maintaining sustainable economic growth without inflation. Bankers do not question the importance of continuing a flexible monetary policy. Rather, the issue raised is how instruments of monetary management can be utilized in such a manner as to avoid unduly restricting the growth of commercial banking. Removal of the competitive handicaps under which commercial banks now operate in the savings field could go a long way toward solving this problem.

Effects on Bank Loans

By governing the reserve position of the banking system, monetary policy has a profound impact upon commercial bank lending operations. The nature of the impact depends partly on the action taken by the Reserve authorities, and partly on each bank's investment, liquidity, and capital position.

When loan demands at an individual bank exceed loanable funds provided by its new deposits, the bank is likely to reduce its holdings of Government securities through runoffs and prior-to-maturity sales. There are limits, of course, to how long and how far a bank will move in this direction, and the maturity distribution of the bank's investment portfolio will play an important role in determining these limits. So, too, will inhibitions about realizing security losses—perhaps some maximum loss figure based upon operating earnings will act as a constraint.

If an individual bank owns mostly intermediate- and short-term securities, potential security losses will not seriously inhibit loan expansion. What proportion of the bank's assets will then go into loans? Several rules-of-thumb have been used to measure the extent to which banks are "loaned up." The most commonly used ratios are the loan-deposit ratio and the capital-risk asset ratio, with risk assets generally defined to include all assets save cash reserves and U.S. Government securities, and sometimes' also excluding federal agency securities and loans insured or guaranteed by federal agencies.

The loan-deposit ratio is a measure of illiquidity, if securities and cash assets are considered to be the primary source of liquidity to meet deposit declines. But it is a rough and imperfect measure of illiquidity, and target or "maximum" loan levels based on this ratio may not be too meaningful. Designating bank earning assets as loans or securities does not adequately define their liquidity. Many bank loans may be readily converted into cash within a relatively short period of time, while some securities that are carried at par can be converted into cash only at substantial discounts when interest rates rise. Moreover, liquidity needs vary among banks according to such influences as seasonal deposit and loan fluctuations, economic conditions in the community in which the bank operates, and the mix of the bank's deposits. Consequently, no single measure of liquidity indicates the extent to which monetary policy limits bank lending by its effect on the liquidity of banks.

The capital-risk asset ratio is a measure of capital coverage; it measures the capital cushion afforded depositors. Its significance is determined in large measure by the quality of earning assets held, so that it is of only limited use when not supplemented by a readily defined concept of adequacy. Capital adequacy is closely interrelated with investment policy, credit standards, liquidity and, most important, general economic and credit conditions. Capital-risk asset ratios, especially where internal policy or fear of supervisory criticism comes into play, may restrain conversion of Government securities into loans and tax-exempt securities (that is, conversion of nonrisk assets into risk assets).

Individual commercial banks respond differently to changes in their loan-deposit, capital-risk asset and liquidity ratios, however these are measured. For example, in recent years the loan-deposit ratios at central reserve and reserve city banks have been considerably higher than those of most other commercial banks. Some banks may adhere rigidly to constraints that rules-of-thumb impose on their asset acquisition. But the more typical reaction is that of an increasing aversion to reducing liquidity further as it falls below some given level.

Monetary control measures affect the several major classifications of bank loans in varying degree. In a period of credit tightness, some would-be borrowers may decide to reduce or defer borrowing because of higher interest rates. But many others are likely to be influenced more by the bright business outlook typical of such periods than by the higher cost of credit. Banks, then, generally must set up criteria for deciding which loan requests to grant. That is, rationing of the limited supply of loanable funds becomes necessary.

Relevant criteria include: long-run effects on profits; long-run deposit growth; the desire to maintain competitive positions in certain areas vis-à-vis other banks in the community or other financial institutions; the desire to meet the community's or customer's "legitimate" loan needs and to maintain a desired public image associated with meeting such needs.

These considerations may give rise to different results for different banks. For example, a particular bank may desire to increase its share of the market for, say, agricultural loans. Consequently it might extend such loans on reasonably favorable terms while cutting back in other loan areas. While it might be cutting back on real estate loans in general, it might utilize farm real estate loans as a means for winning a larger share of crop financing in the area.

In the case of instalment loans, an individual bank may find itself forced, by competitive conditions, to extend more loans than it desires. For example, a large volume of automobile and appliance loans is written for banks by the dealers. Because attempts to reduce dealer commitments may entail the loss of a profitable account and business relationship, in cutting back on such commitments it is necessary to weigh the account potential over the entire business cycle. It is on the basis of such criteria that many banks have favored short-term business loans and loans associated with consumer credit in recent periods of monetary restraint.

The impact of credit policy upon the major classes of bank loans will be considered in the following sections.

Business loans. Extending loans to business borrowers is the traditional function of commercial banks. Such loans are basic to attracting and holding commercial accounts. For the most part, prospective business borrowers are also the best long-term customers of commercial banks. Hence, there is a strong desire to grant applications for desirable business loans, wherever possible. Moreover, the use of lines of credit and other commitments to make loans at future dates virtually requires the banks to increase loans to business as needs expand.

Large corporations operating over a wide area or the entire nation maintain deposits at many banks and are unlikely to encounter great difficulty in securing wanted accommodation even in periods of monetary restraint. If they are unable to get bank credit in the amounts desired, they may have access to the corporate bond market, direct intermediate and long-term financing from insurance companies, and the commercial paper market. But large borrowers must pay the price. Although loan rates are generally lower for large borrowers than for small, this differential tends to narrow during periods of restrictive credit policy and to widen when economic activity becomes slack and easy credit conditions prevail. Deposit balance requirements further accentuate fluctuations in costs to large borrowers, since required balances are likely to be higher and more rigidly enforced when rates are high. Balance requirements are apt to be less rigid for small borrowers.

In the case of smaller and medium-sized business borrowers, the effect of credit restriction is more complicated. One point of view has been expressed by Warren Smith:

> If monetary policy works chiefly through availability and if availability is not a problem for large firms, it follows that when monetary policy is effective in curtailing business spending, its impact must fall mainly on small business.[1]

Even if the premise that "monetary policy works chiefly through availability" is conceded, it can still be pointed out that many large firms are dependent on a single bank for most of their outside financing. In a "tight spot," such firms may find some accommodation from other sources,

---

[1] Report of the Joint Economic Committee Staff Report, *Employment, Growth, and Price Levels* (Washington, December 24, 1959), p. 381.

but their financial position and national reputation may fall short of that necessary to tap impersonal credit markets. Thus, the problem of availability need not be confined to *small* firms. Moreover, even for some of the largest corporations having virtually unlimited access to credit sources, interest-rate considerations remain of major importance.

Small and medium-sized businesses undoubtedly are affected by limits imposed on credit availability. Nevertheless, small businesses that have maintained satisfactory relations with commercial banks are unlikely to encounter difficulties in obtaining short-term credit so long as they are willing to pay the price. The price most likely will be only moderately higher than the price paid in periods of less restrictive monetary policy. Many bankers, apart from state usury laws, are sensitive to interest rate criticism and have psychological barriers to going above 6 or 7 percent on short-term business loans.

Where possible, a banker may pare down the size of a loan request or persuade the borrower that he can do with less credit, perhaps by expanding at a slower pace. Unusual loan requests or requests for term loans on the part of customers may be discouraged or denied by banks. For noncustomers, business loans other than relatively secure, short-term loans may be difficult to obtain in a period of restraint.

Bankers are more apt to use conservative approaches to business loans and tighter credit standards during periods of restrictive monetary policy than at other times. This does not necessarily reflect gloomy economic forecasts giving rise to quality upgrading; indeed, one might more logically expect quality *deterioration* in bank loans during periods of buoyant economic activity. Rather, it is a matter of bankers needing some criterion to guide their rationing decisions in a period of credit stringency. Tighter credit standards afford the opportunity to upgrade the quality of loan portfolios when bank liquidity or risk asset ratios are deteriorating. Tighter credit standards then tend to be applied to large as well as to small borrowers.

However, there are several reasons why small borrowers do not have as much difficulty in obtaining loans during periods of credit restraint as is commonly supposed. For one thing, most banks are themselves "small business" serving only small business borrowers and hence cannot discriminate against these even if they should want to. In addition, the small banks which lend mainly to small concerns are less affected by credit restraint than large banks, and often have sizable excess reserves even during tight money periods. It appears, too, that many banks take into consideration the lesser availability of nonbank credit to smaller firms and hence make extra efforts to accommodate them.

In 1958, the Federal Reserve published background studies and the results of commercial bank loan surveys designed to appraise the adequacy of small business financing and the impact of restrictive monetary policy over the 1955-57 period.[2] Insofar as there was any indication that monetary policy more severely affected bank lending to small business, it stemmed primarily from bank efforts to upgrade the quality of their loans by imposing uniformly stricter credit standards. Other apparent bases for bank credit rationing involved favoring local versus nonlocal or national borrowers, and favoring established over new customers. As a result of the former criterion small businesses might tend to be favored over larger firms, while the reverse is apt to be true (at least to the extent that most new businesses are also small) on the basis of the latter criterion.

During the 1955-57 period of monetary restraint, credit tightness was largely centered at banks in large cities. These banks had less than average deposit growth (central reserve city bank deposits actually declined over the 1955-57 period), while deposits at country banks grew faster than the national average.[3] In addition, growth in loan demand during the 1955-57 period was concentrated at large city banks. Country banks, whose business customers usually are relatively small in size, had least cause to resort to credit rationing. All this suggests that many small businesses may not have been affected seriously by restrictive monetary policy.

While some banks have indicated less willingness to extend term loans in periods of monetary restraint, this unwillingness has not been reflected in bank loan statistics. The proportion of term loans in commercial bank business loan portfolios increased during the 1955-57 period of monetary restraint. Term loans to smaller businesses showed the greatest percentage increase during this period, but most of this increase was accounted for by loans of intermediate maturity for the purchase of automobiles, trucks, farm implements, and other chattels. Such loans normally are made by bank instalment loan departments and, like instalment loans to individuals, tend to be relatively profitable for banks. To some extent, the growth of this form of borrowing may have reflected the inability of smaller borrowers to obtain adequate loan accommodation on an unsecured or otherwise more favorable basis during this period of credit restraint. On the other hand, smaller business firms rarely have access to long-term unsecured credits, and the growth of equipment-secured financing may have reflected a combination of increased business demand and greater flexibility in bank lending policies.

---

[2] The Federal Reserve System, *Financing Small Business,* Report to the Committees on Banking and Currency and the Select Committees on Small Business, U.S. Congress, 2 parts, April 11, 1958 (Washington: U.S. Government Printing Office, 1958).

[3] This presumably reflected, in part, the importance of large corporate, public and foreign deposit concentrations in big city banks. During periods of rising interest rates such deposits are most likely to be economized or shifted to higher-yielding earning assets.

Commercial bank term loans to larger borrowers increased relatively less during the same period. In part, this stems from the reluctance of larger banks to make term loans of large size during periods of credit stringency. In fact, the sensitivity of term loans to changes in monetary policy appears to be confined mainly to loans by large banks to large borrowers.[4]

Consumer credit. The responsiveness of consumer credit to changes in monetary policy has received considerable attention during the past five years. In 1957 the Federal Reserve published an extensive study [5] of consumer credit, focusing attention largely on its sensitivity to general monetary controls and the desirability of establishing selective controls to regulate such credit. The five volumes include a variety of opinions from economists and others, but no basic conclusion on the part of the Federal Reserve. Shortly thereafter the Federal Reserve indicated that it did not feel the need for selective controls over consumer credit, even on a standby basis.

The majority, though not unanimous, view expressed in the Federal Reserve study was that restrictive monetary controls have not had a strong impact on instalment credit.[6] The rapid expansion of instalment credit during the period of restrictive monetary policy in 1959-60 appears to have lent some additional support to this view. There have been dissenters, however. A recent study of the 1955-56 period indicated that those particular banks that were under the greatest restrictive pressure because of poor deposit performance did cut back on their consumer credit extension along with other loans.[7]

Changes in monetary policy may affect the willingness of banks to lend on marginal credits and to extend loan maturities, but such willingness is also affected importantly by loss ratios on outstanding instalment loans and by a bank's appraisal of the economic outlook. Thus, according to the Federal Reserve study, "restrictive lending policies instituted in early 1953 were sustained into 1954 by lender caution in the light of general business developments." [8] Even though monetary policy became progressively more restrictive throughout 1955, the easing of consumer credit terms, which had begun in mid-1954, continued through early 1956. Particularly important during this period was the significant increase in the average maturity on newly-extended automobile loan contracts. It was probably not until mid-1956 that restrictive monetary

---

[4] *Financing Small Business, op. cit.,* Part 2, Vol. I, chap. III.

[5] Board of Governors of the Federal Reserve System, *Consumer Instalment Credit,* 4 Parts, 6 Volumes (Washington, 1957). See especially Vol 2, Part I, pp. 61-73.

[6] For a summary of the case for insensitivity of consumer credit, see Warren Smith, "Consumer Instalment Credit," *American Economic Review,* December 1957.

[7] Paul Smith, "Response of Consumer Loans to General Credit Controls," *American Economic Review,* September 1958, pp. 649-655.

[8] *Consumer Instalment Credit, op. cit.,* Vol 2, Part I, p. 73.

policy induced a significant number of commercial banks to be more cautious in extending instalment loans.

Interest rates on consumer loans generally have been fairly sluggish in responding to fluctuations in money market rates. Consequently, the returns on consumer loans are relatively more attractive to banks in periods of slack economic activity, and as a result one might expect considerable responsiveness to monetary policy. However, offsetting this has been a combination of a secular growth trend in consumer lending and competitive "necessity." Moreover the rate of return to banks, even in periods of restrictive monetary policy, probably makes consumer lending attractive under any circumstances. During the past decade an increasing number of commercial banks have moved into the instalment credit field and those already in the field have widened their dealer relations and their line of direct consumer loans. Turning consumer credit on and off in response to monetary policy changes is not consistent with developing a successful consumer finance business. It is particularly necessary to keep up satisfactory working relations with auto and appliance dealers, for when money is readily available, dealers are likely to be in a position to choose among alternative lenders.

Commercial banks also exercise an important indirect role in the extension of consumer credit through their lending to sales finance and consumer finance companies. The latter are dependent on bank loans for a significant portion of their financing. The largest of the finance companies, in addition to having lines of credit at commercial banks, have ready access to the open money market. As might be expected, finance companies are not favorites of commercial banks because they tend to be heaviest borrowers when other loan demands are strong and they provide little other business for banks. Consequently, some banks are more selective in lending to finance companies than to other borrowers in periods of monetary restraint. Compensating balance requirements have been raised; requests for extensions of credit lines, at times, have been refused; and some existing credit lines have been pared.

Housing credit. Home mortgage loans have been more sensitive to monetary policy than most other classes of loans. True, commercial banks, although important, are far from having a predominant position in mortgage financing; they held slightly less than 15 percent of all outstanding mortgages at the end of 1959. But variations in commercial bank mortgage extensions have accounted for a considerable part of the variations in total mortgage lending. This may be seen in Table 3-1 by a comparison of changes in commercial bank and total non-farm residential mortgage holdings:

The cyclical variability of residential construction can be attributed in large part to the relative inflexibility of FHA and VA insured mortgage

TABLE 3-1
Annual Changes in Non-Farm Mortgage Holdings

Year	Increase in outstandings			Increase in outstandings compared with increase during preceding year		
	All Lenders (Billions)	Banks	Percent of Banks to All Lenders	All Lenders (Billions)	Banks	Percent of Banks to All Lenders
1953	$ 8.2	$0.7	8.5%	–	–	–
1954	10.2	1.3	12.7	$2.0	$0.6	30.0%
1955	13.3	1.7	12.8	3.1	0.4	12.9
1956	11.5	1.1	9.6	-1.8	-0.6	33.3
1957	9.1	0.2	2.2	-2.4	-0.9	37.5
1958	11.7	1.4	12.0	2.6	1.2	46.2
1959	14.9	1.8	12.1	3.2	0.4	12.5

Source: Housing and Home Finance Agency.

loan rates, and the consequent cyclical fluctuations in the differential between these rates and other investment yields.

During periods of restrictive monetary policy, commercial banks tend to be cautious in expanding commitments of funds for long-term purposes. When demands from regular borrowers are high and rising and additional deposits difficult to come by, it is only natural that bankers will avoid tying up funds for long periods of time and thus reducing the number of loan applications which can be met. It is worth noting that long-term loans are generally used to finance major capital purchases—homes, factories, machinery, etc. These are precisely the types of economic activity that show the greatest fluctuations and contribute the most to cyclical instability. Hence, by their inability to meet all requests for long-term credits in boom conditions, banks make an important contribution toward smoothing out the business cycle. This, of course, is one demonstration of the successful application of monetary policy.

The long-term loan trend. The increase in bank loans during the 1950's was far greater than the increase in bank deposits. Recurring resort to a restrictive monetary policy to combat inflation during the decade had a much less restrictive effort on bank lending than would have been the case if the loan-deposit ratio had not been relatively low at the beginning of the decade. However, with the loan-deposit ratio now at a relatively high level, equally restrictive credit policy in the future likely would be much more effective in limiting loan expansion.

In the most recent business upswing, commercial bank loan-deposit ratios reached post-World War II highs, though ratios are still well below those of the 1920's. In the spring of 1961, at the beginning of a recovery period, commercial banks had substantially less liquidity—by virtually any liquidity measure—than at the comparable stage of the previous business upswing.

Commercial banks are thus becoming increasingly sensitive to small changes in their liquidity, and as in the past will become increasingly unable to expand loans during future periods of monetary restraint. However, while loan-deposit or alternative ratios have risen, the willingness of commercial banks to tolerate such increases and to discard rigid rules-of-thumb probably has also increased. It remains to be seen just how much further commercial banks will be willing to go in reducing their liquidity, as measured by these ratios, in the future.

Effects on Bank Investments

As in the case of bank lending operations, the impact of changes in monetary policy on bank investment portfolios is pronounced.

As the preceding section of this chapter indicated, the chief effect of a restrictive credit policy upon commercial banking in the 1950's was to force a contraction of investments to accommodate loan expansion, so that loan-deposit ratios rose sharply. On the other hand, periods of monetary ease cause a rapid expansion of bank investments, since the initiative in expanding investments rests with the banks and not with borrowers. Credit control has thus resulted in a strongly countercyclical pattern of bank investing, with investments expanding in periods of low loan demand and low interest rates and contracting in periods of high loan demand and rising interest rates.

The countercyclical nature of bank security transactions stems in part from the preference of commercial banks for loans compared with securities. Loans generally afford higher returns; they tend to build up present and future deposit relations; their short maturities tend to minimize the risk associated with interest-rate fluctuations. Moreover, bankers view themselves as being primarily in the business of lending rather than investing. Most bankers are familiar with the loan process and credit evaluations, whereas the basis for security-price fluctuations and such concepts as taxable-equivalent yields are less widely understood at some banks.

U.S. Government securities. Short-term Treasury securities are viewed by bankers as secondary reserves to meet cash drains arising from deposit losses. Intermediate and longer-term Treasury and municipal issues will eventually become shorter in term and perform the functions of short-term issues, but in the meantime they afford an outlet for excess funds when loan demand is slack, as well as prime investment media which are particularly suitable for commercial bank investment needs.

During the period immediately following the Treasury–Federal Reserve Accord of 1951, it was fairly widely assumed that relatively small increases in interest rates would tend to lock commercial banks and other financial institutions into their holdings of longer-term investments.

In part, this assumption reflected a belief that commercial banks and other financial institutions were strongly averse to realizing capital losses on investment holdings. However, experience in two periods of monetary restraint (1955-57 and 1958-60) raises some question as to the extent to which the presumed "lock-in" effect inhibits bank lending policies during periods of economic expansion and rising interest rates.

It is clear that the "lock-in" effect is a matter of degree, rather than of absolutes, and there are many variables which influence the extent to which the "lock-in" effect may be realized in any particular period of economic expansion. The most important of these variables are the strength of loan demand; the liquidity position of the banking system; the maturity distribution of investment holdings; and bank attitudes toward capital losses on securities transactions. Analysis of the "lock-in" effect is complicated by the fact that these variables are closely inter-related.

If the "lock-in" effect has been less important in the past decade than some observers had expected, the reason appears to be that large bank holdings of short-term Government securities tended to provide banks with a source of loanable funds without the necessity for taking capital losses on investment securities. Traditionally, during periods of credit restraint, banks have liquidated a large volume of short-term investments to meet loan demand and, as a last resort, have turned to the sale of longer-term issues. Although commercial banks experienced capital losses during the postwar period, this experience does not indicate a lack of aversion to taking capital losses on securities. In fact, the tendency of banks to allow the passage of time to effect a gradual reduction in the average maturity of their portfolio, as well as increased reluctance to purchase higher-coupon, longer-term issues during recent periods of monetary ease, suggests quite strongly that the aversion to capital losses is indeed a significant influence on bank lending policies.

The distinction between the "lock-in" effect and the "liquidity" effect of credit restraint is difficult to make. Bank sales of longer-term issues become necessary only after their short-term portfolios have been reduced to what might be regarded as minimum levels. Under these circumstances, it is difficult to say whether the principal objection to sales of long-term Governments is the capital loss which would be sustained or the further impairment of liquidity which would result.

It must be noted that there are risks to selling longer-term issues in periods of credit restraint which warrant the conservative approach that many banks exhibit. A switch from a longer-term issue into loans frequently may involve shortening the commitment of funds near the cyclical peak in interest rates. If, at the time of the loan maturity, credit demands have slackened and interest rates have declined, a bank may find itself in a poorer position than if it had retained the investment in its portfolio. From the standpoint of long-term growth and long-term earnings, admittedly, additional factors would have to be weighed.

As a practical matter, the greatest significance of the "lock-in" effect may prove to be its long-range impact on bank investment patterns rather than its impact on bank lending in the course of one period of rising interest rates. Modern experience with flexible monetary policy dates only from 1951, and it is evident that the experience during this period has caused banks to become increasingly wary of purchasing longer-term issues during periods of credit ease. This wariness demonstrates quite effectively the reluctance which many banks have toward realizing capital losses on securities transactions. And, in view of this reluctance, it must be assumed that a significant "lock-in" effect has operated to inhibit the conversion of funds from longer-term investments into loans.

While the development of more sophisticated bank investment policies designed to minimize the risks of capital losses may serve to impair the effectiveness of Federal Reserve restraining action in future periods of strong credit demand, other factors should work in the opposite direction. As bank holdings of investments have declined, for instance, banks have become increasingly sensitive to limits imposed by liquidity considerations. As a result, Federal Reserve authorities may be able to achieve a degree of over-all credit restraint with roughly the same pressure on bank reserve positions as was required in earlier periods when investment accounts were relatively large.

State and local government securities. In contrast with the downward postwar trend in bank holdings of U.S. Government securities, state and local government obligations held by commercial banks have risen substantially. During the fifteen years ended December 1960, bank holdings of these latter issues approximately quadrupled. The share of bank investments accounted for by state and local government securities rose from about 4 percent to over 21 percent during this fourteen-year period, while their share of all bank earning assets rose from about 3.2 percent to about 8.8 percent.

The increased attention given to state and local government securities during the post-World War II period can be explained by two interrelated factors: (1) the sharp increase in state and local government borrowing, which gave rise to a rapid expansion in outstanding state and local government debt; (2) the rise in yields on such issues—a rise that has outdistanced that of most taxable securities and has led to taxable-equivalent returns on state and local government securities that have compared favorably with returns available on most other bank-held investments.

However, purchases of tax-exempt securities by commercial banks have not been concentrated in periods of most favorable yield comparisons. Banks have been most prone to add tax-exempts when their liquidity was high and when interest rates were relatively low; that is, at the same time they have added to holdings of U.S. Government securities. Thus, 1954 and 1958, years of monetary ease and heavy bank acquisition of U.S. Governments, were the years during which banks added most to their tax-exempt holdings. On the other hand, during years in which monetary policy was restrictive and banks sold Treasury issues, banks added to their tax-exempts only modestly, or even reduced their holdings as in 1959. This occurred despite the fact that, during such periods of monetary restriction, after-tax return considerations alone would have suggested substantial net acquisition of tax-exempts.

Thus, banks have treated tax-exempt securities much like medium- and longer-term U.S. Government securities—as a source of earnings when loan demand was relatively slack. But, while some banks have used maturing tax-exempts as a source of funds when money was tight, neither maturities of tax-exempts nor prior-to-maturity sales of such securities have been an important source of funds for banks as a whole during periods of monetary restraint.

The Effect on Bank Earnings

Chapter 12 discusses bank earnings in some detail, but it is worthwhile at this point to consider briefly, how they are affected by monetary control measures.

It is widely believed that restrictive credit measures, by raising interest rates, tend to increase bank profits, and that it is for this reason that bankers have in recent years generally supported the policies of the Federal Reserve System. This belief, if not completely false, is at least such a partial truth as to be false in substance. The profits of the commercial banking system are governed largely by the following four factors: (1) the volume of bank earning assets, (2) the average rate of return on loans and investments, (3) operating expenses, (4) gains and losses on security transactions. All of these factors are influenced to an important extent by changes in monetary policies. It is, therefore, quite incorrect to fasten attention solely on interest rates as the only monetary influence upon bank profits.

During a period of restrictive credit policies, rising interest rates, it is true, normally will tend to increase gross operating earnings of banks. However, the effect of this on net profits may be offset or more than offset by the other factors listed above. Restrictive credit policies will operate to reduce, if not eliminate altogether, the rate of growth in earning assets, with resultant adverse effects on total profits. Operating expenses also tend to rise at such a time, largely because the banks themselves have to pay higher interest rates on their time deposits and borrowed funds. Too, banks usually realize heavy losses on security transactions during periods of high interest rates because at such times bond prices tend to be low and banks are under pressure to sell off investments in order to raise funds for meeting increased loan demands.

Conversely, during periods of relatively easy money and low interest rates, the effect on net profits of a lower average return on loans and investments is likely to be offset by the expansion in the volume of bank earning assets, by appreciation in investment accounts, and by the reduction in interest rates paid on time deposits and borrowed funds.

The combined effects of these various factors is for net profits of commercial banks (expressed as a ratio to capital accounts) to be higher during periods of easy money and low interest rates than during periods of tight money and high interest rates. For instance, banks enjoyed substantially higher net profit ratios on the average in the recession years of 1954, 1958, and 1960 than in the other years since 1947.

Notwithstanding the statistical record, however, too much importance should not be assigned to the fact that profit ratios of banks are highest in periods of low interest rates; to some extent banks can and do concentrate their capital gains in these years. All things considered, therefore, postwar cyclical changes in monetary policy probably have not had a great effect on bank profits in general, although, of course, they may have affected significantly the profits of individual banks.

As for the trends in bank profits, it seems likely that these have been held down during the postwar period by persistent inflation and the effects of monetary control measures taken to combat it. Benefits from the substantial rise in the average rate of return on earning assets have been largely offset by rising operating costs, heavy net losses on security transactions (associated with the upward trend in interest rates), and the restricted growth of the volume of earning assets. Although commercial banking is clearly a major growth industry in terms of the services it performs, its average net return on capital is below that of the majority of other major industries. Moreover, this return has shown no tendency to improve during the postwar period, and, indeed, during most years has been substantially lower than it was in 1946.

Commercial bankers do not believe, of course, that the primary purpose of monetary policy is to assure them adequate earnings. But they do feel that this consideration cannot be ignored entirely if the banking system is to continue to attract needed capital and to perform its essential functions efficiently.

The Impact of Monetary Policy upon the Economy

How successfully monetary management has accomplished its basic function and how it might better accomplish it in the future have been subjects for dispute for many decades. No attempt will be made here to resolve all of the difficult problems in this field, nor to describe in great detail how monetary and credit controls operate. Nevertheless, because of their central position in the financial system, commercial bankers may be in a position to throw light on some of these questions. Accordingly, the present section will discuss several of the key problems involved in monetary management as they are seen by commercial bankers.

For purposes of analysis, the mechanics of monetary and credit controls in our financial system may be divided into two parts: (1) the effects of central bank action upon the commercial banks and (2) the effects upon the rest of the economy of the commercial banks' reactions. Preceding sections of this chapter have discussed the first of these subjects; the present section will discuss aspects of the second.

The commercial banking system operates between two crucial variables: the demand for credit from would-be borrowers and their reserve positions as determined by the monetary authorities. The individual banker can adapt to changes in either of these variables in one of four ways.

1) He can make minor changes in his reserve position at his own discretion by building up or drawing down excess reserves and by borrowing or repaying borrowings from his Federal Reserve Bank. This ability provides the banker with a cushion against abrupt changes, but does not enable him to avoid the effects of major changes in either of the two variables.

2) He can modify the composition of his assets, e.g., by selling securities in order to make more loans or by buying securities when the loan demand is weak. This possibility has been discussed in the preceding section. While there is one disagreement as to how far banks are willing to go in this respect, it is clear that major changes in the two basic variables can be absorbed in this way only in part.

3) The banker can vary the interest rates he charges on loans in order to bring the demand for loans into better balance with the available supply.

4) To the extent that these measures do not bring about a perfect balance between demand and supply, the banker is compelled to ration credit in some manner (assuming the demand exceeds the supply).

These reactions of the commercial banks affect interest rates and the supply of credit throughout the credit markets via the familiar process of substitution. Frequently, of course, other sectors of the credit markets respond, not to actual changes in bank rates or the supply of bank credit, but merely to *expectations* of such changes. It is nonetheless true, however, that the banking system is the focal point through which the influence of Federal Reserve policies is exerted upon the economy as a whole, regardless of whether that influence is exerted via expectations or more directly.

One of the most controversial questions in the field of monetary policy is the extent to which borrowing is responsive to changes in interest rates. A number of students have asserted that it is highly interest-inelastic, so that moderate interest-rate changes have little effect on the amount of credit demanded. A number of empirical studies have been made purporting to prove this. On theoretical grounds it is argued that interest costs are usually so small relative to the possibilities of profit or loss as not to be of decisive importance. If this is true, it follows that interest-rate changes are not an effective means for bringing into balance the demand for, and the supply of, credit.

While there is no doubt an element of truth in these arguments, their significance seems to be exaggerated. It is obviously not necessary that *all* borrowers be influenced by interest rate changes but only that a marginal fringe be so influenced. Experience as well as logic suggests that this fringe does exist and that, given a sufficient change in interest rates (of the extent that typically occurs during a cyclical swing), a significant number of potential borrowers will be influenced. These will be mainly long-term borrowers, to whom a difference in interest rates extended over a period of years has a significant effect on total costs. Many corporations, state and local governments, home buyers, and others attempt to do their necessary financing when rates are low.

With respect to short-term bank credit, the factor of "rationing" is probably at least as important as interest rate changes as a means of bringing into balance the demand for and supply of loans. Bankers are generally agreed that when loan demands increase sharply, they do not as a rule raise rates as much as would be justified by the increase in demand, but rather become more selective in granting loan requests. By tightening up on credit standards, they eliminate the riskier or otherwise less desirable types of loans, thereby improving their average quality as well as holding down the total volume.

During the postwar period the volume of bank credit outstanding has never actually declined during periods of credit tightness; it has merely not been allowed to grow at an unwarranted rate. Banks are not compelled to turn down legitimate and normal loan demands. Rather, the need is to reject those demands which will result in excessive or unwise business expansion or speculative activities. During a boom period, some businessmen and investors—particularly small ones—tend to become over-optimistic, and to expand their operations or make investments in the belief that business prosperity will continue indefinitely. To accede to all such credit demands would, in the long run, be a disservice to the borrowers themselves and to the economy as a whole. By tightening up on their lending standards at such times, the banks help to prevent not only excessive credit expansion and consequent inflationary pressures but also unwise investments which would have to be liquidated later, with depressing effects on business activity.

Interest rates must be flexible if they are to perform, however imperfectly, their essential function of bringing into balance the demand for and supply of credit. They must be left free to fluctuate in accordance with changes in basic forces in the credit markets, including the impact of flexible monetary policies. Otherwise, serious imbalances are certain to develop which can result in inflationary or deflationary pressures. Moreover, fluctuations in interest rates, by reflecting changing conditions in the markets for loanable funds, provide the monetary authorities with necessary guides for their actions. To attempt, therefore, to maintain interest rates at artificial and inflexible levels, whether high or low, is to destroy the very foundations of countercyclical monetary policy.

Effects of Changing Velocity

It was pointed out above that the efforts of the monetary authorities to stabilize the economy are tempered to some extent by fluctuations in the velocity of circulation of the money supply. For instance, restriction in the growth of the money supply during expansion periods may be accompanied by a rise in velocity. This is because, as was noted earlier, the difficulty of obtaining desired credit at such times encourages the fullest use of cash balances and also because the rise in interest rates makes it more profitable to shift idle funds out of demand deposits into interest-earning money substitutes such as savings deposits or short-term government securities. Such an increase in velocity tends to offset—in part, at least—the effects of the restrictive monetary policies, since a higher level of aggregate expenditures can be supported by a higher turnover rate as well as by a larger money supply.

The question that naturally arises is whether this offsetting influence is sufficient to nullify the efforts of the monetary authorities. If velocity were able to increase rapidly without limit or hindrance, it would do so. Some students of monetary problems have argued to this effect and have concluded that monetary management is necessarily ineffectual as a result. Others have not gone quite this far but have maintained that velocity is so elastic that only sharp decreases in the money supply can slow the pace of economic activity during boom periods.

Fortunately, there are good grounds for considering these views too pessimistic. Common sense and experience both suggest that drawing down cash balances involves some cost. If working balances are reduced, they have to be managed with greater care. If speculative balances are drawn down, the chances of future advantageous purchases are sacrificed. For each depositor, these increased costs and sacrifices will at some point come to outweigh the return that can be obtained by activating idle balances. This is not to say that there is a fixed ceiling beyond which velocity cannot rise. Rather, the resistance to further increases in velocity grows sufficiently stronger so that, after a time, the restrictive policies pursued by the monetary authorities begin to take hold. The line of least resistance then becomes a slowing down in the increase of spending.

If this analysis is correct, the rise in velocity may delay somewhat the full effects of a restrictive monetary policy or compel the Federal Reserve authorities to take more vigorous action than would otherwise be necessary, but will not in the end prevent them from slowing down the flow of payments. Experience, too, suggests that this must be true, since every tight money period produces widespread outcries from those who are unable to obtain all the credit they desire. It is clear from these outcries that tight money does squeeze, despite the elastic turnover rate.

Whether the increase in velocity during boom periods compels the monetary authorities to reduce the money supply in order to restrain inflationary pressures, or whether a mere slowing of its rate of growth is sufficient will depend on the circumstances in each case. The factors affecting velocity are too diverse to permit easy generalization, but it seems likely that the boom-period increases in velocity since World War II have been much sharper than might be expected in the future. This has been a period during which velocity has shown a marked upward trend, as the economy worked off the excess liquidity accumulated during the war. The increase in velocity during each expansion phase of this period has reflected this secular rise as well as cyclical effects. As a result, it has been necessary to restrict the growth of the money supply more than would otherwise have been necessary. In other words, the degree of restrictiveness of postwar monetary policy was made necessary in part by the excessive expansion of the money supply during the war.

For the future, it is probable that fluctuations in velocity will be less of an obstacle to monetary management. With income velocity about back to the level of the 1920's and nearly double the 1945 rate, further increases, while by no means impossible, should come more slowly than during the past fifteen years. If so, monetary policies may not have to be as restrictive during periods of expansion as they have been. There seems to be little justification for the belief that our monetary stabilization measures are doomed to failure because of short-run fluctuations in velocity.

The Timing Problem

The preceding sections have argued that monetary policy, if employed vigorously enough, *can* influence the total flow of payments and hence over-all economic activity despite the fact that velocity is somewhat elastic and the demand for credit is somewhat interest-inelastic. But whether this influence can be exerted in such a way as to offset cyclical fluctuations in economic activity depends on the ability of the Federal Reserve to time its monetary actions properly.

A number of economists have argued that monetary measures operate with such long lags that they cannot be of much aid in countering cyclical fluctuations. Indeed, it is maintained by some that they may actually intensify such fluctuations by taking effect during the wrong phases of the business cycle. For instance, credit-tightening measures intended to counteract a boom may have the effect rather of intensifying the following recession.

In analyzing this problem, it is necessary to consider separately the various types of lags involved. We may classify them as follows:

First, there is the interval between a cyclical change in economic conditions and the consequent change in monetary policy. Once rather lengthy, this interval has been considerably reduced as the result of improved information on business conditions and the Federal Reserve's gain over the years in confidence, understanding, and decisiveness. We may take this lag to be quite brief and relatively insignificant.

Second, there is the interval between changes in monetary policy and changes in the cost and availability of credit. When banks are provided with additional reserves, they will usually be able to expand their lending operations within a matter of days. Interest rates on bank loans respond somewhat more slowly but, as has been pointed out above, they have less influence on bank borrowers than the availability of credit. Other sectors of the credit markets are likely to be affected by a change in Federal Reserve policy within a few weeks. When speculative forces within the credit markets act to reinforce a shift in Federal Reserve policy, as occurred late in 1957 and again during the summer of 1958, a decisive change in the level of interest rates and the availability of credit throughout all credit markets may be effected very quickly.

Third, there is the time it takes potential borrowers to be affected by the changed credit conditions. This, of course, depends on the situations confronting the individual borrowers. Those who have been unsuccessful in seeking credit during a preceding tight-money period may be in a position to borrow just as soon as credit becomes more available. Those who have already prepared expansion plans and are only awaiting a favorable opportunity to finance them may also be able to act quickly. Others may not be ready to take advantage of the changed conditions for some time.

Fourth, there is the lag between the borrowing and the expenditure of the funds. This, too, may vary considerably. Where the loan is for the purpose of expanding inventories or payrolls, the lag may be very short.

Where it is for long-range investment purposes, the funds will be spent over a period of months or years, but even in these cases the initial effects are likely to be felt quickly as the investment projects are begun.

If we consider these four lags together, it is clear that the effects on economic activity of a shift in monetary policy will be dispersed over a period of time. But what is more significant is that *some* of these effects will be felt quickly. The fact that part of the effects may not be felt for some months does not mean that they are not beneficial. During a depression period, the economy will benefit from whatever stimulating effects occur not only during the entire period of the decline but also during the ensuing recovery period. Such stimulation becomes undesirable only after the economy has approached full employment and inflationary or other boom-period pressures begin to appear. However, before this point is reached the monetary authorities will have reversed their policies and will again be tightening up. Ideally, the dampening effects of this new monetary tightness should begin to supplant any remaining stimulating effects of the previous policy of monetary ease just about the time the economy returns to a reasonably full employment level. There seems no inherent reason why the Federal Reserve cannot come fairly close to achieving this ideal.

Thus, those who argue that monetary policy cannot be effective because it cannot be timed accurately enough are unduly pessimistic. The unavoidable lags involved in the use of monetary policy mean that it cannot *fully* offset cyclical fluctuations in economic activity. But no one ever supposed that it could. The objective of all stabilizing economic policies is merely to *moderate* such fluctuations—to reduce the amplitude of the business cycle. Monetary measures can contribute to this end so long as they have some effect within the intended phase of the cycle. To illustrate the point and to use an extreme and unrealistic example: if a business recession were to last twelve months and the easing of credit conditions did not begin to take hold for eleven months, there would still be something gained by getting recovery started a month earlier.

A few words should be added about the proposal made by some economists that the Federal Reserve System should be divested of its discretionary monetary powers and should instead be instructed by the Congress to provide for a steady increase in the money supply at some prescribed rate. The basis for this proposal is the belief that monetary policy as it has actually worked in the past has been more destabilizing than stabilizing. It is alleged that because of the lags involved, it generally has its effects at the wrong time.

In part, this belief seems to rest on the notion that if some of the effects of a shift in monetary policy occur too late to be useful, the policy as a whole is not useful. But, as has been shown above, monetary measures can make a contribution toward stability if only part of the effects occur during the cyclical phase for which they were intended. It must be admitted that there have been episodes in our history when Federal Reserve actions have had perverse consequences. But these episodes occurred during earlier periods when the theory of central bank control had not been fully developed or when the hands of the Federal Reserve were tied by legislative or other handicaps. Monetary management, as we understand it today, really dates only from the Federal Reserve–Treasury Accord of 1951. The record during this past decade has been good enough to warrant the conviction that monetary policy can be and has been a stabilizing influence.

Even if the Federal Reserve were successful in providing a steady increase in the money supply, it could not (at least, without new powers that would be more onerous than those it now has) control velocity. We have seen that velocity is capable of marked fluctuations over the course of the business cycle, and even if these should prove somewhat less violent in the future, they would still be capable in all probability of causing unacceptably large fluctuations in economic activity. Monetary management, carefully employed, affords a means of offsetting part of these fluctuations in velocity and hence in economic activity. It would be foolish to throw away this stabilizing weapon, merely because it had not always been used perfectly in the past, just at the time we have learned how to use it.

Conclusions

Monetary policy has made an important contribution during the past decade to the growth and stability of our economy. No doubt there have been mistakes, and it has not entirely lived up to the most optimistic hopes for it. Nevertheless, the relative prosperity and stability of the past decade have resulted in no small measure from the judicious exercise of monetary policy. Moreover, with the experience and greater understanding that has been gained, monetary policy should be able to accomplish even more in the future towards attaining the primary economic objectives of sustained growth, stable prices, and maximum employment.

In order to do this, however, monetary policy must remain flexible. Interest rates must not be frozen artificially, and the monetary authorities must be free to adapt their policies to changing economic conditions in accordance with their unbiased judgments. This means that they must not be subject to political pressures or fettered by doctrinal dictates. The present arrangement, under which the Federal Reserve System operates within the framework of government while at the same time being free of partisan political pressures, seems the best that can be devised.

But, although monetary policy has accomplished much and can be expected to accomplish still more, it would be folly not to recognize its limitations. There are some things it cannot do. If the practices of labor unions and management with respect to wages and prices are such as to stimulate strong inflationary pressures of a "cost-push" nature, monetary restraint alone can prevent inflation only at the cost of high unemployment. If the federal budget has unstabilizing effects, these cannot be entirely offset through monetary measures. Monetary policy should not be expected to compensate for all deficiencies in other economic policies. Much of the recent disappointment with monetary controls stems from the fact that it was expected to accomplish too much.

Chapter 4

COMMERCIAL BANKS AND
BUSINESS CREDIT

As noted in the preceding chapter, meeting needs of the business community for short- and intermediate-term credit has been a prime function of the commercial banking system since its origin. In earlier years, banks were the only important institutions equipped to provide this type of credit to businesses, and the formation and growth of banks has gone hand in hand with the spread of commerce and industry. Today, businessmen have access to a number of alternative sources of funds, and banks have entered into other credit areas more aggressively. Yet business credit remains the single most important element in the loan portfolios of commercial banks, and no other group of lenders is equipped to provide the same essential lending service to business, small and large and in all areas of the country, on equivalent terms.

In this chapter, both the role of banks in financing business and the importance to banks of business loans are discussed. In addition, some of the principal techniques of bank lending, the costs, and collateral services provided business borrowers are summarized. Special attention is given to the areas of term lending and lending to small business. Finally, the record of banks in providing credit to business is appraised, and potential problem areas are explored.

Business Loans Defined

A precise definition of "business loans" is difficult because of their heterogeneous character. Historical data, particularly before the late 1930's, are often not available on a consistent basis over long periods of time. Even for the more recent period, business loans have been defined in various ways for different purposes.

In this chapter, the definition used for business loans generally follows that specified prior to the middle of 1959 in the call-report instructions for commercial and industrial loans [1]—i.e., all loans to persons and corporations engaged in manufacturing, mining, oil and gas producing, quarrying, construction, utilities, trade, services, and amusements; to real estate operators or developers; and to sales finance companies. The loans may be used for financing capital expenditures as well as current operations. They may be secured or unsecured, except that mortgage loans for business purposes are included only in the data derived from the special Federal Reserve Surveys of business lending by member banks and in data in Table 4-1 derived from Federal Reserve "flow of funds"

TABLE 4-1
Outstanding Business Financial Liabilities
End of 1959

	Total	Bank Business Loans[a]	Trade Debt	Corporate Bonds	Mortgages[b]	Other
			(Billions)			
Borrower	$278.9	$52.0	$69.2	$79.8	$52.0	$25.8
Nonfinancial corporations	197.1	32.7[c]	53.4	71.6	31.3	8.1
Nonfinancial unincorporated business	56.5	13.0	15.8	-	20.7[d]	7.0
Finance	25.3	6.3	-	8.2	-	10.7
Lender	$278.9	$52.0	$69.2	$79.8	$52.0	$25.8
Commercial banks	65.4	52.0	-	1.2	7.3	4.9[e]
Savings institutions[f]	15.1	-	-	3.6	11.5	-
Insurance companies[g]	76.2	-	-	62.6	13.6	-
Other lenders	122.1	-	69.2	12.4	19.6	20.9
		(Percentage Distribution)				
Total	100.0%	18.6%	24.8%	28.6%	18.6%	9.3%

Detail may not add to totals because of rounding.
[a]This definition of business loans is somewhat broader than that used on call reports, largely reflecting inclusion of some construction loans secured by mortgages and loans to certain financial institutions.
[b]Multi-family and commercial structures.
[c]Includes $1.2 billion of open market paper and $1.7 billion of construction loans secured by 1- to 4-family mortgages.
[d]Includes $5.3 billion of borrowings on 1- to 4-family dwellings.
[e]Security credit extended to the finance sector.
[f]Mutual savings banks, savings and loan associations, and credit unions.
[g]Life and nonlife insurance companies and private pension plans.

Source: Board of Governors of the Federal Reserve System.

[1] In 1959 the definition of commercial and industrial loans for call-report purposes was revised to exclude loans to sales finance companies and certain other financial intermediaries. Those loans amounted to $4.4 billion of the total of $41.5 billion commercial and industrial loans of insured commercial banks (old definition) on June 10, 1959.

statistics. Instalment lending to small businesses is also included within the definition of business loans, although loans of that type sometimes originate in personal loan departments.

The Role of Banks in Financing Business

The principal sources of funds for American business over the years have been equity financing, to a very considerable extent in the form of retained earnings, and depreciation allowances. During the postwar years, however, between 35 percent and 40 percent of business assets have been obtained by the use of borrowed funds.[2]

More than two-fifths of business indebtedness is short- and intermediate-term credit advanced either by banks or by business firms, as reflected in Table 4-1.[3] Business loans of commercial banks alone accounted for roughly 19 percent of the total indebtedness, while trade debt, which consists of accounts payable to other businesses, amounted to nearly 25 percent at the end of 1959.

The remaining indebtedness of business firms consists mainly of longer-term bond issues and the mortgage financing of multi-family buildings and commercial structures. In these areas, too, commercial banks have played a part in business financing, although this type of credit is not ordinarily classified as a business loan. In recent years, commercial banks have participated to a relatively minor extent in the corporate bond market, but a significant part—perhaps one-sixth—of the mortgage financing of business concerns has been handled by banks.

Miscellaneous sources of credit, such as finance companies, factors, individuals, and government lending agencies, together accounted for only about 9 percent of all business indebtedness. For nonfinancial businesses, these miscellaneous sources of funds were equal to only about one-third of their bank borrowings. Moreover, these miscellaneous lenders have frequently obtained from bank loans the funds re-lent to other businesses.

While the business loans of banks, totaling $52 billion at the beginning of 1960, were less than the total outstanding volume of trade credit, there is an important element of double counting in these figures. A significant part of trade credit has in effect been financed by bank borrowing, either by suppliers who in turn extend credit to their customers or by factors

[2] Raymond W. Goldsmith, "Postwar Capital Markets," *Thirty-Seventh Annual Report,* National Bureau of Economic Research, and R. R. Moss, "Financing of Large Corporations, 1951-55," *Federal Reserve Bulletin,* June 1956, p. 586.

[3] The data in Table 4-1 are based on the "flow of funds" estimates by the Federal Reserve Board. They have a broader coverage than the call-report data on commercial bank loans. For example, loans to the finance sector include loans to personal, industrial and other finance companies as well as sales finance companies. At the end of 1959, the flow of funds data yielded an estimate of $52 billion for commercial loans as compared with the Board's estimate of $40.2 billion based on call-report data.

and finance companies which carry a part of the trade credit. Moreover, a bank extending a loan to a business concern often carries a larger share of whatever risks are involved than does a single trade creditor, though the total amount of credit extended the firm by all its suppliers may be larger than its bank borrowings. Consequently, a comparison of the volume of trade credit and bank credit used by American business tends to understate the crucial role of banks in providing external funds to the business community.

Industry Differences in Reliance on Bank Credit

The Federal Reserve has estimated that there were perhaps one and three-quarter million to two million separate bank loans to business outstanding in the fall of 1957. That compares to a total business population in the neighborhood of four million firms.[4] True, some of the individual loans represented different notes of the same business firm. On the other hand, a survey taken at any given date is bound to miss many intermittent borrowers. Thus, the fact is clear that a very large proportion of all business firms rely on banks to provide all or part of their credit needs, and those firms range from the largest to the smallest.

As between different sectors of the business community, however, there are some rather wide differences in the use of bank loans as a means of financing. Some rough indication of these differences is reflected in data for corporate sources of funds developed by the Department of Commerce.[5]

From 1946 to 1957, according to these data, bank loans did not loom especially large as measured against the total sources of funds to corporations—internal and external. In those postwar years, bank loans accounted for 8 percent of aggregate sources for wholesalers and retailers, at the upper end of the scale, but for less than 2 percent in the case of the communications industry. At the same time, retained earnings and depreciation allowances accounted for about 60 percent of the total sources of funds for all nonfinancial business corporations.

The importance of bank financing is more apparent, however, when only external sources are considered. Thus, bank loans provided one-fourth of the external funds raised by trade concerns, and roughly one-fifth of the external requirements of the manufacturing and mining industries, railroads, and other transportation firms. In the financing of the utilities and communications groups, on the other hand, bank loans

---

[4] G. W. Mitchell, "Review of Survey Findings," in *Financing Small Business*, Report to the Committees on Banking and Currency and the Select Committees on Small Business, U.S. Congress, by the Federal Reserve System, Parts 1 and 2, April 11, 1958 (Washington: U.S. Government Printing Office, 1958), p. 360.

[5] Herman I. Liebling, "Financing the Expansion of Business," *Survey of Current Business*, U.S. Department of Commerce (September 1957), p. 12.

accounted for less than 5 percent of the outside funds obtained in these postwar years, reflecting their relatively heavy use of long-term bond financing.

Even these figures tend to understate substantially the role of bank credit in financing industry. Unincorporated businesses, without access to the bond and stock markets, are probably more dependent on banks than corporations. Moreover, the "sources of funds" data merely reflect the net increase in outstandings over the period. Aggregate credit extensions are, of course, much greater, reflecting the turnover of business loans over the course of a year. Fragmentary data suggest, for instance, that the *new* loans of one large bank in the course of a year amount to roughly three to four times its outstanding volume. In a sense, even without a change in the total, banks provide a large pool of revolving credit for business, with repayments by one borrower offsetting the new loans to another. And over the course of a year or several years, the use that any single borrower or group of borrowers has made of that credit pool cannot be adequately measured by changes in its size. Nor can study of the aggregate figures convey the crucial role that a bank loan, as an external source of funds not tied directly to specific purchases from suppliers, can play in the over-all financial planning of a business firm— especially a smaller firm with only a limited choice between alternative sources of funds.

Variations in the use of bank loans by particular industries over a period of time give some indication of the flexibility with which banks can and have shifted funds from one point of need to another. In the years 1947-51, manufacturers placed the greatest emphasis on bank loans, obtaining 10 percent of their gross funds in this way. Transportation other than rail, the railroad industry, and trade followed with 9, 8, and 7 percent of their gross funds coming from bank loans in that order. Public utilities and the communications industry obtained only 4 percent of their gross funds from bank loans.

In contrast, over the years 1952-56, trade concerns rather than manufacturers relied most heavily on bank loans, obtaining 11 percent of their requirements in this manner. In other areas, business use of bank loans ran below their uses in the early postwar years. Corporations in the transportation industry (other than rail) actually repaid bank loans (net), compared with the 9 percent of gross funds obtained by bank loans earlier. Railroads cut back their use of loans from 8 percent of gross funds to 5 percent, and manufacturing from 10 percent to 4 percent.

Reasons for Bank Borrowing

Traditionally, the average industrial or mercantile concern relies on the commercial bank chiefly for assistance in meeting seasonal or other short-run variations in cash requirements. But to an important degree business has turned to commercial banks also to cover longer-term requirements for working capital and fixed assets.

Typically, variations in the demand for bank loans arise mainly from changes in inventory, accounts receivable, and equipment requirements, with inventory fluctuations particularly important. At times, however, funds may be needed for a wide variety of other purposes, such as to meet interest payments on a bond issue at a time when sales are reduced because of a recession, strike, or other development; to cover capital outlays while a program of long-term financing is being arranged; or to acquire other businesses. The funds may be used to acquire assets directly, to reduce liabilities incurred, or to replenish cash already used for the purchase of assets. Sometimes several banks are used, especially where plants are maintained and important selling operations are conducted in different localities, or where needs exceed the lending capacity of individual banks because of legal loan limits or other reasons.

Lending to Financial Intermediaries

In addition to their role in the direct financing of industrial and commercial concerns, commercial banks play a crucial role in providing a large part of the credit needs of certain types of specialized financial intermediaries. These include factoring companies, mortgage companies and, most important, personal loan, sales, and commercial finance companies.

These intermediaries in turn provide specialized financial services to businesses, sometimes in competition with the banks themselves, but frequently in areas that are not considered suited for direct bank financing because of the exceptionally high risk or the highly specialized collateral used. Thus, mortgage companies, as key middlemen in the mortgage market, need access to credit while working out arrangements to place mortgages with permanent lenders. But their credit needs are only one aspect of their services to the mortgage market—services that are somewhat removed from the prime functions of a commercial bank. Similarly, factors have developed techniques for controlling and collecting a heterogeneous group of accounts receivable, particularly in the textile industry, and those special services, while supported by credit extensions, involve much more than a lending function alone. Moreover, other intermediaries have sometimes exploited newer credit areas, as in the field of consumer financing, which banks were unable or unwilling to pioneer for various reasons, such as legal restrictions or the need to avoid areas of potentially high risk before reliable experience had been gained.

By lending to these institutions, the commercial banks have participated indirectly in these specialized areas, and in some cases have become important direct participants as well. Thus it has been estimated that one-half to two-thirds of the funds used by finance companies are obtained by borrowing from banks or by discounting the receivables of their customers at banks,[6] and that close to two-fifths of the funds of the old line factors come from commercial banks.[7] Commercial banks have played an active part also in meeting the needs of mortgage companies for interim financing—commonly known as "warehousing"—between the acquisition and sale of mortgages. The interim requirements of these companies have increased significantly in recent years with the growth in the volume of home financing with federal-insured and guaranteed loans and the desire of institutional investors at times to defer the taking up of those mortgage loans for which they are committed. Commercial banks sometimes lend directly to institutional investors to enable them to take up maturing mortgage commitments pending necessary portfolio rearrangements.

In all these cases, the inherent flexibility of bank lending—the ability to borrow and repay on short notice, the use of various types of collateral, and the absence of the more detailed and rigid requirements imposed on borrowers in the public market—is vital to the borrowing institution involved. Hence the importance of banks to these specialized institutions —which typically experience wide variations in their short-run cash needs—is even greater than the data on outstanding loans itself would indicate. And the volume itself is far from negligible; insured commercial banks at the end of 1960 were lending $7.1 billion to nonbank financial institutions, an amount equal to about one-sixth of their lending to non-financial businesses.

Advantages of Bank Lending to Business

Commercial banks are particularly suited for meeting the current needs of business. Because of their decentralized structure, responsibility for lending is widely distributed, decisions can be reached quickly, and there is recognition of the needs of small business as well as large. Continuing account relationships, whether or not the customer is borrowing, lay a firm basis for sympathetic, informed, and flexible treatment of credit needs as they arise; lending terms and arrangements can be tailored to fit individual needs and charges are often substantially lower than those of alternative sources of funds. Finally, banks, in the normal course of their business, provide many subsidiary services to customers. In fact, the various services provided by banks as custodians of the payments

---

[6] Loring C. Farwell, "Specialized Short Term Financing," *Financial Institutions,* ed. by E. W. Boehmler (Homewood, Ill.: Richard D. Irwin, Inc., 1956), p. 184.

[7] William G. F. Price, "Why Business Firms Borrow from Commercial Banks," *Business Loans of American Commercial Banks,* ed. by B. H. Beckhart (New York: The Ronald Press Company, 1959), p. 51.

mechanism and as lenders are so intertwined that one type could not exist without the other.

One reflection of the flexibility of banks in meeting the needs of their borrowers is the variety of terms under which they lend. Thus, about one-half of the dollar amount of business loans by banks is unsecured. While unsecured loans are more typical of large borrowers, over one-fifth of the smallest loans have no specified collateral, and roughly one-third of all short-term loans to small borrowers are unsecured. For loans with collateral, the security is usually based on plant, real estate, equipment, and inventories (including trust receipts, warehouse receipts, and factor liens). But business loans are also backed by co-maker guarantees, assignment of claims (contracts, accounts receivable, and oil runs), and the pledge of marketable stocks and bonds. Thus, creditworthy businesses are seldom faced with lack of suitable collateral for a bank loan.

Some borrowers obtain temporary advances on direct application, but, if the borrowing is likely to be renewed, the usual practice in the case of short-term needs is to arrange for a "line of credit," permitting quick and almost routine handling of specific loan requests as they arise. In other cases, where the borrowing need may be more prolonged, the bank enters into formal revolving credit agreements that permit reductions and reborrowing for a period of a year or more ahead. Term loans, under which the full sum may be advanced at one time, provide for repayments over a period of one to five years or longer in instalments that are carefully integrated with the borrower's over-all financial plan. More detailed discussion of these arrangements is given in the section on the techniques of bank lending.

Relative Costs of Bank Credit

One measure of the effectiveness with which banks are able to meet the credit needs of businesses is the relative costs of bank borrowing as compared to the costs of other sources of funds. Cost comparisons encounter problems. For instance, the effective cost of a bank loan to a borrower may in some cases include other indirect expenses, such as (1) the purchase of insurance by borrowers, (2) the purchase of future contracts by those pledging inventories, or (3) maintenance of compensating balances which could exceed normal operating cash balances. Similarly, the quoted rate for open market borrowing does not include certain costs of flotation and servicing which are included in the quoted interest rate on bank loans. On the other hand, the borrower may receive valuable services from the lender over and above the use of the funds borrowed.

As a consequence, accurate judgments as to relative costs of borrowing are not possible. The following summary of relative costs of alternative sources of short and intermediate credit is made largely in terms of the nominal payments required.

As shown in Table 4-2, rates on bank short-term business loans in 1959-60 were at their highest levels in thirty years, although still below those prevailing in earlier periods. In March 1960, they averaged 5.34 percent per annum at banks in nineteen large cities and ranged from 6.01 percent for loans running from $1,000 to $10,000 to 5.21 percent for loans of $200,000 and over. These rates compare with a range of 1¾ per-cent to 4¼ percent during the late 1930's, and upwards of 6 percent during some years in the 1920's.

TABLE 4-2
Bank Rates on Short-Term Business Loans,[a] by Size of Loan
Selected Years 1920-1959

		Size of Loan (Thousands of Dollars)			
Year[b]	Total	1-10	10-100	100-200	200 and Over
1920	6.58%	n.a.	n.a.	n.a.	n.a.
1925	4.98	n.a.	n.a.	n.a.	n.a.
1930	4.85	n.a.	n.a.	n.a.	n.a.
1935	2.93	n.a.	n.a.	n.a.	n.a.
1940	2.1	4.3%	3.0%	2.0%	1.8%
1945	2.2	4.3	3.2	2.3	2.0
1950	2.7	4.5	3.6	3.0	2.4
1951	3.1	4.7	4.0	3.4	2.9
1952	3.5	4.9	4.2	3.7	3.3
1953	3.7	5.0	4.4	3.9	3.5
1954	3.6	5.0	4.3	3.9	3.4
1955	3.7	5.0	4.4	4.0	3.5
1956	4.2	5.2	4.8	4.4	4.0
1957	4.6	5.5	5.1	4.8	4.5
1958	4.3	5.5	5.0	4.6	4.1
1959	5.0	5.8	5.5	5.2	4.9

n.a. - Not available.
[a] Annual averages for 19 large cities
[b] Data prior to 1940 not strictly comparable because of revision in series.

Source: Board of Governors of the Federal Reserve System.

Costs of Trade Credit

Use of trade credit beyond the cash discount period of the customary ten days—an alternative to bank loans for many borrowers—is usually relatively expensive. However, despite its expense, it is convenient and is available to firms that may not qualify for bank loans. Under the typical terms, 2 percent may be deducted from a bill if cash is paid within ten days; otherwise, the face amount is usually due within thirty to sixty days. Consequently on an invoice of $1,000, for example, the borrowing business by deferring payment for thirty days, loses a $20 cash discount and thus pays $20 to use $980 for twenty days. This is equivalent to an annual rate of 36.5 percent. If payment is deferred for sixty days, the equivalent rate is 14.5 percent.

If the buyer is permitted to defer payment for a longer period, the annual rate for use of trade credit would be correspondingly reduced. Moreover, some suppliers may make special arrangements with their customers (or some large firms may arrange to extend credit to their smaller suppliers) and these arrangements could reduce the cost of trade credit. However, these special arrangements usually reflect marketing or other considerations that are not related to credit criteria.

Factoring and Commercial Finance Companies

Old-line factoring, in which the credit risk and the collection task are assumed by the factor, involves a twofold charge: (1) a rate of discount (usually about 6 percent per year) for the funds which is applied to the amount of each receivable purchased from the date of acceptance by the factor to its payment date; and (2) a commission for assuming the credit risk and the task of collection, ranging from less than 1 to 2 percent or more of the amount of each receivable handled. These charges, with the accounts outstanding fifty days on the average, would amount to 15 to 22 percent per annum. The effective cost to the borrower may be considerably lower, however, since the factor generally allows relatively high interest on balances left on deposit with him and the customer does not have the expense of conducting a separate credit and collection department.

Charges on accounts receivable loans by commercial finance companies and factors (where they do not accept the task of collection) are usually stated as a specified rate per day on the amount of the receivables pledged. Rates range from one-twenty-fifth to one-fiftieth of 1 percent per day, with a rate of one-fortieth of 1 percent typical. While the rate applies to the full amount of the receivables pledged, the borrower obtains the use of funds equal to only two-thirds to four-fifths of this amount. An advance equal to 70 percent of the pledged receivables with a rate of one-fortieth of 1 percent per day would involve a cost of approximately 13 percent per year. Other loan agreements for accounts receivable loans are stated in terms of an annual rate of interest but these agreements also require the deposit of the funds as the receivables are collected and their application, from time to time, to the reduction of the loan balance. With a stated rate of 6 percent, the effective rate becomes more than 6 percent and possibly as high as 12 percent per year.

Bond Financing

Issuance of bonds, either in the public market or by means of private placement, is an alternative source of funds for larger borrowers with longer-term needs. Table 4-3 gives some indication of the relative nominal costs of bank loans and bond financing over a long period of years. The figures in the Table must be used with reservations, however. The prime rate of banks, while reserved for customers with the highest credit stand-

TABLE 4-3
Interest Rates on Selected Types of Financing
December 1952 - 1960

December	Commercial Bank Prime Loan Rate	Moody's Aaa Bonds	Spread: Aaa Bonds and Prime Rate	Prime Commercial Paper 4-6 Mos.	Spread: Commercial Paper and Prime Rate
1952	3.00%	2.97%	-.03%	2.31%	- .69%
1953	3.25	3.13	-.12	2.25	-1.00
1954	3.00	2.90	-.10	1.31	-1.69
1955	3.50	3.15	-.35	2.99	- .51
1956	4.00	3.75	-.25	3.63	- .37
1957	4.50	3.81	-.69	3.81	- .69
1958	4.00	4.08	+.08	3.33	- .67
1959	5.00	4.58	-.42	4.88	- .12
1960	4.50	4.35	-.15	3.23	-1.27

Source: Moody's Investors Service, and Board of Governors of the Federal Reserve System.

ing relative to other bank borrowers, is available to a much wider range of concerns than an Aaa bond rating. Moreover, there are other costs not reflected in the interest comparison—commitment fees to banks for a term loan, cost of flotation for a public bond offering, and the like. A fair conclusion would be that for larger corporations able to command a national market, bond rates and bank loan rates are generally closely competitive, with one or the other relatively more costly at specific times depending on conditions in the bond market and the banking system. No clear rate advantage is apparent for one or the other over the postwar period as a whole.

Interest cost data are not available for private placements, but in general, rates on private placements seem to run somewhat higher than rates for comparable publicly offered issues. Both forms of bond financing are subject to rigidities that are avoided by bank financing, but both provide funds for much longer periods than is usual in the case of bank loans.

Commercial Paper

Borrowing in the commercial paper market can usually be done at significantly lower rates than those available from banks, as shown in Table 4-3. However, the borrower must absorb certain other issuing costs that would not arise in the case of a bank loan, and access to the market is limited to a relatively few firms of widely recognized standing.

The larger sales finance companies now commonly finance a large portion of their needs by the sale of paper directly to nonbank lenders at rates well below bank rates. The maturity of that paper is set more at the convenience of the lender than the borrower, however, and the finance companies frequently must replace the paper with bank loans at times when seasonal or other factors reduce the available supply of money from other lenders. Moreover, potential lenders often require that finance companies arrange lines of credits with banks sufficient to insure their ability to repay the notes when due.

Other Services of Banks

A borrower obtains many advantages aside from the loan of funds from his relationship with a commercial bank. The bank has a fund of knowledge about its customers and local conditions which enables it to be helpful to borrowers. A bank watches the financial operations of its borrowers with great care and frequently gives the borrowing concern very valuable suggestions. Also, ability to borrow from a bank creates a favorable impression upon suppliers, who know that the concern has successfully met the bank's standards.

Banks provide customers with credit information and trade data about both domestic and foreign opportunities. They effect introductions to other businessmen. They also stand ready to provide business and financial counsel and related services when called upon to do so.

Characteristics and Importance to Banks of Business Lending

During the past few decades, commercial banking has undergone far-reaching changes in the structure of its earning assets, as shown in Chart 2. Prior to the great depression, loans constituted the major portion of earning assets, while holdings of non-Government securities dominated investment portfolios. In the early part of the century, bank loans consisted mainly of short-term credits to business firms, especially for financing the trading and storage of commodities. This was in line with the then accepted principle that commercial banks, with liabilities payable on demand or short notice, should make only short-term "self-liquidating" commercial loans. In 1920, this type apparently constituted about 70 percent of all bank loans. Loans against securities made up most of the rest of the loan portfolios. These security loans, although inconsistent with the "commercial loan theory," were regarded as liquid and readily convertible into cash. The stock market boom of the late 1920's increased the demand for security loans, and in 1929 business loans (which had been fairly stable in volume throughout these years) amounted to less than half of the loan portfolios. Total loans in 1929 constituted over 70 percent of bank earning assets.

During the depression, loans began a downward trend, both in dollar

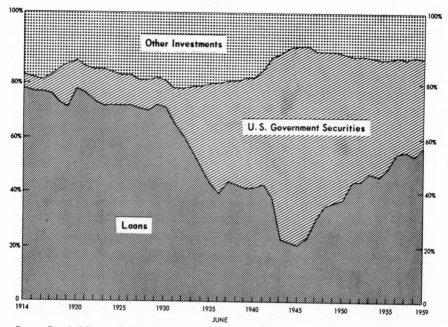

CHART 2

**DISTRIBUTION OF LOANS AND INVESTMENTS
ALL COMMERCIAL BANKS, 1914–1959**
(As % of Total Earning Assets)

Source: Board of Governors of the Federal Reserve System.

amount and relative to bank investments. This trend continued into the war period. With easy money and the great expansion of the available supply of U.S. Treasury issues during the depression and World War II, bank holdings of Government securities expanded severalfold. By the end of the war, bank loans and investments had just about reversed their pre-depression relationship. Less than one-quarter of earning assets were in loans and the remainder were in investments, mainly U.S. Governments.

In the meantime, commercial banks had sought new types of loans as well as investments. They began making consumer credit loans for the purchase of automobiles and other consumer durable goods. Home mortgages accounted for a larger proportion of bank lending. Longer-term business credit—usually repayable in instalments over one to five years— for the purchase of machinery and other equipment found a new place in commercial bank lending.

In 1938 a revision of data reported by member banks of the Federal Reserve System provided for the first time a detailed breakdown of loans. Business loans, although remaining the most important group of loans, by this time accounted for only two-fifths of the commercial bank loan portfolio, while non-farm home loans came to 18 percent and consumer loans to 14 percent, as shown in Chart 3. All other loans (including security credit) came to 28 percent of total loans.

CHART 3

DISTRIBUTION OF MEMBER BANK LOANS
1938–1959
(As % of Total Loans)

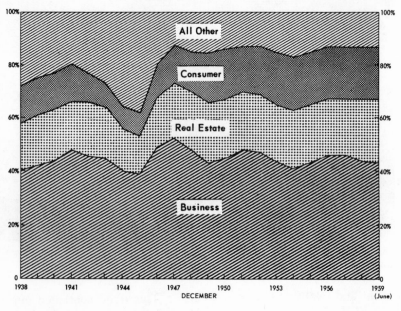

Source: Board of Governors of the Federal Reserve System.

The postwar rise in business activity produced a sharp increase in private demands for credit, and bank loans rose substantially. Banks reduced their holdings of securities, especially Treasury issues, and loans expanded to exceed investments beginning in 1955. Investments, however, are still somewhat more important in the structure of earnings assets than in the 1920's.

Despite the emphasis on the newer types of loans, business loans have maintained their relative position in bank lending in the postwar years, and in periods of rising economic activity business loans assume an even more important place in the structure of bank earning assets. Loans in the commercial and industrial category at the beginning of 1959 were more than four times as large as at the beginning of 1946.

At the beginning of 1960 business loans were over 35 percent of all loans and over 20 percent of earning assets (assets other than cash) of commercial banks, as shown in Table 4-4.

TABLE 4-4
Assets of Commercial Banks
December 31, 1959

Assets	Amounts (Billions)	Percentage Distribution of Earning Assets	Percentage Distribution of Loans
Total	$244.7		
Cash	49.5		
Earning assets	190.3	100.0%	
Loans [a]	110.8	58.2	100.0%
Business	40.2		35.5
Mortgages	28.1		24.8
Consumers	24.2		21.4
Financial institutions	7.9		7.0
Agriculture	5.0		4.4
Securities	4.9		4.3
Other	2.8		2.5
U.S. Governments	58.9	31.0	
State and local government issues	17.0	8.9	
Other securities	3.5	1.8	
Other assets	4.9		

Detail may not add to totals because of rounding.
[a]The various loan items are gross (before deduction of valuation reserves) and do not add to the total which is on a net basis. Gross loans total $113.1 billion.

Source: Board of Governors of the Federal Reserve System.

Loans by Type of Industry

Bank loans to business are distributed over a wide range of industries. Manufacturing and mining concerns account for close to two-fifths, trade for about one-fifth and the various services industries for the remaining two-fifths of the total of business loans, as shown in detail in Table 4-5, based on data in a recent survey of bank loans by the Federal Reserve.[8]

During the postwar years, it can be seen, the proportion of loans obtained by individual industries has changed, reflecting the broad redirection of resources in the economy. Every major business group increased its use of bank credit in the eleven-year period covered, but the service industries increased their loans at a faster rate than borrowers in trade and manufacturing. The decline during the postwar years in the relative importance of trade borrowers occurred entirely in loans to wholesalers.

[8] Carl T. Arlt, "Member Bank Term Lending to Business, 1955-57," *Federal Reserve Bulletin,* April 1959. Other articles in the Survey series in the *Federal Reserve Bulletin* include Caroline H. Cagle, "Security Pledged Business Loans at Member Banks," September 1959; James B. Eckert, "Member Bank Lending to Small Business, 1955-57," April 1958, and "Business Loans of Member Banks," April 1956; and Caroline H. Cagle, "Credit Lines and Minimum Balance Requirements," June 1956.

TABLE 4-5
Business Loans at Member Banks
Amount and Percent, by Business of Borrower
1946, 1955, and 1957[a]

Business of Borrower	Amount (Billions)			Percentage Distribution		
	1946	1955	1957	1946	1955	1957
Total	$13.2	$30.8	$40.6	100.0%	100.0%	100.0%
Manufacturing and mining	5.6	11.3	16.1	42.8	36.8	39.7
Metal and metal products	1.6	3.2	5.5	12.4	10.5	13.6
Petro, coal, chemicals, and rubber	1.1	2.6	3.8	8.0	8.4	9.2
Food, liquor, and tobacco	1.5	1.9	2.4	11.6	6.1	5.9
Textiles, apparel, and leather	0.5	1.7	1.7	3.7	5.6	4.1
Other	0.9	1.9	2.8	7.1	6.2	6.9
Trade	3.9	6.6	8.4	29.5	21.3	20.6
Retail	1.5	3.4	4.6	11.2	11.2	11.3
Wholesale	2.4	3.1	3.8	18.3	10.2	9.3
Services	3.7	12.9	16.1	27.7	41.8	39.7
Utilities	1.2	2.8	4.2	9.3	9.2	10.3
Sales finance cos.	0.8	2.9	3.1	5.9	9.2	7.6
Real estate	n.a.	2.4	3.0	n.a.	7.9	7.3
Direct services	0.5	1.8	2.3	3.7	5.7	5.6
Construction	0.4	1.7	2.0	3.4	5.5	4.9
Other	0.7[b]	1.3	1.6	5.4	4.3	4.0

Detail may not add to totals because of rounding.
[a] As of Nov. 20, 1946; Oct. 5, 1955; and Oct. 16, 1957. Ranked by importance in 1957.
[b] Includes loans to real estate concerns not reported separately for that year.

Source: Board of Governors of the Federal Reserve System.

The relative position of wholesale borrowers dropped significantly, falling from over 18 percent in 1946 to slightly over 9 percent in 1957, paralleling a decline in importance of the independent wholesaler.

While manufacturing and the combined service industries accounted for approximately equal shares of the dollar volume of business loans in 1957, rather marked differences existed in the number of loans to each, as Table 4-6 shows. The service industries accounted for roughly the same proportion of the number of loans as of the dollar volume. But the share of the total number of loans obtained by manufacturing enterprises was less than one-half of their share of the dollar volume, reflecting the larger average size of loans in this field. Borrowing by sales finance companies was most heavily concentrated, accounting for nearly 8 percent of the dollar amount of loans and less than 1 percent of the number. In

TABLE 4-6
Business Loans at Member Banks
Number and Percent, by Business of Borrower
1946, 1955, and 1957[a]

Business of Borrower	Numbers (Thousands)			Percentage Distribution		
	1946	1955	1957	1946	1955	1957
Total	673	1,317[b]	1,281	100.0%	100.0%	100.0%
Manufacturing and mining	116	225	211	17.2	17.1	16.5
Metal and metal products	29	59	59	4.3	4.5	4.6
Petro, coal, chemicals, and rubber	13	28	30	1.9	2.2	2.3
Food, liquor, and tobacco	18	36	30	2.7	2.7	2.3
Textiles, apparel, and leather	16	31	25	2.4	2.3	2.0
Other	40	72	68	5.9	5.4	5.3
Trade	341	517	507	50.7	39.2	39.6
Retail	253	411	395	37.6	31.2	30.9
Wholesale	88	105	111	13.1	8.0	8.7
Services	216	575	563	32.0	43.7	43.9
Utilities	38	44	49	5.6	3.4	3.8
Sales finance cos.	7	13	12	1.0	1.0	0.9
Real estate	n.a.	76	82	n.a.	6.4	6.4
Direct services	76	239	230	11.3	18.2	17.9
Construction	43	105	108	6.4	7.9	8.4
Other	52[c]	98	83	7.7	6.8	6.5

Detail may not add to totals because of rounding.
n.a. - Not available.
[a]As of November 20, 1946; Oct. 5, 1955; and Oct. 16, 1957. Grouped according to importance in dollar volume in 1957.
[b]Revised total is $1,185, but revised breakdown is not yet readily available. This probably does not affect percentage distribution significantly.
[c]Includes loans to real estate concerns not reported separately for that year.

Source: Board of Governors of the Federal Reserve System.

1955 the average loan in this field, at $213,500, was over twice as large as that in any other line of business. The direct services, in contrast, accounted for 18 percent of the number of loans but less than 6 percent of the dollar volume. Like the direct service lines, retail trade accounted for roughly three times the proportion of the number of loans as it did of the dollar amount of loans.

Loans by Maturities

Short loans, defined in the Federal Reserve Surveys as loans of one year or under at the time of extension, remain the largest in terms of number and dollar volume in commercial bank business loan portfolios. Their importance relative to term loans has declined considerably over the years, however. In 1957, short loans represented 62 percent of the dollar amount of member bank business loans, whereas in 1955 they had accounted for 66 percent (almost the same as in 1946) and in 1939 they had been close to 75 percent.[9]

The decline between 1955 and 1957 in the proportion of short loans was offset by a rise in intermediate-term loans (one to five years), as shown in Table 4-7. The intermediate group grew steadily from 1946

TABLE 4-7
Business Loans at Member Banks
Amount, Number and Percent, by Maturity
1946, 1955, and 1957[a]

Original Maturity (Years)	Amount			Number		
	1946	1955	1957	1946	1955	1957
	(Billions)			(Thousands)		
Total	$ 13.2	$ 30.8	$ 40.6	671	1,185	1,281
Short, 1 or less	8.7	20.3	25.2	527	820	801
Intermediate, 1-5	1.8	4.9	7.7	109	268	352
Long, over 5	2.7	5.6	7.7	35	96	127
	(Percentage Distribution)					
Total	100.0%	100.0%	100.0%	100.0%	100.0%	100.0%
Short, 1 or less	65.9	66.1	62.1	78.6	69.2	62.5
Intermediate, 1-5	13.6	15.9	19.0	16.2	22.6	27.5
Long, over 5	20.5	18.1	19.0	5.2	8.1	9.9

Detail may not add to totals because of rounding.
[a]As of November 20, 1946; October 5, 1955; and October 16, 1957.

Source: Board of Governors of the Federal Reserve System.

whereas the dollar volume of long-term loans (five years and over) in 1955 and 1957 was somewhat below their 1946 percentage.

One-half of the dollar amount of short loans, as defined in the Federal Reserve Survey, were granted in 1957 to retail and wholesale trade establishments, the metal products industry, and sales finance companies. In contrast, nearly 50 percent of the term loans in 1957 were concentrated in borrowing by the three industry groups with traditionally heavy fixed capital requirements—the utilities, the petroleum-coal-chemical-rubber

---

[9] The 1939 estimate is based on a Federal Reserve Survey of weekly reporting banks on April 19 of that year. The weekly reporting banks then held about 70 percent of all member bank business loans. See George S. Moore, "Term Loans and Interim Financing," *Business Loans of American Commercial Banks, op. cit.*, p. 213.

group, and the metal products lines. Retail trade and direct service enterprises also were important term borrowers, with 9 percent and 8 percent, respectively, of the term loan total.

Loans by Size of Bank

As might be expected, the larger banks account for the largest portion of bank loans. At mid-October 1957, banks with deposits of $1 billion and over held 45 percent of all member bank business loans. Banks with deposits of $100 million to $1 billion accounted for 35 percent, while banks with deposits of between $10 million and $100 million extended 16 percent of all business loans. The smallest banks (less than $10 million of deposits) accounted for the remaining 4 percent.

The largest banks are generally located in larger financial and market centers and areas that are highly industrialized. It is not surprising therefore that business loans—loans to commerce and industry—have traditionally held a key position in their loan and deposit structure. At Central Reserve City banks, the generally large banks located in New York and Chicago, total loans reached $20 billion by mid-October 1957, of which $14.6 or more than 70 percent were business loans. Business loans amounted to 44 percent of their total deposits.

At Reserve City banks—those located in a number of other large cities throughout the country—business loans accounted for 47 percent of all loans and amounted to 25 percent of total deposits. At country banks, located in smaller communities, business loans were 26 percent of total loans and 12 percent of deposits at that time.

The size of the lending bank is closely related to the size of the borrower. The bulk of the dollar volume of business loans in 1957 was, for the largest banks ($1 billion of deposits and over) to large and medium-sized businesses, and for the smallest banks (under $10 million of deposits) to small and medium-sized business (Table 4-8).

Lending by small banks is, in effect, limited by law largely to small business. For national banks and many state banks, loans to any one borrower cannot exceed 10 percent of capital and surplus. Some states have less rigid restrictions for state-chartered institutions, but all impose some maximum on loans to one borrower.

In all bank-size classes, as would be expected, the largest number of loans, as shown by data as of October 1955, went to relatively small enterprises.

The 1955 Survey also showed that the importance of loans to the several types of businesses varied for banks of different sizes. Loans to manufacturing and mining enterprises accounted for nearly one-half of the business loans of the largest banks (deposits of $1 billion and over), compared to less than one-fifth for the smallest banks (deposits of less than $10 million). Trade loans accounted for close to two-fifths of out-

TABLE 4-8
Business Loans, by Size of Bank and by Size of Borrower, 1957

Size of Borrower	Total	Size of Bank (Total Deposits - Millions)			
		Under $10	$10-$100	$100-$1000	$1,000 and over
			(Billions)		
Size of Borrower					
Amount[a]	$ 40.6	$ 1.7	$ 6.4	$ 14.2	$ 18.3
Small	7.0	0.8	2.1	2.6	1.5
Medium	17.7	0.8	3.4	6.7	6.8
Large	14.7	b	0.7	4.5	9.4
		(Percentage Distribution by Size of Bank)			
Total[a]	100.0%	100.0%	100.0%	100.0%	100.0%
Small	17.2	47.1	32.8	18.3	8.2
Medium	43.6	47.1	53.1	47.2	37.2
Large	36.2		10.9	31.7	51.4
		(Percentage Distribution by Size of Borrower)			
Total	100.0%	4.1%	15.9%	34.9%	45.1%
Small	100.0	11.3	29.7	37.3	21.6
Medium	100.0	4.6	19.5	37.8	38.2
Large	100.0	0.3	4.9	30.7	64.2

[a]Includes some loans for borrowers whose size was not ascertained.
[b]Less than $50 million.

Source: Board of Governors of the Federal Reserve System.

standing loans of the smallest banks but less than one-seventh at the largest banks. Similarly, loans to concerns providing direct services and to construction enterprises were relatively more important to medium-sized banks (deposits of $10 to $100 million) than to larger banks.

Regional Distribution of Business Loans

The fact that larger banks loom most important in business lending—measured both against the total of business loans outstanding and against their own total loans and deposits—is reflected in data for the regional distribution of business lending. Thus, nearly three-fourths of all business loans were made by banks in the five FDIC districts with most concentrated population and industry development. In contrast, banks in those districts held only about 65 percent of total deposits and 67 percent of total loans.

In these five districts business loans amounted to 21 percent of deposits and 44 percent of total loans; in both cases these proportions are significantly higher than for all districts taken together. Available evidence suggests that not only the larger banks but also the smaller banks in these industrialized areas have tended to keep a larger proportion of their assets in business loans than has been true of banks of comparable size in other areas.

Techniques of Bank Lending

A wide variety of techniques has been developed by banks to meet the needs of business customers. These techniques were virtually revolutionized during the 1930's, when the term loan came into prominence and methods were developed for lending to businesses unable to provide traditional forms of collateral. Details of lending techniques, not important for the purpose of this monograph, do demonstrate the flexibility of bank lending in meeting the varied needs of customers. This section confines itself to some highlights of current lending techniques that are applicable to most banks and borrowers.

Loan Agreements

Line of Credit.   A businessman with a temporary need for funds may apply to a bank for a loan for a given short period, perhaps leaving open the question of possible renewal. However, if needs are likely to be recurrent, the bank and the businessman will frequently arrange for a so-called *confirmed line of credit*. The understanding would then be that the business could borrow and pay off loans as needs dictate, but the maximum amount borrowed at any one time would be subject to the limit established by the line of credit. The size of the credit line would, of course, depend upon general considerations of creditworthiness, the business outlook, credit conditions generally, the loan position of the particular bank, and the legal limitation on loans to one customer.

The line of credit is an expression of willingness by the bank to lend up to the indicated maximum for agreed purposes. It is not a contractual obligation and no fee is charged, but banks seldom fail to honor a request for a loan within the credit line unless the circumstances of the borrower change very significantly. While the line is open, the borrower is expected to keep the bank informed of its operations and financial condition and, partly to facilitate that continuing review, the borrower is normally expected to maintain a deposit account at the bank. Sometimes an agreement as to a minimum or average deposit balance is formally or informally agreed upon between the bank and the business.

Under normal circumstances, lines of credit are usually extended for a period of one year, with some expectation that the borrower will repay all indebtedness at some point within that year. Many credit lines are renewed from year to year, but the opportunity for annual review is thus provided.

Some information concerning the practices of member banks in extending credit lines is available from the Federal Reserve Business Loan Survey of 1955. At that time more than one-half of all member banks made a practice of extending lines of credit, and those banks included nearly all the larger institutions with deposits of over $100 million. Use of credit lines diminished progressively as bank size declined, with less than 40 percent of small banks (deposits of under $20 million) making use of the procedure. To some extent that variation may reflect differences in the size and established credit standing of borrowers, since lines are most commonly extended to larger borrowers and well established firms. Moreover, the more informal relationships possible between the country banker and local businessmen may obviate the need for more formal credit lines.

Credit lines are most commonly used for seasonal or other recurring needs for credit, and many include the so-called "floor plan financing" of dealers, inventory and equipment financing, and financing of construction activity. Sales finance companies have received such accommodation more often than any other industrial group.

Revolving Credit.   To avoid the necessity of annual renegotiation, and as a means of obtaining more formal assurance of the availability of credit, some businesses and banks have arranged for so-called *revolving credits.* These arrangements differ from a line of credit in that they are normally for periods of more than a year—sometimes for five years or more—but are similar to a line of credit inasmuch as they provide for fluctuating amounts of short-term loans as needed up to a specified maximum. Unlike a line of credit, the bank charges a fee, often of 0.5 percent per annum on the unused portion of the credit, for its commitment to lend, which is expressed in a formal contractual agreement. Sometimes revolving credits will include a provision for conversion into a term loan at a specified date under certain conditions.

The use of revolving credits is more confined to larger corporate borrowers than is the case with lines of credit. The technique is particularly useful when well established firms engaged in setting up a long-run financial program wish to obtain assurance of the availability of credit over a fairly long period.

Term Loans.   A term loan agreement provides for the extension of credit at a specified time to be repaid over a period ranging from a year to five years or more. The repayment is usually scheduled in periodic instalments; in 1955, 80 percent of term loans of member banks provided for periodic repayments of principal. The schedule of repayments is geared to the potential cash flow of the borrower over the period that the loan is outstanding.

The conditions of the term loan are set forth in a formal agreement between the borrower and the bank. Because of the additional risks involved, collateral is required more frequently than in the case of short-term loans, and the bank may impose certain conditions and restrictions on the operations of the borrower. These might include some agreement as to the maintenance of a specified working capital position, the submission of financial statements at intervals, limits on other borrowing and capital expenditures or sales of assets, and the like.

Term loans have grown rapidly in importance since the 1930's. They are discussed in further detail later on in this chapter.

Collateral Requirements

As mentioned earlier, secured loans account for about one-half of the dollar volume of business lending, but in terms of number of loans they predominate two to one.

The main purpose of collateral or other security is to limit the risk of loss and facilitate collection in the event that the borrower is unable or unwilling to repay the loan at maturity. In some cases where the bank would be willing to extend unsecured credit, the borrower may find it advantageous to use security to obtain a larger loan, a longer maturity, or a lower rate of interest.

In general, collateral in itself is not the determining factor in bank lending today. The character of the borrower, his financial capacities as revealed in the past record and future prospects, and his whole capital position will be the principal factors determining the desirability to a bank of the loan, rather than the ability of the borrower to provide collateral—the value of which is sometimes dependent on the continued functioning of the business as a going concern, in any event. Security requirements may be more rigid, however, in cases where the loan is large relative to the total resources of the borrower, in cases where the security represents the bulk of the firm's available assets, in the case of smaller firms with no established credit rating, and in instances where financial records are inadequate or earnings unsatisfactory.

According to the Federal Reserve Business Loan Survey, in October 1957 less than one-fifth of the amount of bank loans to the largest businesses (assets of $100 million and over) were secured, as compared with almost four-fifths for the smallest firms (assets of under $250,000). However, the size of a business is not in itself the prime factor determining collateral requirements. Requirements for collateral tend to vary from industry to industry because of credit characteristics, and the industries in which collateral is likely to be a part of the loan agreement are composed in large part of relatively smaller concerns. Thus, below average use of secured loans occurred in the typically large-sized areas of sales finance companies, manufacturing, and utilities, while substantial use of secured loans characterized the construction, direct services, and retail trade fields in which small and medium-sized firms are dominant. However, the additional risks often associated with loans to new and smaller businesses tend to result in greater use of secured loans for such firms.

Use of collateral was also common in lending to real estate companies, which by the nature of their business have collateral that is conveniently and customarily used in bank financing and which operate on relatively thin equity.

Another factor influencing the requirement for collateral is the maturity of a loan, since maturity is one of the elements that determine the risk to the lender. Member banks required security on nearly three-fifths of their term loans (original maturity of more than one year) but on only about half of their short loans, according to data from the 1955 Survey.

Type of Security

Certain types of collateral are generally used as security for loans, largely because of their availability and the ease of appraising and handling them. But strides have been made in adapting bank lending to widely varying forms of security.

The types most often pledged against business loans in recent years have been plant and other real estate, equipment, the assignment of claims (including assignment of contracts, accounts receivable, and oil runs), and endorsement. About three-fourths of all secured business loans outstanding in 1955 used one of these four types. Loans backed by inventories, although important in manufacturing and trade, accounted for less than one-tenth of secured loans those collateraled by corporate stocks for slightly over 6 percent, and those backed by life insurance and savings accounts (used mainly by smaller business) for less than 3 percent. Less than 2 percent of all business loans in 1955 had a U.S. Government participation or guarantee.

Balance Requirements

Nearly all banks, in extending credit to their business customers and in deciding upon specific lending terms, will consider their deposit relationships with their customers. These considerations sometimes are more or less formalized in minimum or average balance requirements.

In 1955, about one-fourth of all member banks in the Federal Reserve Survey said that they had minimum balance requirements, and those minimum balances were generally tied in with the extension of lines of credit. Minimum balance requirements are sometimes relatively uniform for all borrowers, but a number of banks require higher balances for some types of businesses (particularly sales finance companies) than for others. Requirements are at times related to the amount of the credit line, to the amount of borrowing, or to both.

These differences make generalization difficult. A minimum or average balance requirement would result in a higher effective interest rate to the borrower where the required balance, or some portion thereof, exceeded his normal need for working funds. However, minimum balance requirements also are a means of encouraging borrowing customers to maintain a principal account relationship with the lending bank, of helping to discourage simultaneous borrowing from other banks when the borrower's needs can be handled by one institution, and of permitting the bank closer surveillance of the customer's operations.

Participations

Banks often make loans in association with other lenders (particularly with other banks). These loan participations may arise because the credit needs of the customer exceed the amount each bank is able to lend to one customer by law. Or they may reflect a desire to spread risks.

Participations provide a means whereby heavy loan demands in some sections or areas of the country can be supplied in part by banks in other areas. Loan participations are particularly common in the case of term loans; in 1955, nearly one-third of the dollar volume of term loans involved two or more banks.

Among large banks, so-called pool arrangements predominate—i.e., a loan is syndicated, or divided, among a number of banks each of which grants a prorata share of the credit to the borrower, and takes a prorata portion of the risk of loss. One bank usually acts as agent for the pool and handles the details. The borrower may or may not give individual notes to each participant.

Small banks seldom participate in pool arrangements, since their loans normally are not large enough to warrant such procedure. However, small banks do offer larger institutions so-called *overline participations,* whereby the initiating bank offers a correspondent a portion of the loan in excess of its own legal loan limit or the line of credit that it feels capable of extending. These overline participations result in city correspondents' taking a portion of larger loans initiated by smaller country banks. They facilitate the extension of credit in relatively large chunks in areas of the country without sufficient banking resources of their own. For other reasons, large banks may give participations in a loan made to a large enterprise to smaller banks, particularly where the borrowing business has branch plants or offices in the communities where the smaller banks are located.

Larger banks also often join with insurance companies, pension funds or other long-term lenders in arrangements whereby the banks provide shorter-term credit and the other lenders meet the borrower's needs for longer-term extensions.

Summary

Over a period of time banks have developed a variety of lending techniques that facilitate the extension of credit to business in needed amounts at appropriate times and places. Some of these techniques—especially participations—help to break down potential barriers in the flow of funds to the point of need—barriers that would otherwise limit the ability of a unit banking system to service a growing economy. Others, like the term loan, enable banks to fill needs for intermediate-term credit, particularly in the case of concerns unable or unwilling to enter the public bond market, on a basis convenient for the borrower and consistent with the bank's need for safety and liquidity. Revolving credit and line of credit arrangements have been developed to assist both borrowers and the banks in planning ahead on a sound basis, with a minimum of uncertainty and time-consuming negotiations. Secured loans remain important, but types of collateral have been adapted with ingenuity to the needs of businesses unable to provide traditional types of security. The flexibility inherent in these techniques, combined with relatively low cost, has been a prime factor enabling banks to retain their position as the basic supplier of short-term funds to business.

Term Lending

Business loans carrying a maturity of more than one year are generally referred to as term loans. Such loans are normally paid off on an orderly basis over the life of the loan. Term loans have grown greatly in importance since the early 1930's. As pointed out earlier, they increased from roughly one-quarter of all business loans at member banks in 1939 to 38 percent in 1957. For some larger banks the proportion is now over 50 percent.

Almost three-quarters of all member banks, large and small alike, had term loans outstanding on the Federal Reserve Loan Survey date in 1957. The largest banks (deposits of $1 billion or more) held more than one-half of the outstanding dollar amount of term loans—a significantly larger share than in the case of short-term loans. But smaller banks have also become active term lenders—banks with deposits of less than $100 million held more than half of the number, although less than one-fifth of the dollar amount.

Bank term loans in 1957 were evenly distributed in dollar volume between those with an *original* term of one to five years and those for longer terms (five years and over). The average size of the longer loans was larger, however, and three-quarters of the number of loans was in the shorter of the two groups, as shown in Table 4-9. The current even distribution of the maturities of the dollar volume of loans reflects a

TABLE 4-9
Business Term Loans at Member Banks
Amount, Number and Percent, by Maturity
1946, 1955, and 1957[a]

Original Maturity (Years)	Amount			Number		
	1946	1955	1957	1946	1955	1957
	(Billions)			(Thousands)		
Total	$4.6	$10.5	$15.4	144	365	479
Intermediate	1.8	4.9	7.7	109	268	352
1-2	0.6	1.4	2.4	58	136	168
2-3	0.3	1.0	1.9	23	78	108
3-4	0.2	0.7	1.2	11	23	31
4-5	0.7	1.7	2.3	17	31	45
Long	2.7	5.6	7.7	35	97	127
5-10	2.3	4.7	6.2	29	83	101
Over 10	0.4	0.9	1.5	6	14	26
	(Percentage Distribution)					
Total	100.0%	100.0%	100.0%	100.0%	100.0%	100.0%
Intermediate	40.2	46.7	50.0	75.7	73.5	73.6
1-2	14.2	13.6	15.6	40.0	37.3	35.0
2-3	6.9	9.5	12.1	16.1	21.3	22.6
3-4	4.8	7.0	7.6	7.5	6.4	6.6
4-5	14.3	16.6	14.8	12.0	8.5	9.4
Long	59.8	53.3	50.0	24.3	26.5	26.4
5-10	50.7	44.9	39.9	20.4	22.8	21.1
Over 10	9.1	8.4	10.0	3.9	3.7	5.3

Detail may not add to totals because of rounding.
[a] As of November 20, 1946; October 5, 1955; and October 16, 1957.

Source: Board of Governors of the Federal Reserve System.

more rapid growth since 1946 in the one-to-five-year group, which then accounted for only two-fifths of term loans.

Historical Background

The reasons for the shift toward longer-term lending by banks in the 1930's are complex. One reason was recognition of the need for a more realistic relationship between bank loan maturities and the period for which funds were needed by the borrower.[10] Many nominally short-term loans in earlier years were made with an agreement to renew or with

---

[10] George S. Moore, "Term Loans and Interim Financing," *Business Loans of American Commercial Banks, op. cit.;* N. H. Jacoby and R. J. Saulnier, *Term Lending to Business* (New York: National Bureau of Economic Research, 1942); and L. S. Ritter, Commercial Bank Liquidity and Medium and Longer-term Bank Loans in the United States, Fifth Meeting of Technicians of Central Banks, Documente de Trabajo No. 2, Banco de la Republica, Bogotá, Colombia, June 1957.

the implied intention to renew clearly understood, and the borrower was in fact in no position to repay his indebtedness at the end of the stipulated term. During the early depression years, attempts to obtain payments of such loans to secure funds to meet deposit withdrawals often failed, since inability of the borrowers to renew loans could have resulted in their bankruptcy. These experiences taught the lesson that the "short" term of a loan was not necessarily an assurance of liquidity for a bank. When business recovery set in after 1933, banks and businesses alike looked to new techniques for relating the nature of the need for funds and the timing of repayment to the terms of the loan instrument. The term loan emerged as the solution.

Another factor was the growth in popularity of term loans among borrowers in the 1930's. Many corporations, for instance, wished to retire high rate bond issues sold in the 1920's, and they turned to banks to avoid the *terra incognita* and added costs of borrowing in the investment market under new rules and regulations imposed by the Security Act of 1933 and the Securities Exchange Act of 1934. In many cases small businesses did not (and still do not) have access to the public security market on attractive terms; yet even small businesses were finding their needs for fixed capital rising as the economic environment changed. Financing with equity securities was very difficult and costly, reflecting the shattering effects of the depression on investor psychology.

At the same time, banks were being attracted to term loans for several reasons. During the later 1930's, large excess reserves encouraged them to seek actively new outlets for their funds. Business demands for traditional short-term loans had shrunk and Government securities provided low yields, enhancing the incentive to make relatively higher rate term loans.

Structural changes in the banking system also facilitated bank resort to term lending. Thus, the presumed lesser liquidity of term loans (vis-à-vis short-term loans) was offset in part by the establishment in 1934 of federal deposit insurance which reduced the likelihood of "runs." Moreover, in the banking legislation of the 1930's, collateral requirements for rediscounting at the Federal Reserve were liberalized, enabling banks to borrow on any sound asset (at a penalty rate). Also, examiners for regulating agencies by agreement in 1938 eliminated the "slow" classification for term loans and adopted instead a policy of evaluating loans on the basis of their "probable collectibility" according to maturity. Another influence favorable to term lending was the experience of the banks during those years with participations in term loans with the Reconstruction Finance Corporation and the Federal Reserve. Satisfactory experience with FHA-insured mortgages also encouraged bankers to extend the amortization feature to other lending areas.

In the years after World War II, continuing heavy demands for term loans were but one reflection of the great expansion in total needs for capital to modernize and expand machinery and plant and to offset the eroding effects of inflation on cash resources. The relatively low cost and convenience of bank financing—particularly in meeting intermediate-term requirements related to equipment purchases—caused borrowers to approach banks for accommodation in preference to other lenders, or as one part of an over-all financial plan that included a simultaneous or subsequent long-term bond issue. At the same time, lessened fears of severe depressions and bank "runs" contributed to the willingness of banks to expand term lending, especially since, at least during the early postwar years, total loan volume remained relatively small. The result was that the growth in term loans exceeded that of short-term lending during the postwar years as a whole.

Purposes of Term Loans

Bank term loans are made for several purposes. They are made to supplement working capital where inventory and receivables cannot be liquidated seasonally because of the long production period involved, particularly in the manufacture of machinery, airplanes, and ships. They are made for expansion purposes where the repayment schedule is supported by a projected cash flow from depreciation, depletion or earnings, or where funds are eventually to be obtained by the liquidation of assets, by refunding in the public market, or by means of loans from other lenders or infusions of new equity capital. Upon occasion, they are made for special purposes, such as to retire debt or preferred or common stock. In these cases the objective is to reduce interest costs, to rearrange maturities in line with the borrower's projected cash flow, to simplify the capital structure or to eliminate restrictive provisions of existing debt agreements or indentures. The retirement of preferred stock substitutes tax-deductible interest payments for nondeductible dividend requirements; while retirement of common stock may be effected to increase the leverage of the remaining stock, to meet personal needs of large stockholders or to buy out interests wishing to withdraw from the business.

In all these cases, the great advantage of a term loan to the borrower is its great flexibility relative to other alternatives. Negotiations can be conducted privately with a lender interested in promoting a sound long-run relationship. Maturities and conditions can be altered to fit shifts in the needs of the borrowing business or a change in its situation. Costs are often lower than those of alternative sources of such funds, funds are borrowed only when needed and can usually be repaid in advance without penalty.

Industrial Concentration

As already noted, term loans are concentrated to an important extent in the three large fixed-capital industry groups—the utilities, the petroleum and rubber group, and metals and metal products firms. Together, these three groups accounted for one-half of the volume of term loans outstanding in mid-October 1957. Other important borrowers were in retail trade, real estate, and the direct service lines.

Competition for Term Loans

In entering the area of intermediate- and longer-term lending to businesses, banks have come into somewhat closer competition with other institutional lenders and the public bond markets, which have traditionally catered to the business concern raising capital for longer periods. But term loans are by no means merely an alternative source of longer-term funds for the business concern. Rather, the bank loan of one to five years or even longer maturity meets certain business needs that often cannot be satisfactorily handled either by short-term lending or by longer-term credits from other institutional investors.

That is true in part because other institutional investors, looking for an assured return over long periods of time, are normally interested in credits with a maturity substantially longer than the average term loan. Moreover, other longer-term borrowing arrangements tend to be more inflexible, and that is particularly true of bond issues sold in the public market. In addition, negotiations involving confidential financial data or future plans would need to be disclosed in public security offerings but can be kept in confidence in negotiating with a bank. So far as nominal interest costs are concerned, bank rates and the rates on new corporate issues have fluctuated in a similar pattern over recent years, with no clear advantage lying with either type of financing over long periods of time.

In periods of easy money, competition between banks and other lenders in providing term credits may be intensified. Under these conditions, banks may tend to lengthen terms in an effort to put their available funds to work, while insurance companies and other institutional investors may be willing to accept credits with shorter maturities and with less onerous prepayment penalties than normal for the same reason. But in periods of easy as well as tight money, banks often work in cooperation with longer-term investors, rather than in competition. Thus, banks may frequently provide credit pending the final negotiation of terms with a longer-term investor; in other cases, banks may handle the borrower's need on an interim basis supported by an actual commitment by another lender to take over the loan at a later date. Similarly, banks may take the shorter portion of a large term loan, while an insurance company, pension fund or other lender provides long-term funds for the remainder.

Term loans can often complement and supplement borrowing in the public bond market as well. Thus, bank term loans are often convenient in permitting a borrower to undertake an expansion program before he is prepared to enter the bond market—either because of a desire to await more favorable market conditions or because he wishes to delay public offering until the extent of his long-term needs may be better appraised. Moreover, term loans are available to borrowers who because of their small size or other factors cannot enter the public market on satisfactory terms.

Term Loans and Bank Liquidity

The rapid growth in term lending since the 1930's, combined with the rise in loan-deposit ratios generally during the postwar period, has sharpened the issue of appropriate standards for bank liquidity under today's circumstances. The term loan concept appears to run counter to one of the traditional precepts of commercial banking of earlier years— that a commercial bank, with its liabilities repayable on demand or short notice, should carry the bulk of its assets in the form of paper that is self-liquidating over a short period of time or readily salable.

This precept was justified on grounds that a commercial bank must at all times stand ready to convert its assets into cash promptly and with a minimum of disturbance—ideally by means of the repayment of loans based upon the movement of goods through the processes of production and marketing to final sale. Moreover, the "commercial loan theory," which provided the theoretical rationale for earlier practices, implied that the volume of bank lending and thus the money supply would automatically expand or contract with fluctuations in business activity.

Even in the decades before the rise of the term loan, however, there was wide recognition of some fallacies in this reasoning. The banking difficulties of the early 1930's emphasized again that the liquidity of the banking system as a whole depends upon its ability to shift assets to other lenders since the economy's need for credit is continuous. The short term of assets alone provides no assurance of large-scale "shiftability" in periods of general market strain. A concerted calling of loans at a time when other potential lenders also want cash can only lead to a severe contraction in employment and real output along with numerous defaults, unless the central bank intervenes to provide funds to the extent required.

Moreover, many nominally short-term loans were not in any real sense self-liquidating even on an individual basis. It was estimated that in 1918 from 40 to 50 percent of short-term unsecured loans were commonly renewed by large city banks, and that the proportion was probably larger for country banks. A special survey of member banks in the

Fourth Federal Reserve District in 1955 suggested that a significant proportion of short-term loans is still regularly renewed by banks today.[11]

This is not to deny the importance of liquidity for an individual bank or the need for banks to maintain a substantial margin of assets that, if needed, can be readily converted into cash without material loss. Staggered short-term loan maturities as well as short-term security holdings are basic to an individual bank's asset structure.

But the term loan itself possesses characteristics that make it useful from the standpoint of planning the liquidity position of an individual bank. The scheduled repayments provide the bank with a cash inflow that can frequently be diverted to other uses, such as meeting deposit drains, more readily than funds theoretically available from the maturity of short-term loans—loans that often must, in fact, be successively renewed if the borrower is to maintain his normal business operations. The advantage of a term loan in this respect is that it is usually a part of a longer-run financial plan, carefully geared to the anticipated income of the borrower, and often tied into the cash throw-off from depreciation. There is a firm expectation on the part of both borrower and lender that the loan will not be renewed and, if well conceived, funds for its repayment will become available from the operations of the business under normal circumstances.

That this cash flow from term loans is not a negligible factor is apparent when it is considered that the average maturity of outstanding term loans has been estimated at between three and four years for banks engaged in term lending for some time. Thus, probably a quarter or more of the funds placed in term loans may be "freed" each year— and those funds are not implicitly committed to renewals.

Another factor that must be considered in evaluating the impact of the growth of term loans on bank liquidity is the relatively rapid growth since World War II in savings deposits and small individual checking accounts—deposits which are not subject typically to sharp swings. In early 1946, for instance, time deposits of individuals, partnerships, and corporations (which are largely savings accounts) and demand deposits of individuals amounted to about 38 percent of all deposits; by 1959 that figure was about 45 percent.

These considerations do not mean that the growth of term loans poses no problem for a bank engaged in a constant effort to protect liquidity and solvency. For one thing, the additional risks in longer-term lending must be matched by equivalent care and sophistication in credit analyses and by maintenance of more adequate capital funds for banks. Equally important, too great a diversion of funds into term loans at a time when

---

[11] Federal Reserve Bank of Cleveland, "Continuous Borrowing Through Short Term Bank Loans," *Monthly Business Review* (September 1956), pp. 6-13.

over-all loan-deposit ratios have become relatively high could threaten the ability of banks to meet legitimate demands for additional short-term credit. The latter area is one in which no other lenders are prepared to meet the demands of businesses, and if banks are to meet their unique responsibilities in that area, they cannot afford to extend their term loan commitments to the point of impairing their flexibility.

In the last analysis, each bank must arrive at its own independent judgment as to its needs for liquidity and capital funds, based upon its own analysis of its deposit structure and its loan portfolio, conditions in its trade area, and the like. The appropriate limits on term lending are likely to vary widely in individual cases. But there are some indications that the growth in term loans has matured to a point where further increases will be more closely dependent on an expansion in total banking resources. And there have been some signs that many banks have taken a more cautious attitude toward extending new commitments in cases where the term loan is clearly in the nature of a substitute for open market borrowing, in order to conserve their funds for more pressing customer credit needs.

Lending to Small Business

Analysis of bank lending to small businesses is made difficult by the absence of agreed definitions as to what constitutes a "small business," by a paucity of statistical information (except for bank lending at certain survey dates since World War II), and—most important—by the lack of objective measures of the extent to which legitimate demands of small business for credit might exceed the available supply. Consequently, investigations in this area permit few categorical conclusions as to the adequacy of available facilities, trends over time, relative costs of credit to small and large borrowers, and the like.

It is clear, however, that commercial banks are, and have been, far and away the most important external source of funds to small businesses, other than trade credits.[12] A sample survey by the Department of Commerce in 1955 revealed that bank loans accounted for nearly 80 percent of all borrowing (exclusive of trade credit) by established small and intermediate-sized businesses, and for 70 percent of the credit needs of newly formed firms.[13]

Given the heavy dependence of small businesses on banks for short-

---

12 V. L. Andrews, S. Friendland, and E. Shapiro, "Who Finances Small Business?" *Financing Small Business,* Report to the Committees on Banking and Currency and the Select Committees on Small Business, U.S. Congress, by the Federal Reserve System, Parts 1 and 2, April 11, 1958 (Washington: U.S. Government Printing Office, 1958), p. 21.

13 Loughlin McHugh and Jack N. Ciaccio, "External Financing of Small and Medium-Size Business," *Survey of Current Business* (October 1955), pp. 15-21.

and intermediate-term credit, it is noteworthy that independent observers have repeatedly indicated that the supply of credit for working capital and other shorter-term purposes appears to be generally adequate to meet the legitimate needs of those concerns. New firms or concerns introducing new lines or processes more frequently report unsatisfied financing needs, but the most urgent needs in that respect appear to be for additional permanent equity capital or very long-term loans, neither of which are supplied by commercial banks. Moreover, the principal problems of small business have to do with management more than with finance.[14]

Volume of Lending

The vast majority of banks are themselves relatively small businesses in terms of capital and number of employees and, by virtue of that fact and the environment in which they operate, a sympathetic orientation toward the problems of small business financing is natural. Of the nearly 13,500 commercial banks in the country, over 8,340 (or more than 60 percent) have deposits of $5,000,000 or under; their capital accounts with few exceptions range downwards from $500,000. Loans to single borrowers at national banks and a number of state banks are limited by law to 10 percent of the bank's capital accounts, or roughly $50,000 or less for these smaller banks. Such banks, for the most part, are located in smaller towns or rural areas. If they are to lend to business at all, they must look primarily to smaller concerns; their whole lending philosophy and their ultimate success as banks are tied into the problems of smaller businesses. This is reflected in the fact that in 1957 nearly one-half of the dollar amount of all business loans made by member banks with less than $10 million of deposits were to firms defined as small by the Federal Reserve.

While less obvious on the surface, larger institutions that account for the bulk of the nation's banking resources are also compelled to remain alert to the needs of smaller businesses. With few exceptions, even the largest banks are heavily dependent on the "retail" business in their immediate trade area as a source of deposits, and the financial health of businesses in their local community is bound to be a major consideration in any event. A branch manager in an extensive branch system is likely to have his principal contacts with small businessmen and, just as in the case of a small unit bank, his success will depend largely on his ability to service their needs. Special arrangements to insure adequate facilities

---

[14] See, for instance, George Garvy, "Observations Based on the Background Studies"; A. D. H. Kaplan and Paul H. Banner, "Adequacy of Small Business Financing: One View" (especially p. 117); and Irving Schweiger, "Adequacy of Small Business Financing: Another View" (especially pp. 139, 148, 149), *Financing Small Business, op. cit.*

for handling small business loans are often found in larger banks. Loans not suitable for handling by means of usual techniques, by virtue of their small size or other special characteristics, may be provided by instalment credit departments, or even by special departments oriented entirely toward small business financing.

This orientation of commercial banks toward the small businessman is reflected in the fact that over three-quarters of the 1.3 million business loans of member banks in 1957 were extended to firms with assets of less than $250,000, and 90 percent were accounted for by borrowers with assets of under $1,000,000 (Table 4-10). Nearly three-fifths of these small business loans involved relatively large banks (deposits of over $100 million), but a higher proportion of small firms than of large ones borrowed at small banks. (Larger borrowers are, of course, virtually compelled to seek loans only from larger banks, accounting for their relative importance in the loans of those institutions.)

TABLE 4-10
Business Loans at Member Banks
by Size of Borrower
1946, 1955, and 1957

Asset Size of Borrower (Thousands of Dollars)	Amount (Bil.)	Number (Thous.)	Percentage Distribution					
			Amount			Number		
	1957		1946	1955	1957	1946	1955	1957
Total	$40.6	1,281	100.0%	100.0%	100.0%	100.0%	100.0%	100.0%
Under 250	6.7	999	25.6	19.5	16.5	88.5	77.5	78.0
Under 50	1.5	505	9.2	4.9	3.6	64.5	42.5	39.4
50 - 250	5.3	494	16.4	14.6	12.9	24.0	35.0	38.6
250 - 5,000	13.1	206	29.0	34.5	32.2	8.3	13.8	16.1
250 - 1,000	6.3	158	n.a.	16.4	15.5	n.a.	10.6	12.3
1,000 - 5,000	6.8	48	n.a.	18.1	16.7	n.a.	3.2	3.8
5,000 and over[a]	20.8	76	45.4	46.0	51.3	3.2	8.7	5.9

Detail may not add to totals because of rounding.
[a]Data for 1957 includes borrowing in the amount of $1.2 billion for which the asset size of the borrower was not ascertained.

Source: Board of Governors of the Federal Reserve System.

As might be expected, the proportionate share of smaller businesses in the total dollar volume of business loans is much less than that of larger borrowers. Borrowers with assets of less than $250,000 accounted for nearly $7 billion, or 16.5 percent of the total in 1957, and the next largest size class ($250,000 to $1,000,000 in assets) accounted for another $6.3 billion (or 15.5 percent). The proportion of loans extended smaller borrowers (measured by asset size) has dropped over the postwar period, but that drop may reflect entirely the upward movement in prices and general growth in business activity over the period which has substantially expanded the asset size of businesses, rather than any real shift in the relative importance of smaller businesses in bank lending.

The volume of commercial bank lending to small business was well maintained during the period of credit stringency that prevailed in the latter half of 1959, according to a spot check made by the Small Business Credit Commission of The American Bankers Association at that time. This check among representative banks found that "countrywide there is a moderate increase in the number and volume of loans being made by banks to business enterprises in the under-$50,000 category."

Differences by Industry

In terms of number of loans, every major industry group shows a heavy concentration in bank lending to smaller businesses. In fact, in 1955 (the latest data available) businesses with assets of less than $250,000 accounted for over one-half of the number of all bank loans in each industry category, except in the case of sales finance companies. Reflecting in good part the marked differences in the size of the typical enterprise from industry to industry, however, there were wide differences in the relative dollar volume of loans extended smaller firms within the various groups.

In an attempt to escape from the difficulties implicit in attempts to rank firms by a uniform standard as to asset size regardless of industry, the most recent Federal Reserve Survey in 1957 established separate definitions for "small" businesses in each industry, based on the size pattern of enterprises in that industry. Thus, in petroleum or metals manufacture, concerns with assets under $5,000,000 were classified as "small," whereas in retail trade or services those under $50,000 were so classified. On that basis, "small" firms accounted for nearly one-fifth of the dollar volume of all business loans. The metals and metal products industry, textile and apparel firms, petroleum, chemical, and rubber concerns, sales finance companies, real estate brokers and developers, and wholesalers all showed above average concentration of loans to small business. In the case of retailers, the direct service fields, commodity dealers, utilities, and construction firms, the proportion of loans to small business was less than average (Table 4-11). The validity of such comparison is, however, impaired by the necessarily arbitrary nature of the size classification used.

Maturity Distribution of Small Business Loans

Small businesses, like large, borrow from banks mainly on the basis of short-term notes. Over recent years, however, term borrowing by

TABLE 4-11
Business Loans of Member Banks
by Business and Relative Size of Borrower,
October 17, 1957

Business of Borrower	Amount (Billions)	Percentage Distribution of Industry Total by Size of Borrower		
		Small	Medium	Large
All	$40.6	17.2%	43.6%	36.2%
Manufacturing and mining				
Metals and metal products	5.5	30.8	34.4	34.4
Petroleum, coal, chemicals, and rubber	3.8	21.3	37.3	37.3
Food, liquor, and tobacco	2.4	20.9	41.8	33.4
Textiles, apparel, and leather	1.7	35.7	47.5	17.8
Other	2.8	14.3	60.9	21.5
Trade				
Retail	4.6	10.9	54.5	32.7
Wholesale	3.0	23.5	57.0	20.1
Commodity dealers	0.8	12.2	36.8	61.3
Services				
Utilities	4.2	-	50.4	43.2
Sales finance cos.	3.1	22.8	35.8	42.3
Real estate	3.0	20.2	23.5	47.0
Direct services	2.3	13.3	53.1	30.9
Construction	2.0	5.1	50.5	40.4
Other	1.6	6.2	43.6	49.8

Figures do not add up to 100 percent because some loans were made to borrowers whose size was not ascertained.

Source: Board of Governors of the Federal Reserve System.

small businesses has expanded rapidly and during that period term loans have constituted a greater portion of total bank borrowings of small business than of larger concerns. Large businesses have relied less on bank term loans because they utilize bond financing to a greater extent, either through public offering or private placement. Extension of inter-mediate-term credit to new and small businesses has been appreciably facilitated during this period by use of the mechanism of instalment loans, on the pattern of consumer instalment paper.

Increased reliance by smaller concerns on term loans was particularly striking during the boom period of 1955-57. Then, term loans of all borrowers increased from 34 percent to 38 percent of total member bank business loans. Term loans to the smallest borrower group (assets of under $50,000) rose from less than 39 percent to 46 percent of total loans of that group, while term loans to the $50,000-$250,000 asset class advanced from under 30 percent to 37 percent.

Interest Charges

Small businesses commonly pay higher interest rates on bank loans than do large firms. That reflects in part the fact that loans to small businesses tend to be small loans, and the costs of processing individual credit applications and administering such loans may be as great as—and sometimes greater than—for a much larger loan. These costs, which must be recovered through the interest charge, are thus more important relative to the "pure" cost of money in the case of loans to small businesses.

Another factor contributing to the higher interest charge for small business loans is the greater risk and uncertainties sometimes associated with such lending. That is particularly the case with respect to new businesses—most of which are relatively small. Roughly 5 percent of the dollar volume and 8 percent of the number of member bank loans in 1957 were to businesses established within the previous two years, suggesting that a significant portion of total small business lending was to relatively new firms. Interest rates on such loans were on the average appreciably higher than on loans to established firms, which tended to raise the average rate for all lending to small businesses.

While interest rates on small loans are typically higher than on large loans, they are also more stable. Thus, the differential tends to narrow in periods of credit restriction when the general level of rates is rising, but to widen in periods of easier money. This tendency was evident in the results of the special surveys of business loans of member banks conducted in 1955 and 1957. In the latter year, average rates for all loans made between June 30 and October 16 ranged from 4.4 percent for the largest borrowers to 6.5 percent for the smallest (assets of less than $50,000), with the over-all average at 5 percent. In each case, those rates were higher than during the summer of 1955 (when the over-all average was 4.2 percent), but the increase for large borrowers was 1.1 percent, while it was only .7 percent for the smallest. Thus, the spread dropped from 2½ percent in 1955 to about 2 percent in 1957.

Interest rate differentials between short- and intermediate-term loans are much more pronounced among small borrowers than large. In 1957, the smallest firms (under $50,000 of assets) paid an average of 8.7 percent for one- to five-year money (including instalment loans), as against 6.1 percent for short-term loans, while firms with assets of $50,000 to $250,000 paid 7.1 percent for intermediate-term credit as against 5.6 percent for short-term. In contrast the average rates were precisely the same (4.4 percent) for the two classes of loan maturities in the case of the largest firms. The differential for smaller concerns reflects both the greater risks inherent in lending for extended terms to small businesses and the wide use of instalment loans (which carry higher effective interest rates) in meeting the intermediate-term credit needs of smaller enterprises.[15]

On the other hand, average rates paid by smaller businesses for longer-term credits (over five years) were actually lower than for short-term credits. The longer loans were frequently secured by real estate and were considerably larger, on the average, than instalment loans—both of which factors tended to reduce the cost.

Other Sources of Credit to Small Business

There are, of course, other sources of credit to small business. Trade creditors supply a sizable volume of external funds to small firms. Finance companies and factors are important sources of short- and intermediate-term credit to small businesses, and life insurance companies provide the latter with some long-term funds. The Small Business Administration makes loans to small firms which are unable to obtain needed credit from private sources on a reasonable basis, and since 1958 the SBA has been authorized to license and help finance investment companies devoted entirely to the financing of small business enterprises.

But even with respect to these other sources of credit to small business, commercial bank financing is usually important indirectly. Firms that extend trade credit to others frequently obtain the funds needed for such financing from banks. Finance companies and factors also depend on commercial banks to provide much of the funds that they re-lend to others. Banks participate, too, in many of the loans made by the Small Business Administration, often advancing large portions of such loans. Moreover, commercial banks have been among the most active sponsors of investment companies under the terms of the Small Business Investment Act.

Appraisal of the Record

A dynamic, growing economy like that of the United States requires a financial system responsive to new credit needs as they arise, able promptly to redistribute funds to points of greatest demand, and alert to the development of new techniques and procedures to facilitate the distribution of credit in an efficient and equitable manner. On these counts, the record of the banks in the area of business lending over recent decades has been noteworthy.

Sweeping changes in the structure of the economy, in the relative importance of various industries, and in the legal and institutional framework of banking since the early 1930's have posed a series of challenges

---

[15] *Op. cit.*, Table 10, p. 405.

to the banks in their capacity as the chief institutional lender to business. One measure of the success with which they have responded can be found in the resurgence of loan volume since the end of World War II. The evidence shows that small businesses as well as large have found supplies of bank credit ample to meet their vastly increased needs for working capital. Regional differences in credit availability and in interest rates charged, while not entirely eliminated, have tended to narrow, and funds have been shifted from sector to sector, and from industry to industry, with few elements of friction.

The evolution of bank lending techniques to keep pace with the needs of modern industry has been striking. Increased emphasis on the flexible use of credit lines and revolving credits and a willingness to experiment with new types of collateral have enabled the commercial banking system to serve better its traditional function of financing the working capital requirements of the business community at a time when these requirements have increased rapidly as a result of both inflation and economic growth. The broadening of the mortgage market over the postwar period to finance a record volume of residential building has been assisted by the pioneering role of banks in financing mortgage market intermediaries. Loan participations have helped the banking system meet the special problems posed by the needs of larger firms within the context of a unit banking system. Perhaps most important, the full development of the term loan has closed a potential gap in the credit mechanism by providing, on reasonable terms, a source of intermediate term credit well suited to the financing of new machinery and equipment. While this development has been of great assistance to both large and small businesses, it plays a particularly crucial role for newer and smaller concerns in view of their limited access to alternative sources of funds.

The rapid postwar expansion in lending has not been accompanied by a commensurate increase in deposits. From 1946 to 1959, business loans nearly tripled, while deposits rose by less than 50 percent. That sharp contrast in the growth rates of loans and deposits looms as the principal problem confronting commercial banks as they enter the 1960's.

At the end of World War II, the banking system was exceptionally liquid. Subsequently, the rapid expansion in business loans (as well as other loans) has caused steady erosion of that excess liquidity over the past fifteen years. Loan-deposit ratios are now approaching the point where either loan expansion must slow down, or deposits must rise at a more rapid pace.

With the age-old banking problem of adequate liquidity moving to the fore once again, many banks have carefully reviewed their lending policies to insure that they will retain the ability to meet needs for shorter-term working capital or equipment purchases. Less essential types of loans—particularly the sort that may be merely temporary substitutes for bond financing, or that could equally well be handled by other institutions—may need to be more carefully assessed, and more frequently rejected, under the circumstances of today.

Expansion of loans has been accompanied by a rising structure of interest rates. One possibility in coming years, if deposit growth is not greater, is that bank lending rates may remain at somewhat higher levels relative to market rates of interest than was the case earlier in the postwar period.

Other problems, current and potential, related to establishing criteria for term loans and an appropriate balance between those loans and other types of business credit, remain to be solved. Lending to financial intermediaries has given rise to new problems—growing in part out of the volatility of demand for such loans. And there is still room for improving old techniques and developing new.

None of these problems can be solved by the business lending officer alone. The ability of the banking system to fulfill its role as by far the most important supplier of business credit in the future depends upon a solution of the broader problem of maintaining the position of commercial banking in the competition for loanable funds.

Chapter 5

COMMERCIAL BANKS
AND CONSUMER CREDIT

Since consumer credit is an important force in our economy, a basic purpose of this chapter is to analyze such credit from the point of view of problems posed for public policy. Implications of the growth and present magnitude of consumer credit for the safety of financial institutions, the financial well-being of consumers, and over-all economic stability will be examined. A major objective is to present data and analysis which might be helpful in judging whether there is a need to regulate consumer credit, either to protect financial institutions or to minimize fluctuations in economic activity. These are matters of concern to bankers as well as to all others who seek an economy characterized by reasonable stability and adequate growth.

The term *consumer credit* will mean credit used by consumers to finance the purchase of goods and services for personal consumption, or to refinance debts originally incurred for such purposes. While data on the use of consumer credit are available in considerable detail, there are some deficiencies. For example, some loans to farmers classified as agricultural credit are undoubtedly used to some extent for consumption purposes, and some automobiles financed with "consumer credit" are used for business purposes. These and other such difficulties in classifications of credit, however, do not lead to major distortions in reported data.

Instalment credit means simply consumer credit scheduled to be repaid in a number of instalments. It includes *automobile paper*, representing credit extended to purchase automobiles (both new and used) and *other consumer goods paper*, which is credit extended to purchase consumer goods other than automobiles. Also included in the term *instalment credit* are *repair and modernization* loans (which are extended on owner-occupied dwelling units) and *personal loans* (normally extended for consolidation of consumer debt, medical and other emergency expenses, education, and travel). The latter category includes loans made under bank revolving credit plans. It should be noted that although instalment loans frequently are made by banks to small businesses, such loans are not considered consumer loans; they are reported by banks as commercial and industrial loans. *Noninstalment credit,* as the term implies, is credit scheduled to be repaid at one time.

Growth of Consumer Lending by Banks

The major role of commercial banks in consumer finance is indicated by the fact that they lend more money to consumers than any other type of financial institution; they also provide more such credit than is extended by retail outlets. This leading position in consumer credit has been achieved by banks even though they were relatively late among financial institutions in entering the consumer credit field on an aggressive basis.

Although aspects of consumer financing long have been associated with the conduct of banking business, the large-scale entry of banks into the field of *direct* consumer lending is a comparatively recent development in the history of commercial banking. The forces which have led to the emergence of direct consumer lending as an integral part of commercial banking activity are numerous and diverse, and the general treatment presented here offers opportunity for little more than a highlighting of some of the more fundamental of these forces.

Prior to the early 1900's, direct consumer lending by commercial banks was conducted on a highly selective basis. Although most banks were engaged in the occasional extension of direct consumer loans, the practice was most generally confined to the accommodation of established bank customers and, as a general rule, was looked upon as an exception to established bank lending policy. Fixed standards governing the extension of such loans and well-defined concepts of consumer lending were absent, and the aggressive use of consumer lending as a means either to bolster earnings or to promote deposit growth was not generally accepted as sound banking policy. While it is true that some banks were much more inclined than others to approve of consumer loan requests, the over-all picture was one of the passive use of consumer lending.

Inevitably, bank attitudes toward consumer lending began to change as the record of experience with these loans, however reluctantly they may have been extended originally, demonstrated their favorable performance. Simultaneously, a number of other factors served to produce a more favorable environment for consumer lending. Sources of personal credit information were being improved, the population was becoming less migratory, and rising standards of living generated greater consumer interest in purchases of the type which lent themselves to consumer financing. These and other developments, including increasing recognition of the applicability of amortization principles to consumer goods, contributed to a slow but persistent erosion of the traditional resistance which most banks had shown toward direct consumer lending. Although the shift in bank attitudes came slowly and not at all uniformly as among individual banks, a number of the larger banks in the nation had established personal loan departments by the end of the 1920's.

Consumer financing by banks received further impetus in the 1930's. Growth in demands for consumer credit associated with the mass appeal of the automobile, favorable experience of banks in consumer lending under programs of government loan insurance, and the combination of low interest rates, large excess reserves, and slack business loan demand served to stimulate bank interest in consumer lending. By the end of 1940, approximately 5,000 banks were actively making consumer loans. The number continued to grow rapidly during World War II, when a low level of interest rates and abundant reserve availability served as strong inducements for greater bank participation in the consumer credit field. Almost 11,000 banks were engaged actively in direct consumer lending by the end of the war. Since that time bank participation in consumer lending has continued to expand, and there are few banks at which the volume of consumer loans is not a relatively important component of total bank assets.

It should be noted that the strong growth of consumer lending, both by commercial banks and other financial institutions, was facilitated by state legislation enacted generally prior to World War I. Such legislation provided for various measures designed to regulate lending practices and to legalize interest charges on instalment loans higher than the generally prevailing 6 percent limit for regular loans. Nearly every state has enacted this type of legislation in recognition of the fact that instalment lending involves special costs and risks, and it has been clear that higher loan rates have been needed to attract to consumer lending the funds of lenders other than predatory "loan sharks." In 1934 it was necessary for most states to pass enabling legislation to permit the extension of Title I FHA loans at a 5 percent discount rate on a monthly repayment basis—a rate equivalent to 9.7166 percent per annum on unpaid principal balances. Many states also allow either a general service charge or fees for credit investigation, late payments, and insurance premiums. Bank lending rates have been, and continue to be, generally as low as—and in a great many cases much lower than—those charged by other lenders.

By making funds available to consumers, banks, as well as others engaged in consumer lending, have filled a real economic need and have done much to hasten the spread of the benefits of our production system throughout the population. The specific ways in which banks have engaged in this lending and the extent of their lending are set forth below.

Initially, banks engaged in traditional forms of consumer lending, but in recent years they have introduced their own innovations. Commercial banking, like other dynamic industries, is today furnishing services that were not significant or even known two decades ago. Many are in the fast growing retail banking field, and include new types of personal loans, special checking accounts, charge account banking, and in-plant banking. Others, such as the lock-box check collection and account reconciliation service, are designed for business customers.

Specialized Checking Accounts. The first specialized checking account plan, called the "Check Master Plan," was launched by the National Safety Bank and Trust Company in New York in 1935. Its purpose was to appeal to customers who were deterred from using checking accounts by minimum balance requirements. The original plan was to charge five cents per check and five cents per deposit, regardless of the size of the depositor's balance. Statements and checks were to be sent out quarterly, since it was not expected that customers would write a large number of checks. The original plan worked well, but other banks were slow to adopt the plan.

About eighteen months after the original service was put into effect, however, Empire Trust Company announced its "Check-O-Matic" plan —ten cents per check and no minimum balance requirements. Within another year, National City Bank of New York offered its system of popular checks, selling a checkbook of twenty checks for two dollars. In time, resistance to the plan melted away. By 1950 an estimated four to six thousand banks were offering this service in one form or another.

Rising costs made the original schedule of charges untenable. In 1950, National Safety was charging ten cents per check and a twenty-five cents monthly maintenance charge, but no charge for deposits and no minimum balance requirements.

A survey taken in 1956 of the twenty-five New York City banks offering this service showed that 52.3 percent of their checking accounts were specialized, yet this 52.3 percent represented only 1.3 percent of total dollars in demand deposits. That same year some banks increased monthly maintenance charges from twenty-five cents to fifty cents per month. At the same time, they agreed to send customers monthly rather than quarterly statements and to imprint the customers' names on the checks. At this time, charges varied from five cents to twenty cents per check, the average falling around ten cents. Monthly maintenance charges ranged from fifteen cents to fifty cents.

Specialized checking accounts have undergone many changes, and there are now many variations of the original concept. As a result, it is often difficult to distinguish between a regular and a specialized checking account.

The special checking account development shows how a new service having broad popular appeal and originating in a single bank will be adopted by a large proportion of the commercial banks in a few years, as investigation reveals both a widespread demand and ways and means of furnishing the service efficiently at a profit.

Charge Account Banking.[1] One of the first bank-sponsored community credit plans in the country went into effect on September 6, 1950, at the Paterson Savings and Trust Company, Paterson, New Jersey. The plan was called "Charge-It," and was developed to meet the demand for a workable credit system which, through a central financing organization, would give customers of smaller retail establishments credit facilities comparable with those of major department stores.

There are many variations of the original plan. Basically, charge account banking operates as follows: The bank takes over charge accounts from merchants for a fee, handles all credit checking, billing, bookkeeping, and collection details, and provides the necessary forms, literature, credit plate equipment, etc. The merchants run no risk of credit loss, do not have to investigate credit applications or maintain extensive bookkeeping facilities, and have immediate cash for the operation of their business upon assigning their receivables to the bank.

For the most part, merchants have given charge account banking plans their wholehearted approval. Among reasons for this are: (1) Accounts receivable have been converted into cash. Money previously tied up in receivables is thus put to more productive use. Cash discounts made possible by charge account banking have in many instances paid the entire cost of the service. (2) Sales have increased since customers are spared the bother, embarrassment, and loss of time usually entailed in opening a charge account at several different stores. (3) Credit costs per unit have been reduced as the credit volume handled has gone up. (4) Valuable selling space previously occupied by a credit department has, in many instances, been made available for sales purposes. (5) With the elimination of credit departments, merchants have been able to reduce the number of employees. (6) All of the merchant's own time can be concentrated on the vital function of merchandising, since he is no longer bothered by credit problems. (7) Accounts receivable losses have been eliminated—the bank absorbs all bad debt losses stemming from accounts receivable.

Charge account banking, born in 1950, has shown considerable growth over the decade, although it is a complex operation that gives rise to a number of problems. In November 1959, there were approximately 110 banks in the United States which operated such a service.

The record of this type of financing has been good. At the end of the third quarter of 1959 the percentage of accounts at the thirty-eight stores

---

[1] The information in this section was drawn heavily from the following references: "Community Charge Account," *Banking* (October 1950), p. 84; "Charge-Account Banking Has Made the Grade," *Bankers Monthly* (November 15, 1957), pp. 42-44; "Charge Account Banking," *Mid-Western Banker* (November 1959), pp. 24-26.

which were over thirty days delinquent at thirty-eight banks varied between 1.1 percent and 16.6 percent. Five had delinquencies in excess of 10 percent of all accounts. About half of the banks had between 2 and 7 percent of their accounts delinquent by over thirty days. These figures are higher than delinquencies on other forms of bank consumer credit. However, bad debt losses have been low. Only four of the thirty-eight banks showed losses of over 1 percent of the volume of credit extended in the third quarter of 1959 and many of the remainder were well below 1 percent. Consumers have not paid charge accounts as promptly as other consumer loans, in part at least because merchants who handle the great bulk of such accounts have been somewhat more lenient in collection practices than financial institutions. The record of banks in this field compares favorably with that of retail stores.

Revolving Credit Plans. Revolving credit for consumers represents a new approach to consumer lending with emphasis on convenience of the borrower. Under this plan a bank will establish a line of credit for a customer which he can use at any time in whole or in part simply by writing a special check against this credit. It resembles a bank letter of credit which enables a customer to draw money at any time by merely writing a check.

A revolving credit plan was inaugurated by the First National Bank of Boston early in 1955 under the name of First Check Credit Plan. By midyear, similar plans had been put into effect by the First National Bank of Dallas, Texas, the First National Bank of Oklahoma City, Oklahoma, and the City National Bank and Trust Company of Kansas City, Missouri. These revolving credit plans have also been designated by such names as "Borrow-By-Check," "Check Loan," "Ready Money."

The operation of a revolving credit account is relatively simple. An application form is filled out which is similar to that for other bank consumer loans. The amount the consumer is able and willing to repay per month on his loan is asked for on this blank. The application is checked somewhat more carefully than a regular application for a consumer loan since it is a continuing line of credit. The line of credit granted is usually about equal to one month's income of the revolving credit applicant. When the bank approves the line of credit and the minimum monthly payment the customer is furnished special checks. These checks become loans when issued by the customer and paid by the bank. The most common rate of charge is 1 percent per month on the outstanding balance in the account at the billing date and a twenty-five cent service charge for each check issued and paid.

These revolving credit plans have several advantages for the customer. They provide a ready source of credit for major household expenditures, dental bills, school tuition, taxes, insurance, vacation expenditures, and the like. Credit is available on a 24-hour-a-day basis without the necessity of coming to the bank to make arrangements for a loan. A loan application is required only at the time the credit is set up, thus reducing the amount of time and paper work needed.

Revolving credit plans have grown rapidly in numbers during the last year. Some information on the results of operations of some of the plans is available from a report to The American Bankers Association which covers sixty banks having such a plan in the first six months of 1959. About half of these banks used a twelve-month repayment period, most of the others had a period not over twenty-four months, but one had a thirty-six-month period. Some offered a choice of two or three periods such as twelve and twenty-four months or in one case twelve, eighteen or twenty months.

The repayments in all but three cases were based on the line of credit, not on the loan volume outstanding. For example, if the line of credit is $600 and the repayment period is twelve months $50 must be repaid monthly even if the loan outstanding is only $250. One-half of the banks charged 1 percent per month on the outstanding debt. Six charged 1¼ percent and one charged 1½ percent. Most of the others charged .90 percent or more but one charged only 6½ percent effective interest per year. Most also charged twenty-five cents per check, but seventeen made no such charge.

The average line of credit ranged from $300 to over $1,000. About half of the banks had an average line between $500 and $800. Most of the accounts had not used more than one-third of their line. Some of the earliest banks to use revolving credit report, however, an average use of about two-thirds of the line, and customers of about 15 percent were "riding the top" of the line. Delinquencies in the sixty-bank sample were very small. About half had none and most of the remainder had 0.5 percent or less.[2]

Revolving credit is an innovation which can be of real service to many customers if it is not abused. Bank loan officers, it is recognized by the industry, will have to watch it carefully to prevent overdrawing of accounts and delinquencies.

On-the-Job Bank Services. After extended study of the problem, banks in a number of areas have announced plans for making their services readily and conveniently available to factory or office employees at their places of employment. More than one hundred banks had such plans in operation early in 1960.

One plan of on-the-job, or in-plant, banking permits an employer to send one check to the bank covering the entire payroll, and the personal checking accounts of the employees are credited for the amounts due them. The bank then deducts, in accordance with instructions from the

---

[2] "Check-Credit Operations," *Banking* (February 1960), pp. 46-47.

individual employees, sums for savings and Christmas Club accounts and personal loan payments due.

Another plan provides that the employer shall deduct specified amounts from each employee's salary or wages and forward one check to the bank for all these deductions. Along with this check go detailed instructions for crediting the individual employee's checking or savings accounts or personal loans due.

A more limited plan involves installation of a small service rack in the plant or office with information on banking services offered, kits containing instructions, forms, and postage-paid envelopes for effecting banking transactions by mail.

The Bank Management Commission of The American Bankers Association has summarized the advantages of on-the-job banking to employees as follows: (1) Provides confidential credit service. (2) Makes more complete financial services available. (3) Offers qualified, professional assistance. (4) Spares the necessity of visits to bank. (5) Makes available a low cost credit service with the added advantage of preferential rates on payroll deduction loans. (6) Encourages thrift. (7) Provides financial counsel if employees have to borrow. (8) Through use of a checking account, establishes a credit standing for the employee in his community.

The advantages for employers are listed as follows: (1) Relieves the company of responsibility, moral or legal, inherent with credit unions. (2) Reduces employer bookkeeping, accounting, and housing expenses normally associated with credit unions. (3) Reduces employee absenteeism, or time off to transact personal banking business. (4) Reduces employee requests for salary advances. (5) Offers employers the means of making an additional fringe benefit available to employees through preferential rates on bank loans. (6) Encourages thrift and develops better employees. (7) Eliminates much of the need for the company to become involved with employees' financial problems and minimizes possibilities of wage assignments. (8) Eliminates possible friction resulting from one employee attempting to borrow from another.

Volume of Bank Lending to Consumers

Two important developments are apparent in consumer credit trends. One is the rapid increase in total consumer credit, following a sharp decline during World War II. The other is the fall in the relative importance of noninstalment credit in this total. These facts are clearly reflected by the data in Table 5-1. The more rapid growth of instalment credit may be attributed to its use in financing more and more types of goods and services, and to an increase in the number of individuals and family units making use of such credit.

TABLE 5-1
Instalment Credit as Percent of Total Consumer Credit
Selected Years, 1941-1960

(Dollar amounts in millions)

Year	Total Consumer Credit	Total Instalment Credit	Instalment Credit as Percent of Total
1941	$ 9,172	$ 6,085	66.3%
1945	5,665	2,462	43.5
1950	21,395	14,703	68.7
1955	38,882	28,958	74.5
1960	56,049	43,281	77.2

Source: Board of Governors of the Federal Reserve System.

Paralleling the strong postwar growth in consumer credit has been a significant increase in the relative importance of commercial banks as consumer lending institutions. It will be noted from Table 5-2, for example, that the percentage of total consumer credit held by banks has increased steadily from 25.0 percent in 1945 to 35.9 percent in 1960.

TABLE 5-2
Consumer Credit Held by Selected Institutions
Selected Years, 1941-1960

Year	Total Consumer Credit (Millions)	Percent Held by		
		Commercial Banks	Other Financial Institutions	Retail Outlets
1941	$ 9,172	26.4%	31.7%	41.9%
1945	5,665	25.0	19.5	55.5
1950	21,395	34.3	29.1	36.6
1955	38,882	34.0	36.6	29.4
1960	56,049	35.9	38.7	25.4

Source: Board of Governors of the Federal Reserve System.

Over the same period the percentage of total consumer credit extended by "other financial institutions" has increased even more. This increase, however, has been divided among sales finance companies, consumer finance companies, credit unions, savings and loan associations, mutual savings banks, and industrial loan companies. Consequently, the increase on the part of commercial banks has made them the principal type of consumer financing institution, and this has been the case in both total consumer credit and the instalment credit sector (Table 5-3).

A noteworthy development in the postwar period has been a decline in the relative importance of retail outlets, including automobile dealers, as consumer lending institutions. A number of significant factors underlie this trend, but several are particularly worthy of mention. First, increases

TABLE 5-3
Instalment Credit Held by Selected Institutions
Selected Years, 1941-1960

Year	Total Instalment Credit (Millions)	Percent Held by					
		Commercial Banks	Sales Fin. Cos.	Credit Unions	Consumer Fin. Cos.[a]	Other Fin. Inst.	Retail Outlets
1941	$ 6,085	28.4%	29.5%	3.3%	-	12.5%	26.3%
1945	2,462	30.2	12.2	4.2	-	25.5	27.9
1950	14,703	39.4	25.2	4.0	8.8%	2.9	19.7
1955	28,958	36.6	29.2	5.8	9.2	3.7	15.5
1960	43,281	37.9	25.7	9.0	9.7	4.3	13.4

[a]Consumer finance companies were included with "other" financial institutions until September 1950.

Source: Board of Governors of the Federal Reserve System.

in price levels and growth in sales volume in the post-World War II years substantially increased working capital needs of retailers, who found it more difficult and costly to hold their customers' paper. At the same time, financial institutions were in a favorable position to increase consumer lending in the postwar years, especially those immediately following the end of the war. The postwar resumption of peacetime production of consumer durables in the face of enormous pent-up demand was a major influence on consumer credit, of course, and banks entered this period holding large quantities of Government securities which were converted into loans as the postwar surge in credit demands gained force. Other types of financial institutions also were in a good position to accommodate consumer credit demands, and sales finance companies in particular found a ready market for their obligations among insurance companies, banks, business corporations, and other investors with loanable funds.

A change in the composition of consumer credit has also been a factor in increasing the role of financial institutions, including banks. Instalment credit to finance consumer goods other than automobiles has decreased relative to other consumer financing and, since a substantial proportion of such financing is done by retail stores, this decline has reduced the relative importance of total financing by retail outlets. Further, there has been a larger proportion of cash purchase of consumer goods other than automobiles as consumer incomes have risen. A growing tendency for residential mortgages to include financing of household equipment, and the more general use of open-end mortgages which make possible the financing thereunder of purchases made in later years also have tended to increase the relative importance of financial institutions as sources of consumer credit. Financial institutions have had some advantage, too, because they specialize in the credit-granting function.

Federal regulation of consumer credit at times in the past, and the tendency for increasing state regulation, have multiplied record-keeping and administrative problems in this field, and retail stores have found it increasingly difficult and costly to attract and hold personnel qualified to handle instalment credit extension and collection.

Finally, it must be mentioned that aggressive efforts by banks and finance companies to expand their business by making credit conveniently available to consumers have resulted in ever-increasing volume for them.

All of the foregoing have affected the relative positions of financial institutions—particularly of banks—in direct lending to consumers. The statistics presented, however, do not give a complete picture of bank participation in consumer financing. In addition to lending directly to consumers, banks also supply a substantial amount of credit to sales finance companies and to consumer finance companies, thereby financing the consumer indirectly. At the end of 1960, weekly reporting member banks in leading cities in the United States had $4.3 billion in loans outstanding to personal and sales finance companies. (The amount for all commercial banks would be only moderately higher, since loans of this type are heavily concentrated at larger banks.) Banks indirectly finance consumers, also, by purchasing open market paper issued by sales finance companies, by accommodating businesses on an accounts-receivable basis, and through other forms of business lending.

The importance of bank credit as a source of funds for sales finance and consumer finance companies is indicated by ratios compiled by the First National Bank of Chicago on sales and consumer finance companies which have lines of credit with that bank. These include companies that account for the bulk of the business in these fields. On June 30, 1959, the sales finance companies in this sample obtained 45 percent of their resources from bank borrowing and 13 percent from open-market borrowing. The consumer finance companies in the sample got 36 percent of their resources from bank borrowing and 5 percent from open-market borrowing.

The effect of combined direct and indirect consumer financing by banks has been to make banks the source of more than 50 percent of all consumer credit. In attaining this position, banks have allocated to consumer loans an ever larger proportion of their total assets, and consumer loans have become a larger part of total bank loans. Thus, at the end of 1941 consumer loans accounted for 11.4 percent of total loans at all insured commercial banks. By 1945 the percentage had decreased sharply to 5.5 percent, as consumer loans declined while total loans increased somewhat; but following World War II the ratio of consumer loans to total loans resumed its upward movement. By the end of 1960, the proportion had risen to 17.1 percent.

These percentages, derived from aggregate figures, do not indicate the extent to which consumer lending has become a part of total lending in some of the commercial banks. Reference to Table 5-4 will give a fairly clear picture of the major role consumer loans had attained in some banks by 1959 and the relatively minor importance of consumer loans in others. It is clear that large banks have tended to hold a lower percentage of consumer loans, relative to total loans, than do the medium-size and small banks. In 1959, about one-half of all insured banks had from 10 to 30 percent of their loans in consumer loans.

TABLE 5-4
Distributions of Insured Commercial Banks
Within Size Groups According to Their Individual Ratios
of Consumer Loans to Total Loans (Gross), June 10, 1959

Ratio of Consumer Loans to Gross Loans	Total	Number of Banks with Deposits (in millions of dollars) of					
		Less than 2	2 to 10	10 to 50	50 to 250	250 to 1,000	1,000 or more
Zero	151	106	43	1	1	-	-
Above zero to 9.9%	2,493	1,179	1,135	142	25	4	8
10.0 - 19.9	3,737	1,215	1,997	410	80	27	8
20.0 - 29.9	3,049	751	1,579	553	121	42	3
30.0 - 39.9	1,974	411	1,031	422	97	13	-
40.0 - 49.9	966	206	492	230	36	2	-
50.0 - 59.9	417	88	210	109	10	-	-
60.0 - 69.9	186	57	90	35	4	-	-
70.0 - 79.9	72	21	34	16	1	-	-
80.0 or more	52	20	22	10	-	-	-
Lowest ratio for any bank	.0%	.0%	.0%	.0%	.0%	5.3%	3.9%
Highest ratio for any bank	99.9	99.9	99.6	97.5	70.8	45.3	24.3

Source: Federal Deposit Insurance Corporation.

Other measures of the relative importance of consumer lending within commercial banking are shown in Table 5-5. These data pertain to instalment credit at 330 commercial banks, which hold approximately 50 percent of total instalment loans extended by all commercial banks, and which have reported to The American Bankers Association Instalment Credit Committee. The figures, as do those in Table 5-4, indicate the relatively greater emphasis on instalment credit among the smaller banks, as indicated by the higher ratios of such loans to deposits and to total loans. In addition, the data highlight the substantial contribution of instalment loans to the gross income of banks.

The variations in individual bank consumer lending activities indicated by Tables 5-4 and 5-5 reflect a variety of influences. In many cases those banks with a high proportion of consumer loans were organized initially as so-called industrial banks, designed especially for consumer lending.

TABLE 5-5
Significance of Instalment Credit Outstanding
by Size of Banks, 1960

Total Deposits (Millions of dollars)	Ratio of Instalment Credit Outstanding to Deposits	Ratio of Instalment Credit Outstanding to Total Loans Including Mortgages	Ratio of Instalment Loan Income to Gross Income from All Loans
Up to 10	16.53%	29.18%	37.91%
10 - 25	14.75	26.78	36.36
25 - 50	15.13	24.22	34.28
50 - 100	11.83	22.59	34.27
Over 100	9.72	16.87	25.24

Source: Based on reports in 1960 from 330 banks to the Instalment Credit Committee of The American Bankers Association.

While in some cases these banks have broadened the scope of their operations to embrace other commercial banking functions, they continue to do a great deal of consumer financing. Local competitive conditions have been a factor also. The extent to which individual banks actively are engaged in direct consumer lending often is influenced by the presence or absence of other competing financial institutions and by the strength of local demand for consumer credit.

In many banks, as was noted earlier, direct consumer lending has been developed as an appropriate and profitable banking function along with other services which characterize "retail banking." Other banks have not stressed consumer credit, preferring instead to concentrate on the traditional commercial banking functions and, in some cases, to adhere almost exclusively to "wholesale" banking. While such banks may have engaged relatively little in direct consumer lending, they nevertheless have provided a great deal of credit indirectly through loans to finance companies and through other forms of business lending. This, of course, is not reflected in the data on instalment credit as shown.

A further breakdown of the aggregate data reported by 330 banks to the Instalment Credit Committee of the ABA is provided by Table 5-6, which indicates the relative importance of the various types of consumer loans in these banks (considered representative of the commercial banking system as a whole). It will be noted that automobile, repair and modernization, personal, and appliance loans are the most important from the point of view of bank income.

These will be discussed briefly in the following section to indicate the relative importance of commercial banks in each type of lending and to set forth the factors that have affected the position of banks.

Automobile Lending

Automobile credit has come to be the largest single type of instalment credit, and a significant development during the past decade has been

TABLE 5-6
Distribution of Consumer Instalment Loans
at 330 Banks, 1960

Class of Loans	Number	Dollar Amount	Gross Income	Average Loan
Total	100.00%	100.00%	100.00%	$ 538
Personal loans	23.16	13.52	14.31	1,007
FHA Title I	11.82	9.99	8.85	940
Modernization - own plan	8.53	7.09	7.67	1,408
Automobile - direct	13.62	18.87	17.96	1,542
Automobile - indirect	18.15	24.95	22.52	437
Appliances	13.04	5.67	10.66	3,134
Mobile Home	2.30	6.49	6.17	
All other instalment-retail	9.38	13.42	11.86	2,092

Source: Based on reports in 1960 from 330 banks to the Instalment Credit Committee of The American Bankers Association.

the increasing relative importance of banks in automobile financing (Table 5-7).

Several influences have contributed to the rising share of the automobile credit market which is served directly by commercial banks. It is due in part to vigorous efforts by many commercial banks to develop this business; another influence has been the changing relationship of dealers to sales finance companies. Most dealers now have financing re-

TABLE 5-7
Automobile Credit
Selected Years, 1941-1960

(Dollar amounts in millions)

Year	Total Outstanding	Percentage of Total Held by			
		Commercial Banks	Sales Finance Companies	Other Financial Institutions	Auto Dealers
1941	$ 2,458	31.9%	55.5%	5.0%	7.6%
1945	455	45.9	36.0	11.9	6.2
1950	6,074	40.7	48.7	5.9	4.7
1955	13,472	39.4	51.4	5.6	3.6
1960	17,866	45.0	43.1	9.0	2.9

Source: Board of Governors of the Federal Reserve System.

lations with several finance companies as well as with one or more banks. The several lenders offer different terms and rates, enabling a dealer to meet the credit needs of individual customers having differing requirements. Some customers are attracted to bank financing which requires a sizable down payment and a repayment period generally not over thirty-six months by the lower financing costs which customarily are involved. The desire to serve such customers has led dealers to develop financing arrangements with banks, and this has helped to increase the banks' share of total automobile financing.

The increased share of automobile financing by "other financial" institutions (i.e., institutions other than banks and sales finance companies) is due almost entirely to increased activity in this area by credit unions. These institutions have made vigorous efforts to attract such business, the number of credit unions has greatly increased, and resources available for lending have grown rapidly.

Insofar as bank automobile financing itself is concerned, there has been a general increase since 1953 in the volume of automobile paper purchased from dealers, while the amount of direct automobile loans has risen rather slowly. Purchased paper as a percentage of total bank holdings of automobile paper rose from 54.3 percent in 1953 to 65.5 percent in 1960. This shift reflects deliberate efforts on the part of banks to attract this type of financing, which has advantages both for individual banks and for automobile dealers. Banks obtain automobile paper in volume at a lower cost than when each loan is handled individually for the prospective borrower and, in addition, get many of the preferred risks. Banks also use the dealer relationship involved as a step toward promoting a closer lending and deposit relationship with automobile dealers—an important consideration, as banks have become highly competitive in obtaining deposits to assure growth and capacity to meet the needs of their communities.

From the point of view of the automobile dealer, the practice of selling a substantial part of his paper to a bank places him in a position to arrange financing more efficiently and promptly for individual customers as the need arises. This is extremely important in the highly competitive automobile market. The dealer also obtains financing for his inventory of cars and is in a better position to negotiate for other financing which may be needed. Furthermore, banks have followed the sales finance companies' practice of setting up part of the financing charge as a reserve for losses, and if the dealer's loss experience is good, part of this reserve reverts to him as profit.

Home Repair and Modernization Loans

Most banks were introduced to the consumer loan field through home repair and modernization loans under Title I of the FHA, and banks have always made a major portion of such loans (Table 5-8). In addition to making a substantial volume of repair and improvement loans under the FHA insurance program, many banks also have chosen to carry on lending programs without such insurance. This is indicated by the data in Table 5-6.

The portion of repair and modernization loans not made by commer-

TABLE 5-8
Repair and Modernization Loans[a]
Selected Years, 1941-1960

(Dollar amounts in millions)

	Total Outstanding	Percentage of Total Held by	
		Commercial Banks	Other Financial Institutions
1941	$ 376	42.8%	57.2%
1945	182	60.4	39.6
1950	1,016	82.1	17.9
1955	1,689	79.2	20.8
1960	3,008	71.9	28.1

[a]Repair and modernization loans held by financial institutions only; holdings of retail outlets are included with other consumer goods paper.

Source: Board of Governors of the Federal Reserve System.

cial banks is made largely by savings banks and savings and loan associations. However, these institutions typically have preferred longer term loans and investments and generally have not sought actively to acquire a larger share of repair and modernization loans.

Bank Lending for the Purchase of Other Consumer Goods

Banks do a substantial volume of financing of consumer goods other than automobiles, such as appliances, television sets, radios, mobile homes, and boats. Since the individual amounts borrowed (except on mobile homes) are smaller, charges are usually somewhat higher than in the case of automobile financing. The percentage of such loans held by banks has been declining, and the percentage held by other financial institutions rising, in recent years (Table 5-9). Sales finance companies, consumer finance companies and credit unions all have increased their share of such consumer durable-goods financing. Sales finance companies have been especially active in this field, since it affords an outlet for their funds in years of slow automobile sales and offers somewhat higher rates of return than are available in the more highly competitive auto-financing field.

Consumer finance companies also have acquired increasing amounts of such paper. They are experienced in handling some of the more marginal credit risks frequently encountered in this type of lending, and they have a rate structure which permits handling such paper in small dollar amounts for each contract.

The growing role of credit unions in this field may be attributed to their cost advantages over consumer finance companies, as well as to their ability in many cases to handle such business more conveniently for the buyer.

TABLE 5-9
Other Consumer Goods Paper
Selected Years, 1941-1960

(Dollar amounts in millions)

| Year | Total[a] Outstanding | Percentage of Total Held by | |
		Commercial Banks	Other Financial Institutions
1941	$ 1,929	16.0%	10.5%
1945	816	14.0	5.4
1950	4,799	30.3	15.3
1955	7,634	26.7	20.6
1960	11,215	24.0	29.1

[a]Includes retail outlets.

Source: Board of Governors of the Federal Reserve System.

Personal Loans

As indicated in Table 5-10, bank holdings of personal instalment loans, expressed as a percentage of such loans held by all financial institutions, have declined in recent years. Several factors account for this decline in the banks' proportion of personal instalment loans. Credit unions have expanded their activity in this field, and sales finance companies have

TABLE 5-10
Personal Instalment Loans
Selected Years, 1941-1960

(Dollar amounts in millions)

| Year | Total Outstanding | Commercial Bank Holdings | |
		Amount	Percent of Total
1941	$ 1,322	$ 471	35.6%
1945	1,009	312	30.9
1950	2,814	1,037	36.9
1955	6,163	1,916	31.1
1960	11,192	3,505	31.3

Source: Board of Governors of the Federal Reserve System.

entered the personal loan field, either directly or through subsidiaries, to obtain the advantages of diversification of loan business and also, in some cases, to earn a higher rate of return. The share of consumer finance companies in personal instalment lending has declined somewhat because of this competition and because of the smaller average size of their loans.

Summarizing, this section has presented data in sufficient detail to show the amounts and types of consumer credit outstanding and the important role of commercial banks in providing this credit. Since consumer credit now represents an important and substantial share of total bank lending, bankers are concerned with the effects of this credit on the economy and with the problems of public policy that arise therefrom. This is particularly true because of continuing discussions of the advisability of subjecting consumer credit to selective credit controls. These broader aspects of consumer credit are discussed in the following section.

Consumer Credit Control

Consumer instalment credit regulation in the United States has been in effect during three relatively brief periods. In each period, except toward the end of the third, wartime or other limitations on the flexible use of the major instruments of monetary policy gave rise to the necessity for reliance on selective credit controls.

The first use of selective controls on consumer credit was in World War II. The purpose then was to curb inflationary pressures, to promote savings to finance the defense program, and to complement the program of diverting productive resources to defense industries. Regulation W of the Board of Governors of the Federal Reserve System, which became effective September 1, 1941, and was terminated in November 1947, imposed minimum down payments and maximum permissible maturities for each type of goods generally sold under instalment contracts.

Instalment credit regulation was reimposed in 1948 because of inflationary pressures and rapid growth of bank credit at the time. At a special session of Congress called to consider anti-inflation legislation, a joint resolution was passed authorizing the reimposition of consumer credit control until June 30, 1949. In scope and coverage the new regulations were similar to those in effect during 1947. By early 1949 a temporary slackening in demand for both durable and nondurable goods had become evident, however, and relaxation of terms preceded the expiration of consumer credit controls on the specified date.

With the outbreak of hostilities in Korea in June 1950, the President requested the reinstatement of consumer credit control. This request resulted in the passage of the Defense Production Act of 1950 and, under its terms, Regulation W again became effective on September 18, 1950. The regulation was suspended on May 7, 1952, because of increased production of consumer goods and a slackened demand. The Board of Governors recommended the continuation of such controls on a standby basis, for subsequent reinstatement if needed, but the authority for such regulation was eliminated by Defense Production Act amendments passed in 1952.

During these three periods, the enforcement of regulations was made the responsibility of the Federal Reserve System. The experience of these three unusual periods has served as the basis for many of the arguments that have been presented for and against reinstatement of consumer credit regulation as a means of achieving certain public policy objectives and as a supplement to general credit control.

Before taking up these arguments, it is well to consider the reasons why consumer credit has grown so tremendously in the postwar period. The increase has been due in large part to the satisfaction of demands built up during the depression and the war, especially for automobiles and other consumer durables. In this connection, it is relevant to note that the most rapid growth in consumer credit took place between 1945 and 1950. The rise since then has been at a slower rate. Moreover, the rise in consumer prices, growth in the economy, generally high levels of employment, rising wages, and the accompanying increase in the purchasing power of consumers made substantial increases in consumer credit inevitable. Gains in consumer income, particularly in discretionary income, have encouraged consumers to acquire the high-cost durable items which normally are purchased with credit. These economic developments have been accompanied by the extension of instalment-plan purchasing to new types of goods and services. For example, instalment loans have been made generally available to finance the acquisition of airplanes, boats, and trailer homes, and to finance education and travel.

The growth of consumer credit has been speeded, also, by the extension of maturities on consumer loans. Since the 1920's maturities have been increased from a generally prevailing twelve months to the thirty or thirty-six months which are common today. The extension of maturities has kept monthly repayment requirements low and has thus stimulated the demand for consumer durables. In many cases, longer maturities also have been accompanied by lower down payments. Although these two developments account in part for the increase in total consumer credit outstanding in the past, it is doubtful whether lenders will further reduce these requirements significantly.

In examining the trend of consumer credit and the implications attendant thereto, the close interrelationships between shifting consumer spending patterns and the rapid development of consumer credit facilities cannot be ignored. Cause-and-effect relationships between these two stimulants to consumer credit use are difficult to disentangle, but it is apparent that each has made a major contribution to the growth in consumer credit outstanding. In part, the effectiveness of instruments of national economic stabilization in holding cyclical economic fluctuations within moderate bounds has promoted a greater willingness on the part of consumers to commit future incomes for consumer debt repayment, and relative stability in income and employment has exerted a strong influence on the attitudes of financial institutions concerning the soundness of direct consumer lending. It is clear that these influences—greater willingness of consumers to borrow and greater willingness of lenders to lend—have reacted upon each other in a highly complementary manner to promote the strong upward trend in consumer credit use.

In view of the importance which consumer credit has assumed, two basic questions are involved in considering the advisability of imposing selective controls on its use. First is the question of whether unregulated extensions of consumer credit have led (or permitted) consumers to assume a dangerous burden of debt which, at some point in the future, will jeopardize the stability of the economy. Second, and aside from the question of the magnitude and relative burden of the volume of consumer credit outstanding, there is the question of whether variations in the use of consumer credit constitute a source of cyclical instability which ought to be regulated.

It must be stressed that measurement of the burden of consumer debt requires reference to other relevant factors in the economy, mainly personal income, personal consumption expenditures, liquid assets, total private debt, and commitments of consumers other than consumer debt. In taking these factors into account, the following observations are relevant.

1) As shown in Table 5-11, both total consumer credit and the instalment credit component as a percentage of disposable personal income have grown substantially in the postwar period. It should be noted, however, that most of the increase was realized prior to 1955; there has been only a moderate increase since that time.

2) Total consumer credit and instalment credit outstanding as a percent of personal consumption expenditures also have risen. Again, however, most of the increase occurred in the early postwar years.

3) Since the end of World War II, consumer debt has generally increased at a rate much faster than consumer liquid assets. But the ratio of debt to liquid assets has been increasing more slowly since 1950 than in the early postwar years, and more recently the rise in debt has fairly closely paralleled the growth in liquid assets.

4) Total consumer credit outstanding as a percentage of net private debt has risen from 4.3 in 1945 to 9.6 in 1960 (Table 5-12). The major portion of this rise was realized, however, by the end of 1952. Since then there have been only fractional fluctuations in this percentage, and it was lower at the end of 1960 than in 1956.

5) The ratio of fixed commitments of consumers to disposable income was not much higher in 1959 than it had been prior to World

TABLE 5-11
Consumer Credit Related to Consumer Income and Expenditures
1947-1960

(Dollar amounts in billions)

	(1)	(2)	Consumer Credit (3)	(4)	(5)	Installment Credit (6)	(7)	(8)
Year	Disposable Personal Income	Personal Consumer Expenditures	Total Outstanding	As % of col. (1)	As % of col. (2)	Total Outstanding	As % of col. (1)	As % of col. (2)
1947	$170	$165	$12	7.1%	7.3%	$ 7	4.1%	4.2%
1948	189	178	14	7.4	7.9	9	4.8	5.1
1949	190	181	17	8.9	9.4	12	6.3	6.6
1950	208	195	21	10.1	10.8	15	7.2	7.7
1951	227	210	23	10.1	11.0	15	6.6	7.1
1952	239	220	27	11.3	12.3	19	7.9	8.6
1953	252	233	31	12.3	13.3	23	9.1	9.9
1954	257	238	32	12.5	13.4	24	9.3	10.1
1955	274	257	39	14.2	15.2	29	10.6	11.3
1956	293	270	43	14.7	15.9	32	10.9	11.9
1957	309	285	45	14.6	15.8	34	11.0	11.9
1958	318	293	46	14.5	15.7	34	10.7	11.6
1959[a]	337	314	52	15.4	16.6	40	11.9	12.7
1960	354	328	56	15.8	17.1	43	12.1	13.1

[a] Includes Alaska and Hawaii for the first time.

Sources: U.S. Department of Commerce and Board of Governors of the Federal Reserve System.

TABLE 5-12
Consumer Debt Related to Net Private Debt
Selected Years, 1941-1960

	Net Private Debt (Billions)	Consumer Debt (Billions)	Consumer Debt As % of Private Debt
1941	$139	$ 9	6.5%
1945	140	6	4.3
1946	154	8	5.2
1947	180	12	6.7
1948	201	14	7.0
1949	212	17	8.0
1950	251	21	8.4
1951	282	23	8.2
1952	307	27	8.8
1953	330	31	9.4
1954	348	33	9.5
1955	403	39	9.7
1956	439	43	9.8
1957	468	45	9.6
1958	500	46	9.3
1959	548	52	9.5
1960	582	56	9.6

Source: U. S. Department of Commerce.

War II. Fixed commitments include payments due on instalment debt, payments on mortgage debt, taxes, insurance and pension payments, and rental payments.

The major difficulty with all of the foregoing measures of the relative size of consumer debt is that they provide aggregates and do not reveal the burden of debt to individual consumers. While up-to-date data are lacking, 1959 investigations indicate that close to 20 percent of all spending units devote 20 percent or more of their disposable income to instalment payments. Further, if all fixed commitments of consumers (as referred to above) are taken into consideration, it appears that about one-half of all spending units are committed for 20 percent or more of their income and a considerable number are committed for 40 percent or more. There is no doubt that the spending units with heavy commitments are those in the lower age brackets and lower income brackets, among whom unemployment during recessions hits hardest. This is to say that for both lenders and borrowers there is risk exposure which, while it cannot be measured precisely, might be considered to some degree a potential danger. It is a mistake to assume, however, that this risk is at all unique in the consumer credit field, or that it has qualities making it especially appropriate for regulatory supervision. Almost all credit-lending activities involve risks which expose both the borrower and the lender to possible loss. Individually, these risks have implications, however small in importance, for over-all economic stability; and collectively they have significant implications. In the consumer credit field, no less than in any other areas of credit, recognition of the dangers and risks involved takes the form of restraint on the part of borrowers and reasonable credit-extension policies on the part of lenders. One may question whether such restraint will be exercised in the case of consumer credit, and whether the individual decisions of consumers and lenders will add up to a collective influence which is at all times consistent with the welfare of each, but the same is true of other types of credit, also.

It cannot be argued, of course, that the measures of the relative burden of consumer credit cited above permit the determination of purely objective judgments. Nevertheless, the trends which have been noted in the relationships of consumer debt to consumer income, expenditures, and liquid assets do not provide a basis for believing that the level of consumer credit has become dangerously high.

Experience with consumer credit sheds some light on the question at hand. Consumer instalment credit repayments, as related to new extensions, have remained at a high level in the postwar period.

Repayments have not fallen below 85 percent of extensions in any year. The repayments percentage was more than 100 in 1958, when a net reduction in consumer credit occurred, and on a number of occasions has been well over 90 percent (Table 5-13). This experience would appear to attest to the basic soundness of consumer credit.

The delinquency rate of bank instalment credit furnishes an additional indicator of the safety of consumer credit. This rate, defined as the per-

TABLE 5-13
Instalment Credit Repayments Related to Credit Extensions
1950-1960

Year	Consumer Instalment Credit Extensions (Billions)	Repayments (Billions)	Repayments as a % of Extensions
1950	$21.6	$18.4	85.6%
1951	23.6	23.0	97.5
1952	29.5	25.4	86.1
1953	31.6	28.0	88.6
1954	31.1	30.5	98.2
1955	39.0	33.6	86.2
1956	40.2	37.2	92.7
1957	42.5	40.3	94.6
1958	40.8	40.9	100.3
1959[a]	49.0	43.4	88.5
1960	50.3	46.9	93.2

[a]Extensions and repayments include data for Alaska and Hawaii beginning with January and August 1959 respectively.

Source: Board of Governors of the Federal Reserve System.

centage of loans on which payments are thirty days or more overdue, rarely rose above 2.5 percent between 1948 and 1954, and since 1954 has fluctuated between 1.5 percent and 2.0 percent. This good record has been achieved, admittedly, in a period that has not included an economic setback of serious proportions but has included four downturns which qualify as recessions.

It should be noted that most consumer lending is done by financial institutions which generally are soundly financed and which could survive far larger delinquencies and losses than have been experienced in the postwar years. In a major downturn delinquencies and losses unquestionably would rise, but it is difficult to see how any probable level of losses in this field could impair the orderly functioning of our financial system. In the absence of a serious threat to financial institutions which engage in consumer lending, there appears to be no justification for special statutory or regulatory restraints on consumer credit as a means of protecting the financial soundness of lending institutions.

In the final analysis, it is perhaps no exaggeration to say that the safety of any given level of consumer credit is determined to a large extent by the degree of cyclical instability to which the economy is subject. The current level of consumer credit might prove excessive indeed in the event of a sharp and prolonged economic recession, for there can be little doubt that under such circumstances the burden of carrying the present level of consumer credit could be greatly increased. It would appear more reasonable, however, to consider the volume of consumer credit in the light of our postwar experience, which has featured moderate and relatively short-lived periods of economic adjustment. Repetition of this experience in the future cannot be taken for granted, of course, but there are reasons for believing that such results will remain within the area of achievement if national economic stabilization tools are wisely and flexibly administered. Quite aside from the use of general instruments of economic stabilization and their implications for consumer credit burdens, it may also be noted that the general capacity of consumers to meet fixed obligations has also been strengthened in recent years by such specific developments as minimum wage legislation, unemployment insurance and supplementary unemployment benefit, health insurance, and a number of other influences on the stability of consumer incomes.

A major question, however, is whether consumer credit should be subjected to special controls on the ground that it contributes to economic instability. While this is not the place to make an exhaustive analysis of this problem, it is appropriate to set forth what appear to be fair conclusions from extensive studies of consumer buying, consumer credit, and business cycles over the past three decades.

It is clear that the availability of consumer credit provides consumers with a much wider area of discretion in the timing of durable goods purchases than would be the case if they were limited to cash transactions. Changes in the volume of consumer buying, financed in part by consumer credit, are theoretically capable of initiating economic upswings or downswings more or less autonomously, but it is generally true that such changes occur in response to other fundamental forces influencing the direction of economic changes. Consequently, the use of consumer credit commonly is thought to permit the accentuation of economic fluctuations—to contribute to the intensity of a boom during the upward phase of the business cycle and subsequently, when consumers are forced to devote current income to the repayment of debts incurred earlier, to increase the severity of the ensuing adjustment. This is but another way of saying that consumer buying is quite noticeably pro-cyclical, a characteristic which is attributable only in part to the fact that consumers may rely upon consumer credit facilities in scheduling their purchases. It is to be noted that even in the absence of consumer credit facilities, the relationships between aggregate economic activity and consumer income levels doubtless would give a pro-cyclical pattern to consumer buying in any event.

Analysis of postwar business cycles casts some doubt upon the importance of changes in consumer spending as an *initiating* force in economic upswings and downturns, although there is no question of the importance of these changes in influencing the course of economic developments once the general direction of change has been established. There is little question that the use of consumer credit may intensify a boom, or that excesses in the use of consumer credit may lead to a subsequent intensification of the recession. Nevertheless, these characteristics of consumer credit are by no means unique. Precisely the same characteristics are present in business credit for inventory accumulation and for plant and equipment expenditures, in mortgage credit, or indeed, in any type of credit. If, therefore, there is no clear evidence that consumer credit is distinctive as an unstabilizing factor in our economy, special regulation of such credit cannot be justified on that ground.

There remains, however, another question. Assuming consumer credit is not a special source of instability, is it largely immune from general credit controls and does it, therefore, require selective controls in order for monetary policy to be effective?

The basic question is whether or not consumer credit is substantially unaffected by general credit controls, particularly in periods of tight money. While it may be said fairly that there is no conclusive evidence which can permit an unassailable answer to this question, there is pertinent evidence; and there have been developments which shed light on the issue.

It is clear that there have been periods, for example, in the first three-quarters of 1956, when consumer credit grew less rapidly under conditions of credit restraint than it did in previous periods of easier money. Still, over the postwar years, and particularly since the restoration of flexible monetary policy in 1951, consumer credit has shown remarkable strength and almost uninterrupted increases. Superficially then, it would appear that recurring periods of credit restraint have not curbed the growth of consumer credit.

Several factors are pointed to by those who argue the immunity of consumer credit from general credit controls. One of these is that finance companies are exceptionally good credit risks and therefore are acceptable borrowers at banks and elsewhere at all times (including periods of credit restraint when banks are observing more selective credit standards). It is claimed that this ready availability of funds to finance companies means that consumers at the retail level as well as dealers always have access to the funds they require. It is argued, further, that consumer borrowers are relatively insensitive to changes in interest rates and financing charges—that they are concerned primarily with down payments and monthly payments and are not deterred from borrowing even when rates tend to rise. It is pointed out, also, that in past periods of credit restraint, there has been little evidence of more stringent terms at the retail level. That is, down payments generally have not been increased, maturities have not been shortened, and rates rarely have shown rapid increases.

Despite the foregoing points, all of which have some validity, there is evidence that consumer credit is affected by general credit controls. The degree to which consumer credit is affected, however, is as impossible to measure as is the effect of general controls on any particular type of credit.

It may be noted that the postwar rise in consumer credit may be more eloquent testimony to the strength of demand for such credit than to its immunity from the effects of general credit controls. Surely, when available credit becomes scarce, the relative strength of competing demands is a factor which will influence credit allocation. There can be no doubt that there has been a tremendous demand for consumer credit in the postwar period. The manner in which lenders have responded to this demand is a relevant consideration in judging the effectiveness of general credit controls.

In periods of credit restraint banks must allocate available credit among the several types of demand for it. This is done, of course, with an eye to the most profitable loans and investments, but also with other considerations in mind. Banks must accommodate their business customers as well as their consumer borrowers, and they must bear in mind the potential for future deposit growth represented by the various kinds of borrowers. When one considers the fact that business lending generally is better calculated to serve these ends than is consumer lending, it is clear that banks cannot afford to ignore the practical implications of diverting funds to consumers which might otherwise be used in accommodating business loan requests. Moreover, tangible evidence of bank attitudes in this respect is to be found in the tendencies toward less consumer lending promotional activity during periods of credit restraint. It is noteworthy that some of the new consumer credit plans of banks (such as check credit) originated in periods of easy money when banks were seeking outlets for excess funds and turned to consumer credit as a source of additional business. This type of promotion plan has spread less widely when the banks have been pinched for funds.

As has been indicated above, it is argued by some that the effects of tight money on bank lending do not reach the finance companies to which banks lend substantial sums. This, however, is a generalization which overlooks some significant influences on bank lending. It is clear that banks have been unwilling in credit restraint periods to increase the lines of credit they make available to finance companies on a continuing basis. While, admittedly, the very large finance companies may not always have been obliged by their need for funds to use fully their bank lines of credit, it is nevertheless true that marginal loan companies (from the standpoint of credit-worthiness) have found their access to bank credit significantly limited. Furthermore, banks generally have not been willing to open new lines of credit for finance companies which have not previously been customers. It seems clear also that banks have, in the past, sought to induce their finance company borrowers to adhere more strictly to sound lending terms and standards of credit-worthiness in periods of credit restraint.

It has been noted that periods of credit restraint have not been accompanied by general consumer credit rate increases at the retail level. Rates, however, do play a role. Banks charge higher rates to the dealers they finance with direct loans, and higher rates are charged to finance company borrowers. Even the largest finance companies pay more for borrowed funds when the prime rate rises.

The reactions of finance companies to tight money periods have also been significant. There is evidence that when finance companies have found their bank sources of credit somewhat limited and bank credit available only at higher costs, the immediately available alternative has been open market borrowing by means of commercial paper sold, frequently to nonbanks, at higher rates. But in periods of tight money, this source has not always produced all of the desired funds and finance companies have shifted to long-term financing, thereby adding to demands on the capital markets. When this has happened, the finance companies have experienced higher borrowing costs. In many cases they have resorted to subordinated debentures, and they have found that they could not obtain as favorable prepayment terms as they could obtain on such borrowing in other periods. Further, borrowing in the capital markets in the face of limited supplies of loanable funds has meant that finance companies, generally speaking, have had to accept more restrictions on their discretion in the handling of their funds. At some point, rising interest rates and other costs of borrowing must deter borrowing.

It seems reasonable to conclude from the foregoing that credit restraint, by bringing about a combination of rising costs, somewhat stricter credit standards, and more limited availability of funds, does affect consumer lending. The restraint is, of course, most clear in the case of the marginal borrowers—both individuals and finance companies—just as it is, it may be added, in any other field of credit. The effects of restraint may not reach consumer credit as quickly as some other types of credit, but it must be recognized that not all areas of credit can be influenced equally and at the same time by credit policy. In any case, it does not appear that a persuasive case can be made for selective consumer credit controls on the ground that this credit escapes general controls.

There remains, nevertheless, the argument that because consumer credit is largely concentrated in relatively few institutions, and because there is considerable uniformity in lending practices, such credit is peculiarly susceptible to controls. Further, it is argued that such controls should be instituted to provide monetary management with a useful, supplementary tool.

Few would question that controls, strictly applied, could curb growth of consumer credit—or permit it to expand when such would appear desirable. Obviously, however, this would be accomplished at the price of further limitations on free choice in our economy. It would be far more desirable to have monetary policy aim at achieving relative stability in aggregate demand and output and to rely on market forces for the allocation of bank credit, savings, and resources in accordance with the choices of producers and consumers.

Chapter 6

COMMERCIAL BANKS AND
AGRICULTURAL CREDIT

Agriculture has always used substantial amounts of credit. It has been and may remain a capital-deficit industry for two basic and very important reasons: One arises from the very nature of the institutional organization of farming—the other from the fact that the functioning of the industry is governed by the seasons.

First, there are less than four million separate farm operating units, most of them organized as individual proprietorships. The typical ownership pattern is title in fee simple by the individual, with a relatively small proportion of tenancy. This means that the financial history of the typical farm is tied to the life cycle of its individual owner. In most cases, a farm needs to be refinanced each generation to effect a change in the ownership at the retirement or death of an owner. Thus there will be substantial long-term debt in agriculture, so long as the present pattern of fee simple ownership of family farms persists.

Second, farming is a biological process, with production and marketing tied to the seasons. The seasonal nature of production costs and of farm marketings, separated as the two frequently are, necessitates substantial and repeated use of production or operating credit. This is not the result of poor management; it is a very essential part of modern agriculture. Indeed, many of our highest income farmers are the heaviest users of operating credit.

Thus, large and continued demands for credit in one of our basic industries lend a special significance to those of our financial institutions which have demonstrated a willingness and capacity to supply the necessary credit. Notable among these are the commercial banks.

In this chapter, we discuss the important economic factors which have affected the demand for agricultural credit in recent decades, and describe the manner and extent to which commercial banks have adapted to the needs of farmers by supplying not only credit but a variety of services as well. We review also the role of government agencies and

190

CHART 4

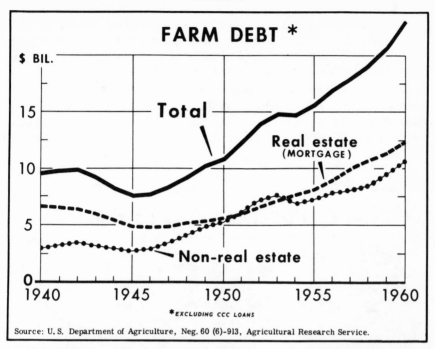

FARM DEBT *

Source: U. S. Department of Agriculture, Neg. 60 (6)-913, Agricultural Research Service.

nonbank lenders in order to demonstrate the major extent to which agriculture relies upon commercial banking for its credit needs. Finally, we appraise the probable changes ahead in agricultural finance and discuss the implications for future credit needs.

Economic Changes Affecting Demand for Agricultural Credit

Farmers now use record amounts of credit. Total farm indebtedness was estimated at $25.4 billion as of January 1, 1961.[1] A little more than half of this was real estate debt (Chart 4). About $1.3 billion of this debt was owed by farmers to the Commodity Credit Corporation, representing price support advances made on commodities placed under government storage. In reality, these were not loans in the traditional credit sense, but rather "guaranteed sale prices" advanced to farmers by the Commodity Credit Corporation or, in the case of commercial banks, guaranteed by the Commodity Credit Corporation. After adjusting total agricultural indebtedness downward by the $1.3 billion of CCC paper, the total indebtedness at the beginning of 1961 was estimated at $24.1 billion, still a record figure.

There are a number of reasons for the rising trend in farm indebtedness.

---

[1] Department of Agriculture.

Rising Asset Values

The total value of assets in American agriculture on January 1, 1961, was estimated at $206.1 billion. This was up from $53 billion in 1940, an almost fourfold increase. Estimated value of real estate as of January 1, 1961, was $136.5 billion, up from $33.6 billion in 1940; more recently the dollar value of farm land increased by more than two-thirds from the 1947-49 period to 1959 (Chart 5). In thirteen states the increase was more than 75 percent in those years. Non-real estate investment in physical assets was $52.0 billion in 1960, compared with $15.2 billion in 1940.

CHART 5

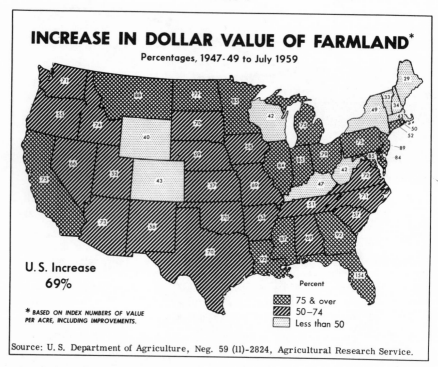

Source: U. S. Department of Agriculture, Neg. 59 (11)-2824, Agricultural Research Service.

Higher Production Costs

In addition to vastly higher asset values, prices of farm inputs have risen almost continuously since 1940 and have come increasingly from non-farm sources (Charts 6 and 7). These purchased inputs, such as power equipment, pesticides, and fertilizers, have substituted for more land and more labor as farm production has increased. They call for increased amounts of credit for the successful farmer.

Increased values and higher costs, coupled with the declining number of farm workers, have raised capital requirements per worker phenome-

CHART 6

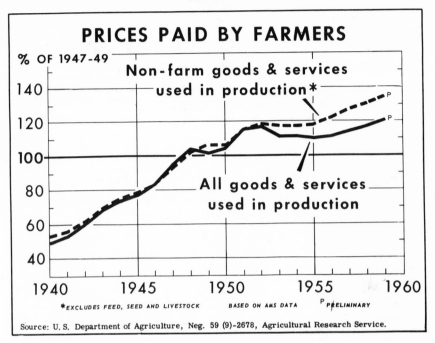

PRICES PAID BY FARMERS

% OF 1947-49

Non-farm goods & services
used in production*

All goods & services
used in production

*EXCLUDES FEED, SEED AND LIVESTOCK   BASED ON AMS DATA   P PRELIMINARY

Source: U. S. Department of Agriculture, Neg. 59 (9)-2678, Agricultural Research Service.

nally. In 1940, the total investment per farm worker averaged only $3,413, but by 1960 the average was $21,303, representing a sixfold increase (Chart 8).

Today, family farms in the Corn Belt represent investments of up to $200,000 or even in excess of one-quarter of a million dollars. On farms like these, investment per worker is nearly always in excess of $50,000 and sometimes runs as high as $100,000.

It is apparent that technological progress and shifts in farm organization have stimulated investment in farm machinery and structures, reduced the number of workers needed on farms, and tremendously increased credit requirements. This, however, has not resulted in an excessive use of credit. Indeed, while farm debts have risen to record heights, they are still only 12 percent of the value of farm assets as contrasted to 19 percent in 1940 (Chart 9). This means, therefore, that with farmers having almost an 88 percent equity in their total production plant, American agriculture, as an industry, is probably more solvent than most major American industries. Danger, of course, can come when individual indebtedness situations get out of line.

The declining number of farms, the decreasing number of farmers, and the increasing size of farms do not mean agriculture is a "declining"

CHART 7

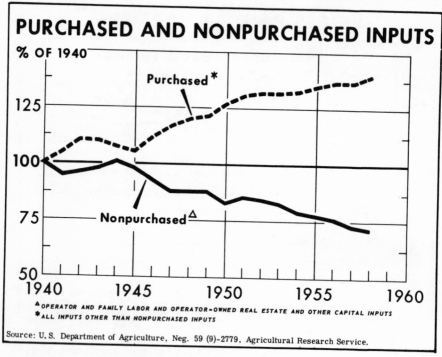

PURCHASED AND NONPURCHASED INPUTS

% OF 1940

Purchased*

Nonpurchased△

Source: U. S. Department of Agriculture, Neg. 59 (9)-2779, Agricultural Research Service.

△OPERATOR AND FAMILY LABOR AND OPERATOR-OWNED REAL ESTATE AND OTHER CAPITAL INPUTS
*ALL INPUTS OTHER THAN NONPURCHASED INPUTS

industry. American agriculture is an expanding industry in every important respect save one—number of people required to run our farms.

Our agricultural plant each year uses more capital, more science and technology, more managerial capacity, more purchased-production inputs, more specialized marketing facilities, and more research than ever before.

Agri-business Also Requires Financing

As a consequence of these developments, we can no longer regard agriculture as the simple production of food and fiber. We must include those businesses that supply our farmers with items used in production, as well as the processing and distributing concerns that handle the food and fiber produced. Employment in these enterprises, called "agri-business," when combined with workers on the farms, comprises nearly two-fifths of our nation's total labor force. This total has not changed much in the last decade or so, because the trend toward fewer workers on farms has been accompanied by increasing numbers of workers in agriculturally related businesses.

The farm plant in America purchases each year from off-farm sources

CHART 8

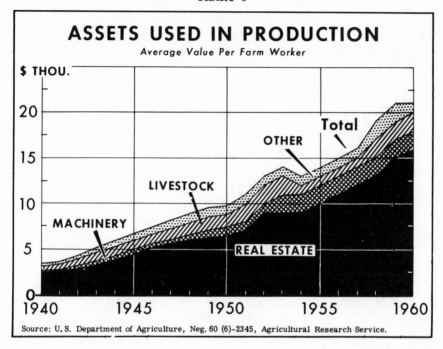

ASSETS USED IN PRODUCTION
Average Value Per Farm Worker

$ THOU.

20

15

10

5

0

MACHINERY

LIVESTOCK

OTHER

Total

REAL ESTATE

1940   1945   1950   1955   1960

Source: U. S. Department of Agriculture, Neg. 60 (6)-2345, Agricultural Research Service.

approximately $17 billion worth of goods and services used in farm production. To this it adds a value of about $17 billion on farms, which means that the total farm produce leaves the farm gate valued at about $34 billion. Processing and distribution add another $45 billion to this, making a total output of approximately $80 billion. While it is not the purpose of this chapter to discuss the financing of agri-business, it is sufficient to note that this essential part of modern agriculture also requires growing amounts of credit which must come in large part from commercial banks.

Development of Bank Lending to Agriculture

Many commercial banks were formed for the specific purpose of serving farmers. Today, nearly two-thirds of the 14,000 commercial banks in the United States are located in towns with populations of 5,000 or less. These rural banks are close to the people they serve, and have ranked high among farm credit lenders both in number of institutions and in volume of credit extended. Here we give a very brief review of major trends in the development of this bank credit over the past half century.

The volume of agricultural loans by commercial banks expanded rapidly between 1911 and 1921, reaching a high of $5.3 billion in the

CHART 9

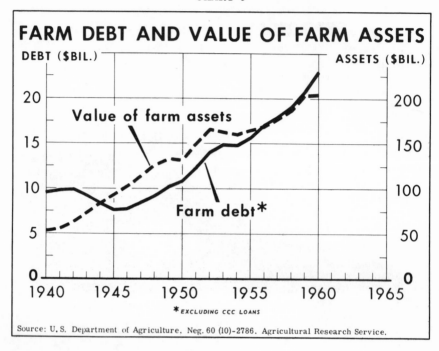

FARM DEBT AND VALUE OF FARM ASSETS

DEBT ($BIL.)   ASSETS ($BIL.)

Value of farm assets

Farm debt*

*EXCLUDING CCC LOANS

Source: U. S. Department of Agriculture. Neg. 60 (10)-2786. Agricultural Research Service.

latter year. The total then declined during the agricultural recession of the 1920's, to $3.5 billion in 1930. A further marked decline was experienced following 1933, when much of the credit was transferred to the newly formed Farm Credit Administration agencies. Subsequently, bank loans to farmers expanded fairly rapidly to present high levels [2] (Table 6-1).

In the early part of this century, especially after establishment of the Federal Reserve System, banks, in addition to making loans, were an important factor in bringing outside capital into agricultural communities to meet peak seasonal demands for credit. The Federal Intermediate Credit Banks were established in 1923, in an effort to augment this flow of outside capital into agriculture. However, as will be pointed out later, these credit banks were not very effective until the establishment of the Production Credit Associations in 1934. It remained, therefore, for commercial banks to carry the principal load during this entire period in meeting the non-real estate credit needs of agriculture.

Many banks experienced substantial losses on farm loans during the depression years, and these were primarily responsible for the closing

---

[2] Present bank lending to agriculture will be reviewed in detail in the following section of this chapter.

TABLE 6-1
Agricultural Loans Held by All Operating Banks
January 1, Selected Years, 1911-1961

(Millions)

Year	Total	Non-Real Estate Loans[a]	Farm Mortgage Loans[b]
1911	$1,816	$1,338	$ 478
1915	2,352	1,606	746
1920	4,658	3,454	1,204
1921	5,317	3,870	1,447
1925	3,874	2,674	1,200
1930	3,488	2,491	997
1935	1,340	841	499
1940	1,669	1,135	534
1945	1,827	1,377	450
1950	3,989	3,052	937
1955	5,871	4,660	1,211
1956	5,823	4,477	1,346
1957	5,488	4,102	1,386
1958	5,461	4,047	1,414
1959	6,422	4,910	1,512
1960[c]	6,650	5,019	1,631
1961[c]	7,369	5,678	1,691

[a]Includes CCC loans.
[b]State and national banks, 1911-30; insured commercial banks, 1935-45; all operating banks, 1950-61.
[c]Includes Alaska and Hawaii.

Source: Department of Agriculture.

of a large number of country banks. Some writers and political figures of those days were strongly critical of banks for curtailing their credit extension to farmers. In retrospect, however, it is clear that the great majority of country bankers were forced to tighten up on lending because of declining deposits, shrinking security values, vanishing equity ratios, and a host of conditions associated with the general depression.

It is noteworthy that several desirable changes in bank lending policies grew out of this experience. For example, amortization of real estate loans became prevalent, and more attention has been given to estimates of income and expenses in connection with budgeted loans.

The contribution which commercial banks have made to agricultural development cannot be measured merely by the extent to which they have channeled credit into agriculture. They have been able to give quick service with a minimum of red tape, they have been accessible to farmers, and they alone have provided checking accounts and other banking services in thousands of local communities.

Further, the friendly counsel of the country banker on matters both financial and nonfinancial has been of inestimable value to hundreds of thousands of farm families. The country banker, knowing his customers and holding their confidence, has been a kind of "silent" partner of the farmers in his community. This relationship, through the years, has been of genuine assistance in agricultural development. More recently, this aid to agriculture has been vastly improved by the addition of more and better trained agricultural specialists to bank staffs, including those of correspondent banks as well as country banks. This will be discussed more fully below.

Present Day Bank Agricultural Lending

Types and Amounts of Loans

Ninety-two percent (12,106) of all insured commercial banks had some type of agricultural loans outstanding on January 1, 1961.[3] Eighty-seven percent of these banks had non-real estate farm loans, 86 percent had real estate farm loans, and a great majority had both types of farm loans. In a few states, 100 percent of all the banks had some agricultural loans; at the other extreme, the figure was as low as 58 percent for New Jersey banks. In thirty-four states 90 percent or more of the banks had agricultural loans.

The fact that banks are a major source of agricultural credit in every state is clearly shown by data in Chart 10, giving the volume of agricultural loans held by all operating banks as of June 10, 1959 and as of June 15, 1960. The total of such loans for the United States in mid-1960 was $6.9 billion, excluding CCC guaranteed loans.

More detailed data on agricultural lending by commercial banks are available from the Federal Reserve System Agricultural Loans Survey as of June 30, 1956.[4] At that time about 2.3 million borrowers had $5 billion of farm loans outstanding at insured commercial banks in the United States, and all farm debt (exclusive of Commodity Credit Corporation price support advances) totaled some $18.5 billion. About $5.7 billion of farm debt was held by all financing organizations other than banks, and an estimated $7.7 billion of loans and other farm credits were held by individuals, merchants, and the like. Thus, in 1956, commercial banks held more than one-fourth of total farm credit. They were by all odds the largest single group of farm financing organizations.

Commercial banks serve a preponderance of small agricultural borrowers, as would be expected, but large as well as small farmers are served, with the larger farmers utilizing the greatest amounts of credit

---

[3] *Agricultural Credit and Related Data*, Agricultural Committee, American Bankers Association, June 1961.

[4] The data in this section were reported in the *Federal Reserve Bulletin* for November 1956 and January, February, and March 1957.

CHART 10

AGRICULTURAL LOANS HELD BY ALL OPERATING BANKS
EXCLUDING LOANS GUARANTEED BY COMMODITY CREDIT CORPORATION

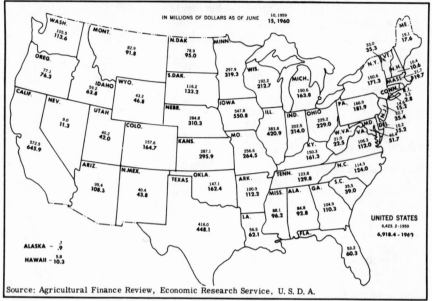

Source: Agricultural Finance Review, Economic Research Service, U. S. D. A.

(Table 6-2). The 53 percent of borrowers with loans of $1,000 or less represented less than 10 percent of the total amount of loans. The 10 percent of the borrowers with debts of $5,000 or more had slightly more than 50 percent of all farm loans outstanding.

A large majority of the 2.3 million borrowers obtained loans for seasonal purposes. Only about 200,000 borrowers had bank loans for the purpose of buying real estate. Of the $5 billion of bank loans outstanding in 1956, loans to pay current expenses and to buy feeder livestock constituted 38 percent of the dollar volume. Loans to finance intermediate term investment—purchase of other livestock, machinery, etc.—were about 33 percent of the total. Loans to buy farm land were 17.5 percent, and loans for repayment of debt and for "other" purposes made up the remaining 11.5 percent. (See Table 6-3.) Banks provide about three-fourths of the institutional credit used for these purposes (Chart 11). On the other hand, banks furnish only about one-sixth of all farm mortgage credit, for nonbank sources are most frequently used for this longer term type of credit (Chart 12).

The most common maturity for current expense loans was six months or less (including demand notes); 64 percent of the dollar volume of these loans was in this maturity group. Thirty-nine percent of the loans to finance intermediate term investment were for six months or less, 26

TABLE 6-2
Distribution of Banks' Farm Borrowers by Type and Amount of Credit Extended
June 30, 1956

Type of Borrower and Amount of Debt	Number of Borrowers		Amount of Debt	
	(Thousands)	Percentage distribution	(Millions)	Percentage distribution
Total	2,268	100.0%	$5,050	100.0%
Under $250	438	19.3	60	1.2
$250-$499	353	15.6	126	2.5
$500-$999	416	18.3	289	5.7
$1,000-$1,999	416	18.4	584	11.6
$2,000-$4,999	410	18.1	1,269	25.1
$5,000-$9,999	155	6.8	1,055	20.9
$10,000-$24,999	65	2.9	943	18.7
$25,000 and over	14	.6	722	14.3
Borrowers with loans to buy farm land	205	100.0%	1,089	100.0%
Under $250	4	1.8	1	.1
$250-$499	7	3.3	3	.2
$500-$999	18	9.0	13	1.2
$1,000-$1,999	35	17.0	50	4.6
$2,000-$4,999	72	35.3	234	21.5
$5,000-$9,999	45	22.0	313	28.7
$10,000-$24,999	20	9.9	289	26.5
$25,000 and over	3	1.6	187	17.1
Other borrowers	2,063	100.0%	3,960	100.0%
Under $250	435	21.1	60	1.5
$250-$499	346	16.8	124	3.1
$500-$999	397	19.3	276	7.0
$1,000-$1,999	381	18.5	534	13.5
$2,000-$4,999	337	16.3	1,035	26.1
$5,000-$9,999	110	5.3	742	18.7
$10,000-$24,999	45	2.2	654	16.5
$25,000 and over	11	.5	536	13.5

Detail may not add to totals because of rounding.

Source: Board of Governors of the Federal Reserve System.

percent matured in nine months or one year, while 34 percent had more than one year maturity. Of the loans to buy farm land, 42 percent had a maturity of more than five years.

Chattel mortgages (or conditional sales contracts) were used to secure 43 percent of the dollar amount of all farm loans outstanding in 1956, and this constituted about 60 percent of the dollar volume of loans not secured by real estate. Real estate was security for 27 percent of all loans, while unsecured loans made up 22 percent of the total dollar amount. Remaining loans were endorsed or otherwise secured.

Interest Rates

Generally speaking, commercial banks are competitive with other lending institutions with regard to interest rates. The interest rate, of course,

TABLE 6-3
Purpose of Farm Loans Outstanding at Banks
June 30, 1956

Purpose of Loan	Number of Notes (Thousands)	Percentage distribution	Amount of Loans (Millions)	Percentage distribution	Average size of note
Total	3,528	100.0%	$5,050	100.0%	$1,431
Current expenses	1,697	48.1	1,903	37.7	1,121
Feeder livestock operations	134	3.8	497	9.8	3,717
Current operating and living expenses	1,564	44.3	1,406	27.8	899
Intermediate-term investments	1,325	37.6	1,685	33.4	1,271
Other livestock	234	6.6	447	8.9	1,911
Machinery, etc.	723	20.5	781	15.5	1,081
Consumer durable goods	215	6.1	138	2.7	641
Improvement of land and buildings	153	4.3	319	6.3	2,076
Farm real estate purchase	216	6.1	883	17.5	4,086
Repayment of debt	152	4.3	346	6.9	2,274
Other, or not ascertained	137	3.9	233	4.6	1,699

Detail may not add to totals because of roundings.

Source: Board of Governors of the Federal Reserve System.

varies with type and size of loan. The average rate of farm loans not secured by real estate was 6.4 percent in 1956. Loans for intermediate-term investments carried somewhat higher rates than other type loans. Interest rates varied inversely with the size of loan.

Loans secured by real estate averaged about one percentage point lower than non-real estate loans. This was partially a reflection of the larger average size of loans secured by real estate. When loans of the same size were compared directly, real estate loans were about one-half of a percentage point lower in interest rates than non-real estate loans (Table 6-4).

In areas where agriculture is characterized by small units and variable incomes, as in some regions of the South, rates are sometimes higher because of poorer risks and higher loaning expenses than in areas with larger farms and more stable incomes, like the Corn Belt. Likewise, areas with highly seasonal demands for loans are likely to have higher rates than those with fairly stable loan demands the year around.

Bank rates on farm loans are influenced by competition with other

CHART 11

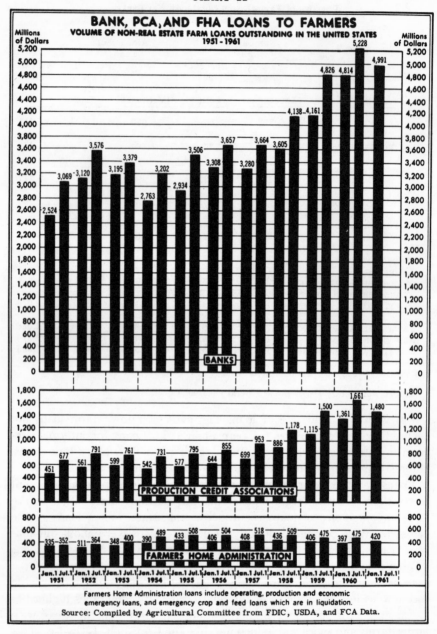

BANK, PCA, AND FHA LOANS TO FARMERS
VOLUME OF NON-REAL ESTATE FARM LOANS OUTSTANDING IN THE UNITED STATES 1951 - 1961

Farmers Home Administration loans include operating, production and economic emergency loans, and emergency crop and feed loans which are in liquidation.
Source: Compiled by Agricultural Committee from FDIC, USDA, and FCA Data.

lenders, primarily the agencies supervised by the Farm Credit Administration, insurance companies, and individuals. However, banks are better able than governmental or cooperative lending institutions to

CHART 12

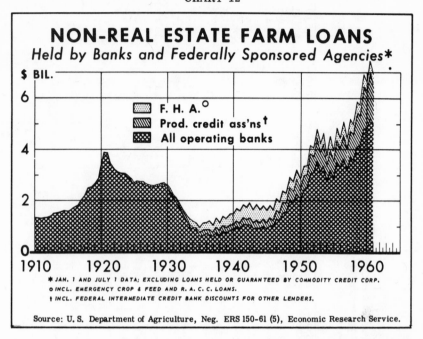

NON-REAL ESTATE FARM LOANS
Held by Banks and Federally Sponsored Agencies*

$ BIL.

F. H. A.°
Prod. credit ass'ns†
All operating banks

1910   1920   1930   1940   1950   1960

* JAN. 1 AND JULY 1 DATA; EXCLUDING LOANS HELD OR GUARANTEED BY COMMODITY CREDIT CORP.
° INCL. EMERGENCY CROP & FEED AND R. A. C. C. LOANS.
† INCL. FEDERAL INTERMEDIATE CREDIT BANK DISCOUNTS FOR OTHER LENDERS.

Source: U. S. Department of Agriculture, Neg. ERS 150-61 (5), Economic Research Service.

adjust the rates among individual borrowers, depending on credit ratings, repayment records, and size of loan. This accounts in substantial measure for the variation in rates among bank loans to individuals.

Other Forms of Credit for Farmers

Farmers occasionally use consumer credit set up on the typical instalment repayment plan. When they do use credit to purchase consumer goods, repayment is not on a monthly basis but is geared to the time of selling farm produce. The most frequent exceptions to this are loans to dairy farmers who have a regular monthly income from sale of milk.

Other Bank Services to Agriculture

In recent years large numbers of banks have added to their staffs an agriculturally trained man who is often known as the "farm representative" of the bank. More than 1,000 such men are employed by banks in the United States. An unknown additional number of bank employees, without specific agricultural training, do a great deal of farm counseling.

These "agricultural men" not only make farm loans, but spend a great deal of time counseling farmers about their farm operations and financial programs. They assist in organizing and financing livestock sales, farm sales, and the like. They help bring purebred and high-producing livestock

TABLE 6-4

Interest Rates[a] on Farm Loans at Insured Commercial Banks By Specified Size, Purpose, and Security
June 30, 1956

Security and Purpose of Loan	Total	Size of loan[b]							
		under $250	$250-$499	$500-$999	$1,000-$1,999	$2,000-$4,999	$5,000-$9,999	$10,000-$24,999	$25,000 and over
No farm real estate mortgage	6.4%	7.4%	7.4%	7.4%	6.9%	6.6%	6.0%	5.7%	5.3%
Current expenses	6.2	7.2	7.1	6.8	6.5	6.2	5.9	5.7	5.3
Intermediate-term investments	6.9	8.1	8.1	7.6	7.4	6.9	6.1	5.8	5.5
Farm real estate purchase	5.5	7.5	7.2	6.4	6.2	5.9	5.6	5.2	4.7
Repayment of debt	6.3	7.3	7.4	7.1	6.8	6.5	6.2	5.6	5.1
Other, or not ascertained	6.0	7.1	6.9	6.5	6.2	6.2	5.6	5.7	5.5
Farm real estate mortgage	5.4	7.4	7.7	7.0	6.4	5.8	5.2	5.0	5.1
Current expenses	6.2	7.7	7.5	7.1	6.9	6.1	5.8	5.7	5.3
Intermediate-term investments	5.7	7.6	8.5	7.5	6.6	5.9	5.4	5.2	5.2
Farm real estate purchase	5.2	6.4	7.0	6.3	6.1	5.6	5.0	4.9	5.0
Repayment of debt	5.4	7.2	6.7	6.5	6.1	5.7	5.3	5.3	5.0
Other, or not ascertainable	5.5	6.7	7.3	6.9	6.4	5.9	5.4	5.2	5.5

[a]Annual averages.
[b]When originally made or (if renewed) when last renewed.

Source: Board of Governors of the Federal Reserve System.

into a community, and finance its distribution to well-qualified farmers. In some cases they perform farm management services for landlords, and assist with the management of the farms in the trust department. They are helpful with income tax management and farm accounting problems.

Many bankers recognize that it is to their long-run advantage to aid in general improvement of agricultural production. Thus, they cooperate with local agricultural leaders in educational endeavors such as 4-H clubs, and FFA groups. Closely related is the practice of some banks of providing educational scholarships to farm youth.

Bankers also seek to improve the general level of agricultural production by furnishing farm outlook and production data to their farmer customers. Some of these materials are prepared by bank staff members while others are purchased in newsletter form.

Insofar as credit is concerned, banks have enhanced their services and are continuing to do so in two important ways.

First, they have supplemented their own resources by placing loans or participations therein with their correspondent banks, thus drawing on pools of bank credit available outside their own communities. This has created a need for agriculturally trained specialists in more and more city banks, a need which banks are meeting effectively.

Second, closely allied with the foregoing bank lending activity is the servicing of life insurance company farm mortgage loans. As mentioned previously, banks often are not in a position to furnish large amounts of long-term real estate credit, but through arrangements with life insurance companies they can make such loans available to farmers, to the advantage of both borrower and lender.

An area of growing importance in agriculture is the trust services offered by commercial banks. Not only may trust services aid in tax problems, in the inheritance and transfer of farms, but also in providing a means whereby non-farmers may invest in farm businesses which are competently managed.

The Government's Role in Agricultural Credit

Reasons for Government Assistance

The reasons for governmental assistance in providing credit to private sectors of the economy are (1) to counter depressions, (2) to provide needed services when private credit sources are unwilling or unable to extend the funds, (3) to meet emergency conditions, and (4) to give preferential treatment and to accelerate the flow of funds to some sector of the economy. All four of these motives have entered into government programs for granting credit aid to agriculture.

Specifically a variety of government and government-sponsored institutions have been established to provide price support loans on farm products, production credit for the growing season, intermediate credit to help finance purchases of equipment and other supplies, and long-term mortgage credit. Each of these types of agricultural credit is discussed in the following sections.

Commodity Credit Corporation Loans

The Commodity Credit Corporation, entirely owned by the government, was created in 1933 and authorized to make advances on a variety of agricultural commodities in connection with government-sponsored price support programs. The CCC also provides a type of storage facility loan to further these programs.

The CCC is an integral part of the U.S. Department of Agriculture. It has a maximum borrowing authorization of $14.5 billion at any one time. In practice, whenever its obligations push hard against that figure and additional commodities are coming under price support loans, Congress usually appropriates a sufficient sum to make up a stated amount of losses, which restores the capacity to borrow and to meet current price support obligations.

When the levels of price support for particular commodities are announced by the Secretary of Agriculture, the CCC offers farmers non-recourse "loans" at the stated levels. The farmer, in turn, gives a chattel mortgage or warehouse receipt as security, and must provide acceptable storage for the commodity. At maturity of the loan the borrower may pay the loan and redeem the commodity if its price has risen in the meantime, or he may deliver the commodity to the CCC in full settlement of the loan and accumulated interest. It is obvious, therefore, that CCC loans of this kind are not "credit" in the conventional sense.

While the bulk of CCC loans on price supported commodities have always been carried directly by CCC, there is an arrangement under which commercial banks and other financial institutions may participate. The CCC forms a pool for each crop year for all producer notes evidencing price support loans on certain commodities, and issues "certificates of interest" against them. When a commercial bank participates in disbursing price support non-recourse loans to farmers, the CCC issues to the financial institution a "certificate of interest" equal to the amount of disbursement. CCC will thereafter purchase at its option, or at the option of the holder, any outstanding certificates of interest at their face value plus interest earned thereon.

CCC paper has sometimes been fairly attractive to commercial banks, especially when competitive interest rates were relatively low. For example, on January 1, 1955, commercial banks held $1.7 million worth of this paper fully guaranteed by CCC. The Production Credit Associations have participated from time to time in CCC paper, but to a limited extent.

Intermediate Credit Banks and Production Credit Associations

The twelve Federal Intermediate Credit Banks (FICB) were organized in 1923 to serve primarily as banks of discount, not to make direct loans to farmers. They are authorized to purchase or to discount the farm paper of Production Credit Associations (PCA), state and national banks, trust companies, livestock loan companies, and certain other agricultural financing institutions. A few commercial banks have used this discount privilege, but the principal business of these credit banks is with the Production Credit Associations.

Production Credit Associations were created as permanent organizations under the Farm Credit Act of 1933. As of January 1961, there were 489 PCA's in the United States, privately organized and managed by farmer-borrowers as agricultural cooperatives. They are supervised and assisted by the Federal Intermediate Credit Bank of their district. Loanable funds are obtained by discounting farmers' notes with or borrowing from the Federal Intermediate Credit Banks.

PCA's are organized to make loans for general agricultural purposes of a short-term or intermediate-term nature in any agricultural county in the United States. Loans outstanding as of December 31, 1960 were $1,480 million. This was a near record high volume.

The average size PCA loan per borrower made in 1960 was $7,749 for the entire country. During 1960, a total of 334,773 borrowers were served in the United States in the amount of $2,594 million. This means that the PCA's reached about one-seventh as many farmer borrowers as did the commercial banks. It is estimated that in 1960, PCA's served about 9 percent of all farmers in the United States, as contrasted with nearly 50 percent served by commercial banks.

Although Production Credit Associations were rather heavily subsidized with interest-free government capital in their early years, a great majority of these associations have retired all the government capital and are now completely farmer-borrower owned. As of January 3, 1961, 469 associations of the total 489 were entirely owned by their farmer members and operated without direct federal subsidy. These PCA's charge competitive interest rates based on the cost of money in the central money markets where the FICB debentures are sold, plus the cost of making and servicing the loans. For example, during 1960 the average cost of PCA loans to borrowers amounted to 7.25 percent. In many instances interest costs (including loan service fees) on PCA loans run above commercial bank costs for comparable loans. This situation varies from region to region.

The Production Credit Associations, in the main, make the kind of loans that are eligible for commercial bank financing, and they have grown relatively faster in total loan volume than have commercial banks during the past ten years. The willingness of the associations to lend sums with maturity up to five years has strengthened their competitive position. Of the PCA loans outstanding at mid-1960, 14 percent had maturities of two to five years. Commercial banks have sometimes been reluctant to expand their lines of credit to individual farmers or to make longer-term farm loans of a capital type, although more than a one-third of bank agricultural loans outstanding are of intermediate term. In recent years strong demands for bank credit from other classes of borrowers who rely on bank credit have been partly responsible for the relatively greater gain in PCA loans to agriculture.

In earlier years, commercial banks were strongly critical of PCA's because of their government subsidy to operate in the same field as commercial banks. However, now that most of them are subsidy-free and meet their tax obligations, they have become another strong competitor at the local lending level. Some of them have a great deal of equity capital which has been accumulated through the years. Where this is true, they are particularly strong competitors for banks having relatively limited capital resources.

While PCA loans may once have offered a distinct advantage to borrowers, especially at times in their early history when bank credit was tight, it is doubtful if in most instances a competitive advantage exists today. However, the presence in any agricultural community of another strongly capitalized, soundly managed, permanent cooperative credit organization works to the advantage of the farmer borrowers, and gives them a choice of sources of production credit. It is apparent that with PCA volume after twenty-seven years of service being one-fifth the agricultural loan volume of commercial banks, and with PCA's reaching only about 9 percent of the total number of farmers, commercial banks continue to occupy a very dominant position in supplying the short- and intermediate-term credit needs of farmers.

Government Lending Agencies

Two other principal governmental lending agencies for farmers are the Farmers Home Administration and the Rural Electrification Administration (REA). The latter really is not a credit agency in the generally accepted sense, although it does disperse large amounts of credit to electric and telephone borrowers to construct electric power distribution facilities and telephone services. It is primarily a mechanism to implement the organization of local REA's, and lends directly to them, at a nominal rate of interest, funds borrowed from the U.S. Treasury at 2 percent. Although the REA itself does not lend directly to individual farmers, "consumer facility" loans are made by the REA to its distribution borrowers for re-loan to individual consumers. These loans are for wiring, plumbing, and water systems and are made for five years at a 2 percent rate to the distribution borrower. The record of repayment in its loans has been good.

The Farmers Home Administration actually had its inception during the mid-1930's, but was created formally in 1946 when the former Farm Security Administration was terminated. The Farmers Home Administration, theoretically at least, does not compete with commercial banks, Federal Land banks, life insurance companies, or production credit associations. It was created to make higher risk loans than are considered justifiable by other lending agencies. On the other hand, the FHA lends only in situations where the borrower has good prospects of becoming eligible for credit of the quality acceptable to commercial banks or production credit associations. When a Farmers Home Administration borrower improves his credit standing to the point that he is eligible for a commercial loan, he is supposed to "graduate" to a commercial bank, a land bank, a Production Credit Association, or the like.

FHA loans carry a great deal of personal supervision. They are high cost loans with no intention that the agency will be self-supporting on the loans it makes. Loans are made at 5 percent interest for purchase of feed, seed, fertilizer, livestock, machinery, and the like, and are repayable in one to seven years. Farm ownership loans are made to help farmers buy, enlarge, or develop family type farms. These loans are repayable over a forty-year period with a 5 percent interest rate.

Obviously, these loans are below current competitive rates. Even so, when the borrower's credit position improves to the point that he qualifies for a regular commercial loan, he is supposed to make the shift.

Private lenders may advance funds for farm ownership loans through FHA. Loans may not exceed 90 percent of the value of the farm and are fully insured by the government. Payments are amortized over forty years at 5 percent, of which 4 percent goes to the lender. Lenders have the option of selling the paper to the government after five years. Insured loans outstanding as of January 1, 1961 amounted to only $190.7 million. In recent years, with relatively high interest costs, these loans have not been attractive to commercial banks and other investors.

On January 1, 1961, the total outstanding volume of operating loans made by FHA was approximately $420 million. In the main, these loans are not competitive with loans from banks, and in most areas bankers actively cooperate with the Farmers Home Administration program because it permits the financing of worthy cases which have reasonable prospects of success, but which cannot meet loan requirements of most

CHART 13

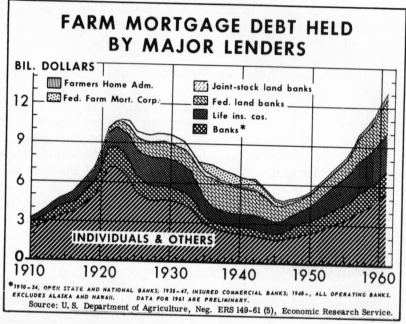

FARM MORTGAGE DEBT HELD BY MAJOR LENDERS

BIL. DOLLARS

▦ Farmers Home Adm.   ▨ Joint-stock land banks
▦ Fed. Farm Mort. Corp.   ▨ Fed. land banks
                             ▮ Life ins. cos.
                             ▨ Banks*

INDIVIDUALS & OTHERS

*1910-34, OPEN STATE AND NATIONAL BANKS; 1935-47, INSURED COMMERCIAL BANKS; 1948-, ALL OPERATING BANKS. EXCLUDES ALASKA AND HAWAII.   DATA FOR 1961 ARE PRELIMINARY.
Source: U. S. Department of Agriculture, Neg. ERS 149-61 (5), Economic Research Service.

bankers. As such borrowers improve their financial position, commercial banks and other lending institutions will in most instances serve their credit needs.

Long-Term Lending to Farmers

As has been pointed out previously, commercial banks have never been a major factor in the long-term real estate mortgage field (Chart 13). Commercial banks have accounted for only a modest portion of our mortgage borrowing because of the lack of liquidity of such loans, and because of losses on such lending in the past, particularly during the long period of real estate price decline from 1920 to 1935.

Many of the intermediate term agricultural loans made by commercial banks for production purposes are secured by mortgage. In recent years, more than one-half the bank farm loans secured by real estate have been made for purposes other than land purchases.

The sources of outstanding farm mortgage loans have compared as follows (Table 6-5) on January 1st of each of the years listed.

Commercial banks held 10 percent of outstanding farm mortgages in 1930 and 11 percent in 1961. As with other kinds of long-term lending, the future position of commercial banks in this field is largely dependent upon the volume of savings deposits that they will receive in the future.

Life insurance companies have always been aggressive lenders in the

TABLE 6-5
Mortgage Loans to Farmers
Selected Years 1930-1961

(Millions)

Lenders	1930	1940	1950	1961
Total	$9,630	$6,586	$5,579	$14,802
Banks[a]	997	534	937	1,691
Life insurance companies	2,118	984	1,172	2,984
Federal Land Bank[b]	1,202	2,723	965	2,539
Farmers Home Administration	--	32	193	484
Joint stock land banks	638	92	c	--
Individuals and others	4,675	2,221	2,312	7,103

[a]1930, state and national banks; 1940, insured commercial banks; 1961, all operating commercial and savings banks.
[b]Includes Federal Farm Mortgage Corporation loans.
[c]Less than $1 million.

Source: Department of Agriculture.

farm mortgage field, and will probably continue to be so. The long-term character of their investment requirements makes them ideally suited for long-term lending on farms.

The twelve Federal Land banks have been for many years a principal source of long-term farm mortgage credit. They were organized in 1917 as permanent institutions by authority of the Federal Farm Loan Act of 1916. They are cooperative in character; all of their stock is owned by Federal Land Bank Associations all of whose stock in turn is owned by their farmer-borrowers. Consequently, they are entirely owned by their borrowers. They lend funds that are obtained primarily by the sale of consolidated farm loan bonds in the open money market.

Their loans are secured by first mortgages on farms and ranches and may exceed 65 percent of the appraised normal value of the property by the amount of stock which is paid for out of the loan. Loans held by the Federal Land Banks as of January 1, 1961 totaled $2,539 million. While it may be maintained by some commercial bankers that Federal Land Banks are in competition with them, it would appear that commercial banks have about as many long-term loans as they desire. Federal Land Bank loans usually are made for as long a term as thirty-three years; most insurance companies will make loans for twenty years or longer, although in both instances, normal pay-out has been for a much shorter term. Very few commercial banks would care to make a loan that long. It probably would not be prudent to do so.

Traditionally, individuals have furnished large amounts of farm real estate credit. This has been due to the willingness of land owners to finance land when they sold it. Increasingly, there are tax advantages to sellers of land to finance purchases. This has been done with mortgages as well as contract sales of land. Much of the low-equity financing of land has been done, and will continue to be done, by individuals.

It is anticipated that the insurance companies and the Federal Land Banks, among institutional lenders, will continue to dominate the long-term farm mortgage field.

Appraisal of Public Policy in Agricultural Credit

Although the federal programs for supplying credit to agriculture have to a considerable extent achieved the goals mentioned above, they have proved very costly and the farm problem still remains far from being solved. The federal agencies have provided credit to agriculture in times of emergency such as drought and flood, and have greatly expanded the availability of long-term and other credit facilities to farmers. Some of these activities, however, could have been financed by private financial institutions. Furthermore, the REA makes loans at 2 percent interest, whereas the Treasury which supplies the funds has to pay a considerably higher rate. The cost differential is being borne by the taxpayer. Some of the projects financed by REA should be carried out by private companies.

In some respects, however, it would seem that the public interest has not been well served by the government's agricultural lending programs. First, as is the case with most Federal credit programs, agricultural lending has grown steadily, regardless of economic conditions. Moreover, no effort has been made to coordinate financial aid to agriculture with fiscal and monetary policies designed to smooth out the business cycle and promote sustainable economic growth.

Another problem, but one harder to document, is that the lower cost and increased supply of credit available for agriculture have tended to bring about an unduly large allocation of economic resources to agriculture.[5] This has intensified the problem of dealing with agricultural surpluses. In addition, since the demand for farm products is relatively inelastic, the ease with which credit could be obtained has tended to keep uneconomic units in operation and thus to reduce the percentage of the total national income received by farmers.

The farm problem is complex and is further aggravated by political considerations and pressures. On the whole, the credit activities of the government and its agencies have been helpful to the farmer and to the attainment of desirable public objectives, but at a very high cost to the taxpayer. Some of the policies and procedures are in need of overhauling. A considerable part of the funds now supplied by the government and its

---

[5] See Saulnier, Halcrow, and Jacoby, *Federal Lending and Loan Insurance*, National Bureau of Economic Research, 1958.

agencies might well be furnished by the commercial banks and other private lenders.

Changes Ahead in Agricultural Finance

The principal changes ahead in financing agriculture will be associated with changes in the institutional pattern of agriculture itself.

There are five fundamental characteristics of the current agricultural adjustment which are pertinent.

1) Capital requirements per farm and per worker have increased to the extent that it has become increasingly difficult for an individual, during his productive years, to accumulate a sufficient amount to finance an economically-sized operating unit. This will become increasingly true in the decade ahead. Moreover, in view of the inheritance tax structure, it is becoming increasingly difficult for a parent to transfer such a unit to his son without substantial operating or financial disruption.

2) Management has become the key factor in successful farm operation. This is in sharp contrast to a generation or two ago when the farm unit was much more self-sufficient than now, with much less capital involved, with less science applied, and with many fewer critical managerial decisions to be made.

3) The trend toward larger and fewer commercial farm units will continue. This trend has been pronounced during the past decade. It will be accelerated in the decade ahead. All the power of government and politics cannot stop it. Nor should it.

4) The commercial farm will increasingly assume the characteristics of a manufacturing establishment, with the manager assembling "packages of technology" which have been produced by others on a custom basis. The share of total farm receipts spent for production items will increase still further. The gross margin per dollar of receipts will become narrower, and profit will depend increasingly on volume. Agriculture is changing from a way of living to a way of making a living. It is changing from a business of arts and crafts to a business undergirded with large amounts of science and technology.

5) The process of "rurbanization" will accelerate. Rural and urban cultures will intermingle in countless communities within commuting distance of industrial centers. A new community culture will emerge in which the farmer will tend to lose his vocational identity, just as the lawyer, the doctor, or the machinist now loses his in his community.

There are two principal implications of these forces of general interest to lenders.

First, there will be growing pressure on the combination of owner-manager-operator in one man as the typical institutional pattern of farm operation. We have departed from this pattern in the majority of other major business sectors in America. Time was when we had many family entrepreneural foundry shops, tailor shops, boot makers, corner grocery stores, and, yes, even automobile assembly plants. These have given way primarily to larger units with more and more capital, with higher levels of management, with more specialization of labor, and, if you choose, with a higher degree of integration.

Usually when such changes have occurred, opportunities for profit and higher living standards have increased for owners, for managers, and for workers. Some individuals were injured in the adjustment but, on the whole, society gained.

We have noted that today's farms have very large amounts of capital. It is not necessary to dwell at length on the difficulty of passing such units intact from father to son, in addition to pausing at least to catch one's breath as one passes the tax collector. If the son has to face the prospect himself of providing the necessary capital structure, perhaps by paying off two or three heirs in the family, he may choose to spend more of his current income in living and less in saving. This means that he will not only be willing, but anxious to enter into some kind of financial arrangement whereby a third party puts up some of the capital, or perhaps becomes a financial partner on a permanent basis at the time of his father's death.

Managerial capacity is even more difficult to pass from father to son than is accumulated capital. Management is now the critical factor in successful farm operation. And this means a highly specialized kind of management.

Fathers do not necessarily breed managerial capacity into their sons. A generation or two ago it was not difficult for a son to apprentice under a father, and take over the family farm, provided the son had a strong constitution and a propensity for hard physical work. The latter factors are no longer limiting. The limiting factor is now managerial capacity.

It is equally true that fathers do not necessarily breed vocational preference into their sons. With the growing tendency for farm youth to be educated beyond the high school, many farm-reared youngsters will have their vocational preference tipped away from the "three-in-one" farmer their father was. They might prefer to train themselves for manager, for manager-operator, for part owner-operator with some "integrator" supplying part of the capital and part of the management, or for some combination of these. In any event, whatever direction the future takes, the man with the higher level of managerial capacity on the farm is going to need more capital from outside sources. Commercial banks can aid in supplying it.

The second implication of the changing times is that our typical system of fee simple ownership by individual operators will be under increasing pressure. This is a logical deduction from the analysis in the preceding paragraphs. Nevertheless with any process of refinancing there is usually a shift in management and operation, seldom accomplished without considerable disruption of the farm as a going concern. This disruptive process in transfer will increase as the size of the unit grows, as financing becomes more difficult, and as the importance of maintaining a unit large enough to be economically efficient increases.

Industry has met this problem with divisible shares of ownership, the holders of which in many cases are not even remotely related to management or to operation. This permits passing ownership from one generation to the next without disrupting management or operation. It permits the accumulation under single management and single operation, or under single management and multiple operation, of units so large as to be beyond the capacity of the ordinary individual to accumulate in his productive years and yet large enough to attain the economies associated with scale of operation. The pressure is in this direction in commercial agriculture.

This does not necessarily mean the growth of corporate farms. The same result may be accomplished in a number of other ways. We shall see the growth of family shares of ownership of the family farm, instead of placing the family farm in an estate to be sold as a unit. The family shares will be transferable, so that one of the heirs, wishing to convert his inheritance to some other form of property, can sell his share to a third party who may be entirely outside the family. In this way, the farm unit will remain intact.

Thus, what starts off as essentially "family owned" may end up as a farm under group ownership, but still a single unit and a single operation with single management for the entire unit. Increasingly, on units of this kind, management may be provided by a professional management group standing between the individual owner and the operator of the farm and the capital will be supplied by outside agents.

This may alter the traditional entrepreneurial risk-taking function of the individual farmer. It may even move him in the direction of a quasi-riskless, semi-guaranteed wage earner. But this is not necessarily bad, per se. He may become, and frequently is, better off this way than he was before.

Commercial banks will be called on increasingly to meet the operating credit needs of these specialized, highly efficient, well-managed commercial farms. We will need to develop criteria for assessing the managerial capacity of this kind of farmer in much the same way as one analyzes the management of a commercial concern applying for credit.

Management will be far more important than collateral security behind the farm loan in the future.

There will continue to be opportunities to extend credit to part-time farmers on smaller units who also have off-the-farm jobs. This will be especially, true within commuting distance of the larger urban centers. Loans of this kind can often be treated like consumer loans with repayment schedules on an instalment basis to be paid at least partly from off-the-farm wages.

Conclusion

The logical conclusion to this analysis is that agriculture will need and use increased amounts of credit in the decade ahead. This credit will be extended increasingly to the larger, better-managed units on a basis similar to that used in extending credit to any other business institution. Managerial capacity of the operator will loom more important in loan analysis than collateral security.

The credit institutions that are progressive and can adapt their lending operations to the changing needs of the times will get the business.

A strong and progressive commercial banking system is needed by American agriculture to assist in supplying the credit our farmers must use in the decade ahead. In many ways, the commercial banking system is strategically situated to serve the increasing credit needs of agriculture. Banks are located throughout the country and are readily accessible to farmers. Informed local bankers are aware of changing agricultural credit needs in their own communities and they are in a good position to evaluate the management necessary to go with capital. Alert bankers also have the opportunity of financing businesses which, in turn, provide financing to farmers. This indirect financing has grown in importance in many areas.

Questions have been raised about whether inadequate capital may prevent banks from adequately financing agriculture. While the capital position of some banks may need strengthening, the progressive small banker is, in a sense, as large as his correspondent. Correspondent banks provide resources when required to supplement the lending facilities of rural banks. Furthermore, the rural banker can develop working relationships with an insurance company or other long-term lender and thus provide farm real estate credit in large amounts.

While federal farm lending agencies have greatly expanded their activities during the past generation, commercial banks have retained the leading place in serving short- and intermediate-term credit needs of farmers. They have achieved this by adapting credit terms, rates, and service to the requirements of these specialized borrowers. As farm units require more capital, technical knowledge, and managerial ability, commercial banks will be in position to increase the usefulness of their services to agriculture.

Commercial banks are able to offer short-term, intermediate-term, and farm real estate credit as a "one-stop" service. No other commercial institution is able to offer this complete "package" of farm credit.

Chapter 7

COMMERCIAL BANKS
AND HOUSING CREDIT

Residential mortgage lending activities at commercial banks have grown from a position of ancillary importance in the mid-1920's to a leading role in commercial bank lending operations today, largely as a result of institutional changes which have improved the quality of mortgages as investment instruments, progressive liberalization of restrictions governing commercial bank mortgage lending, and strong postwar demands for mortgage credit. This chapter provides an abbreviated discussion of the broad influences which have shaped the evolution of modern mortgage lending practices, the relative importance of commercial banks in the field of mortgage finance, and the principal factors which condition the attitudes of individual banks toward mortgage lending. Data and discussion which highlight the impact of changes in over-all credit conditions on bank mortgage lending also are presented.

In contrast with the brief historical and analytical treatment described above, the major portion of the chapter is devoted to a discussion of existing characteristics of the mortgage market, and to an appraisal of these characteristics as they relate to the capacity of the market to accommodate the growth in demand for mortgage funds which seems to lie ahead. Serious obstacles to the smooth functioning of the market are pointed out, and recommendations which would promote an improved market structure are advanced. It is stressed that structural changes in the market can be designed to permit a smooth and adequate flow of savings into the home-financing sector of the credit market in such a way as to assure the advantages accruing from a free-market allocation of funds.

Development of Mortgage Lending by Commercial Banks

During the era before the Civil War, bank financing of the purchase and construction of residential properties was quite common, but the earliest experience of banks in this type of lending tended to be unfavorable at times. The recurrence of periodic speculative excesses in real estate and construction, followed by deflation of real estate values and numerous mortgage defaults, served to inject an element of serious risk into residential mortgage lending and contributed to growth of the view that residential mortgages were undesirable as bank assets, especially in the newly settled frontier areas.

This view found reflection in the National Banking Act of 1863, which contained no authority under which national banks could engage in mortgage lending. Most state-chartered banks were permitted to make such loans, but their willingness to do so was conditioned strongly by earlier loss experiences. Nevertheless, such lending assumed significant proportions in the latter half of the nineteenth century and sentiment inevitably developed for redressing the lack of equality between national and state banks in the real estate lending field. The first step in this direction was taken with the passage of the Federal Reserve Act. This act permitted national banks to make mortgage loans on improved farm land, and in 1916 the authority was broadened to include one-year loans on urban properties. Successive liberalizations of regulations governing mortgage lending followed, and in 1927 national banks obtained authority to make residential mortgage loans up to 50 percent of a property's value, with maturities up to five years. This step promoted sharp growth in mortgage lending by banks. Between 1927 and the culmination of the boom in 1929, national banks increased their non-farm real estate loans by 45 percent.

Defaults on home mortgage loans, of which commercial banks held $2.2 billion in 1930, were common during the early 1930's, and it became clear that fundamental changes in real estate mortgage lending were essential if commercial banks and other prudent lenders were to participate in this field of lending on a large scale.

By providing for such changes, the National Housing Act of 1934 proved a landmark in the development of home mortgage lending by commercial banks as well as by other lenders. In the first place, it made available to lenders home mortgage loans that, in the event of default and foreclosure, were exchangeable for Government-guaranteed bonds or cash. Second, and more important in the long run, the act required that insured mortgages be fully amortized, so that a precedent was set for the general adoption of this basic reform in mortgage terms. With a sustained flow of amortization receipts providing a substantial degree of flexibility to lending institutions, and with the development of a secondary market for government-underwritten mortgages imparting a measure of liquidity to such loans as well, the attractiveness of home mortgages to commercial banks was greatly enhanced. Finally, FHA-insured mortgages were exempted from the restrictions as to maturity and percentage of loan to value of mortgaged property that otherwise applied to mortgage loans extended by national banks.

These changes had far-reaching implications for bank participation in home-mortgage lending, but depressed economic conditions in the latter part of the 1930's and the transition to a war economy in the early 1940's delayed their full impact. With the restoration of a prosperous peacetime economy, however, home-mortgage lending by commercial banks provided impressive testimony of the substantial shift which had occurred in bank attitudes toward mortgages as outlets for loanable funds. The volume of non-farm residential mortgage loans held by commercial banks advanced in every year after 1946, rising from $5.2 billion to $20.4 billion in 1960. During the same period, such mortgages held by commercial banks rose from 3.4 percent of bank assets to 7.9 percent, and from 15.0 percent of commercial bank time deposits to 28.5 percent. (In view of the fact that the 1946 ratios were lower than prewar levels, it is necessary to point out that the 1960 ratios also are significantly higher than those recorded in the 1930's.) These statistics underscore the extent to which mortgage lending has come to occupy a role of leading importance in bank lending and investing operations.

The expansion of bank mortgage lending has been facilitated, of course, by further relaxation of the restrictions on mortgage lending imposed in earlier periods. As a result of successive legislative amendments, national banks can acquire FHA-insured and VA-guaranteed home mortgage loans without regard to statutory restrictions on percentage of property value loans, maturity, or total amount of mortgages held. Conventional loans, i.e., those not endorsed by a government agency, if amortized by maturity, may equal 75 percent of the appraised value of a home and have a maturity up to twenty years. The total of such conventional loans held by national banks may not exceed a bank's capital and surplus or 60 percent of savings and time deposits, whichever is greater. Regulations on state-bank mortgage lending vary rather widely, but they generally are related to capital and surplus and often are more restrictive than the regulations applicable to national banks.

Commercial banks have also expanded their construction lending and short-term financing of mortgage companies since 1945, as the demand for such accommodation has soared with the sharp rise in the volume of home building and the growth of large-scale contracting and mortgage-servicing organizations that require a large volume of funds for their operations. In areas where shortages of funds to finance home ownership prevail, some commercial banks have undertaken the origination, sale, and servicing of mortgages to attract additional institutional funds into the mortgage market.

The Place of Mortgages in Bank Portfolios

Commercial banks are one of the four major mortgage lending institutions which, combined, hold four-fifths of all non-farm mortgage loans outstanding in the United States. The non-farm mortgage holdings of these institutions, the bulk of which are residential mortgages, at the end of 1960 are shown in Table 7-1.

TABLE 7-1
Non-Farm Mortgage Holdings
December 31, 1960

	(Billions)
Total	$152.9
Savings and loan associations	60.1
Life insurance companies	38.8
Commercial banks	27.2
Mutual savings banks	26.9

Source: Board of Governors of the Federal Reserve System.

Commercial banks are unique among the important sources of mortgage credit in the diversity and scope of their lending operations. Savings and loan associations were organized for the exclusive purpose of channeling savings into home mortgages. Mutual savings banks also specialize largely in mortgage lending. Life insurance companies invest the bulk of their funds in corporate obligations and in mortgages, favoring one or the other of these two outlets for their funds as relative yields indicate.

Commercial banks, by contrast, seek to serve all the credit requirements of their communities. Where a large demand exists for business, agricultural, or consumer credit, commercial banks may not feel justified in placing a large part of their resources in long-term mortgage loans that are to be amortized slowly over a long period of years unless they can attract a substantial volume of savings deposits. The credit needs of a community undergo constant variation. An institution that seeks to serve all types of credit needs, therefore, requires a large measure of flexibility in its portfolio. Mortgage loans, despite the great advantages of regular amortization and the development of some secondary market facilities, provide considerably less portfolio flexibility than other classes of loans having much shorter maturities or marketable securities.

Savings Deposits and Mortgage Lending

As noted above, a key factor affecting the amount of mortgage loans that individual commercial banks feel justified in making is the volume of savings deposits held. There are several reasons for this. First, savings deposits are quite stable in character. As a result, such funds can be placed in large part in mortgage loans without fear that heavy withdrawals will give rise to a liquidity problem. Second, and more important from the viewpoint of serving a community's credit needs, savings deposits usually show a steady rise from year to year, so that placing a substantial part of savings-deposit gains in mortgages will not prevent a bank from expanding its loans to other classes of borrowers.

Mortgage loans are attractive to banks with a large volume of savings deposits even when they give a lower net rate of return than some types of short-term lending. Banks require a stable income from most of the assets acquired with savings deposits because interest must be credited regularly on such deposits. A portfolio of long-term amortized mortgages provides such stable income whereas short- and intermediate-term loans may not. The real estate loans of all commercial banks at the end of 1960 aggregated 28.5 percent of their savings and other time deposits (Table 7-2). (It is to be recognized that a substantial portion of total time deposits represents relatively volatile corporate and government balances, which do not lend themselves to mortgage investments.)

The ratio of mortgage loans to total loans varies widely among banks, reflecting variations in both the relative importance of savings deposits and in the credit needs of individual communities. Large city banks often find that demands for commercial and consumer loans are so heavy that they limit accommodations to the real estate sector largely to interim construction financing and other loans to contractors. Such loans are, of course, highly important to residential construction. By contrast, banks in growing suburban areas may devote a large part of their loanable funds to mortgage loans, since these may well constitute the chief credit need of such communities.

At the end of 1960, real-estate loans of New York City, Chicago, reserve city and country member banks, and of nonmember banks compared as shown in Table 7-3.

The fact that savings deposits are a much larger proportion of total deposits in country and nonmember than in city member banks, and that they are far more important in reserve city banks than in New York and Chicago banks, indicates again the close relationship between mortgage lending and savings deposits discussed previously.

Bank Mortgage Lending and Credit Conditions

The volume of commercial bank mortgage lending varies with credit conditions. This variability is reflected in part by the data in Table 7-4, which show relatively large year-to-year fluctuations in the volume of net mortgage loan extensions at commercial banks and significant swings in the extent to which commercial banks participated in each year's in-

TABLE 7-2
Residential Non-Farm Mortgage Loans Held by Commercial Banks at Year-End, 1946-1960

Residential Non-Farm Mortgage Loans Held by Commercial Banks

Year	Total					Conventional			FHA-VA		
		As Percent of					As Percent of			As Percent of	
	Amount (Billions)	Total Residential Non-Farm Mortgage Debt	Total Bank Assets	Comm'l. Bank Time Deposits	Total Bank Loans and Investments	Amount (Billions)	Total Conventional Mortgage Debt	Residential Non-Farm Mortgage Debt Held By Comm'l. Banks	Amount (Billions)	Total FHA-VA Mortgage Debt	Residential Non-Farm Mortgage Debt Held By Comm'l. Banks
1946	$ 5.2	18.5%	3.4%	15.0%	4.5%	$ 2.9	13.3%	55.8%	$2.3	36.5%	44.2%
1947	6.9	20.4	4.4	19.5	5.9	3.5	14.6	50.7	3.4	34.7	49.3
1948	8.1	20.5	5.2	22.5	7.1	3.9	15.0	48.1	4.2	30.9	51.9
1949	8.7	19.4	5.4	23.8	7.2	3.9	14.0	44.8	4.8	28.7	55.2
1950	10.5	19.6	6.0	28.3	8.2	4.8	15.2	45.7	5.7	25.8	54.3
1951	11.3	18.4	6.4	29.5	8.6	5.0	14.4	44.2	6.3	23.7	55.8
1952	12.1	17.6	6.4	29.5	8.5	5.4	13.6	44.6	6.7	22.9	55.5
1953	12.9	16.7	6.8	28.8	9.0	5.9	13.1	45.7	7.0	21.8	54.3
1954	14.2	16.3	7.1	29.3	9.2	6.7	13.1	47.2	7.5	20.7	52.8
1955	15.9	15.8	7.6	31.8	10.0	7.7	13.3	48.4	8.2	19.1	51.6
1956	17.0	15.2	7.9	32.6	10.4	8.4	13.1	49.4	8.6	18.0	50.6
1957	17.2	14.2	7.8	26.9	10.2	8.7	12.5	50.6	8.5	16.5	49.4
1958	18.6	14.0	7.8	28.3	10.1	9.9	12.7	53.2	8.7	15.8	46.8
1959	20.3	13.7	8.3	30.7	10.7	11.0	12.4	54.2	9.3	15.7	45.8
1960	20.4	n.a.	7.9	28.5	10.2	11.7	n.a.	57.4	8.7	13.8	42.6

n.a. - Not available.

Source: Housing and Home Finance Agency and Board of Governors of the Federal Reserve System

TABLE 7-3
Real Estate Loans by Classes of Commercial Banks
December 31, 1960

| | Real Estate Loans | |
Class of Bank	Amount (Thousands)	As Percent of Total Loans and Investments
Member banks:		
New York City	$ 868	3.1%
Chicago	196	2.8
Reserve City	9,005	14.3
Country	12,449	18.3
Nonmember banks	6,205	18.3

Source: Board of Governors of the Federal Reserve System.

TABLE 7-4
Annual Increase in Commercial Bank Holdings of Non-Farm
Residential Mortgages as Percent of Total Increase in
Mortgages of All Holders, 1947-1959

| | Increase in Commercial Bank Mortgages | |
Year	Amount (Billions)	As Percent of Increase in Total Non-Farm Residential Mortgage Debt All Holders
1947	$1.7	30%
1948	1.2	21
1949	.6	11
1950	1.8	21
1951	.8	10
1952	.8	11
1953	.8	10
1954	1.3	13
1955	1.7	13
1956	1.1	10
1957	.2	2
1958	1.4	12
1959	1.8	12

Source: U.S. Housing and Home Finance Agency.

crease in mortgage debt. The variability in these data is directly related to the fact that commercial bank mortgage lending is affected strongly by shifts in over-all credit demands. Net redemption of public-debt securities in the late 1940's enabled commercial banks to expand mortgage as well as other loans without causing any considerable increase in total loans and investments. But in years like 1956-57, heavy demands from business and consumer borrowers tended to limit expansion of mortgage loans at some banks. Moreover, commercial banks alone among lending institutions are affected directly by Federal Reserve credit control measures. Restraining credit actions late in 1952 and early in 1953, and again in 1955-57, caused a sharp decline not only in new mortgage lending by the commercial banks but also in their share of the annual increase in residential mortgage debt. As would be expected, there is a noticeable tendency for changes in mortgage lending at commercial banks to lag somewhat behind changes in credit conditions. The 1960 decline in mortgage lending reflected credit-policy measures adopted in 1959, for example, and the sharp decline in commercial bank mortgage lending in 1957 reflected the cumulative effect of credit restraint imposed in the preceding year as well as in 1957.

Mortgage Origination and Servicing by Commercial Banks

One activity which commercial banks perform in the housing finance field—and an activity which is often overlooked—consists of loan origination rather than permanent lending. The improved liquidity of mortgages and the establishment of a national secondary market, combined with significant imbalance in the supply of mortgage credit in fast-growing areas, has led to active sale of mortgages by originating banks to other institutions. The latter have included life insurance companies, mutual savings banks and other lenders located in the northeast—where the relative amount of loanable funds is traditionally more plentiful—and FNMA, plus a scattering of pension funds, eleemosynary institutions, universities, and the like. Following the sale of the loan, the originating bank may expect to retain the servicing of the loan and combine this operation with the servicing of its own mortgage loans.

No data are available which bear directly upon the volume of bank mortgage-origination activity. However, data on the net change in bank portfolios and the volume of bank mortgage recordings indicate that the volume of mortgages sold by banks during the postwar years has increased, especially in periods of monetary restraint.

Differences of opinion exist concerning commercial bank mortgage-origination activities. Occasional sales of mortgages by banks from their permanent portfolios are obviously necessary and desirable, both as a way to replenish the supply of mortgage funds in the bank's locality and for intelligent management of a bank's investment funds. In certain areas, however, mortgage banking facilities have not been adequate, and local banks sometimes have taken the lead in tapping outside sources of funds by originating mortgages for sale in the secondary market to meet fast-growing demands for housing credit in their areas.

Some have argued that banks, especially large ones with branches in smaller communities, can most efficiently perform the origination and servicing function due to their experience with mortgage lending and servicing, their correspondent relations in other areas, and their easy and knowledgeable access to national money markets and secondary mortgage markets. Others take the position that banks are lenders, not brokers, and question whether they should actively seek to build up an origination and servicing business simply for its own sake. The brokerage function is an important one and, if done properly, requires specialized skills and personnel. Mortgage companies specialize in this function and so have the advantages of specialization where they compete with commercial banks, as do all specialized financial institutions. Commercial banks possess the advantages of multipurpose financial institutions, but many make extensive use of the services of mortgage companies when they wish to dispose of mortgages to nonbank lenders or acquire mortgages from them. It is safe to conclude that mortgage companies will hold a major place in mortgage origination and servicing. However, with its other financing services to builders and its flexible staff and equipment for servicing, a bank can compete for mortgage origination and servicing on an equal basis with specialists by providing the requisite facilities and personnel.

The Future of Mortgage Credit

All indications point to the probability that the United States economy will experience substantial growth and expansion during most of the 1960's and 1970's. During the decade of the 1960's gross national product is expected to increase by almost 50 percent, population is expected to increase by approximately 35 million, and the number of families is expected to grow by about 11 million. An endless array of such statistics could be cited, all pointing in the direction of favorable growth in economic aggregates generally and, more specifically, in the direction of larger housing requirements and increased mortgage credit demands.

The real problem is how this demand can be satisfied most effectively. Meeting the greater expected demand for housing will depend in large measure upon our ability to produce and our ability and willingness to save. Even within the framework of an adequate supply of savings, however, there exists the problem of allocating savings and credit among the various credit-using sectors of the economy. Consequently, if we are to assure an adequate flow of credit into the mortgage sector, it is extremely important that the instruments of mortgage credit be as attractive as other credit instruments if they are to compete for the available supply of loanable funds.

It is difficult to say how much of the total available supply of credit *should* be used for residential mortgages. It is fairly obvious, however, that if the supply of private mortgage credit is "insufficient" in the light of either social or economic considerations, then public policy is likely to be used for diverting funds to the mortgage market. Since the excessive use of public policy to divert funds into special sectors of the economy may introduce distortions and rigidities which interfere with the viability of the over-all economy, however, it is of the utmost importance that the market mechanism be made to function effectively in the field of housing. In other words, the mortgage as an instrument of credit—both in the primary market and in secondary markets—must be made so effective that it can compete on an equal footing with other credit instruments for the available supply of funds.

Insofar as adequate housing credit for the 1960's is concerned, therefore, two issues are raised. Will the total supply of savings be adequate? And will the share of savings going to those financial institutions which supply the main stream of mortgage credit be adequate? As to the first, the total supply of savings will depend to a large extent upon our success in maintaining stable economic growth, in controlling inflation, and in avoiding excessive unemployment.

The answer to the second question, relating to the adequacy of the flow of funds into mortgage-lending institutions, is likely to depend upon how effectively we deal with changes in methods of savings and investment which already have become obvious and are likely to become more important. One of the most significant of these changes is the increasing extent to which savings are tending to flow into new types of savings pools which have not been tapped effectively by the mortgage market. Included within this category are pension funds, mutual funds, social security payments, and other outlets for savings funds. If we are to assure that the savings accumulated in these pools are free to move into mortgage credit in response to greater housing demand, a number of problems in the primary and secondary market for mortgages must be overcome. This becomes apparent upon an examination of the structure of the mortgage market.

The Structure of the Mortgage Market. The mortgage market, one of the more complex components of the capital market, is burdened with a number of imperfections. The chief participants in the market are savings and loan associations, insurance companies, commercial banks, and savings banks. To these may be added individual investors and mortgage companies, which also play a significant role in the market's functioning. There is, however, little uniformity in the operations of the different types of financial institutions, reflecting largely significant differences in structure, state and federal laws, experience, and development. Historically, as noted earlier, savings and loan associations have invested a large share of the savings which they hold in residential mortgages. Having been organized specifically for this purpose, this is not surprising. Savings and loan associations invest in all types of mortgage loans, but they have shown little interest in government-endorsed mortgages. This is due largely to the fact that they have been anxious to earn as high a yield as possible, a consideration which has compelled them to place heavy emphasis on conventional mortgages. Savings and loan associations are restricted by law to originating mortgages on properties located within a narrow range of their home office. Thus they have not played a direct role in transferring funds from capital-surplus areas to capital-scarce areas.

Insurance companies, in contrast, operate on a national basis, and have therefore become important in originating mortgages on a nationwide basis. Although many smaller companies confine their mortgage lending to a regional basis, larger companies are of strategic importance in channeling funds from capital-surplus to capital-scarce sections of the nation. Savings banks are essentially long-term investors in mortgage credit. They presently are prevented by law from buying and selling conventional mortgages on a nationwide basis, but they are important traders in government-endorsed mortgages. Mortgage companies have become prominent in the field of mortgage credit mainly since the end of World War II. Their chief function is to serve as a middleman between short-term and long-term investors and, frequently, to service mortgages.

Because of the different characteristics of its major participants, the mortgage market itself is characterized by a lack of uniformity in investment practices and, more important, by seriously inadequate facilities for secondary trading in outstanding mortgages. The absence of a broad secondary market has contributed to an uneven flow of mortgage funds, a development which some observers (including The American Bankers Association) regard as a major problem in mortgage finance. Moreover, the absence of a strong secondary market for conventional mortgages also renders mortgages less liquid (in the sense of being less marketable) than they otherwise would be.

Problems of the Primary Mortgage Market

The development of a properly functioning secondary mortgage market, it seems clear, is a prerequisite for assuring adequacy of mortgage funds in the future. Commercial banks are not alone in seeking marketability and liquidity in their investments. It is clear that such new pools of savings as pension funds can be more effectively tapped for mortgage funds if the mortgage is made a simpler and more marketable credit instrument.

Ideally, an effective secondary market requires uniformity in the primary mortgage market. At present, however, the mortgage market lacks uniformity and is highly compartmentalized. Specifically, the smooth functioning of the market is impeded by the following characteristics: (1) interest-rate rigidities in government-endorsed mortgages; (2) the personal and highly local element of the conventional mortgage; (3) considerable variations in the terms of lending among the various financial institutions; (4) considerable differences in the investment latitude granted the various lenders; and (5) variations in state laws regarding mortgage credit, of which the foreclosure procedure is only one example.

Unlike other important long-term credit instruments, the mortgage is a highly differentiated and personal credit instrument. This is especially true of the conventional mortgage. Government endorsement in the form of insurance and guarantees gives mortgages a far more impersonal status. The conventional mortgage, thus handicapped, cannot easily be traded on a secondary market. Every conventional mortgage differs from every other conventional mortgage as to borrower, property collateral, and the policies and practices of the lenders. As a result, differences in state laws governing such matters have made it more difficult for the natural development of a secondary market to occur. It is likely, however, that certain basic changes in the marketability of the conventional mortgage can be accomplished, in which case many of the laws which now serve as obstacles to the mortgage market will gradually disappear. Such was the case with the FHA mortgage which, partially as a result of being made impersonal, was granted exemption from the many obstacles to which the conventional mortgage remains subject.

Some of the laws which serve as obstacles to the mortgage market, and to the supply of mortgage credit in general, discriminate as to the different types of financial institutions. There appears to be little logic in these existing discriminatory laws. Loan-to-value ratios, maturities, and savings-to-mortgage ratios vary greatly in both federal and state laws applicable to the different types of lenders. In many instances, such laws reflect the absence of a properly-functioning secondary mortgage market. It is fairly clear, however, that the elimination of these obstacles must await the development of a complete program which would remove the basis for their existence.

In addition to the existing discrimination in laws applying to different lenders, there is another factor which serves as an obstacle to the marketability of mortgages. Foreclosure procedures vary from three weeks to over two years in the different states, and costs may exceed $1,000. The lender, of course, has to maintain the property in a saleable condition, and the differences in foreclosure terms have caused many lenders to discriminate against mortgages originated in certain states. In many states a mortgagor may redeem a foreclosed property within a stated period which may be as long as two years; although such redemption rights are rarely exercised, their existence is of importance to the mortgagee. For example, the lender is not reimbursed by FHA until the property in question is no longer subject to redemption privileges.

Another factor of importance to the mortgagee, and one which serves as an obstacle in the primary mortgage market, is the fact that mortgage lenders often are taxed—in the form of income, franchise, or capital stock taxes—for "doing business" in a particular state although they may be located elsewhere. In a number of states such taxes have kept many mortgagees from doing business there.

When it is considered that the majority of the nation's commercial banks are quite small, it is not surprising that the obstacles and complexities characteristic of the mortgage market have served to keep many banks less active in mortgage lending than would otherwise be the case.

Problems of the Secondary Mortgage Market

The secondary mortgage market is very thin, if we exclude transactions based on firm commitments and transactions in which the originator warehouses the mortgage for a permanent investor. Secondary mortgage activity in government-endorsed mortgages amounts to less than 2 percent a year of the total of outstanding mortgages, and such activity in conventionals is much less than 1 percent. The reasons for the thinness in the true secondary market for residential mortgages were analyzed in the previous section. It was shown that the conventional mortgage is too personal an instrument of credit for widespread national marketability. In addition, there are legal barriers which serve as obstacles to certain institutional investors in absorbing mortgages originating outside of a relatively small geographic region.

Apart from the advantages imparted by government backing, one important reason for the higher rate of activity for government-endorsed mortgages is the existence of Fanny Mae. In 1955, for example, when secondary market activity in FHA and VA mortgages totaled perhaps $800 million, Fanny Mae bought $411 million and sold $62 million. In 1957, when the mortgage market was much tighter, Fanny Mae bought $1,096 million and sold only $3 million. In 1958, when mortgage funds were more abundant, Fanny Mae bought $623 million and sold $482 million.

The lack of marketability of conventional mortgages and the interest-rate rigidity of government-endorsed mortgages reduces the competitiveness of potential investors. Among the investors which largely refrain from investing in mortgages, especially conventional mortgages, are pension funds. These funds are experiencing rapid growth and, in recent years, have devoted an increasing portion of their funds to mortgage investments. Nevertheless, the relative importance of their mortgage holdings remains small, and steps which would stimulate pension fund participation in the mortgage market appear to be desirable.

The creation of a well-organized secondary mortgage market would place the mortgage on a level of equality with other important instruments of credit. In summary, such a market could offer numerous advantages.

First, it would tap potential mortgage funds which at present do not flow into mortgages for reasons which are technical and can be corrected. Such a market could permit the development of mortgage-backed instruments of credit, for example, which would appeal to pension-fund trustees and other investors unwilling to tackle the problem of administering a residential-mortgage portfolio. A strong secondary market in conventional mortgages would in time appeal to investors who find cyclical variations in the supply of VA and FHA mortgages an investment handicap. It is also quite likely that the investment preferences of such institutional investors as life insurance companies would be influenced by improvements in the residential-mortgage market. In particular, life insurance companies might find mortgage-based securities attractive at such times when they shift investment emphasis from mortgages to other types of obligations.

Second, it would increase the mobility of mortgage capital between capital-scarce and capital-surplus areas. This is a fundamental requirement of a properly working capital market.

Third, a poor market mechanism adds to the costs of lending by increasing charges for risk and administrative operations. An effective mortgage market would lower costs.

Fourth, by increasing the liquidity of the mortgage, an effective secondary market would contribute flexibility to portfolio adjustments.

Fifth, national marketability of conventional mortgages, together with active trading in these mortgages by a trading institution, could help assure that the flow of funds into the mortgage market would not be too severely restricted by artificial barriers during periods of rising interest rates, and also could help communicate the effects of credit ease more quickly to the mortgage markets and the construction industry during periods of declining economic activity. While there is no desire to shelter the mortgage market from the impact of credit restraint, there are sound reasons for believing that interest-rate rigidities on government-backed mortgages now operate as a handicap to the mortgage market in competing for funds during periods of high interest rates. With government-backed mortgages having fixed rates, a rise in market rates during periods of economic expansion drives such mortgages to a discount; and, with some lenders reluctant to invest in deep-discount mortgages, borrowers often have been forced to secure loans on a conventional basis or not at all. Lending terms on conventional mortgages, however, are less favorable than on government-backed mortgages. Thus, this shift to conventional mortgages has the effect of reducing demand for housing. In addition, rising market rates sometimes narrow the gap between more marketable debt instruments and conventional mortgages (because of the lag in mortgage rates) to a point where the necessary allowance for mortgages servicing and administration costs (about two-thirds of 1 percent) disappears. Consequently, investors who are permitted by law to invest in corporate securities and other high-quality investments with fixed maturities have tended to shift funds out of mortgages.

By permitting the liberalization of terms on conventional mortgages, the establishment of institutions to guarantee and undertake secondary trading in these mortgages would tend to render residential construction activity less vulnerable to shifts from government-backed mortgage financing to conventional financing. It must be re-emphasized that such a cushioning influence would not be designed to isolate mortgage credit from the impact of monetary policy, but would merely help overcome existing artificial barriers to the effective functioning of the market mechanism in the area of housing credit.

As noted earlier, the establishment of an active secondary market for conventional mortgages also would contribute to more prompt easing in mortgage credit during periods of economic decline. In such periods, mortgage lending rates tend to lag somewhat behind other market rates in their downward movement. In view of this pattern, a secondary market organization which financed its mortgage purchases with the proceeds of debentures and other marketable issues would experience the development of a more profitable spread between rates on its debentures and mortgage lending rates. Under such circumstances, a secondary market organization probably would be able to step up its purchases of mortgages more quickly than most other institutional investors. A quicker diffusion of money market ease throughout credit markets could therefore be encouraged, and a faster transmission of ease to the residential mortgage market.

As indicated earlier, it seems likely that an effective secondary market would help liberalize mortgage lending terms. That factor, as well as the issuance of mortgage-backed debentures by a trading organization, probably would enable housing to claim funds which otherwise might not have been available to it. It should be borne in mind, however, that such a change in the allocation of resources would result from an improved market organization—not from subsidies or other artificial means. It should also be remembered that if the supply of housing funds is to remain adequate and in private hands, the structural changes in our savings pattern which have occurred must be met with the best possible *free* market organization in mortgage credit.

Private Enterprise and the Proper Role of Government in the Mortgage Market

Unquestionably the federal government has contributed much since the 1930's to strengthening the mortgage as an instrument of credit. There is no question, either, that many of the innovations introduced in the 1930's by the federal government have rightfully come to have a permanent place in our economy. Examples of these are the Housing and

Home Finance Agency, with its subordinate agencies such as FHA and Fanny Mae, and independent agencies such as the Federal Home Loan Bank System. In the 1930's the private mortgage market was so weakened that intervention by the federal government became inevitable. HOLC was established for the purpose of purchasing mortgages, often poor ones, from lenders who could not hold them in their own portfolio. Many basically good mortgages were saved in this way, and the mortgage market was given much-needed support.

The conventional mortgage, which suffered greatly from this experience insofar as acceptability was concerned, had to be supplemented by another kind of mortgage if housing was to be financed adequately. The upsurge in home ownership among middle- and low-income families undoubtedly received strong impetus from the revisions in mortgage-lending practices which were initiated in the 1930's.

There is no question but that government housing policies and programs inaugurated during the 1930's subsequently have been used, and to an increasing extent, to carry out narrowly defined welfare functions in the field of housing and mortgage finance. The insurance of mortgages at preferential rates for certain types of housing provides only one illustration of this tendency. Without touching on the merits of such programs, one may note that important distinctions need to be made between that sector of housing and mortgage finance which can stand on its own feet and that much smaller sector which, it is argued, could not be financed adequately without special government support. Unless this distinction is made, government subsidies and assistance are likely to be extended to areas of housing where they are not needed—leading to inefficiencies and interfering with national programs both in mortgage finance and in housing. A second important consideration is that those sectors of housing which presumably need and deserve government support most likely would encounter more serious opposition if, through the indiscriminate application of subsidies and support, assistance is extended to areas where it is not really needed.

Measures designed to make the conventional mortgage as liquid and as marketable as the government-endorsed mortgage would constitute direct recognition of the distinction noted above. This could be accomplished if the principles and practices upon which the FHA and Fanny Mae were founded were applied to the conventional mortgage. With adequate capitalization, good management and proper supervision, privately-owned and publicly-supervised counterparts to FHA and Fanny Mae could be created. Considerable attention now is being given to such a plan, which gives explicit recognition to the distinction which needs to be drawn between areas where private enterprise can operate effectively in a free-market environment and areas where direct government intervention is deemed to be in the public interest.

Chapter 8

COMMERCIAL BANK FINANCING
OF SECURITY MARKETS

The Role of Credit in the Security Markets

The security markets perform a number of vital functions in the conduct of the economy. They are an essential link in the savings-investment process by which a large proportion of personal savings is invested in corporate and Government securities either directly or through savings institutions. They are a very important source of liquidity, enabling financial institutions, corporations, and individuals to obtain cash when required through sales in the open market of securities they own. New security offerings are the main source of borrowed funds to governments and a major source of capital to business.

Ready access to credit is essential to the functioning of the security markets. Credit is required for:

1) *Financing the underwriting and distribution of new offerings of securities.* Security issues are of relatively large size in relation to the capital funds of underwriters and dealers, so that investment houses must rely upon borrowing to clear transactions and to finance inventory.

2) *Financing dealer inventories of outstanding securities.* The making of markets in outstanding bonds and unlisted stocks, and the conduct of the business of specialists and odd-lot dealers on exchanges, involve the carrying of fluctuating and at times relatively large inventories of securities. Security dealers can carry such inventories only if they are able to borrow freely for shorter or longer periods as funds are required for this purpose.

3) *Financing security purchases by individuals.* The liquidity of the security markets is dependent in large measure upon the ability of would-be buyers to obtain credit to help finance their purchases of securities. The quality of marketability, vital to buyers and holders of securities, requires a broad market with many potential buyers. The breadth of the market is greatly expanded when purchases can be made with borrowed funds as well as for cash.

The term "security loan" can be defined narrowly to include loans for the purpose of purchasing or carrying securities or, more broadly, all loans collateralized by stocks and bonds regardless of their purpose. It does not cover loans on other collateral whose real purpose, unknown to the lending bank, is to buy or hold securities.

Loans secured by stock or bond collateral may be made for a wide variety of other purposes as well as for purchasing or carrying securities. The pledge of securities as collateral gives added protection to the lender, so that borrowing is facilitated and relatively better terms are obtainable by the borrower.

In recent years, the Federal Reserve statistics on security loans have been confined to loans for the purpose of purchasing or carrying securities. The regulation of security credit under the Securities Act of 1934 applies only to loans made for this purpose, and published statistics of security credit now include only such loans. Unsecured loans also may be incurred for purchasing or carrying securities, but the great bulk of the loans made for this purpose are secured by stocks and bonds as collateral.

Loans to purchase or carry securities are commonly referred to as "purpose loans," while security collateral loans, the proceeds of which are used for other purposes, are described as "nonpurpose loans."

Security loans as a class differ from other major types of lending because the largest part of such advances are payable on demand, although in fact they are infrequently called. Long before the money desk on the New York Stock Exchange was abolished in 1946, the call-money market in New York City had disappeared. The New York banks have for years financed their "street" customers in much the same manner as their commercial customers have been accommodated.

"Street loans" have a high credit standing because of the excellent solvency record of "street" borrowers as well as because they are secured by marketable collateral.

Security Lending by Commercial Banks

The typical security loan is secured by readily marketable collateral, and the lender can call for additional collateral whenever the market value of bonds or stocks pledged as collateral falls below the specified ratio to the amount loaned. Failure to furnish additional collateral or to reduce the loan gives the lender the right to sell collateral to reduce or pay off the loan, with any excess realized over the amount due the lenders being payable to the borrower.

History of Bank Security Lending

Because of these characteristics of call loans on securities to brokers and dealers, they became a chief source of liquidity for the commercial banking system of the United States in the nineteenth and early twentieth centuries.

New York City banks in particular, holding balances of other banks throughout the country that could be withdrawn at any time, found call loans on securities very suitable for their needs in view of the scarcity of other liquidity media at the time. However, the necessity for large-scale calling in of security loans on occasions of very heavy withdrawals of funds from New York banks by other institutions, and the forced selling of pledged securities that resulted, produced several "money panics" during the century before 1913. These experiences were one reason for the concentration of bank reserves in the Federal Reserve banks under the Federal Reserve Act.

Following the establishment of the Federal Reserve System, the importance of call loans on securities as a source of liquidity for the commercial banking system was very greatly curtailed. Nevertheless, the strong demand for such loans that developed during the 1920's, with the great expansion of activity in financial markets in those years, caused an expansion of security lending to unprecedented levels. At the peak of the stock market boom, however, banks held down the volume of their security loans, while the readiness of borrowers to pay high rates of interest brought a flood of offerings of funds "for the account of others" into the stock market to satisfy demands for such loans.

In recent years security loans have become a much smaller proportion of total loans of commercial banks because of a decline in demand for such credit. Margin regulation under the Securities Exchange Act of 1934 has limited the demand for credit for purchasing or carrying securities. Private placements of security issues with insurance companies have reduced the volume of financing of new public offerings of bonds that would otherwise have been required. In the Government security market large corporations have provided funds through repurchase agreements, reducing the need of dealers to borrow from banks. Foreign bank agencies have also become substantial sources of security credit, particularly as large dollar deposits have been shifted to Canadian and Swiss banks because those institutions have offered higher rates on time deposits than New York banks were allowed to pay under interest rate ceilings imposed by the Board of Governors of the Federal Reserve System.[1]

From the commercial banks' viewpoint, the relatively stable demand for security loans in the post-World War II period, which has been in marked contrast with the rapid expansion of other credit demands, has

---

[1] Foreign bank agencies favor security loans as an outlet for dollar time deposits received by their parent institutions because of the relative ease with which such loans can be made, as well as their high quality and liquidity. A net effect of the shift of time deposits to foreign banks because of the interest rate ceiling has thus been to channel additional funds from meeting other credit needs into security loans.

been a favorable development in several respects Business loans are regarded as a more desirable earning asset because of the larger compensating balances and other types of business they usually provide for banks. Consumer loans give a higher rate of return. The limited demand for security credit has enabled banks to expand business and consumer loans to a greater extent than might have been the case if larger borrowing needs and higher rates on security credit had attracted a larger volume of funds into such loans. The very wide fluctuations in the volume of security loans in the past, with rapid expansion in boom periods and sharp contraction in recessions, gave rise to problems for bank managements and added to instability of bank earnings.

Short-term U.S. Government security issues have replaced security loans as the chief liquidity medium of commercial banks. The ample supply of these issues available, their nonrisk asset status, and ability to use them as collateral for advances from the Federal Reserve Bank enhance their attractiveness for this purpose as compared with call loans on securities.

While the relative importance of security loans to the commercial banking system has thus declined greatly as compared with earlier periods of banking history, commercial banks remain the most important source of credit for the security markets. At times other lenders, such as foreign bank agencies in New York, account for a substantial part of the total volume of security credit extended. However, other lenders provide funds only at times when it is to their advantage to do so, whereas the commercial banks constitute the assured, continuous source of credit for the security markets.

The importance of commercial banks to the orderly financing of the security markets is far greater, therefore, than statistics on the volume of such loans or the proportion of bank lending to total security credit outstanding at any one date would indicate.

Security loans in the narrower sense of the term comprising advances for the purpose of purchasing or carrying securities, are made for four main purposes: (1) To clear the underwriting and distribution of public offerings of securities. (2) To finance inventories of dealers who make markets in outstanding securities, primarily bonds and over-the-counter stocks. (3) To finance stock exchange firms that carry margin accounts for customers. (4) To help finance directly purchases of securities by individual investors or speculators.

In addition, as was mentioned earlier, loans on security collateral may be made for purposes other than purchasing or carrying securities.

Financing Underwriting

The underwriting and distribution of new offerings by security dealers is made possible only by the readiness of large commercial banks in financial centers to advance a high percentage of the value of such offerings between the date the issuer is paid and the date investors make payment for the new securities.

The capital of security dealers is of moderate size in relation to the underwriting commitments they undertake. Hence, billions of dollars of new tax-exempt and corporate securities can be underwritten and distributed each year only because the commercial banks that specialize in such lending stand ready to advance a very high percentage of the value of the securities to clear them pending distribution.

If a new issue is oversubscribed, the dealers in the underwriting and selling groups can quickly repay their borrowings. But if the issue is "sticky," the dealer may want to bank his participation until he can dispose of it.

These factors make loans to finance the underwriting and distribution of security issues a highly volatile form of credit. The volume of new security flotations, the trend of prices and the attitude of investors affect the magnitude of the demand for such credit and the period for which loans will be outstanding. The commercial banks specializing in such lending, by standing ready at all times to finance a volume of new issues equal to a number of times the underwriter's net worth, perform as essential a part in the underwriting process as the security dealers themselves.

Financing Dealer Inventories

The making of effective markets for outstanding bonds and for over-the-counter stocks requires dealers in these securities to carry substantial inventories. Only because of the ability of dealers to take positions in these securities can they absorb offerings and satisfy bids readily.

By far the largest volume of credit to carry inventories is required by dealers in U.S. Government securities because of the magnitude of trading in Treasury obligations. While commercial banks are the mainstay of the supply of credit for Government security dealers, as of other security dealers, other lenders find this market so attractive at times as to provide the larger part of the credit required to carry Government securities both for dealers and for others. However, these nonbank sources of such credit may and do withdraw from the market from time to time, and at such times dealers have to shift their borrowings to commercial banks. In fact, one reason why nonbank sources are used so freely for such borrowing is the knowledge that commercial banks stand ready to provide credit when wanted. The two major nonbank credit sources are foreign bank agencies and corporations seeking liquid investments for their excess cash holdings. Much of the credit used to carry U.S. Government securities takes the form of a sale of the securities to these lenders under repurchase agreements.

While dealer inventories in outstanding securities do not undergo as wide and erratic fluctuations as does the volume of new security offerings, they do vary a good deal with the trend of prices and the volume of trading. In the market for state and local obligations, for example, dealers offer the securities carried in their inventory for sale through a Blue List of Current Municipal Offerings that is published daily. Since the offerings in the Blue List have frequently exceeded $300 million, it is apparent that municipal bond dealers' borrowings can average a quarter of a billion dollars or more to carry total inventories, including issues that may not be advertised in the Blue List.

Financing Stock Exchange Firms

Member firms of the New York Stock Exchange carrying margin accounts rely upon bank loans for the larger part of the funds they require to finance the debit balances of customers. Credit balances maintained by other customers, of course, reduce the amounts that need to be borrowed from banks.

On June 30, 1960, member firms carrying margin accounts reported total bank borrowings of $2,279 million. Of this total, banks in New York City advanced $1,157 million or almost 51 percent, while U.S. agencies of foreign banks advanced $806 million and U.S. banks outside New York City advanced $316 million.[2]

Dealer vs. Broker Loans

Statistics of bank loans for purchasing and carrying securities to brokers and dealers, as published, comprise both loans made to a dealer on securities belonging to him and loans made to a broker on customers' securities to finance margin accounts. Neither the weekly statistics on such loans published by the Federal Reserve for reporting member banks in leading cities nor the monthly report of borrowings by members of the New York Stock Exchange distinguish between dealer and broker borrowings. This could lead to misleading interpretations of fluctuations in the reported volume of loans to brokers and dealers outstanding.

Thus, a major increase or decrease reported in loans to brokers and dealers may be interpreted as evidence of increased or decreased public speculation in securities with borrowed money, whereas it may be caused by extension or repayment of one-day loans to clear large stock or bond issues.

Statistics of loans for purchasing and carrying securities to brokers and dealers do not show the specific purposes for which such loans are made, and so can lead to mistaken conclusions as to what a given change in the volume of such credit signifies.

---

[2] *Federal Reserve Bulletin* (September 1960), p. 1069.

Financing Individual Security Purchases

Commercial banks make loans for the purchase or carrying of securities to others than brokers and dealers. A large proportion of such loans is made for carrying bonds and unlisted stocks. Bank lending on securities to individuals supplements rather than competes with the facilities provided by stock exchange firms through their margin accounts, which are used chiefly to carry listed stocks. Stock exchange members may not carry unlisted securities on margin.

Net debit balances due New York stock exchange firms by their customers on June 30, 1960, aggregated $3,185 million. For all commercial banks, loans for purchasing or carrying securities made to others than brokers or dealers on June 15, 1960 aggregated $1,739 million. "Purpose" loans by all banks to others than brokers and dealers were thus only a little over half the net debit balances due stock exchange firms by their margin account customers on that date.

Volume of Security Loans

Loans for purchasing or carrying securities by all commercial banks in the United States aggregated $5,117 million on December 31, 1960, or 4.2 percent of all bank loans outstanding. Security credit thus makes its several major contributions to the economy while absorbing but a small percentage of the lending resources of the commercial banking system. This is made possible by the fact that this moderate amount of bank credit facilitates the functioning of the security markets, through which a large part of the savings of the American people is channeled into long-term investment.

Nonpurpose Loans

Statistics are not published regularly on the volume of bank loans made for purposes other than purchasing and carrying securities but secured by the pledge of stocks and bonds as collateral. A survey made by the Board of Governors of the Federal Reserve System showed that on October 5, 1955, a total of $1,349 million or 8.6 percent of the dollar amount of all secured business loans and 4.4 percent of all business loans of member banks had stocks and bonds pledged as security.[3] Since there has always been a substantial volume of borrowing on securities for business purposes, particularly by concerns that seek to borrow for expansion sums in excess of their unsecured lines of credit, the small proportion of loans for business purposes that is secured by stocks and bonds is significant. These data do not indicate that margin regulation has

---

[3] "Security Pledged on Business Loans at Member Banks," *Federal Reserve Bulletin* (September 1959), pp. 1114-1129.

given rise to a substantial volume of "nonpurpose" security loans from banks to provide funds that are in effect utilized to purchase or carry securities.

Regulation of Security Credit

Selective control over security credit through margin regulation by the Board of Governors of the Federal Reserve System was enacted into law as an aftermath of the great expansion of such loans in the late 1920's and their drastic deflation in the early 1930's. That expansion and contraction of security credit contributed materially to instability both of the security markets and of the economy was the conclusion of Congressional inquiries in the early 1930's.

The Federal Reserve authorities had adopted a restrictive credit policy in 1928 and 1929 to check the speculative boom, and particularly the rapid growth of security loans, at that time. Nevertheless, security credit continued to expand during those years as borrowers paid high rates of interest to obtain additional collateral loans. The arguments that the volume of such loans had proved unresponsive to a restrictive credit policy and that the continued rapid expansion of security credit had lessened the effectiveness of over-all quantitative credit control were key reasons for the adoption of selective security loan control in the Securities Exchange Act of 1934.

Regulation of security loans, its advocates maintained, was required to safeguard the stability of the economy. An expansion of security loans stimulates economic activity as does any increase in the use of credit, since the funds borrowed by security buyers are transferred to sellers of securities, and when spent by the latter are added to the stream of business and consumer spending. However, when security loans are increased on a large scale, the supply of funds for other types of borrowing may be contracted, particularly if a restrictive credit policy is being pursued by the Federal Reserve authorities. Moreover, in the event of a major decline of security prices such as occurred in the early 1930's, large-scale forced liquidation of security loans exerts a depressing effect upon the whole economy as funds are diverted from spending to repayments of security loans.

The lack of responsiveness of security credit to Federal Reserve policy in 1928-29 was not due to any lack of cooperation of commercial banks with the expressed objectives of Federal Reserve policy, however. The opposite was the case, as Table 8-1 shows.

It can be seen from the Table that New York City banks reduced lending to brokers in 1928 and 1929. And since an estimated one-half of the loans to brokers made for the account of out-of-town banks in 1929 were actually for the account of their nonbank customers, it is evi-

TABLE 8-1
Brokers' Loans By and Through Reporting Member Banks
in New York City
Selected Dates 1928-1929

(Millions)

Date	Total	For Own Account	For Account of Out-of-Town Banks	For Account of Others
Jan. 25, 1928	$3,788	$1,275	$1,472	$1,041
Jan. 30, 1929	5,559	1,091	1,853	2,615
Oct. 2, 1929	6,804	1,071	1,826	3,907

Source: Board of Govenors of the Federal Reserve System.

dent that commercial banks cooperated fully with the expressed wishes of the Federal Reserve authorities to limit lending to brokers at that time. However, the eagerness of the public to buy securities on credit in 1928 and 1929, and its willingness to pay high rates of interest for such credit, attracted a flood of funds from nonbank lenders which made overall credit restriction ineffective so far as security loans were concerned.

When the boom came to an end, these "other" lenders called in their loans on a large scale. The commercial banks were called upon to expand their brokers' loans to replace funds that had been loaned by outside lenders to avoid a "money panic" that would have added to an already severely strained financial situation.

The high quality and liquidity of security loans at the time explain why nonbank funds could be attracted in very large volume for such lending, with borrowers willing to pay quite high interest rates. In 1929, the renewal rate on the New York Stock Exchange rose as high as 12 percent, and the new loan rate to 20 percent. These rates of interest attracted corporate, foreign, and individual lenders into this market in large numbers.

The Banking Act of 1933 gave added powers to the Federal Reserve authorities to control bank lending on securities by giving the Board authority to limit the percentage of a member bank's capital and surplus that may be loaned on security collateral, and to suspend rediscounting privileges of member banks that increase their security loans to an extent deemed excessive. These powers were never used, however, as Congress adopted a radically different approach to selective control over security lending with the enactment of the Securities Exchange Act of 1934. Since nonbank rather than bank lenders were chiefly responsible for the great expansion of such credit in the late 1920's, it was concluded that regulation, to be effective, would have to be directed to the *demand* for security credit from all sources, rather than to the *supply* of such credit from commercial banks as was done in the Banking Act of 1933. The Securities

Exchange Act of 1934 regulates the demand for security loans by limiting the amounts that may be borrowed to purchase or carry securities.

The Banking Act of 1933 did halt security lending for the account of others by making it unlawful for member banks to act as agents of non-banking lenders in placing security collateral loans to brokers and dealers. The New York Clearing House had already barred its members from handling such loans in 1931.

Regulation Under the Securities Exchange Act

The emphasis in security credit regulation under the Securities Act of 1934 has been placed on restriction of demand for credit to finance margin trading. Care has been taken to minimize interference with credit extensions for underwriting new security offerings and for financing the operations of dealers and brokers, as well as the making of security collateral loans for purposes other than purchasing or carrying securities.

Selective control of security credit by the Board of Governors of the Federal Reserve System is authorized by Sections 7 and 8 of the Securities Exchange Act of 1934. Section 7 states that such regulation is "for the purpose of preventing the excessive use of credit for the purchase or carrying of securities."

The provisions of the statute apply specifically to extensions of credit by brokers or dealers, but the Federal Reserve Board is also authorized to issue rules and regulations applicable to other lenders "for the purpose of purchasing or carrying any security registered on a national securities exchange." It is under this provision of the law that the Board of Governors issued its Regulation U, which first became effective May 1, 1936. This regulation specifies minimum margin requirements for bank loans to customers to purchase or carry listed stocks, so that margin requirements on listed equities have been the same whether such credit is extended to customers by brokers and dealers or by banks.

The statute specifies that regulation of margins on bank security loans shall apply only to loans on equity securities registered on national exchanges. It does not apply to bank loans on other securities, or to loans "to a dealer to aid in the financing of the distribution of securities to customers not through the medium of a national securities exchange." Regulation U excepts bank loans to brokers or dealers collateralized by securities carried for the account of customers. This permits stock exchange member firms carrying margin accounts to borrow from banks by pledging a smaller amount of securities than customers must maintain in their margin accounts, thus permitting brokers to retain securities for making transfers and deliveries and as collateral for additional borrowing when needed in their business.

It is thus apparent that margin regulations affect directly only bank loans secured by stocks and made to customers for the purpose of purchasing or carrying listed stocks. Specific exemptions are made for loans to assist in the distribution of new security issues, for financing dealers trading in bonds and unlisted stocks, and for financing brokers who in turn are extending credit on margin to their customers.

It is due to the flexibility thus provided in the law and Regulation U that selective security credit control has interfered much less with the banks' functions in facilitating security underwriting and trading than was feared when margin regulation was first proposed.

Experience with Margin Regulation

Minimum margin requirements have been changed a number of times by the Board of Governors of the Federal Reserve System under Regulation U. Between November 1937 and February 1945 they were as low as 40 percent. They were as high as 100 percent in 1946, and were held at 90 percent between October 1958 and July 1960. In its annual reports, the Board of Governors of the Federal Reserve System, identifying the criteria it uses in determining what constitutes "excessive use of credit for the purchase or carrying of securities," has cited: (1) the volume of security credit outstanding; (2) the volume of speculative activity; (3) the price action of the stock market; and (4) general economic and credit conditions.

During the period since 1934 when margin regulation has been effective, there has been no repetition of the large-scale expansion of security credit that occurred in the later 1920's, although stock prices advanced during the 1950's at a rate comparable to that of the 1920's. The relative stability of the volume of security loans at a level far below that of the late 1920's contrasts with the rapid rise of business, consumer, and mortgage loans to new record-high levels. While at times the question has been raised whether margin regulation has unduly curtailed the liquidity of the stock market, experience during the 1950's indicated that, at least under favorable conditions of a strong upward trend in prices, the effect has not been as great as had been feared. Whether margin regulation would prove unduly restrictive under less favorable economic and financial conditions, future experience alone can demonstrate. The degree of promptness exercised by authorities in reducing margin requirements when market conditions become less favorable will largely determine whether the regulation will prove unduly restrictive.

A problem that arises under selective regulation of security credit is a shift of borrowing to unregulated sources at times when high margin requirements are in effect and a strong desire exists to carry securities on credit. Security loans were offered in 1959, when the minimum margin requirement under Regulations T and U was 90 percent, from such unregulated sources as factors and lenders located abroad with much smaller margins, but at high interest rates.

The Board of Governors of the Federal Reserve System has taken steps toward expanding the scope of security credit regulation to curtail the ability of would-be borrowers to obtain credit through unregulated channels or in unregulated forms.

Administrative Problems in Security Credit Control

Borrowers can avoid the impact of margin requirements in obtaining credit on security collateral by: (1) Pledging exempt securities, including U.S. Government and tax-exempt securities, for credit from either brokers or banks. In the case of banks, exemption is extended to loans on bonds and on unlisted stock, where the proceeds are not to buy listed stocks. (2) Borrowing for purposes other than purchasing or carrying securities and diverting funds, directly or indirectly, to security purchases. (3) Resort to unregulated lenders.

There has been no conclusive evidence to date that the volume of credit obtained by these expedients has been large. However, since avoidance of margin regulation by these means could lead on a future occasion either to an excessive expansion of security credit or to a distortion of the flow of funds into certain types of securities merely to escape margin regulation, the problem has been repeatedly studied by the Federal Reserve authorities, and measures to prevent these possibilities have been taken.

The chief instance of relatively large-scale borrowing to carry tax-exempt securities on thin margins occurred in the Government security market in 1958. A Treasury–Federal Reserve report on that episode noted that the "speculation financed by credit created a particular problem in this instance because there were large blocks of holdings acquired by newcomers to the market who bought or made commitments to buy Government securities on very thin margins—or in many cases on no margin at all." Adverse effects on the stability of the Government securities market, rather than the volume of security credit involved, concerned the authorities in this case.[4]

In 1960, the Comptroller of the Currency instructed national bank examiners to require the banks to have at least 5 percent margin on loans or repurchase agreements on Government securities, although a lower margin may be held adequate for loans on issues with short maturities or where special circumstances prevail. Explaining this action, he said that "extension of credit without adequate margin for the purpose of carrying speculative positions in Government securities was a contributing factor to the disruptive fluctuation in Government security prices during the late spring and summer of 1958." The New York State

---

[4] "Summary of the Treasury–Federal Reserve Study of the Government Securities Market," *Federal Reserve Bulletin* (August 1959), p. 865.

Banking Department subsequently extended this requirement to state-chartered banks under its jurisdiction. By these steps, a limited measure of margin control was extended to lending on Government securities without ending their statutory exemption under the Securities Exchange Act of 1934. This course of action avoided the inflexibility that might result from efforts to prevent a repetition of the 1958 episode in the Government security market through ending the exempt status of U.S. Government securities under that statute. The New York Stock Exchange has had a 5 percent minimum margin requirement of its own on the carrying of Government securities in margin accounts for customers by its member firms.

Closer control over "nonpurpose" loans by banks was provided for by the Board of Governors of the Federal Reserve System through amendments to Regulation U effective June 15, 1959. It is now required that a borrower's "nonpurpose" statement must be signed, as accepted in good faith, by the officer of the lending bank. If the borrower's statement merely states what is not the purpose of the loan, it is to be supported by a memorandum or notation of the bank's lending officer describing the purpose.

Publicity given lending on thin margins at very high interest rates by factors and by banks in other countries attracted attention in 1959 and 1960 to the possibility of increased resort to such unregulated lenders, particularly by persons seeking to buy control of publicly owned enterprises with small cash outlays. Regulation U was amended to provide that reports could be required from "every person engaged in the business of extending . . . credit for the purpose of purchasing or carrying securities registered on a national securities exchange," and such reports were called for in 1960. This was regarded as a step toward possible regulation of security lending by others than brokers, dealers, and banks, where they could be brought under regulation either directly or indirectly. In the case of factors who lend on listed stocks, indirect regulation has been attempted through limiting their use of bank credit.

The basic problem of administration of selective credit control is to make it effective without unnecessary or harmful restrictions upon borrowers and lenders. As control is extended to cover previously exempted transactions and additional credit sources, however, new complications may result. An example was the action of the Board of Governors of the Federal Reserve System on March 8, 1960 in withdrawing an amendment to Regulation U made on June 15, 1959 that had been designed to tighten control over loans secured by listed stocks which were claimed by the borrowers to be for purposes other than purchasing or carrying securities. The amendment was withdrawn after it had been in effect for some months, it was stated, "in order to avoid administrative problems arising under the provision."

Implications for Selective Credit Control

Security credit regulation is the only type of selective credit control now exercised by the Federal Reserve authorities. Experience with such regulation has been used as an argument for proposals to adopt other selective controls. On the other hand, it has been argued that the absence of other selective controls justifies ending margin regulation by the Board of Governors of the Federal Reserve System.

The validity of both contentions rests on the assumption that security credit does not have unique characteristics of its own, but resembles other types of credit in essential respects. The following characteristics of security credit have been cited, however, which qualify its comparability with other forms of credit.

First, speculative borrowers may expand the amount of their security loans without restraint in a period like the late 1920's, when widespread optimism prevails and people are confident that security prices will rise. At such times, many speculators and investors do not look on this borrowing in the light of a debt calling for plans for repayment, but rather as a mere incident to their security trading activities.

Second, the ability to pyramid speculative security purchases when prices rise, since larger sums can then be borrowed on pledged securities automatically, is another special characteristic of the use of credit to carry securities.

Third, a rise in interest rates does not restrain speculative borrowing when an advance in security prices is confidently expected, since the added interest cost seems inconsequential when compared with the amount of anticipated appreciation in securities purchased.

Fourth, lenders are concerned primarily with collateral value rather than with the credit standing of the borrowers and the usual measures of ability to repay such as income, cash flow, and other liabilities.

Fifth, the high quality and liquidity of security loans, and the relative ease of arranging and administering them because of the ease of checking on current value of collateral, can cause a very rapid expansion in their volume when borrowers, in their eagerness to obtain additional credit, offer to pay high interest rates to nonbank lenders for such loans. This was demonstrated in the late 1920's.

Security credit is sometimes compared to consumer credit in discussions of qualitative credit control. The above recapitulation of the special characteristics of security lending indicates that the two types of credit are highly dissimilar, so that no valid analogy can be drawn. The consumer borrower is made acutely aware of the existence of his debt from the start by the obligation to make periodic repayments, and if he incurs excessive debt the need for curtailment of the use of credit is promptly brought home to him as he makes instalment payments. By the same token, lenders to consumers are promptly alerted to excessive credit extension by an increase in delinquencies. They must analyze the borrower's ability to meet his payments as they fall due, to minimize risks of default and loss. Thus, the conditions governing use of consumer credit require constant self-discipline by both borrowers and lenders, which can be absent in security borrowing and lending when a protracted rise in security prices and confidence in further price advances make both borrowers and lenders willing to expand the use of such credit and minimum margin requirements do not exert a restraining influence.

These considerations make the existence of selective control of security credit, and experience with such control, irrelevant to the issue of whether other forms of selective credit control should be considered.

Chapter 9

COMMERCIAL BANK FINANCING
OF INTERNATIONAL
TRADE AND INVESTMENT

The international financial transactions of the United States have increased tremendously since the outbreak of World War I. In the period between the two world wars the United States became the greatest creditor nation of the world and the dollar the most important currency. American investments abroad, both direct and portfolio, rose materially, and New York City became probably the most important international financial center for the maintenance of international liquidity of foreign governments and central banks.

In this development the commercial banks of the country have played an important role. They are the principal institutions through which international payments are made. They hold in one form or another a considerable part of the international liquidity of both foreign governments and financial institutions, and they play a significant role in assisting business concerns in developing foreign trade and investments abroad.

The present scope of international operations of American commercial banks with their numerous branches, agencies, overseas banks, and correspondent relations abroad is in sharp contrast to the situation which prevailed prior to World War I when most international trade, including that of the United States, was financed in sterling through the London money market and the dollar acceptance for all practical purposes was unknown. Today, American commercial banks finance not only the foreign trade of this country but also a considerable portion of the world's trade in which the United States is not involved. They cooperate with the federal government and the various international financial agencies in the development of the less economically advanced areas of the free world, and they play an important role in the movement of short- and long-term funds from one country to another. This chapter will analyze the role of the commercial banks in international finance, the functions they perform in solving the problems that confront private enterprise, the United States and foreign governments, and central banks.

Volume and Nature of Business

Role of the United States

Practically all U.S. transactions with foreign countries, as well as some of those among foreign countries, are financed through the international departments of U.S. commercial banks and foreign bank agencies located in the United States, chiefly in New York City. The United States is not only the largest exporter and importer of goods but also the world's most important source of international long-term capital. The volume of U.S. business with foreign countries is indicated by the Department of Commerce balance of payment figures for 1960 which show disbursements from the United States (exclusive of military aid) of $31.4 billion and U.S. receipts from foreign countries at $27.6 billion, i.e., a total volume of $59 billion.

U.S. banks have increased their credits to foreign firms, banks, and governments from $563 million at the end of 1945 to $4.2 billion on March 31, 1960. This accounts for about 10 percent of total U.S. private investments abroad.

Foreign-owned short-term dollar assets held at U.S. commercial banks, foreign bank agencies, or at the Federal Reserve Banks as reported at the end of 1945, were $6.9 billion. At the end of March 1960 these short-term assets aggregated $16.4 billion made up of $8.0 billion in deposits, $6.4 billion in U.S. Treasury Bills and Certificates, and $2 billion in commercial paper, bankers' acceptances, and other short-term assets. (This amount does not include $3.3 billion of short-term dollar assets held by international institutions, of which all but $90 million kept as deposits were in U.S. Treasury Bills and Certificates.) The deposits and securities kept at the commercial banks by foreign central banks, commercial banks, corporations, and individuals serve as a basis for the credit lines granted to them and for the services rendered to the foreign customers. The services provided by American commercial banks range over the whole gamut of banking activities, including investment advisory and custodial services.

In recent years foreign owned deposits, particularly time deposits, have proved to be somewhat volatile for American banks, especially those in New York. To a large extent, generally rising short-term interest rates have induced foreign holders of deposits to shift into government securities and money market instruments. No over-all loss of deposits to the American banking system has resulted, but deposits have been dispersed throughout the banking system and have been lost by the banks to which foreign governments and their nationals look for loans and other banking services.

Regulation Q, with its 3 percent maximum interest payable on time deposits, has made it impossible for U.S. banks to raise the rate they pay on time deposits and thus compete with short-term investments.

It should be noted, also, that at times such as in 1960, generally higher levels of interest rates in foreign money markets have led to a substantial outflow of short-term funds from the United States. These dollars going abroad, when purchased by foreign central banks as residual buyers in foreign exchange markets, have led to loss of monetary gold for the United States. This can be expected to happen in the future whenever rate differentials between the United States and foreign countries, allowing for the cost of eliminating foreign exchange risks through forward exchange transactions, enable investors to realize a higher rate of return.

Although New York is the most important international financial center of the country, there are about 100 U.S. commercial banks with foreign departments. These banks range upward in size of total assets from $100,000,000, and are located in every major city. The volume of business being transacted by non-New York commercial banks is growing steadily. This is a sound development not only for the banks involved but also for U.S. industry which has increased its investments abroad materially and thus requires nationwide foreign department service.

Financing of International Transactions

The international transactions of the commercial banks are handled by their foreign departments which are able to render practically every banking service abroad that the Head Office provides at home. In addition, they deal in foreign exchange and finance international trade by issuing commercial letters of credit, accepting domestic and foreign drafts, and by collecting and discounting foreign and local drafts. They take deposits of foreign customers, facilitate foreign outward and inward remittances, issue travelers letters of credit, sell travelers checks, and sell foreign currencies.

Foreign departments render extremely valuable services to their customers by providing up-to-date information about political, economic, and social conditions in foreign countries, including foreign exchange control regulations as well as export-import regulations, and by supplying current credit information about foreign firms. The foreign departments also furnish American business concerns with valuable information about legal and economic conditions relating to investments abroad.

Financing international trade, however, is the most important function performed by the foreign department of a commercial bank. Not only does the bank often carry the burden of financing a transaction until the exporter or importer is able to pay, but it also renders valuable assistance in avoiding or reducing credit and exchange risks. Without the assistance of commercial banks, international trade would be either materially reduced or in many instances could not be carried on at all. This is particularly true when foreign currencies are subject to considerable fluctuations or are surrounded by rigid exchange restrictions.

Commercial Letters of Credit

The risk inherent in foreign trade has always been greater than in domestic business because of the differences in trade usages, laws, currencies, customs duties, ever changing governmental regulations, and the usually larger distances between buyers and sellers. This geographical fact alone ties up funds for longer periods than is the case in domestic transactions. It is also more difficult to obtain reliable and up-to-date credit information about foreign buyers or sellers than domestic ones. Consequently, special methods of financing have been evolved to facilitate international trade in order to reduce or eliminate these risks and difficulties.

The commercial letter of credit is one instrument that serves these ends effectively. It is used to cover both imports and exports to and from the United States as well as financing trade between points outside the United States. Thus, a U.S. bank may issue a letter of credit covering, for example, a shipment from Japan to South America when U.S. dollars are the medium of payment.

While the specific arrangements for international trade transactions may vary considerably, there is a basic function for the commercial letter of credit. It is a document originated by a bank on behalf of a customer who may be an individual, firm, or corporation, and who is usually an importer of goods. The document, addressed to a party who is usually an exporter of goods, authorizes him to draw a draft up to a specified amount on the bank which issues the letter of credit. The issuing bank undertakes to pay the draft when it is presented or it agrees to "accept" the draft and pay at the end of a stated period, in which case a banker's acceptance, as discussed below, is created. The effect of this arrangement is to substitute the bank's credit for that of the importer, assuring the exporter of receiving payment in cash or in a readily marketable bank acceptance when he has complied with the terms of the letter of credit. Through this device the burden of financing goods transported, warehoused, processed, or marketed is shifted from the buyer or seller to a bank and/or the money market. Most letters of credit handled by U.S. banks are in U.S. dollars; however, many American importers often ask for letters of credit issued in other currencies.

In order to standardize the documents and terminology used in international trade, the Thirteenth Congress of the International Chamber of Commerce fixed a "Uniform Customs and Practice for Commercial Documentary Credits." The forty-nine articles of this document define the various types of commercial letters of credit, related transportation credits, and insurance documents. The articles also state the liability of the banks negotiating the documents, and contain regulations interpreting the terms commonly encountered in the documents. Except as otherwise expressly agreed, these definitions and interpretations of commercial credit terms and procedure are adhered to officially by the banks in most countries of the world. In the United States the "Revised American Trade Definitions—1941" is also widely used.

Bankers' Acceptances

As indicated above, a time draft is frequently drawn on a bank as a result of a letter of credit. Such a draft, when accepted by the bank, becomes a bankers' acceptance. "Acceptance" by the bank means that the bank promises to pay the holder of the draft—whoever he might be— the face amount at the maturity date. These instruments may come into being, of course, in a number of ways other than as a result of a letter of credit. Regulations A, B, and C of the Federal Reserve Board describe how, and for what purposes a bankers' acceptance can be created. Because a bankers' acceptance is a direct obligation usually of a prime bank the acceptance has a ready market and is a popular medium for investors.

At present the acceptance business is concentrated in the hands of forty to fifty financial institutions located in major financial centers (mainly in New York) who do the bulk of accepting, but at any given time from 120 to 130 banks have acceptances outstanding. New York also has the principal bankers' acceptance market of the country.

At the end of 1960, the total amount of outstanding dollar acceptances was $2,027 million, exceeding the previous record of $1,732 million reached in December 1929. Of the total amount, $662 million were held by accepting banks (of which $490 million were their own bills and $173 million were bought in the open market), the Federal Reserve Banks held for their own account $74 million and $230 million for foreign correspondents (notably central banks), and the balance of $1,060 million was held by "others," i.e., non-accepting banks, foreign bank agencies, insurance companies, and other institutions. Of the total amount of dollar acceptances, $403 million were created to finance imports into the United States, $669 million were based on exports from the United States, $122 million to supply dollar exchange, $308 million to finance goods stored in or shipped between points in the United States, and $524 million for goods warehoused in or transported between points in foreign countries.

Acceptances created to supply dollar exchange are also permitted under Federal Reserve Regulations for U.S. banks. Member banks may accept drafts with a maturity of not more than three months drawn by banks of certain countries even though no actual shipment of goods is underlying the transaction. The list of countries published by the Board includes all Latin America, Australia, New Zealand, the Australian dependencies, and Indonesia. Banks of these countries are able, by drawing bills on U.S. banks, to obtain dollars during periods in which, because of the highly seasonal nature of their main exports, their sales to the United States are of a low volume. The proceeds of future sales to the United States during the exporting season are used by the foreign banks to pay the American banks, thus enabling them to meet outstanding acceptances.

Collections

In addition to financing exports and imports by letters of credit and bankers' acceptances, banks assist American traders in many other ways. A good example is the handling of collection items. Exporters in many cases ship on a documentary draft basis. The U.S. banks finance exporters on the basis of loans against these outstanding collection items. Loans are made on the basis of such bills which have actually been forwarded by the bank.

Longer-Term Credits

Certain exports are of a nature that require extended payment. Because of intensive competition from exporters of other nations the list of goods for which longer-term credit is asked is growing longer. (Government organizations for assistance of this variety will be discussed later on.) Commercial banks have made, and are continuing to make, loans to assist exporters in this regard. These loans, however, are in effect loans to the foreign buyer since the U.S. exporter usually sells his receivables to his bank without recourse. The terms of these sales vary but usually there is a certain percentage paid with the order, an additional payment on shipment, and the balance is paid over several years with fixed payment periods evidenced by interest bearing notes. Some U.S. banks have lines of credit specifically available to foreign corporations for just such operations. Indeed, some exporting companies will consult with their bankers prior to making sales based on long-term credit to ascertain whether the subsequent sale of the notes is possible, the exact form the note should be in, and what foreign guarantors are required, if any. Purchase by banks of this type of paper requires a thorough knowledge of the debtor, the guarantor, and the foreign country involved.

Loans to Foreign Governments

Some U.S. banks, particularly the large ones, make loans directly to foreign governments, corporations, and individuals which are not directly connected with U.S. trade. U.S. banks with foreign branches obviously engage in direct lending operations in the countries in which their branches are situated.

Foreign central banks borrow from commercial banks against gold but most frequently on their own credit and for a wide variety of purposes. Banks tailor their loans to meet the specific needs of foreign central bank borrowers.

Loans to foreign governments can take the form of a stabilization credit to strengthen a country's foreign exchange reserves. These are usually made by a consortium of U.S. banks or in some cases by an individual bank. They may also be short-term credit facilities made available to foreign governments for special imports due to unusual international events such as the closure of the Suez Canal. An unpublished study by one New York bank shows that since the beginning of 1958 American commercial banks have extended direct loans or standby credits to foreign central banks, governments, or their agencies in more than fifty different countries.

Borrowing in Several Centers

Certain foreign firms are large enough to command credit in money markets other than their own. There are many large European or other foreign companies which have outgrown their own banks and can get the credit they need for at least their external functions from the cheapest money market available. The list of these companies is long but each, although well known, requires an adequate and thorough examination and must pass the same credit tests as a domestic firm. In addition, when U.S. rates are attractive, foreign firms which are not well known here will obtain the guarantee of a foreign bank that is well known, in order to contract loans in the American market.

With the restoration of the international money market and with the return to practically full external convertibility of the leading currencies of the world not only has the international flow of funds been increased but also loans tend to move to those centers where money can be obtained at the lowest rate. During the postwar period New York has been a center of relatively easy money, and many loans to foreigners have been made there covering transactions not involving the United States.

Travel Assistance

Another function of the foreign department is to assist tourist and commercial travelers. The amount spent by American travelers abroad is enormous and is growing rapidly. On long or expensive trips, a traveler, in addition to travelers' checks will also carry a traveler's letter of credit.

Travelers' checks are sold by most U.S. banks with or without a foreign department. A few sell their own checks directly or through correspondents. Most, however, sell the travelers' checks of the American Express Company, Thos. Cook and Co., or one of several well-known large banks. These are honored without question all over the world.

American Depositary Receipts

The commercial banks have played an important role in enabling American investors to buy securities of foreign corporations and have thus contributed to the economic development of many countries.

While the buying and selling of foreign U.S. dollar bonds does not differ in its mechanics from trading in domestic obligations, dealing in foreign stock certificates involves delays, risks, and expenses not encountered in buying and selling equities of domestic corporations. Other obstacles to investing in shares of foreign corporations are varying customs, laws, and regulations, as well as the complex procedure in the actual handling of foreign securities.

In practically all European countries, the use of bearer stock certificates with attached dividend coupons predominates. Americans accustomed to holding stock certificates registered in their names and receiving by mail dividend checks, subscription rights when issued, voting proxies, annual reports, and notices about certain corporate activities are averse to holding bearer certificates.

This situation called for an instrument that would come close to the standardized American registered negotiable stock certificate. The Guaranty Trust Company of New York in cooperation with several leading brokers in New York and abroad and in collaboration with several stock exchanges, created in 1927 the American Depositary Receipt (ADR). This registered negotiable receipt for a stated number of shares of a foreign corporation attained immediate acceptance by American investors. It contributed to making New York an international security market. The shares of British, German, Italian, South African, Dutch, Belgian, Australian, and other foreign corporations are today traded regularly in New York.

The mechanics of the ADR's are simple. The trust departments of large New York City commercial banks (the Depositaries), upon receipt of advice from their branches or correspondent banks abroad that a stipulated number of shares of a certain foreign corporation has been deposited with them for account of a U.S. resident, issue a registered negotiable receipt to the named beneficiary. Safekeeping, transferability, dividends, options, rights, etc. are all handled by the banks involved. Holders of ADR's may at any time demand their shares, and sales to others can take place here with all the necessary formalities being observed.

In March 1960, there were outstanding American Depositary Receipts for about 80 million shares of 128 leading foreign corporations. The growth in size of many corporations located in the European Common Market and in the Free Trade Area countries will require additional capital and the ADR will enable Americans to participate in the expansion of existing production facilities and in the development of new industries. The elimination of double taxation by the Tax Conventions between the United States and some foreign countries, under which holders of ADR's may claim credits on their federal income tax returns for the applicable foreign tax withheld at the source from dividends, has made investment in foreign stocks more attractive.

At the end of 1960, there were 305 foreign securities—stocks and bonds —with a market value of $6.4 billion listed on the New York Stock Exchange. The list of 305 issues includes stocks of twenty-four foreign companies incorporated in nine countries. Of these, four stocks with a reported volume of more than thirteen million shares were among the forty most active issues on the Stock Exchange in 1960.

Institutions and Mechanics of International Banking

The volume of international financial transactions of the United States has grown rapidly since the end of the war. This coupled with the vast economic aid and extensive loans granted by the U.S. government to foreign countries has necessitated the enlargement of the foreign departments of American banks, the opening of branch banks abroad, as well as the establishment of a number of special governmental financial institutions. In its international financial transactions, a commercial bank has the choice of using the facilities of correspondent banks in foreign countries, opening branches and representative offices abroad, or organizing affiliates and specialized subsidiaries (overseas banks) abroad.

Many American banks feel that foreign correspondents, with their expert knowledge of their country's customs and methods of doing business and often operating a network of branches, can offer a better service than their own overseas branches. On the other hand, the proponents of foreign branches or subsidiary banks maintain that American branches and banks abroad are in a better position to serve the growing needs of American business. All banks engaged in international finance have a network of correspondents abroad even when they operate foreign branches. Only relatively few, however, have branches or overseas institutions.

In choosing a foreign correspondent the American bank is guided by two basic criteria: first, the credit worthiness of the bank; second, the ability of the bank to render first-class services. Since trade flows in many directions and dollars are used for a great deal of its financing, U.S. banks are called upon to extend credit to or through their foreign correspondents. The services which a foreign correspondent renders to an American bank are of vital importance. The American bank, therefore, must have confidence in the judgment of the correspondent staff, its accuracy in examination of documents, and preciseness in following instructions. Furthermore, since American banks act as advisers to business concerns in their international transactions they want to feel certain that the information which the foreign correspondent will furnish them will be accurate and up-to-date. The American bank expects its foreign correspondent to have a thorough knowledge of the various regulations and restrictions under which the banks operate.

American Branches Abroad

Of the approximately 100 American banks with foreign departments, eight have branches overseas. The pioneer and leader in the field of foreign branches was the First National City Bank of New York. This bank, as of June 1960, had eighty-two branches abroad in twenty-six countries, representing the widest network of United States foreign branches. The Bank of America N.T. & S.A. and its affiliate, the Bank of America International N.T. & S.A., has nineteen branches and owns the majority of the Banca d'Italia, an Italian commercial bank. The Chase Manhattan Bank has twenty-six branches most of which are in the Caribbean area. The First National Bank of Boston has fifteen branches in three Latin American countries and the Morgan Guaranty Trust Company has branches in Paris, Brussels, and London. Bankers Trust Company, Chemical Bank New York Trust Company, and Manufacturers Hanover Trust Company, each has one or two branches in London. In addition to branches, most of the above-mentioned banks have resident representatives or affiliated institutions abroad. The only major New York bank without branches abroad, although with representatives, is the Irving Trust Company.

The arguments for branches overseas may be briefly summarized as follows: (1) they are of help to the foreign country; (2) they provide the subsidiaries of U.S. corporations with a more sympathetic audience, an easier flow of funds, and a source of profitable business; (3) they aid traveling businessmen and tourists; (4) they provide a better source of credit information and can provide immediate on-the-spot evaluation of economic conditions. Against this are ranged the argument that (1) foreign branches often offer unfair competition to local banks; (2) U.S. business subsidiaries abroad in many instances are inclined to support local banking institutions; (3) local bankers have a wider knowledge of business opportunities and of tourist facilities and know more about local businessmen; (4) traveling bank officers and correspondents combine to produce up-to-date economic knowledge. Some countries disapprove of foreign bank branches while others prohibit them entirely. There would seem to be no definite answer as to which system is the most profitable and desirable. The best that can be said in this regard is that if the arguments were preponderantly on one side or the other, there would be either no U.S. banks with foreign branches or there would be considerably more. The above arguments do not generally apply to London which, as one of the greatest international financial centers of the world, has attracted foreign branches and overseas banks from all over the world.

Edge Act Corporations

There is, however, another method whereby a U.S. bank can obtain some of the advantages of a foreign branch without incurring as many of the risks. In 1919, Section 25(a), commonly known as the Edge Act, was added to the Federal Reserve Act. This provision of the Federal Reserve Act authorized the Board of Governors to charter corporations "for the purpose of engaging in international or foreign banking or other international or foreign financial operation . . . either directly or through the agency, ownership, or control of local institutions in foreign countries. . . ." Directors and majority ownership must be by U.S. citizens but such corporations are not permitted to carry on any part of their business in the United States except such that is incidental to its international or foreign business.

An Edge Act corporation may not have outstanding at any one time liabilities in the form of debentures, bonds, or promissory notes in excess of ten times its paid-in capital and surplus. Thus an Edge Act Corporation may have acceptances outstanding at any one time up to ten times its capital and surplus, while a member bank may accept drafts for merchandise trade or warehousing only up to the amount of its capital and surplus plus an additional 50 percent for the purpose of creating dollar exchange. The aggregate amount of stock held by a national bank in Edge and "agreement" corporations must not exceed 10 percent of the bank's capital and surplus.

Under Regulation K, an Edge Act corporation may be either a banking corporation or financing corporation, thus separating deposit banking from other financing activities. The Board of Governors may permit a banking corporation to change to a financing corporation, and vice versa.

A *banking corporation* may receive demand and time deposits within the United States only when they are incidental to, or for the purpose of carrying out transactions abroad. Such deposits are subject to the same reserve requirements as if the corporation were a member of the Federal Reserve System, but in no event may the reserves in the aggregate be less than 10 percent of such deposits. It may deal in spot and future foreign exchange, issue letters of credit, accept drafts or bills of exchange, receive for collection abroad checks, drafts, coupons, and other securities, and collect such instruments in the United States for foreign customers, and buy and sell securities for the account and risk of customers abroad. With the permission of the Board of Governors, it may purchase the shares of other corporations engaged in foreign banking activities. A banking corporation is not permitted to issue its own obligations, except promissory notes due within one year evidencing borrowing from banks. It must not engage in issuing, underwriting, selling, or distributing securities, except to such limited extent as the Board of Governors may, upon application of the corporation, approve.

A *financing corporation* may not engage in banking, i.e., receiving and paying out deposits or accepting drafts or bills of exchange, except when it is required by the Secretary of the Treasury to act as fiscal agent of the United States. It may finance itself by issuing debenture bonds, promissory notes, or other obligations. While the corporation has outstanding unsecured obligations (except promissory notes), loans or other credit extended or guaranteed by it may not have a maturity exceeding ten years. Upon application of the corporation, the Board of Governors may grant it the power to buy and hold shares in prescribed amounts in generally designated types of foreign corporations not engaged in banking.

The corporation may not engage in underwriting, sale, or distribution of securities in the United States, except the issuance of its own securities. There were, at the end of 1959, six active Edge Act corporations of which one was organized in 1930; the remaining five were formed in the years 1949 through 1959. Three operate as "banking corporations" and three as "financing corporations." The home offices of these corporations are located in New York City. Three corporations had no subsidiaries or foreign branches; one had a branch in France and an English fiduciary affiliate that maintains a branch in Canada; one had a subsidiary, organized under the laws of Panama; and one operates branches in France, Germany, Guatemala, Hong Kong, Lebanon, Malaya, and Singapore, maintains an agency in Guatemala, and owns substantially all of the stock of a bank organized under the laws of Italy and operating in that country. Since the end of 1959, several more Edge Act corporations of both types have been established.

Agreement Corporations

Under Section 25 of the Federal Reserve Act a national bank with a capital and surplus of not less than $1 million may, with the approval of the Board, invest up to 10 percent of its capital and surplus in the stock of one or more corporations—federally or state-chartered—engaged in international or foreign banking. In order to qualify its stock for purchase by a national bank the corporation must sign an agreement with the

Board of Governors that it will conduct its business in such manner as the Board may prescribe. Corporations that have entered into such an agreement are referred to as "agreement" corporations.

Agencies of Foreign Banks

In New York City, the leading financial center of the country, there are a number of agencies of foreign banks. At the end of 1959, twenty-six banks of twelve countries maintained twenty-nine agencies in New York. In addition, there are also seven branches of foreign banks in San Francisco. While foreign agencies are restricted by New York State law from accepting deposits subject to withdrawal by check, they are permitted to engage in most international financial transactions. They are permitted to buy and sell foreign exchange, issue letters of credit, accept drafts, and remit funds abroad. They also buy and sell securities for account of their head offices and customers abroad. Foreign bank agencies thus compete with foreign departments of domestic banks for financing the business between the United States and the rest of the world as well as transactions among foreign countries. The agencies of foreign banks have an advantage over their American banks because they are not subject to most of the regulations affecting American banks. On April 10, 1960 the State of New York enacted a law permitting foreign banks to open branches or convert their agencies into branches in the state and to subject themselves to supervision by the State Banking Department. Since enactment of this law one foreign bank agency has become a branch. Only banks of countries extending the same privileges to New York State banks qualify for New York branches.

Government Agencies

The huge amounts of capital required for the rebuilding of the war-shattered economies of Europe and for the development of the economically retarded areas abroad, coincident with the heavy post-World War II domestic demand for short-, intermediate-, and long-term funds, could not be met by private sources alone. In addition, the risks involved in loans to some borrowers abroad, such as lack of currency convertibility, expropriation, and war could not be assumed by private financial institutions. Such hazards, at least, had to be assumed by governmental agencies.

The U.S. government and international financial agencies in existence prior to World War II and those created shortly thereafter with which U.S. banks cooperate are deeply involved in this problem. The motives of the U.S. agencies are the promotion of U.S. trade abroad and the strengthening of the economies of the various countries.

The principal U.S. agencies are the Export-Import Bank of Washington (Eximbank), the Development Loan Fund, the International Coopera-

| | Export-Import Bank | | International Cooperation |
	Dollars	Foreign Currencies	Foreign Currencies
Purpose	Facilitate U.S. exports and imports	Help foreign development and expand markets for U.S. commodities and goods	Help development and production by providing funds for imports
Resources	$7,000,000,000	Up to 25% local currency payments for agricultural commodity sales	Proceeds of U.S. government sales
Nature of Loans	1. Project loans to purchase U.S. goods or services 2. Exporter credits	1. U.S. companies affiliates or agents 2. The above or local companies for agricultural commodities	Loans for development projects
Nature of Guarantees	Full or partial guarantees to partial lenders	n.a.	n.a.
Relation to Other Sources of Loans	May not compete with private sources which are available on reasonable terms	n.a.	n.a.
Who May Borrow	U.S. and foreign private enterprises and foreign governments of the "free world"	U.S. private enterprises, subsidiaries, affiliates or agents and, for agricultural purposes, private companies in the debtor country	Foreign governments who receive U.S. surplus agricultural commodities
Where Must the Money be Spent	Generally in the U.S.	In country whose currency is loaned	Principally in country whose currencies is owned

262

14
Financial Agencies

Administration Investment Guarantees	Development Loan Fund		Commodity Credit Corporation
	Dollars	Foreign Currencies	
Help U.S. firms in making and insuring investments	Assist in development and production in secondary economies		Facilitate export of surplus agricultural commodities
Authorized up to $1,000,000,000 in guarantees plus borrowing	As Congress votes	Loan repayments plus other U.S. local sales	Cash sales (or 3 years with Documentary Letter of Credit confirmed by U.S. bank)
n.a.	To governments or U.S. or foreign firms for economic development		As above
For U.S. private investors against inconvertibility of earnings or invested capital, and against confiscation, nationalization, or war	Full or partial guarantees to private lenders		n.a.
n.a.	May not compete with private sources and must take into account other free world sources such as Eximbank, IBRD, etc.		n.a.
n.a.	U.S. and foreign private enterprises and foreign governments of the "free world"		U.S. export firms
n.a.	Any "free world" country but U.S. is to be given preference	In country whose currency is loaned unless otherwise agreed	U.S.

	International Bank for Reconstruction and Development (IBRD) "World Bank"	International Monetary Fund IMF
Purpose	Assist the development of resources and production in member country	Assist in the maintenance of exchange stability
Resources	Capital subscriptions to member countries and bond issues. ($1.9 billion is paid in. $16 billion is callable)	In gold $3 billion, in member country currencies $10.6 billion, subscriptions receivable $.7 billion
Nature of Loans	Medium and long-term project loans to member countries or public and private entities guaranteed by governments	"Standby" stabilization credits or short and medium term loans to overcome foreign exchange difficulties
Nature of Guarantees	May issue guarantees to private lenders but has not as yet	n.a.
Relation to Other Sources of Loans	May not compete where private sources are available at reasonable rates	n.a.
Who May Borrow	Private or public entities in member countries	Governments of member countries
Where Must the Money be Spent	Within member countries Plus Switzerland	No limitations

264

International Finance Corporation IFC	International Development Association IDA	Inter-American Development Bank IADB
Assist private productive enterprises in member countries	Assist economic and social growth in less developed countries	Assist basic economic development in member countries
Capital subscriptions by member countries of $93.7 million and sale of investments	Capital subscription by member countries of $1 billion	Authorized $1 billion (850 for "ordinary operations and 150 for "Fund for Special Operations")
Investment (not in capital stock) in private productive enterprises only	Great flexibility in loans and repayments	Making or participating in direct loans to member governments or private firms in those countries
n.a.	May issue guarantees to private lenders	May issue guarantees to private lenders
May not invest where private capital is available at reasonable rates	Due to nature of loans is not competitive with other sources	Cooperates with all other loan and capital sources
Private entities in member countries	Public or private entities in member countries plus public international organizations	Public or private entities in member countries
Member countries	Member countries	No limitations

tion Administration, and the Commodity Credit Corporation. The leading international agencies are the International Bank for Reconstruction and Development (IBRD), the International Monetary Fund, International Development Association, the International Finance Corporation, and the Inter-American Development Bank. All of these were created by special laws and are dependent on one or several governments for their continued viable existence.

The charts of these organizations based primarily on information derived from the *Foreign Commerce Weekly* of February 8, 1960 give at a glance a summary of the activities of some of these agencies (Charts 14 and 15).

The Commodity Credit Corporation is really not a risk-taking institution; however, it has been of assistance in promoting exports of U.S. surplus agricultural commodities. The two agencies of the international group which have been most active and have had sufficient experience to establish a pattern of repayments are the Eximbank and the IBRD. In the Eximbank's more than twenty-five years of operation, only a few loans, totaling about $3 million, have been losses. This is less than .05 percent of all the loans made. The IBRD with fourteen years of operation has loaned more than $5 billion in more than fifty countries and territories. The bulk of the international agency loans in the past has been in U.S. dollars although now other "hard" currencies are being used. Most of the "soft" currency loans stem from holdings of the U.S. government abroad. These arise from payments in local currency to the U.S. government by foreign governments (counterpart funds) from sales of surplus agricultural commodities and from similar transactions.

The various agencies, by assuming credit risks which ordinarily cannot be assumed by private banking, have created an environment in which commercial banks can properly play their role in the financing of international trade and investments. The commercial banks cooperate in credits to foreign firms, banks, or governments in the form of (1) a direct loan by a single bank or by a syndicate of banks, guaranteed by one of these agencies participating in the project; (2) joint bank participation in the loans extended by the IBRD with the commercial banks taking the earlier maturities; (3) purchases from the IBRD bonds related to loans previously made by the bank, usually without the latter's guarantee; (4) loans to foreign borrowers guaranteed by the IBRD (or some other agency) which does not itself participate in the lending; (5) loans to borrowers abroad without guarantee of the IBRD for financing projects devised under supervision of the bank, which in turn vouches for their economic soundness. The banks also assist the IBRD indirectly through underwriting its U.S. dollar bond issues and buying and holding these bonds. In addition, the commercial banks are extending loans and stand-by credits to foreign borrowers under guaranty agreements with the Eximbank. Recently, changes in the Eximbank facilities have been made to include short-term (180 day) political risk guarantees and also to encourage exports by expanding participation and cooperation with private banks in granting medium-term credit to exporters.

Government Aid

There are also direct governmental appropriations which are outside the framework of these agencies. These can be for anything from direct budgetary support to such projects as airfields, highways, etc., which benefit the whole economic structure. Other countries either via direct appropriation, loans, guarantees, or insurance systems may participate with the U.S. government, firms, or banks in these transactions. U.S. banks have utilized the export credit systems existing in foreign countries as the basis for loans made to U.S. companies, their foreign subsidiaries, or to foreign corporations directly.

Loans to underdeveloped countries are also being made by the United Nations Special Fund, by the European Investment Bank (an agency of the European Common Market), private institutions (such as the Transoceanic-AOFC Ltd), and by American groups jointly with Swiss, British, German, French, Dutch, Italian, or Belgian interests. These groups usually pool their capital resources and technical skill for the financing of projects which individual institutions could not undertake because of the size and amount and the considerable risk involved. Private foundations of a quasi-charitable nature including The Ford Foundation and various Rockefeller funds, contribute significantly to the economic and social development in various areas thereby improving the climate in which U.S. business and banks operate abroad.

The credit experience on these loans so far has been good, which is one of the justifications for the relatively low rates at which some of them are made.

Conclusion

The future of the foreign departments of U.S. banks is dependent on the expansion or contraction of international trade and finance. In this respect the foreign department differs from the other departments of U.S. banks. Hence, a recession in business within the United States will affect only part of its operations unless there is a world-wide economic slump. It is impossible to predict the future course of world trade and economic development. Assuming that developments during the next ten years will be similar to those of the last five, there are certain trends which appears likely to continue.

As standards of living increase throughout the world, the volume of international trade will grow. Although the patterns of this trade may shift and the types of commodities traded in may change, the gross volume of goods and services interchanged among the countries of the world will rise considerably. Since 1949 the total general imports into the United States have risen from $6.6 billion to $15.3 billion in 1959. Exports, including military and economic aid shipments (which, it should be pointed out, keep a variety of U.S. workers employed) have grown from $12.1 billion to $17.6 billion having reached a high point of $20.9 billion in 1957.

It is almost axiomatic that economic development leads to increased trade and that the increase is greatest between those countries which are the most developed. It is also certain, granted relative international political stability, that foreign trade will increase. We can be partners in it as we choose. But whether we are or not, it will grow. Government interference by tariffs and quotas may be undertaken from time to time for valid social and economic reasons, but the only effective solution to the variety of problems created in an expanding world economy is intelligence, foresight, and imagination making itself felt in increased, economically competitive production.

The foreign department of U.S. banks, their foreign branches and subsidiaries have well-trained personnel who can advise and assist U.S. industry in the growing and changing pattern of international trade and finance.

Because of the large amount of direct investments abroad, foreign operations are becoming a growing part of the earnings of many U.S. companies. Despite the political difficulties in various parts of the globe there is a stronger and stronger tendency for U.S. firms to invest abroad. The reasons are virtually the same as those which caused expansion or relocation of productive facilities within the United States. These reasons include lower operating costs, rapidly growing demand, higher yields on investments, access to raw materials and markets, protection of investments, favorable taxation, assurance of remittance of profit, and repatriation of earnings. The growth of international economic units such as the Common Market and the European Free Trade Association has created conditions which are attractive to U.S. corporations. This grouping of separate political entities into an economic unity is likely to continue in one form or another.

In addition, various countries have found that U.S. capital can aid materially in their economic development. India, for example, has radically changed its approach to foreign investors and has enacted legislation specifically designed to attract new foreign funds. This legislation combined with the substantial market potential and the relative political stability of the country has caused several U.S. firms to invest in India and many others to consider seriously the possibilities.

The foreign departments or the foreign branches can be of considerable help in this regard by bringing together the interested parties, supplying names and backgrounds of potential partners, making introductions to the government departments concerned, assisting with economic studies and surveys, providing historical experience of other investors, and by performing many other services.

The growing economic strength of Europe and Japan and the need of capital in free Asia, Africa, and Latin America have changed the pattern of the flow of funds from unilateral and bilateral transactions to multilateral ones. This trend will, in all likelihood, continue. The international financing organizations will contribute in ever growing amounts to the rising demand for higher living standards in the depressed areas of the world. The competition between the free world and the Communist world will probably intensify in the coming years and the U.S. government and U.S. industry not only have a tremendous opportunity during this period but a frightening obligation.

Chapter 10

COMMERCIAL BANK
PORTFOLIO INVESTMENTS

Flexibility provided by the investment portfolio is one of the major reasons for the proven ability of commercial banking to adapt to changing economic conditions.

In depression and wartime, when the government becomes the chief borrower, the banking system best serves the economy by expanding its investments. When the economy is marked by healthy growth and a vigorous demand for loans such as prevailed in the 1950's, investment portfolios are reduced, providing funds to satisfy pressing demands for loans from business and consumers.

The investment portfolio also enables individual banks to meet their special needs, which vary with size and local economic conditions. Thus, a country bank frequently faces relatively large seasonal flows of funds, its small staff specializes in local lending, and its investment portfolio is usually conducted along relatively simple, standardized lines.

At the other extreme, a large city bank faces less pronounced seasonal fluctuations in deposits and loans but is apt to encounter wider cyclical swings in loan demands and greater resistance to deposit growth during periods of tight credit. These banks have more opportunity to increase their rate of return on investments by taking advantage of changing yield differentials among classes of securities and among issues of the same class.

Banks of all sizes, however, and under whatever prevailing economic conditions, must consider the functions of safety, liquidity, and income in managing their portfolios. This chapter will, therefore, discuss these functions, review the investment opportunities open to banks, and discuss the principles and problems involved. It will conclude with an appraisal of portfolio management policies.

Functions of Investment Portfolios

No segment of a commercial bank's earning assets can be effectively administered without reference to the bank's other earning and non-earning assets. The management of a bank's funds is an integrated problem.

The investment portfolio is the focal point at which conflicting factors influencing the management of the bank's funds are resolved, and an optimum balance is sought between the objectives of safety, liquidity, and income, each of which may call for different decisions in the choice of assets.

First and foremost, commercial banks have a basic responsibility to make certain that their funds are employed with safety. The investment portfolio provides the means for limiting the bank's over-all risk exposure.

Second, since by far the greater part of commercial bank liabilities is in the form of demand deposits, adequate liquidity is required to meet anticipated withdrawals of these deposits and to provide a margin of safety for the unforeseeable. A bank needs adequate liquidity, also, to be able to satisfy the legitimate credit needs of its customers and to provide portfolio flexibility should a rise in interest rates make available attractive investment opportunities. The part of the bank's investment portfolio that constitutes its secondary reserve (liquidity account) is the prime source of such liquidity.

Finally, bank management can never forget that commercial banking operates in a competitive free enterprise system, and that only if the stockholders who furnish its capital receive a reasonable profit on their investment will it be possible to attract the capital needed to maintain a sound and vigorous banking system. The bank's bond account, consisting of securities not included in the secondary or liquidity reserve, is an important source of earnings, particularly when demand for loans is at an ebb.

Desired risk balance is sought in the whole investment portfolio; liquidity is provided by the secondary reserve portion, while the part here called the bond account is an important source of income to the bank.

Risk Balance—The Whole Investment Portfolio

Enough assets involving no credit risk should be included among the bank's investments at all times to hold within reasonable bounds its over-all risk exposure—including risks assumed in loans. To provide proper balance for a bank's total assets, for example, it may need to hold a larger volume of U.S. Government securities than would be needed solely to provide liquidity.

It is this necessity for limitation of risk exposure that the supervisory authorities have in mind when they use "risk asset ratios" in the analysis of a bank's capital structure. Basically, risk assets are assets other than cash items and U.S. Government securities; other definitions are refinements of this concept. The ratio of capital accounts to risk assets (however defined) provides a statistical indication of risk exposure. It is far from an accurate or complete measure in itself, for it cannot take into consideration many factors pertinent to capital adequacy—such as competence of management, degree of risk exposure per dollar of loans or the nature of the community within which the bank is located. Nevertheless, risk asset ratios provide a statistical indicator of risk exposure that can be adjusted for these other factors, and so they serve as benchmarks for further analysis.

The amount of risk which can, and should, be assumed varies sharply from bank to bank. It depends on the needs and characteristics of the local community, on the type of business done by the bank, the trend of loans, the bank's deposit structure, its capital position, and the competence of management.

Liquidity—The Secondary Reserve

As noted earlier, liquidity may be defined as the ready availability of funds. Liquid assets are those which can be converted at any time into cash easily, quickly, and without significant loss.

The need for liquidity is not confined to the banking system, but is a special problem for banks for the reasons noted above. Among these, having funds available for favorable investment opportunities is in most cases within the control of the bank itself. Therefore, the basic liquidity needs with which the banker must concern himself arise from deposit withdrawals and an expansion in loans.

The solution of a bank's liquidity problem has two aspects which are simple to state, but extremely difficult to apply. One is an appraisal of the probable magnitude and timing of deposit withdrawals or loan expansion. This involves many uncertainties, yet this appraisal must be translated into a specific policy decision as to the amount of liquid assets needed. The second aspect of the problem is the selection of assets to provide the degree of liquidity deemed necessary.

Paradoxically, the bank's cash assets, although technically fully liquid, can be used only to a very limited extent for meeting losses of funds. These primary reserves (cash, deposits with correspondent banks and Federal Reserve banks, and cash items in process of collection) are the working balances used in the day-to-day operation of the bank. Since they are nonearning assets, they will ordinarily be held only in the amount needed.

Cash in vault is completely sterile, earning no return, and commercial banks generally endeavor to hold it to minimum levels. The amount of vault cash needed varies widely among banks, depending on payrolls, community customs, distance from source of supply at the Federal Reserve bank or correspondent bank, and many other factors. Too, the needs of a given bank can vary because of seasonal factors.

Excess stocks of vault cash are costly to a commercial bank because of the greater need for protective measures and insurance to which they give rise and, most important, because of income lost through failure to invest the funds. The authority recently granted by the Federal Reserve for member banks to count their vault cash as part of their legal reserves has reduced the cost of holding excess cash for many banks and has provided material relief for many small country banks which frequently hold large amounts of currency. Nevertheless, there remains adequate incentive to hold stocks of currency and coin to a minimum. Consequently, there is virtually no usable liquidity in most banks' holdings of vault cash.

Balances with correspondent banks provide the exception to the non-earning nature of cash assets. While these deposits earn no interest, the city correspondent banks provide many services in return for holding them. In any event, the country correspondent would have to obtain these services in one way or another, and by a cash fee if necessary.

The size and number of correspondent bank balances depend on the services which the country bank desires from its correspondents. City correspondents require of the country bank only sufficient balances to earn enough to cover the cost of services rendered by them plus a reasonable profit on the account. A city correspondent is not going to turn away excess deposits left with it, and country banks sometimes let these accounts rise to levels which are not necessary for the services demanded, especially when loan demands are slack and deposits are holding up well. Such excess balances can be used to provide liquidity to meet subsequent losses of funds. Normally, however, balances are held at levels commensurate with services rendered and offer only a very limited source of liquidity.

Required reserve balances at the Federal Reserve Bank are not available for either use. While a loss of deposits by a bank frees the legal reserve held against the funds withdrawn, this is no help since a deposit loss is several times as large as the reserve freed. Excess reserve balances, however, represent free cash and so are available for liquidity needs.[1]

Cash items in process of collection are the object of a continuing drive on the part of banking to speed conversion into cash. Since they are held to a minimum at all times, they are not a source of planned liquidity.

Since a bank's cash assets can be counted only to a very limited extent

---

[1] If a bank has an adequate liquidity reserve for potential deposit losses, then a decline in deposits would free the legal reserves held against such deposits for other liquidity uses, as discussed below.

among liquidity assets, a *secondary reserve* of short term, readily marketable, high quality assets must be maintained. This provides the bank with its real source of liquidity. The secondary reserve is used in an accordion-like fashion, expanding to take up the slack when deposits increase faster than lending opportunities and contracting as necessary to meet deposit withdrawals or loan increases.

Comparatively few assets meet the three tests—short maturity, ready marketability and high quality—that must be met for inclusion in a bank's secondary reserve. Short-term U.S. Government securities which obviously qualify on all three counts, constitute the vast preponderance of the secondary reserves of the banking system today. Other readily marketable short-term securities of prime quality are also included in the secondary reserve of many banks.

In addition to securities, other short-term assets of high quality used in the adjustment of a bank's reserve position are considered part of its liquidity account. These include short-term loans made to very strong borrowers with whom the banker-customer relation is of less than usual significance, and who have ready access to other sources of funds to pay off their short-term borrowings. Most popular among these are the money market loans—short-term loans to prime credit risks, Federal funds sold, Government securities bought under repurchase agreements with Government security dealers and other banks, bankers' acceptances held, call loans to security brokers and dealers, and open-market commercial paper. Any borrowings, purchases of Federal funds or resale agreements will be deducted in computing the net amount of assets in the secondary reserve.

Although bankers agree that "short maturity" is an essential feature of assets comprising the secondary reserve, there is considerable difference in the definition of "short" in this context. There is room for policies which are at once different and yet appropriate for the situation at hand. Since the secondary reserve is planned to meet potential needs for liquidity, the maturity of assets in this reserve should be related to the needs they are expected to fill. These needs differ from bank to bank, and hence the composition of the assets used in meeting them can also differ. Furthermore, some banks are better equipped than others to use repurchase agreements with Government security dealers and other particular market instruments such as bankers' acceptances in adjusting their reserve positions. The important thing is that the nature and magnitude of a bank's liquidity needs be realistically appraised, and that the composition of the secondary reserve be planned specifically to meet those needs.

Maturities of securities in the secondary reserve should be tailored to the anticipated size and timing of needs which can be foreseen—such as the seasonal needs which loom so large in the secondary reserve planning of most small rural banks. Since it is not possible to tailor maturities precisely to meet other needs, it is customary to aim for a reasonable spread of maturities over that period of time which management decides is "short" enough to be suitable for a secondary reserve. There is general agreement that assets other than U.S. Government securities should, to be so considered, mature within one or two years. (Maturities of any loans in the secondary reserve, being by their nature much shorter, are usually measured in days instead of years.) The limit on Governments is generally either one or two years, but may be as much as five years. In any event, the bank should hold enough maturities within the one-year limit to meet all those needs for funds which it feels are most likely to arise within that period of time. Of course, assets bought to meet seasonal needs will have maturities of less than a year.

Logically, the definition of what is to be included in a bank's secondary reserve should have some influence on its size. If the definition is more liberal the reserve should be larger, to allow for possible delay or loss in marketing the assets when cash is needed.

Measuring Liquidity Needs

Determining the size of the liquidity account is an exacting problem of commercial bank portfolio management. If it is larger than needed, it will unduly penalize earnings. If it is smaller, it may force liquidation of longer-term investments at depressed prices in unfavorable markets and so cause substantial losses. There is no certain way of determining the appropriate size for the secondary reserve, but constant vigilance, good judgment, and careful appraisal of probabilities provide the basis for setting a range for the liquidity account which will meet potential needs for liquidity without undue sacrifice of earnings.

The most difficult part of the problem is to estimate probable liquidity needs realistically. Periodic appraisals are required of prospective deposit and loan movements. These can start with a study of deposit and loan trends for all banks throughout the country, local banks as a group, and the individual bank concerned, with an analysis of the factors shaping deposit and loan demand behavior at the time. The bank's capital structure is then considered—the more ample the bank's capital cushion, the less urgent its need for a wide margin of liquidity to avoid realizing security losses to raise cash. Consideration is also given to Treasury and Federal Reserve policies, and gold and currency movements. With probable developments in these areas in mind, the trend of deposits and loans can be estimated within reasonable limits for the foreseeable future, at least for the next year or two. These estimates should be subjected to continuous reappraisal, and revised as often as seems appropriate.

Essential in determining a bank's liquidity needs is a full and detailed knowledge of the bank and the influences which bear upon the course of its business. This knowledge comes from careful quantitative evaluations;

it will not suffice even in the smallest banks to appraise probable needs for liquidity by "feel." A "feel" for the individual characteristics of the bank is indeed essential; the portfolio manager must have an intimate knowledge of the character of the bank's business, of community needs and characteristics, and of the neighborhood and environment within which the bank operates. But in addition he must know his bank in a manner possible only through evaluation of the basic statistical data.

The statistical detail required for competent management of the small bank's funds is vastly different from that necessary to manage investment operations of a multi-billion dollar institution. In either case, key data are best presented in a clear, simple form to guide decisions. Easiest to maintain and easiest to visualize comprehensively are a few basic charts that throw light on the salient pertinent trends.

First and foremost, the bank must know its deposit structure in as much detail as possible. Total deposits can be charted over a period of several years to point up seasonal movements, growth trends, behavior of deposits during recessions, and other changes. In the large bank this must be on at least a weekly basis and is sometimes on a daily basis; in the small bank a monthly chart suffices although a weekly chart is better. This basic chart can be supplemented by detailed quantitative information on all components of deposits, either charted or in figures. If the bank is to have an adequate secondary reserve policy, such information must provide answers to such questions as the following:

What is the share of time deposits? Time and savings accounts are much more stable in the short run than demand deposits, although their cyclical fluctuations are sometimes larger. Large time deposits, particularly those of foreign origin, are very sensitive to interest rate differentials. From mid-1959 to mid-1960, for example, yields available on short-term Governments were substantially above maximum rates commercial banks were permitted to pay on time deposits. As a result, foreign-owned time deposits in commercial banks fell sharply.

How many deposit accounts does the bank have? Because of the law of averages, a great many small accounts are likely to be far more stable than a few large ones. The stability of a bank's deposits tends to vary inversely with the size of the average account.

Who are the large depositors? How stable are their deposits? The relatively large depositor can create a liquidity problem if he withdraws a large proportion of his account. A continuing record of the balances in the accounts of the large depositors will indicate their probable behavior.

What other unstable accounts does the bank have? Interbank deposits, public funds, and special accounts such as uninvested trust funds are notoriously unstable. Bankers should seek to be familiar with the status of each such account and the conditions under which it is likely to be drawn down.

Is the bank retaining its proportionate share of the business in its trade area? The bank's deposits can be charted as a percentage of total deposits of banks in its competitive area. If the bank is losing ground in relation to its competitors, a larger secondary reserve may be needed to offset any lag in deposit growth behind loan demand.

Records of this sort are vital in planning the secondary reserve portfolio; they furnish the statistical background for qualitative analysis. In making his decisions the banker draws upon the entire range of his knowledge of the economic outlook, both national and local, including current developments in U.S. government fiscal policy and Federal Reserve monetary policy, and their implications.

Armed with the best available information concerning his bank's deposit structure and those eventualities which could affect it, the banker must make a quantitative estimate of the lowest level to which deposits might fall under unfavorable circumstances. This level is sometimes termed the "deposit floor." The difference between the current level of deposits and this probable minimum deposit level is the potential amount of deposit decline for which provision must be made in the secondary reserve account. Obviously this amount will vary with seasonal, cyclical, and other developments. When deposits are at a seasonal peak the bank must allow for enough liquidity to meet the next expected seasonal withdrawal of deposits; for the seasonal low of deposits little or no provision need be made. The same is true of liquidity reserves planned to meet other needs—when these needs have been met, secondary reserves will inevitably be at low levels.

In addition to the estimate of liquidity needed for deposit declines, it is necessary also to estimate liquidity needed to meet potential expansion of the loan account. Maturing loans provide enough liquidity to renew outstanding loans or to make new loans in equal volume, so provision needs to be made in the secondary reserve only for a net increase in the bank's loan volume.

Banks, of course, have a clear obligation to their customers and to their communities to make, within the limits of their lending ability, such sound loans as are needed to finance the growth and development of their trade areas. This loan demand cannot be turned away arbitrarily when the bank finds itself in a tight position. Legitimate customer demands for credit must be met if the community is to maintain its position in the economy and if the bank is to fulfill its proper function. Thus the bank has every incentive to make as many sound loans as it can, consistent with adequate provision for risk balance and liquidity. The difficulty is to arrive at a reasonably good estimate of the direction and magnitude of future changes in loan demands.

In estimating potential loan demands over the foreseeable future, the starting point is full and detailed knowledge of the bank's existing loan portfolio and of the factors which may affect its growth. As in the case of deposits, statistical information is essential. Charts are generally the easiest way to obtain a comprehensive picture of the quantitative aspects of the loan account and its components. The large bank needs a more detailed statistical record than the small bank, but it is not necessary for either to keep a complex array of charts. Basic, of course, is the total loan volume, which can be charted for several years on a monthly or weekly basis (excluding such loans as short-term money market loans held largely in the secondary reserve). Examination of such a chart reveals much about the pattern of loan expansion over a period of years, over the business cycle, and on a seasonal basis. In addition, a record of each of the major loan components can be maintained to analyze potential changes in each of them.

In projecting potential loan demand, many factors are considered. National and local business conditions and outlook are of major importance. Lending limitations imposed by law and regulation, as well as policies of the bank's management, must be taken into account.

The basic technique is the same as that of anticipating changes in the deposit level. After taking into consideration pertinent factors, an estimate is made of the maximum level beyond which the loan account is not expected to increase during the planning period. This maximum is sometimes called the "loan ceiling." The difference between the present level of loans and this probable maximum for the planning period represents the amount for which provision must be made in the bank's secondary reserve.

At best, estimates of loan ceilings and deposit floors can only be approximate, and therefore allowance must be made for a margin of error. This can be done by making liberal estimates, or by adding some reasonable amount after the estimates have been made.

Thought may be given also to the possibility of an increase in reserve requirements, although this instrument of Federal Reserve policy has not been used in recent years. A bank would have to dip into its secondary reserves for funds to meet an increase in reserve requirements. Securities held for this more remote contingency can be of longer maturity than the rest of the secondary reserve. Whatever provision is made for a margin of error or possible increase in reserve requirements, it cannot be made by chance. It must be a considered decision, even where the contingency is remote.

Once estimates have been made of the probable deposit floor and loan ceiling, the size of the secondary reserve can be determined in the following manner.

1) Compute the difference between current deposits and the estimated deposit floor, and the difference between current loans and the

estimated loan ceiling. The sum of these differences, plus whatever extra margin of safety is decided upon, represents the total potential loss of funds for which provision must be made in the secondary reserve.

2) From this total subtract any deposits with the Federal Reserve Bank or correspondent banks in excess of legal requirements and minimum acceptable balances. A further subtraction can be made for the amount of legal reserves that would be released by a decline in deposits to the estimated deposit floor. The resulting balance is the amount required in the liquidity account.

The carrying out of secondary reserve policy, once established, is largely a matter of timing. Secondary reserve securities are bought or sold promptly as surplus funds become available or as funds are lost as a result of day-to-day changes in deposits and loans. Conceivably, sales of securities to meet declines in deposits and increases in loans might result, at times, in almost completely eliminating the secondary reserve, but such an event need not be cause for concern. The secondary reserve was established for just such contingencies and so is to be used when needed. Not to do so, in an effort to maintain some specific pattern of maturity distribution, would penalize a bank's income and lead to the unwise and costly practice of making changes in longer-term investments in response to temporary fluctuations in deposits and loans. On the other hand, a reduction of the secondary reserve to an inadequate level in the light of a *current reappraisal* of liquidity needs is justifiable cause for concern, and requires prompt action to increase the secondary reserve to a level found to be presently desirable. Such action must be taken promptly, unless sufficient securities in the investment account will shortly become part of the secondary reserve through the shortening of maturity due to the passage of time.

Changes in the size of the secondary reserve are made also in the light of periodic reappraisals of liquidity needs. When an appraisal shows that the secondary reserve is larger than needed, the excess can be utilized to buy longer term securities for inclusion in the bond account. Conversely, when it is found that the secondary reserve is too small, the deficiency can be corrected by selling securities from the investment account and using the proceeds to increase assets in the secondary reserve. Corrections are made promptly or slowly as needs may indicate.

Accurate anticipation of needs for funds facilitates the task of selecting securities to sell to meet a loan expansion or deposit contraction. Cash is provided by currently maturing securities bought for that purpose or by sales of very short maturities. When the bank is faced with a need for cash that was not anticipated, however, a choice must be made as to which securities are to be sold from the investment account. This decision can be made in conjunction with a reappraisal of the bank's liquidity needs. The process of deciding what to sell is about the same as that of deciding what to buy. If the bank were buying securities with excess funds rather than selling them to obtain funds, it would review its portfolio to see how nearly its maturity structure matches its anticipated liquidity needs, and would also consider possible effects on its income tax liability. The interest rate structure—current and prospective—would be the final determining factor as to which security would be the most advantageous to purchase. Similarly, the bank needing to sell securities considers its liquidity needs, its existing maturity structure, its tax status and the current and prospective interest rate structure.

Earnings—the Investment Account

The investment account comprises all securities not held in the secondary reserve. Its basic functions are to provide earnings for the bank and to contribute to appropriate balancing of risks in the bank's assets. Any potential liquidity in the investment account is a comforting bonus. This account does, in fact serve as "liquidity in depth" in providing funds to supplement the secondary reserve.

The maturity distribution in the investment account reflects management appraisal of interest rate prospects, and is subject to change in the light of periodic reappraisals. A bank will buy for its investment account securities which it believes it can hold and would be willing to hold to maturity, although it will effect switches as favorable opportunities arise. Ten years is frequently suggested as an appropriate maximum maturity for a bank, but longer maturities are held when the bank's management does not feel disturbed if such securities show book losses because interest rates have risen.

In intent, the investment account is the bank's residual asset account. Intentions and developments often differ, however, for even the most alert management cannot foresee all contingencies which will influence a bank's needs for funds over the next five, ten, or fifteen years. The investment account has served as a "last ditch of defense" for banks subject to an exceptionally protracted liquidity strain, and it will doubtless serve this purpose again.

When it can be accomplished without undue sacrifice of yield or risk of price depreciation, banks find it desirable to have maturities in the investment account spaced over the years so that the account is not unduly concentrated in any one maturity range. The shorter maturities become available for the liquidity account as they move nearer to maturity. If the liquidity account does not need replenishing from this source, shorter maturities can then be sold and the proceeds used to purchase new securities maturing near the end of the favored maturity range.

The extent to which a bank can space its maturities is limited in practice by the available supply of securities in various maturity ranges, by relative yields, and by the regularity with which funds become available for investment. No arbitrary pattern, even though theoretically desirable, will be adhered to which would either unduly reduce income or, greatly increase the risk of loss. When yields for particular maturities are out of line, spacing of maturities will be adjusted accordingly.

Banks with more than usual investment know-how may invest some of their surplus funds in issues of good quality, as distinct from top quality. This will be done, however, if capital funds or reserves are sufficiently large to permit, without embarrassment, write-downs or charge-offs that could become necessary. Banks have to be more careful than most financial institutions in assuming risks in their investment portfolios. They operate with a relatively small margin of capital, and a comparatively small added risk in the investment account looms large in relation to capital funds. They cannot afford in most cases to take on substantial risks in addition to those assumed in the loan account.

In selecting securities for their investment accounts, commercial banks assume two completely different types of risk—credit risk and market risk. Credit risk involves the risk that the borrower may fail to pay interest or principal when due. Through careful analysis and supervision of its investment portfolio, the bank can minimize the risk of acquiring investments of inadequate quality and can quickly dispose of any that threaten to deteriorate in quality. Professional rating services serve as a starting point in quality analysis, but these are not clairvoyant. Since they frequently follow rather than lead the market with rating changes, supplemental analysis is essential.

At best, credit risks cannot be completely eliminated from portfolios that include other than U.S. Government securities. But the element of risk which cannot be eliminated can be spread by following the basic tenet of diversification, so that no serious loss will be incurred if one investment or group of investments should go sour. Diversification of holdings which carry an element of risk takes several forms. Dividing holdings of securities among municipal obligations and railroad, public utility, and industrial obligations is a first step. Since a recession will typically hit one industry harder than another, or an entire industry may begin a permanent decline because of competitive or other reasons, holdings of industrials in particular have to be well diversified. Economic changes may cause a temporary or lasting decline in the economy of an entire geographic area, affecting the credit of governmental units as well as business concerns; geographic diversification is therefore desirable.

Diversification in the investment portfolio is affected by a bank's other assets. Most of a bank's loans and a good part of its municipal bonds are generally concentrated in the bank's trade area. Diversification by area and industry, however, can be obtained by purchasing obligations of other corporations and municipalities. It follows, of course, the lower the average grade of obligations held, the greater is the need for diversification. United States Government obligations transcend the need for diversification because they are based on the credit and taxing power of the federal government.

While the principle of diversification is important, the law of averages is no substitute for good credit judgment. Carried to extremes, diversification can lead to averaging down of quality of investment portfolios in which the number of items becomes so large as to preclude the close watching essential to successful portfolio management. The greater the number of issues and the wider the geographic and industrial diversification, the more competent the supervision of the account must be.

Market risk is the risk of capital loss from a decline in price because of a rise in interest rates. Although a given interest rate change results in a substantially larger price change for securities of longer maturity, short-term interest rates usually undergo wider swings than long-term rates. For example, on April 21, 1958, the 3½ percent Treasury bonds of 1990 (then a thirty-two-year issue) were selling at 106 24/32 to yield 3.16 percent. By the end of 1959, following a sharp rise in interest rates, this issue was selling at 84 20/32 to yield 4.41 percent. The yield increased 1.25 basis points and the price declined more than twenty-two points—a book loss of one-fifth of the value of the investment in just over twenty months. Over the same period of time, the yield on the 2½ percent bonds of 1961 (three and one-half years from maturity) rose from 2.10 percent to 4.95 percent and their price fell from 101 8/32 to 95 18/32. The increase in yield on the shorter issue was 136 percent and on the longer issue 40 percent—less than one-third as much. Yet a bank buying both issues in April 1958, and selling them at year-end 1959 would have taken about four times as much loss on the longer bond.

The relation between shorter- and longer-term interest rates reflects in part the market's appraisal of the probable future trend of interest rates. When a rise in rates is expected, many lenders favor short maturities so that funds will be available to buy long-term investments when the expected decline in price occurs. At the same time, borrowers try to borrow at long term while the lower rates prevail. This tends to concentrate the supply of funds in the short end of the market and the demand for funds in the long end, with the result that short-term rates will be low relative to long-term rates (an "upward sloping yield curve"). Conversely, when the market reflects expectations of a decline in interest rates, short-term rates may rise above long-term (a "downward sloping yield curve"). Thus actions of lenders and borrowers will in each case accelerate the effected change in long-term rates.

Fluctuations in short- and long-term interest rates, and consequent changes in security prices, make necessary the conceptual division between the secondary reserve account and the investment account. Because short-term rates are often lower than long-term rates, and because longer-term issues are subject to wider price changes, a secondary reserve for liquidity (in which earnings are a minor consideration) is necessary, and an investment account for longer maturities that will provide higher earnings over a period of time is also required.

Commercial banks, in their investment account, are investors rather than traders in bonds. While investment officers may seek to improve the over-all return realized on the portfolio by occasional switches, they generally favor a spacing of maturities and do not as a rule attempt to anticipate market swings by drastic portfolio switching.

The principle of diversification can thus be adapted to the interest rate as well as the credit risk. *Diversification over time* is provided by spacing maturities in the investment account.

Regulation of Bank Investments

Regulations governing state-chartered banks differ from state to state, but in general they are consistent in approving purchase of high-grade bonds and in prohibiting purchase of stocks. Nationally chartered banks, and state banks which are members of the Federal Reserve System, are also permitted to invest in high quality bonds and prohibited from acquiring stocks, with some exceptions. Purchase of stock is permitted

1) in acquiring Federal Reserve Bank stock as required by membership in the Federal Reserve System;
2) when it represents ownership of the bank's quarters (but not in excess of the bank's capital without special permission);
3) in a safety-deposit corporation (up to 15 percent of the bank's capital and surplus);
4) in banks organized to do a foreign banking business (up to 10 percent of capital and surplus);
5) when acquired as collateral incident to the default of a borrowing customer;
6) in small business investment companies (up to 1 percent of capital and surplus);
7) in the Federal National Mortgage Association.

Limitations on the amount of securities which can be held by member banks were imposed by the Banking Acts of 1933 and 1935. Holdings of securities of any one issuer (except U.S. Governments, general obligations of state and local governments, and specified U.S. Government Agency issues) were restricted to a maximum of 10 percent of capital and surplus, and total loans and investments to all affiliates were limited to 20 percent of capital and surplus. Member banks were also required by the Banking Act of 1933 to sever all connections with security affiliates, and were prohibited from participating in the underwriting of new issues of securities other than Federal Government obligations, Federal Agency issues, and general obligations of municipalities.

The regulation of the Comptroller of the Currency governing the quality of investment securities serves as the basis for judging minimum standards of quality which are generally used by all supervisory agencies. This directive, first issued in 1936 and revised in 1938 and 1957, outlines the basic principles banks are expected to observe in acquiring securities:

1) Securities must be marketable reasonably quickly at a fair value.
2) Securities be distributed publicly, or be
    a) marketable because of the fact that other securities of the issuer have adequate public distribution,
    b) of less than ten-year maturity with amortization of 75 percent of the debt before the ten years expire, or
    c) sound and salable special revenue municipal obligations.
3) Trustees for securities issued under trust agreements must be banks or trust companies independent of the issuer.
4) Securities must be in the form of bonds, notes, or debentures.
5) Banks can deal in securities (other than those of federal, state, and local governments and certain federal agencies) only to the extent of purchases for their own account, and for their customers on specific orders of the customers.
6) Purchase of predominantly speculative securities or securities in default is prohibited.
7) Premiums paid for securities must be amortized.
8) Convertible bonds may be purchased if convertible at the option of the holder and if the price paid provides a yield in line with that of non-convertible securities of similar quality and maturity.
9) Adequate credit information must be kept on file.

These regulations do not apply to securities acquired through foreclosure of collateral pledged for loans.

Further supervision of bank investments is exerted by examiners in classifying securities owned by banks into four groupings.

Group I includes "investment securities," specifically the first four ratings (of nine) used by professional bond rating agencies. It also includes unrated securities of equivalent quality. Examiners value these securities at cost and do not take account of either appreciation or depreciation in their reports. This makes it unnecessary for the bank to absorb book loses on investment grade securities unless the securities are actually liquidated in the market.

Group II includes other bonds not in default. These are valued at market prices (averaged over the preceding eighteen months) and half of any depreciation from cost is deducted by examiners in computing the bank's net sound capital.

Group III consists of bonds in default.

Group IV consists of stocks. These are carried at market value, and net depreciation from acquisition cost must be written off as losses.

These laws and regulations provide the general framework within which each bank is free to pursue its investment policy. They provide restrictions rather than guidance for managing the portfolio. The supervisory authorities have emphasized that final responsibility for sound and prudent investment policy lies at the door of bank management.

The Volume of Commercial Bank Investments

At year-end 1945, investments of all commercial banks aggregated almost $98 billion, following huge wartime purchase of Government securities. Early in 1946 a sharp decline began, first because of Treasury debt repayment and then as loan demands increased during the first few postwar years. Bank investments have not regained the level reached at the end of World War II. Since 1950 the total has fluctuated fairly widely, but the trend has been slightly upward mainly because of increases in holdings of municipal securities. At year-end 1959, commercial bank investments were about $79.4 billion.

The volume of commercial bank investments, as noted earlier, varies with seasonal and cyclical fluctuations in the demand for loans, which in turn vary with economic fluctuations. In the period of rapid expansion of loans from late 1954 through 1957, commercial banks reduced their holdings of securities by more than one-tenth and thus obtained over half of the funds needed for the expansion of loans. In 1959 three-fifths of the funds used to finance a sharp loan increase came from sales of securities.

Because of this use of investments as a reservoir of funds for meeting demands for loans, the ratio of investments to total earning assets tends to vary even more widely than the dollar amount of investments. In early 1946, when deposits were at the high level produced by wartime Treasury deficit financing, and when loan demand was still relatively light, investments accounted for four-fifths of the earning assets of commercial banks. By 1959, loan expansion had cut this ratio almost in half and investments amounted to just a little more than two-fifths of earning assets.

Seasonal changes in economic activity influence the ratio of loans to earning assets in much the same manner as changes growing out of the business cycle. When a commercial bank is faced with a seasonal increase in loans or decline in deposits (and only too frequently they occur simultaneously) it meets the need for funds by reducing its investments. Conversely, when seasonal pressures ease, investments will be built up again.

Major developments such as wars profoundly influence the proportion of securities in earning assets. The commercial banking system is typically used to create that part of the funds needed for war finance which is not raised by taxation or by borrowing from the public. Since civilian production and consumption are restricted in a war economy, deposits created by bank purchases of Government securities provide more than enough funds to meet needs and there is little loan demand. Almost all of the increase in assets of the commercial banking system during World War II was in investments.

The ratio of investments to earning assets is strongly affected by Federal Reserve policy. An easy Federal Reserve credit policy encourages an increase in investments, primarily since loan demand is likely to weaken at such times. A restrictive credit policy puts pressure on banks to reduce investments in order to acquire the funds to finance loan expansion, because banks are essentially lending institutions.

U.S. Government Securities as Bank Investments

U.S. Government securities are by far the most important part of the secondary reserves of today's banking system, and a substantial part of the investment account of commercial banks.

One of the prime reasons for the commercial banks' preference for Governments, as noted above, is their superior quality. There is no credit risk in Government securities. Maturing issues are either refunded or retired. Because of the vast taxing and borrowing powers of the federal government, there is no question of its ability to service its obligations— though inflation in the economy may result from inadequate reliance on taxes.

In a bank's secondary reserve the attributes of liquidity and safety are paramount; yield is only incidental. Short-term Governments represent the ultimate in both liquidity and safety. Bankers learned in the early 1930's that commercial loans and corporate and municipal securities could not be depended upon as sources of liquidity under conditions then prevailing because of both market and credit risks. In 1953, they found that they could not rely on long- and medium-term Governments, since these decline in price as interest rates rise.

In the investment account, safety and yield are first in importance and liquidity is a secondary consideration. Although Governments have the highest quality of any class of investments, the yield they give at times is not far below that of other riskier investments.

Many other reasons explain why banks are attracted to Governments.

They enjoy a broad market; substantial sales can usually be effected without causing material changes in price, and the cost of buying or selling is comparatively small. The spread between the bid and asked prices of dealers is minuscule in comparison to that for many other securities. The very large size of Treasury issues enables banks to buy and sell particular maturities in small or large amounts. The unquestioned quality of Governments and the ease of transfer or pledge causes them to be the most widely used of all investments as collateral for public deposits or as the basis for borrowing under repurchase agreement or from the Federal Reserve banks. The fact that Governments are available in large or small denominations helps reduce bookkeeping, storage, and similar costs. And since analysis of the borrower's credit is unnecessary, the small bank is about as well set up to invest in Governments as is the large bank.

In the past the interest on some issues of Federal Government and Agency securities has had the additional attraction of complete exemption (from normal tax and surtax) or partial exemption (from normal tax only) from Federal income taxes. No new issues have been exempted from taxation since 1941. At present there is only one partially exempt Government issue still outstanding—the 2¾ percent bonds of December 1965-60. The last outstanding Agency tax-exempt issue matured in 1946.

Although Governments have many advantages as investments for banks, including the absence of credit risk, they are definitely subject to market risk. For example, the 2½ percent bonds of September 1967-72, widely held by banks, have sold as high as 109 18/32 and as low as 78 10/32 since their issue in 1941. If a bank makes adequate provision in its secondary reserve account for its liquidity requirements, however, it will not have to sell bonds and realize losses unless it chooses to do so.

Obligations of U.S. Agencies as Bank Investments

Another outlet for banks' funds is investment in the non-guaranteed issues of Federal Agencies. While these are not obligations of the U.S. government or guaranteed by it, they do involve a moral obligation of the federal government, and payment at maturity is regarded as beyond question. At this time, available issues include those of the Federal Intermediate Credit Banks, the Federal National Mortgage Association, the Federal Land Banks, the Banks for Cooperatives, and the Federal Home Loan Banks. These securities have the advantage of high quality and a better yield than can be obtained on Governments—ranging from ¼ percent to ¾ percent more. Most issues are comparatively small, however, so that marketability is relatively limited, especially during periods of credit tightness. For this reason they cannot be counted on to lend liquidity to the bank's portfolio except as they mature.

Over the past few years the volume of these securities has increased substantially. Commercial banks probably held upwards of one-fifth of the total amount outstanding in 1959.

Tax-Exempt State and Local Obligations as Bank Investments

High rates of Federal income taxation make tax-exempts a desirable element in most commercial bank investment portfolios. Interest earned on obligations of state and local governmental units is fully exempt from federal taxation. This provides a substantial incentive for taxpayers in high tax brackets to purchase such securities. The extent to which banks find it profitable to buy tax-exempts varies directly with the marginal tax rate which they pay. For example, a 3 percent tax-exempt yield is equivalent to a taxable yield of 6.25 percent for a bank paying the maximum 52 percent tax rate, but it is equivalent only to a 4.28 percent yield for a bank in the 30 percent tax bracket.

Commercial banks compete in the purchase of these securities with individuals paying high income tax rates (mutual institutions are little interested because of the very favored tax position they enjoy). Market prices of these securities reflect their tax-exempt status to some extent, and yields are lower than pre-tax yields of taxable securities of equivalent quality and maturity. In recent years, however, flotations of municipals have expanded sharply and the demand from high bracket investors has not been sufficient to absorb the supply. As a result, yields of tax-exempt bonds have risen closer to those of taxable issues, and most banks can earn a substantially larger after-tax return from municipals than from taxable securities. This has provided a very large market for the placement of state and local security issues.

Of the $64 billion of municipals outstanding at year-end 1959, commercial banks owned more than one-fourth. Individuals comprise the largest group of holders of municipals, but commercial bank holdings are the next largest. They hold considerably more than all other private corporate holders combined.

Many municipal obligations are of the very highest quality, although the range between the best and the poorest municipal is substantial. Since there is such a wide range in quality of municipals, the supervisory authorities have generally agreed that only the four highest ratings of securities are acceptable for bank investment. Few banks, however, find it advisable to move out beyond the first three classifications.

The main attractiveness of municipals is their high effective yield after taxes; they can usually give a better after-tax yield than mortgages. Moreover, since they are generally available in serial issues, it is possible to find the right maturities to fit into a bank's portfolio. Then, too, commercial banks generally feel that they have an obligation to support municipal issues originated in their trade areas. This has public relations advantages; it can be a factor in acquiring or holding public deposits, and the local bank is in an excellent position to note promptly factors which could cause deterioration in the quality of the securities.

In spite of the obvious advantages of tax-exempts, there are important difficulties. One is that the bank may be subjected to pressure to buy or hold larger quantities or lower quality issues than are appropriate. As a matter of fact, many of the more than 3,000 counties in the United States find that the local bank is the principal market for their securities. If necessary, local banks will on occasion take losses from the sale of other securities in order to help finance the local high school or municipal building. Local securities have something of the character of loans, and credit can safely be extended in this form only if it would be safe to extend the same amount of money as a loan. This is particularly true in the case of small local issues which are not marketable. Furthermore, issues of governmental units in the bank's trade area augment the geographic risks of the loan account, thus forcing banks to forego the benefits of geographic diversification.

Municipals are typically limited in salability because of the necessarily restricted size of each issue. Four out of every five issues are for less than $1 million. Since these bonds are usually issued with serial maturities, the size of individual maturities may be quite small. Further, because tax exemption of interest is the major attraction, a relatively small number of buyers (those in high tax brackets) provide the chief market for most issues. As a matter of fact, the purchase of municipals other than the best known and favored names involves an immediate potential loss because of the substantial spread between bid and asked prices stemming from this limited marketability. The spread may equal or exceed a year's interest, and can cut into the realized yield considerably if the issue must be sold before it matures. Since these bonds can be hard to sell in a depressed market, they cannot in any event be counted on to provide liquidity except as they mature. Banks usually buy municipals with the intention of holding them to maturity.

Paradoxically, commercial banks find that one great disadvantage in holding municipals is the fact that they are so popular with banks. Since banks make up a very large share of the total market for municipals, prices of municipals react very sensitively to changes in bank demand for them. Accordingly, the prices of municipals move widely in response to varying degrees of credit tightness, falling when banks are short of funds and rising when banks have more money to invest. Prices of municipals also fluctuate with changing valuation by investors of the yield value of the tax exemption privilege. Such valuation changes may be due either to changes in rates or to changes in earnings of potential purchasers which place them in higher or lower marginal tax brackets.

The yield curve on tax-exempt securities does not necessarily parallel that of U.S. Government securities. Hence, it may be possible to obtain a significantly greater return by choosing carefully among different available maturities on the basis of yield.

Municipals differ widely as to the nature of the issuing agency, which may be a sovereign state, a small school district, or any governmental unit between these extremes. For example, no state except New York may be sued without its consent, a fact which could make it more difficult to force payment through the courts than in the case of a local government unit.

Tax-exempt issues vary in desirability with the sources of funds to be used for servicing the debt. Most desirable are general obligations which tap the "full faith and credit" and total taxing power of the issuer for payment. Some general obligations, however, are subject to specific and potentially crippling limitations on funds available for debt service. For example, their servicing may be subject to the application of a maximum limit on the tax rate which may be applied in the locality (limited tax bonds), or payment may be limited primarily to a specific tax source (special tax or special assessment bonds), even though backed additionally by the full faith and credit of the issuer.

Revenue bonds of municipalities, which are payable from income derived from some specified facility or activity, have expanded greatly in volume in recent years. Because of the restricted source of funds for servicing these obligations, they are considerably less favored as investments for commercial banks. (Bonds primarily payable from specific revenues may be backed additionally by the full faith and credit of the issuer, in which case they are appropriately classed as general obligations.)

Public housing authority obligations are very high quality municipals, regardless of the size or location of the issuer. Although the primary source of payment is the net rental income of the issuing local housing authority, they are in effect backed by the full faith and credit of the United States government since they are fully underwritten by the Public Housing Administration. The PHA in turn has $1.5 billion authority to borrow from the Treasury. These bonds are particularly attractive for banks since they provide the tax exemption feature of municipals coupled with the very high quality of Federal Agency obligations.

The question of the appropriate volume of tax-exempt securities to hold is a difficult decision for banks. Sometimes banks have paid more for the tax exemption feature than it is worth to them, particularly during the war and early postwar years. Because of the higher after-tax yield on municipals, a moderate-sized bank in the 52 percent tax bracket may increase such holdings unthinkingly to the point where it drops into the

30 percent tax bracket whereupon the after-tax yield may be no higher than taxable investments of similar quality.

Although the volume of tax-exempts held varies widely from bank to bank, rules of thumb to serve as guides are used by investment officers. Maximum percentages range from 5 percent of assets to as much as 15 percent and vary from time to time with changing conditions. A commercial bank generally will hold only as large a volume of municipals as it feels its staff can adequately supervise. It will seek to insure that (1) the obligations are of good quality; (2) the bank's risks are adequately diversified; (3) the bank has no need for the funds as secondary reserves; (4) it is still in a tax bracket where it nets more after-tax income by holding tax-exempts than by holding taxable obligations.

Corporate Securities as Bank Investments

During World War II and the immediate postwar years, commercial banks increased their holdings of corporates in their search for income-yielding assets. Even in these years, however, corporates were not an important part of commercial bank assets, and they have declined further in relative importance over the past decade. The term loan has proved for most banks a much more desirable medium for granting longer-term credit to business than corporate bond purchases.

Commercial bank holdings of corporates now average less than 1 percent of their loans and investments, and amount to something less than 2 percent of long-term corporate debt outstanding. Commercial banks generally hold eight or ten to fifteen times as large a volume of municipals as of corporates.

Yield is an attractive feature of corporates, particularly for banks with low earnings and in a low tax bracket. Corporates appeal to a bank which has a chronic deficiency in loan demand with a corresponding chronic surplus of funds for investment, since they give higher before-tax yields as a rule than other classes of securities, and many of them are of top quality.

Supervisory agency regulations limit bank investment in corporates to the four top ratings, but most banks confine their purchases to a more restricted range. In the 1930's losses were heavily concentrated in issues below the first three grades.

Corporate bonds are similar to term loans made to the same corporations, with two obvious exceptions. First, most bonds are issued with maturities longer than those acceptable for term loans. Second, bonds are issued in marketable form. However, at times when a bank is under pressure to sell its "marketable" corporates to acquire additional liquidity, other banks and other investors also may be under pressure to sell, so that prices are depressed.

Commercial banks compete in the market for corporate bonds with investing institutions like life insurance companies which have highly trained staffs of bond specialists. The average banker is a specialist in making loans. Except where he has access to a competent staff trained in investment analysis, he is likely to be quite cautious in his attitude toward corporate bonds as bank investments. However, a number of banks, including small banks, have staffs engaged in loan and trust work or they have outside sources of advice that enable them to invest with safety in high-grade corporate securities.

One type of corporate security which has been very attractive to banks is the shorter maturities of railway equipment securities, although their quality varies significantly with the credit standing of the issuer. There are several different versions of equipment financing arrangements. Basically, each plan achieves in one way or another the objective of retaining for the investor actual title to specified railway rolling stock while the railway pays for its use. The securities, which represent participation in the ownership of the equipment, are issued on a serial basis, usually covering fifteen years or less. They are a claim on current income—taking precedence over servicing of outstanding mortgage bonds—and in addition they represent ownership of equipment which in case of default can be resold or released to other railways.

Each separate maturity of an equipment issue, while equal in quality to others, in effect has a separate market. It must be sold to a buyer who is willing to take that particular maturity of that particular issue. Thus it may take some time to sell such obligations, even in a favorable market, and they cannot be counted on for liquidity except at maturity.

The directive of the Comptroller of the Currency governing investment permits national banks to invest only in those convertible bonds which sell on a basis comparable to that of similar bonds that do not have the convertible feature. Since this is the basis for similar regulation on the part of other supervisory agencies, the regulation in effect applies to most banks. This restriction, applied with some flexibility, stems from the fact that banks are not permitted to acquire stocks as investments; to pay a substantial premium for the conversion feature in essence would be to pay for the stock. Since the market normally attaches value to the convertibility feature, however, convertibles seldom sell at yields equivalent to similar bonds without this feature.

Convertibles can give the holder substantial profits when the conversion privilege causes appreciation in price, and they can prove very attractive investments for banks with access to expert investment counsel. This class of securities had a poor record during the depression, however, and prudence and the supervisory authorities combine to keep commercial banks from being substantial purchasers of convertibles.

Bank Portfolio Management Problems

Pledged Securities

Major portfolio management problems can arise from the requirement in federal and a majority of state laws that Government or municipal obligations be pledged as collateral for public deposits. When the demand for loans is strong, a bank holding substantial public deposits may find its ability to serve credit needs hampered, not only because a large part of its investment portfolios is pledged as collateral for public deposits, but also because such pledged securities are not available as a liquidity source for meeting net losses of other deposits. As a result, another large part of the investment portfolio must be held for liquidity. In 1960, about "half the Government bond portfolio" of New York City banks was pledged against public deposits.[2]

Whatever justification the requirement that specific securities be pledged against deposits of public bodies may have had in the past when the risk of bank insolvency was a material factor, the many safeguards of the strength of the banking system that have been developed call for critical reconsideration of this provision of law. It could interfere significantly with the future ability of banks to adjust their lending and investing to changing credit requirements.

Gains and Losses on Security Sales

One of the most widely misunderstood aspects of the management of commercial bank investment portfolios is the net losses on sales of securities that result from the inherent nature of the operations of commercial banks. A surprising number of individuals—including directors in many smaller banks—feel that depreciation of securities is a sign of poor portfolio management, and that realized losses should be avoided at all costs. Actually, losses in the investment account will have to be taken at times in the best managed investment accounts.

Losses in the investment portfolio result from the unique role banks play in our economy. They are the focal points through which the Federal Reserve moves to foster growth and prosperity when it creates additional reserves. Banks can then expand their assets and deposits. In periods of recession loan demands are usually slack, hence asset expansion will take the form of acquisition of investments. During periods of prosperity, by contrast, the Federal Reserve restrains undue expansion and inflation, by keeping the banks short of reserves, so that banks must dispose of

---

[2] From address of A. C. Simmonds, Jr., President of the New York State Bankers Association, before its Investment Seminar, September 30, 1960.

securities to obtain funds to meet the expanding loan demands of their customers.

Commercial banks typically find that they have funds to buy securities in volume most often during recessions when interest rates are low and security prices are high, while they have to sell investments to make customer loans during boom periods when rates are high and prices low. Over the long run, therefore, net losses on investment transactions are almost inevitable.

The Treasury recognized the special nature of net security losses for commercial banks in the early years of World War II, when it recommended to Congress that banks be permitted to deduct such losses in computing income for tax purposes. This provision of the law eases the impact of net losses taken on sales of securities by banks in declining markets. For a bank in the highest (52 percent) tax bracket, 52 percent of a net loss on sale of investments is offset by reduced tax liabilities, while the bank bears 48 percent of the loss. This helps the Treasury in its debt management operations, for banks have more incentive to purchase and underwrite Treasury securities when net portfolio losses are cushioned by the tax treatment. This provision also makes it more feasible for banks to hold longer-term Governments, thus helping the Treasury in its continuing battle to lengthen the average maturity of its outstanding debt obligations. The tax treatment of net security losses by banks has a countercyclical effect to the extent that it encourages purchases of securities which add to the money supply during recessions, while subsequent sales of securities to meet loan demands during recoveries absorb loanable funds of nonbank lenders.

Accounting, in bank earning statements, for gains and losses on sales of securities presents problems. Profits on the sale of securities are deducted from losses in computing net profit or loss from sales of securities each year, and the difference determines whether the bank has had a "profit year" or a "loss year." Since fluctuations in interest rates are the principal determinant of whether banks as a group experience net profits or losses on sales of securities, most banks report net losses during recovery years, while net profits usually result during recession years. Since net profits on the sale of securities held six months or longer are taxable at the capital gain rate of 25 percent, while net losses are deductible from taxable income, banks usually try to minimize taking both profits and losses during the same year.

Net losses or profits from the sale of securities are an erratic influence on the net income reported by a commercial bank where they are charged or added directly to earnings. Since wide variations in reported profits can affect the ability of a bank to attract capital and may confuse investors, many reports to stockholders separate loss or gain from sales of securities from net current operating earnings. Net operating earnings after taxes give a better measure of recurring earning power, while bond profits are placed in a reserve against which bond losses are charged when the bank has to sell securities in an unfavorable market.

From time to time banks find it to their advantage to revamp the composition of their investment portfolios. Bankers frequently switch between issues to realign their maturity structure or to acquire securities that are available on a favorable yield basis. Such opportunities become more common when bond markets are depressed due to exuberance in business. The wise bank uses such periods to extend maturities at improved yields to avoid the need to do so when prices are higher and yields are less attractive.

The banker who spots a weakening of loan demand in time to lengthen his portfolio somewhat is in a better earnings position when interest rates subsequently soften. And the banker who holds largely short maturities at the beginning of a period of resurgent loan demand will have to take smaller losses liquidating investments to obtain loanable funds. If he misjudges, he incurs book or realized losses as a result of such switches.

The high degree of liquidity maintained by the commercial banking system involves a substantial cost to the banks in the form of reduced earnings. If a bank concentrates its funds in short maturities during a recession, it has to accept a relatively lower yield. If it tries to reach out for longer maturities to obtain a higher yield, it may well have to take capital losses later when business conditions improve and bonds are sold to obtain cash for loans. The cost of maintaining adequate liquidity, however incurred, must be accepted as part of the cost of business lending.

Appraisal of Bank Portfolio Management Policies

Mankind has always fallen short of perfection in its endeavors, and management of bank portfolios is no exception to the rule. Nevertheless, portfolio management has been largely responsible for the banking system's contribution to the credit needs of the economy in the last two decades of world war and rapid economic expansion.

Where individual banks have had relatively poor investment results, they have shown up either in income lost through maintenance of excess liquidity or in capital losses incurred when insufficient liquidity forced sales of securities at unfavorable prices.

The bank which consistently achieves a good record in the management of its investments is the bank which takes the trouble to know as much as possible about its deposits and loans and the whole complex of factors influencing them, and which applies a high degree of skill in using this knowledge to plan for its liquidity needs. It is rare that good investment performance is the result of chance.

One reason for relatively poor results in investment portfolio management is a lack of clear understanding of the purposes that a bank's investments serve. This could result, for example, in the purchase of a five-year bond to meet a known seasonal need. Another obvious example is undue lengthening of maturities or lowering of quality in order to increase investment earnings because of a temporary decline in total earnings. A second reason is a poor choice of individual securities, often because of inadequate analysis of credit risks. In either case the bank may find itself "frozen" into holdings of securities which can be sold only at substantial loss when funds are needed.

Specific problems faced by commercial banks in managing the investment portfolio vary over the cycle and as basic conditions change. Managements have learned to maintain a flexible attitude, so that investment policies can be modified to meet new situations as they arise. Problems of portfolio management are substantially different today from those of the 1920's, the 1930's, or of a decade ago. Loan demands, which for two decades were relatively light, took on a new lease on life in the 1950's. Except during recessions, demands for loans are now so great that banks are hard put to satisfy their customers' needs. The result has been a contraction of bank security holdings to a point where it is doubly essential for banks to use intelligent planning in their portfolio policies.

As already noted, the heart of the commercial banking function is the making of loans. Banks specialize in taking the risks involved in providing funds directly to borrowers on the basis of an assessment of their ability to repay. Backed by an array of credit files, reports, and knowledge gleaned by personal contact with the borrower and his affairs, banks are in a position to make loans to businesses which cannot readily or do not want to resort to financing through bond or stock issues or other open market instruments. Small business and consumer lending are other fields of specialization. Commercial banks are currently performing these major economic functions much of the time at close to capacity levels. The great expansion of loans has meant that commercial banks have lost a large part of the big liquidity cushion in the investment portfolio they possessed during the earlier postwar years. A further rise in loan demand or a drop in deposits of individual banks, particularly when interest rates rise, cannot be coped with as easily now. Banks thus face a much greater challenge in adjusting their operations to the effects of the business cycle.

We cannot know how banks will manage their investment portfolios to meet new problems as they develop in the future. We do know from experience, however, that skillful planning for liquidity to meet future loan demands and deposit fluctuations is good alike for the banks, for their customers, and for the economy.

Chapter 11

COMMERCIAL BANKS AND
THE TRUST FUNCTION

Development of the Trust Business

Although the development of fiduciary services may be traced to antiquity, the first corporate fiduciaries in the United States were organized primarily as insurance companies in the early years of the nineteenth century. Before long it became evident that the trust business was also closely allied to banking. Initially, the trustor's equity resembled a share in a present-day investment company, but by the mid-nineteenth century trust deposits had become very similar to savings accounts. Thus, the business became a combination of savings banking, trusteeship, and insurance. As growth led to specialization, the banking and trustee functions developed together while the property and life insurance businesses became centered in companies organized exclusively for these purposes.

Alongside of the personal trust activity, corporate trust transactions emerged in the mid-1800's. A trust company was named trustee for a railroad mortgage as early as 1839. The corporate trust business was stimulated by a ruling of the New York Stock Exchange in 1869 requiring that all listed stocks be registered by an independent registrar acceptable to the Exchange, and a trust company was usually appointed.

There was a period during the 1850's and the 1860's when companies were organized to engage only in trust work. But, with the growth of industrial corporations, the market for additional services developed rapidly and more corporate fiduciaries entered the commercial banking business. By the 1880's and 1890's, banking functions had become integrated with trust company activities. To counter the increased competition, many state banks sought and obtained trust powers. In addition, in the early 1900's, some national banks established state-chartered affiliates to administer trust business. Section 11(k) of the Federal Reserve Act, passed in 1913, permitted national banks to apply for trust powers. While technically the Federal Reserve was given the authority to permit national banks to perform these services, actually the operations of the trust divisions of these banks were governed by the laws of the state in which each bank was domiciled. The Federal law clearly recognized the sovereignty of the states in this area, granting trust powers only when not in contravention of state or local law. The language of the original provision of the law was inadequate, but this was rectified by an amendment in 1918. After two favorable United States Supreme Court decisions confirming the legality of both the original and revised versions of section 11(k),[1] only one major obstacle to national bank fiduciary business remained, in the form of their limited (fifty-year) charters. This was removed when the national banks were granted perpetual charters by the McFadden Act of 1927.

In the course of about one hundred years of development, therefore, corporate fiduciary services became largely integrated with commercial banking. While there still remain a number of trust companies whose banking functions are merely incidental, the bulk of the trust services in the country are performed as a part of the wide range of commercial bank activities.

The Contribution to Personal Financial Security

There are numerous occasions when an experienced individual acting as executor or as trustee can be exceedingly valuable, especially if the individual was a close friend or relative of the decedent and familiar with his personal affairs. There are also certain advantages to be gained from the appointment of a bank as a corporate trustee or co-executor and co-trustee with an individual. These include the financial responsibility afforded by the bank's capital, supervision and examination by federal and/or state authorities, continuity, impartiality, trained personnel, and economy of operation.

Financial Responsibility

A commercial bank or trust company must meet the minimum capital requirements of the state in which it operates in order to act as a fiduciary. Also, trust property is segregated from the other assets of the bank and not subjected to the risks of banking operations. Under ordinary circumstances, the capital of the bank may be considered as an assurance of financial responsibility. As a consequence, corporate fiduciaries are seldom required to obtain the surety bond often required of individual trustees at considerable expense to the funds under administration.

---

[1] *First National Bank of Bay City v. Fellows on the Relation of the Union Trust Company*, 244 U.S. 416, 426 (1917) and *Burnes National Bank of St. Joseph v. Duncan*, 265 U.S. 17, 21 (1924).

Supervision and Examination

A bank or trust company may engage in the trust business only if specifically authorized to do so. If the institution is a national bank, permission must be obtained from the Board of Governors of the Federal Reserve System. If it is a state bank or trust company permission must be obtained from the designated official, usually the superintendent of banks.[2]

Regulation. Once trust powers have been granted, the bank becomes subject to the regulations, state and/or federal, which apply to corporate fiduciaries. While Regulation F of the Board of Governors of the Federal Reserve System is applicable in its entirety only to national banks, it has become a widely used standard for state supervisory authorities as well. This regulation has been designed to include many of the accepted principles of the law of estates and trusts as well as other principles and policies of an administrative or protective nature.

Examination. To insure that regulations are being carried out and that a bank is acting properly in its fiduciary capacity, the supervisory authorities (Federal Reserve Banks, Federal Deposit Insurance Corporation, Comptroller of the Currency, and state banking departments) subject the trust department to periodic examination.

Audit. The trust department of a commercial bank is also subjected to periodic audit. Larger banks employ auditors who continuously inspect trust department as well as banking department transactions of the institution. In addition, Regulation F requires that every national bank with a trust department must have an annual audit made by a committee of the board of directors or by auditors responsible only to the board of directors.

Deposit of Securities. Wherever the laws of a state require corporations acting in a fiduciary capacity to deposit securities with state authorities for the protection of trust funds, national banks so acting are required to make similar deposits. If for any reason a bank is unable to meet its obligations, the beneficiaries have a first lien on these securities in addition to their general claim against the bank.

Continuous Existence

In most states a private trust [3] is limited in duration to a life or lives in being and twenty-one years, but this span may exceed the ability of an individual trustee to carry out the duties he has assumed. In this event,

---

[2] In a very few states a bank or trust company obtains its authority to engage in trust activity directly from its charter.

[3] Trusts established for charitable, educational, or humanitarian purposes may be exempt from the rule against perpetuities and may have an indefinite life.

the administration of the trust may be temporarily interrupted, and an accounting required at the expense of the principal of the trust. The commercial bank's trust division, on the other hand, has the distinct advantage of "perpetual" life. While a designated trust officer in charge of a particular trust may not be able to serve throughout the life of the trust, the testator or settlor may be confident that an experienced trust specialist will replace him.

Accessibility

The services of the commercial bank trust department are usually available at the main office of the bank. In addition a number of the large, multiple-office systems have established trust departments in some of their branches. In any event, a competent member of a trust department's staff is virtually always available for consultation.

Metropolitan banks have assisted rural banks in making fiduciary services available wherever they are needed. Large institutions in some cases provide training programs for the trust personnel of smaller institutions and they are prepared to advise their correspondents on trust problems.

Specialists

Trust administration is very complicated and even the exceptional individual would have a difficult time mastering all of its technicalities. A man may serve as a trustee but once or twice in his lifetime, hence, his experience is invariably quite limited. The employees of a bank's trust division, however, handle trusts continuously. The officers and staff of this department are trained for the tasks which must be performed, frequently becoming experts in particular areas of trust activity.

Group Judgment

The person who appoints a commercial bank as trustee obtains the benefits of group as well as individual analysis of his estate. The larger trust departments usually have an officers' investment committee. This group, which is composed of specialists from the various divisions of the trust department, is responsible for the over-all supervision of personal trusts. It reviews the portfolio changes that are suggested by members of the staff, and the decisions are submitted to the board of directors or to a committee of the board serving as a trust committee.

Regulation F of the Board of Governors of the Federal Reserve System requires that all investments of trust funds by the trust department of every national bank must have the approval of its board of directors or the trust investment committee. All of the assets in each fiduciary account must be reviewed at least once a year to determine the advisability of retaining or disposing of them. Leading state institutions also follow the basic principles of this regulation.

Impartiality

An individual trustee is frequently under pressure from his personal relationships with the beneficiaries of a trust and open to charges of favoritism toward one of the interested parties. The appointment of a corporate fiduciary minimizes the danger of personal influences. It ensures that every effort will be exerted to carry out the wishes of the trustor by impartially observing the provisions of the trust agreement. This does not imply a lack of concern with the welfare of the trust beneficiaries, for the trust officer will employ every means at his disposal to assist them.

Economy

Although the fees of fiduciaries administering court trusts are fixed by statute or by court ruling and may be the same whether the trustee is an individual, the trust department of a commercial bank, or a trust company, a corporate trustee may prove to be considerably more economical than an individual trustee.

Among the savings effected by naming a corporate trustee are these: the corporate trustee usually does not have to post bond; the bank trust department has access to services of all departments of the bank (clerical, accounting facilities, vaults, investment department, and other like services); and it has on its staff the specialists needed to render the required services.

Volume of Commercial Bank Personal Trust Business

It was not until 1958 that adequate data concerning the volume of personal trust accounts handled by banks were gathered. Earlier attempts to collect such data had proved unsuccessful because trust departments have no uniform method for carrying or reporting trust assets. Trust assets are carried on the books of trust departments in one or more ways: (1) cost or inventory value, (2) unit control value (arbitrarily set), or (3) market value as of the date of the last trust investment committee review. For this reason, data taken from trust ledgers generally have no real relationship to the current value of the trust property.

The American Bankers Association in 1959 and 1960 published the first two of a series of studies of personal trust accounts. Data about asset holdings in all personal trust accounts, administered by banks whose total trust assets were estimated at $10 million or more, were obtained through

TABLE 11-1
Market Value of Asset Holdings of All Personal Trusts [a]
Administered by Banks with Trust Assets of Ten Million Dollars
or More, 1958 and 1959

(Dollar amount in billions)

	1958		1959	
	Amount	Percent	Amount	Percent
Total	$49.7	100.0%	$57.2	100.0%
U.S. Government securities	2.5	5.1	2.6	5.1
State and municipal securities	7.8	15.7	7.8	15.7
Corporate bonds	2.3	4.7	2.6	4.7
Mortgages	0.7	1.3	0.7	1.3
Preferred stocks	1.3	2.6	1.3	2.6
Common stocks	30.7	61.7	37.2	61.7
Common trust fund participations	2.1	4.3	2.6	4.3
All other assets	1.9	3.8	1.9	3.8
Cash	0.4	0.8	0.5	0.8

[a] Year to year changes reflect a combination of fluctuations in market prices and investment policy decisions.

Source: The American Bankers Association.

a carefully planned probability sample. Estimated totals were $49.7 [4] and $57.2 billion in 1958 and 1959, respectively. The banks included in this study represented about 98 percent of all personal trust department assets in the United States.

The first comprehensive data on income and capital gains of personal trusts, derived from income tax data for the calendar or fiscal year 1958, were published by the Internal Revenue Service in 1961.[5] Total income of bank administered trusts amounted to $1,846 million, or 61 percent of the income of all trusts, and capital gains of bank administered trusts were $538 million, or 65 percent of those of all trusts.

Personal trust departments of commercial banks in 1958 and 1959 ranked fourth in terms of total assets among leading financial institutions —after commercial banks, life insurance companies, and savings and loan associations. If only those assets over which the banks had sole investment responsibility were included, the personal trust divisions of all commercial banks would rank behind mutual savings banks, property insurance companies, and investment companies.

---

[4] This figure ($49.7 billion) is subject to a sampling tolerance of $2 billion at the 95 percent confidence level. For 1959 the sampling tolerance is $2.7 billion. For this study current values of living trusts, testamentary trusts, guardian accounts, and funds of incompetents were included. Estates, personal agencies, custody and safekeeping accounts, investment advisory and management accounts, pension and profit-sharing trusts, corporate trusts and agencies, unfunded insurance trusts, and the insurance portion of funded insurance trusts were excluded.

[5] U.S. Treasury, Internal Revenue Service, *Fiduciary, Gift, and Estate Tax Returns,* computed from returns filed in 1959.

Types of Personal Trust Business

Numerous categories of personal trusts have developed because of the varying duties of trustees, the character of the different trust instruments, and the method of creation of the trust. While each of these classifications is significant, the division according to character of the trust instrument is probably of the greatest general interest. All trusts in this category may be subdivided into two main classes—testamentary and living.

Testamentary Trusts

The testamentary trust is created by will and becomes operative only at the death of the testator. Except for limitations which are imposed upon gifts for charitable purposes in some states, a testator may create a trust under his will for the benefit of any person, corporation, association, or institution that is capable of owning property. However, the most common practice is to create a testamentary trust for the immediate members of the testator's family and his dependents. It will relieve the beneficiaries of the responsibilities and problems associated with managing securities and real estate. .It is frequently used to meet the varied requirements of children, especially to avoid the necessity for guardianships of the property of minor beneficiaries.[6] The corporate fiduciary administers the trust for the benefit of the beneficiaries and ultimately distributes the property in accordance with the terms of the will.

Living Trusts

A living trust is a trust created and made operative during the lifetime of the creator for the benefit of himself or a third party. The third party may be a person, a corporation, a public institution, or any organization or association which is legally and actually capable of receiving the benefits of property.[7]

There is nothing distinctive about the property placed in a living trust. It may include, as in a trust under will, any kind of property that can be owned. Depending upon the desires of the settlor, a living trust may be revocable or irrevocable. A living trust is frequently established to obtain the specialized property management and investment services of a bank's trust division. Thereby the individual who is not well versed in these arts can devote his full time to his own interests with the assurance that his financial affairs are being professionally administered.

---

[6] In most states a trust is more economical than a guardianship, and in all states a trustee can be given wider powers than a guardian possesses.

[7] Living trusts are sometimes referred to as voluntary trust, immediate trusts, and *inter vivos* (between living persons) trusts. Each of these terms is correct and may be employed, especially to indicate different point of emphasis.

Insurance trusts, which have many of the characteristics of testamentary trusts, are among the popular forms of living trusts. The creator deposits his life insurance policies with a trustee, and the agreement provides for the administration of the proceeds of the policies. It has become quite a common practice in some sections of the country to establish an unfunded or funded insurance trust or other living trust into which other property "pours over" under the will of the settlor.

Estates

A principal service, and the source of most testamentary trust business, is the administration of estates as executor, co-executor, or as an administrator. The assembling of assets, payment of debts, settling of tax liabilities, and distribution of the property either outright or to testamentary trusts are the major responsibilities of the executor. Each step in settling a decedent's estate involves expert care and attention to detail. Familiarity with procedures, experience, and judgment are the necessary ingredients for efficient execution of the testator's instructions.

Estate Planning

The field of estate planning has been developed by trust departments as a method of eliminating possible future problems of estate administration, as a service to existing customers, and as a means of bringing the facilities of the bank to the attention of potential customers. It has been demonstrated repeatedly that this kind of forward planning, in which the testator, his lawyer, and his executor collaborate, can be of great benefit to the family concerned.

Personal Agencies

Closely related to the personal trust activities of commercial banks are their personal agency functions. The two fundamental differences between a trust and an agency involve title to the trust property and termination of the agreement. Under the trustee relationship title to the property passes to the trustee; while in an agency the title remains in the principal. In regard to termination, a trust does not have to terminate on the death of the trustee or the beneficiary; however, an agency arrangement terminates on the death of the principal.

Although in acting as agent a bank would perform many of the same services as a trustee, these services generally are performed only upon the customer's instructions.[8] Moreover, the agency arrangement is often extremely flexible in contrast with the provisions of many trusts. In most cases, completion of a simple instruction form establishes an agency,

---

[8] The agency agreement may specify certain services which are to be provided by the bank without consultation with the principal.

and the instructions may even be modified by letter. In addition, the account can be closed at any time the customer desires.

Three examples of agency services which are supplied by commercial bank trust departments and by trust companies will be mentioned.

Custodian. As custodian a bank holds a customer's securities safely in its vault. Coupons are cut and collected, and dividends are received. In turn, the income may be deposited to the customer's account, sent to him, or otherwise distributed according to his instructions. Purchases and sales of securities are executed as desired by the principal, records of all transactions are maintained, maturing and called bonds are collected, and rights and conversion privileges are exercised at the request of the customer. For an additional fee, special services such as preparing a year-end statement of income and expenses classified for income tax purposes are provided by the corporate fiduciary.

Managing Agency. The managing agency includes the services rendered to a custodian account, and in addition the fiduciary provides management and advisory services for real property or securities. These services may be as extensive as the customer desires. However, like the custodian account, the agreement may be entered into and rescinded with a minimum of formality.

Probably the best example of the managerial agency is found in the securities area. A customer who would like to relieve himself of the problems of managing his portfolio for a period of time turns this responsibility over to a bank's advisory service. The staff of the corporate fiduciary will then make recommendations for retention, sale, exchange, or conversion of securities held and for the purchase of new securities. The frequency of these reviews will depend upon the terms of the agency agreement. Usually, unless the agreement calls for only limited investment service, the corporate fiduciary as advisory custodian will give the customer's securities substantially the same degree of care and attention that it gives the securities in its trust accounts.

Escrow Agent. Persons participating in a business transaction may consider that it is advisable to deposit cash, securities, documents, or other property with a disinterested but responsible third party. The "third party" selected may be a commercial bank trust department which is instructed to hold the property until specified conditions set forth in the escrow agreement have been fulfilled. The fiduciary then delivers the property in accordance with the agreement. This arrangement is especially useful when real property is involved, for weeks or even months may pass before the transaction is consummated.

Other Personal Trust Services

Among other services, the corporate fiduciary may be appointed guardian of the property of a minor or committee of an incompetent person. It frequently supplies special custody services for an individual who is appointed as sole executor, administrator, trustee, guardian, or committee. Because this person is usually unfamiliar with the technical aspects of his new duties, the bank's trust department may relieve him of all the routine administrative duties and those responsibilities of his office which do not involve the exercise of discretion.

The 1955 ABA "National Survey of the Size of Trusts" [9] noted that 43 percent of all testamentary, living, and life insurance trusts of 862 reporting banks had an annual income of less than $1,200. Nearly two-thirds of the trusts earned less than $3,000 and over four-fifths earned less than $7,000. Thus corporate fiduciaries provide a considerable service for individuals in the middle income as well as the higher income brackets. Some of the large banks of the nation have begun promotional efforts to obtain estates as low as $5,000.[10] Since, in addition, banks are actively engaged in administering the ever-growing pension and other employee benefit trusts, it appears that trust services are being increasingly directed to assist the man of modest means.[11]

Development of Personal Trust Business

The total assets of personal trust departments of commercial banks and trust companies have steadily increased throughout most of the period since 1900. Chart 16, which is based upon the best available estimates, provides some indication of the rate of this expansion as indicated by the growth of trust accounts (excluding estates, agencies, and insurance trusts).

On the whole, the rate of growth has been more moderate during the past twenty years, reflecting the twin influences of terminations of old trusts and highly progressive estate and gift taxes on large fortunes. Nevertheless, many trust men are gratified by the recent expansion of personal trusts. Among the replies of a small sample of bankers in leading cities across the nation, who were sent questionnaires as a part

---

[9] See "National Survey of Size of Trusts," *Banking* (February 1956), pp. 56 and 168; "Small Trusts Make Up Bulk of Business," *Trusts and Estates* (February 1956), p. 102; *The Trust Bulletin* (February 1956), p. 2.

[10] For examples, see *The Trust Bulletin* (February 1945), p. 27; *American Banker* (May 13, 1954) and *Ibid.* (January 21, 1958).

[11] In the past, bankers found that only too frequently the administration of very small estates was unprofitable; but they realized the individual needing skilled assistance the most was often the person who had accumulated only a small estate. To provide an adequately diversified investment medium at a reasonable cost, banks developed the common trust fund. Essentially, the commingled or common trust fund is an investment pool operated and maintained by a bank or trust company exclusively for the purpose of combining the funds of many small fiduciary accounts in a larger investment fund. The common trust fund is invested and managed as a unit and yet, in every other respect, the individuality of each account is retained.

CHART 16

ESTIMATES OF THE TOTAL MARKET VALUE OF PERSONAL TRUST ACCOUNTS
ADMINISTERED BY COMMERCIAL BANKS AND TRUST COMPANIES, 1900–1959

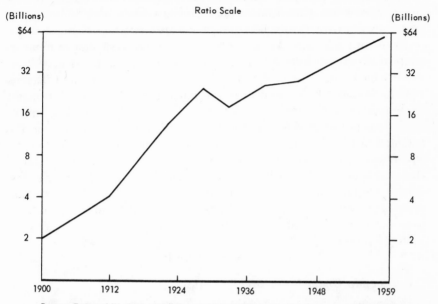

Source: Raymond W. Goldsmith,"Financial Intermediaries in The American Economy since
1900," Appendix B (mimeographed); and the surveys of personal trust accounts by the ABA.
The Goldsmith data have been adjusted to make them more comparable with the recent ABA
survey. However, the data for the earlier years are, at best, only rough estimates. Bench
mark dates used in the graph are 1900, 1912, 1922, 1929, 1933, 1939, 1945, 1949, 1952, 1958,
and 1959.

of this study, there were references to a doubling or even tripling of
personal trust business in their institutions during the past decade.

No definite national trend in the growth of personal trusts as opposed
to corporate trusts or other services is as yet suggested in the trust statistics gathered by four Federal Reserve Banks.[12] In New England, the
surveyed banks in 1958 and 1959 obtained about one-half of their trust
department income from personal trusts. The personal trust divisions also
continued to dominate in the data compiled by the Federal Reserve
Banks of Atlanta and Dallas. In New York City, the largest earnings outside of the corporate trust divisions of banks studied were obtained from
personal agencies.

During the past decade the personal trust business has expanded substantially but the market for these fiduciary services may be even more
promising in the future. In many large cities in the nation corporate

---

[12] The Federal Reserve Bank of San Francisco made trust department income and
expense surveys in California from 1950 through 1955, but this work has been dis-
continued.

fiduciaries handle as little as one-tenth and seldom more than one-third of the dollar volume of the estates passing through probate. In rural areas the figure is probably considerably less. Generally, there has been a tendency for banks to administer a far greater percentage of the larger trusts than of the smaller ones. In the years ahead, however, the medium-sized trust should become a far more important element of the personal trust business. While the huge estates are declining in number, estates valued at $60,000 and more reported for tax purposes have been steadily increasing. The total has nearly doubled during the past decade.

As in the past, there will continue to be keen competition for the right to manage the accumulated wealth of individuals. Open-end investment companies are expanding vigorously and the variable annuity has the potential of being a strong competitor for the funds which would otherwise flow into the hands of trustees or into investment advisory accounts. Hence, although there will be an expanding number of possible customers for fiduciary services, aggressive educational and business development programs will be necessary, if the commercial bank trust department is to participate fully in this growth.

Corporate Trust Business

Trusteeship Under Indentures [13]

The Trust Indenture Act of 1939 provides that issues of debt securities, with certain exceptions,[14] may not be offered for sale to the public unless they are issued under an indenture which conforms to specific statutory standards designed to safeguard the interests of the purchasers.

At least one of the trustees must be a bank or trust company with a combined capital and surplus of at least $150,000. If any trustee acquires a conflicting interest, it must eliminate the conflicting interest or resign. Prior to default, the trustee is not liable except for those specific duties outlined in the indenture but, once default has occurred, the trustee must exercise the rights and powers vested in it by the indenture and use the same degree of care and skill as a prudent man would exercise under the circumstances in the conduct of his own affairs. The provisions of the Trust Indenture Act are also closely integrated with other acts affecting securities, and the Act is administered by the Securities and Exchange Commission.

---

[13] An indenture is simply an agreement setting forth the terms and conditions under which the credit is extended. It is sometimes called a mortgage, a trust mortgage, a deed of trust, a trust agreement, a debenture agreement, a collateral trust agreement, or merely an agreement. The designation usually depends upon the type of financing instrument involved.

[14] Many securities, such as those issued under an indenture which limits the aggregate principal amount of securities at any time outstanding thereunder to $1,000,000 or less are exempt from the provisions of the act. (See Section 304 of the act.)

The commercial bank trust department serving as a trustee under an indenture finds its duties are different from those of a trustee under a living or testamentary trust agreement. In the personal trust arrangement, the trustee has possession of certain trust property which he holds and administers for the benefit of designated beneficiaries. On the other hand, a corporate trust does not provide for possession or right to possession of the trust property unless default occurs. Even then the rights of the trustee are limited. Ordinarily, the indenture does not give the trustee discretionary powers, and there is no recourse to the courts to obtain directions before proceeding in a doubtful situation as can be done by the personal trustee. The beneficiaries of a personal trust are usually known by the trustee. The beneficiaries of a corporate trust (bondholders) are constantly changing, and frequently the trustee must make important decisions affecting their interest without being able to consult with them.

The trustee under an indenture serves as intermediary between the borrower and the lender during the life of the loan. However, its primary duty is, within limits, to protect the bondholders. It receives and holds the collateral security, if any. It certifies by countersigning each bond that it is part of the authorized issue. It may operate a sinking fund to retire part of the bonds before maturity. It endeavors to ensure that the obligor complies with all the terms of the indenture. It handles the redemption, conversion and payment of the bonds, and the cremation of all canceled bonds. In the event of default, it takes such action as it feels will best protect the interest of the bondholders. When the bond issue has been redeemed completely, the trustee executes a final release under the indenture.

Since the passage of the Trust Indenture Act of 1939, indentures involving over $50 billion have been qualified by the SEC.

The corporate trustee today contributes far more to the floating of a successful bond issue than the few services which are described above. The leading trust institutions are staffed with personnel who have had invaluable experience in the administration of trust indentures and who are aware of a vast number of problems which might arise if an indenture is inadequately drawn. Their advice is sought frequently in the drafting of agreements, for a small technical change before an indenture becomes operative may save considerable time and/or expense in the future.

During the past decade (1949-59) over $30 billion of corporate bonds and notes have been privately placed.[15] These contracts, under which an issuer sells long-term debt obligations to one or more institutional investors, do not require that the indenture be qualified by the SEC.

There is little reason to believe that there will be a substantial reduc-

---

[15] *SEC 25th Annual Report, op. cit.,* pp. 226-27.

tion in the need for the services of corporate fiduciaries under indentures in the 1960's. The bulk of the new money secured from the sale of corporate securities (of all types) in the 1950's was obtained to purchase plants and equipment, and if the projections of growth in the American economy which have been made are even reasonably correct, the corporations' needs in this area are far from satiated.

Transfer Agent and Registrar

Essentially, the relationship between a firm and its transfer agent is that of principal and agent. The transfer agent's duties consist of verifying the signatures of the officers of the corporation who are authorized to sign stock certificates; of issuing original stock and transferring outstanding shares; of establishing the identity of the transferor; and of checking his authority to transfer the stock. The agent also has numerous miscellaneous duties such as holding unissued certificates, disposing of canceled certificates, handling replacement of certificates lost, stolen, or destroyed, keeping stock records, and disbursing dividends.

Registrar. The duty of the registrar is to ensure that all shares outstanding are authorized. Its obligation includes checking every new stock certificate issued by a corporation or by its transfer agent against the old certificate being canceled. If an original issue is involved, the registrar verifies that only the authorized number of shares is issued. Unlike the transfer agent, the registrar does not pass on the propriety of transfers but merely checks against overissues; hence, its fees are usually considerably less than a transfer agent's.

Other corporate services. A corporate fiduciary may serve as coupon paying agent (or fiscal agent), paying coupons and registered interest when due, withholding federal tax, and providing numerous other fiscal services. The bank trust department may serve as a depositary for the securities of a firm in reorganization, issuing the new securities on the terms provided in the plan. It may also serve as an exchange agent, a stock redemption agent, sinking fund agent for bond and preferred stock issues, custodian for investment companies, subscription agent for securities offered through rights, and in many other important capacities.

Development of Corporate Agency Business

New York City, as the leading capital market of the nation, is the center of most corporate agency activity. Corporate trusts and corporate agencies combined accounted for over 43 percent of the trust department income of eight large New York City banks in 1959. Some other cities boast important exchanges, such as those in Chicago and San Francisco, but compared with the New York and American Stock Exchanges their volume is small.[16] Nevertheless, to some of the banks in these cities, this is a fairly significant source of trust department income. Moreover, banks in other sections of the nation have noted an expansion in their corporate trust business under indentures and under corporate agency agreements. This has accompanied the decentralization of industry, the growth in the number of publicly owned corporations, the spread of security ownership and the expansion of business in general.[17] However, there is a negative side to this activity as well. Banks in some areas have found growing numbers of firms shifting the trading of their securities from regional to national markets. In addition, mergers of local firms with large listed corporations have also reduced the rate of growth of corporate agency income, especially of some larger banks in the Southwest.[18]

It is extremely difficult to provide even an educated guess regarding the volume of corporate agency activity in the United States. However, one can appreciate the magnitude of the transactions of registrars and transfer agents by perusing the published SEC data for the volume of shares traded on exchanges. In 1958, for example, the exchanges reported turnover reached 1.4 billion shares with a 38.4 billion dollar volume of sales.[19] Since the New York Stock Exchange, which requires that both a transfer agent and a registrar be located in the financial district of New York, handled over 71 percent of the share volume and 85 percent of the dollar volume, the significance of corporate agency duties in New York City are readily discerned. Of course, many firms act as their own transfer agent.[20] But, most companies listed on the NYSE appoint a bank or trust company for this purpose because their corporate trust divisions have the specialists and equipment to perform this function most efficiently. Also, in cases of stock dividends and splits, which have become quite common of late, a corporate fiduciary has the facilities to distribute the new shares quickly and efficiently.

The amount of stock transfer work for the average listed firm has risen substantially during the past twenty years. As a result, a great many of these companies have turned to the commercial bank trust divisions for this service. Also, continued growth of corporate enterprise and movement away from the family corporation should result in even greater

---

[16] The combined market value of shares sold on the Pacific Coast and Midwest Exchanges ($1.8 billion) equaled only about 5 percent of the NYSE and American Stock Exchange Volume ($35.5 billion) in 1958. *SEC 25th Annual Report, op. cit.,* p. 246.

[17] For example, the *Business Review* (July 1958), p. 5, of the Federal Reserve Bank of Dallas mentions the expanding volume of corporate trust and corporate agency business being handled by banks in that District.

[18] Federal Reserve Bank of Dallas, *Business Review* (July 1960), pp. 3-4.

[19] *SEC 25th Annual Report, op. cit.,* p. 258.

[20] Listed firms cannot act as their own registrar, however.

utilization of the corporate agency departments of commercial banks and trust companies in the future.

Employee Benefit Plans

Pension Trusts

Banks act as trustee of a probable three-fourths or more of the assets of noninsured pension funds. This would suggest a current volume of bank-trusteed business, at book values, in the range of $20 to $25 billion for the pension trusts of business firms. The phenomenal growth in these funds during the past decade from less than $6 billion has in effect created a major new market for trust service.

Private pension plans differ materially in their terms and provisions. Thus (1) the benefits may be fixed by formula in relation to compensation and length of service, (2) the contributions may be fixed, or (3) neither benefits nor contributions may be fixed by the terms of the plan.

At the present time, the great bulk of corporate pension plans are the first type, commonly called "level-of-benefit" plans. Practically all of the plans adopted by single companies, either unilaterally or through collective bargaining, specify a level of benefits which will be paid to employees as they fulfill service requirements. Some companies prefer to shift this obligation to a life insurance company through the systematic purchase of a contract to provide the promised benefits. Over the years, however, employers have increasingly preferred to fund the long-term commitment contained in the pension plan through a trust fund. Neither the company nor the trustee normally guarantees that the trust fund will produce sufficient funds to meet all benefit payments, so that the promises made in a "level-of-benefit" plan are supported merely by a bundle of collateral represented by the fund itself.

A basically different situation arises when the amount of contributions is fixed under a collective bargaining agreement. Each employer is then obligated to pay into the pension fund during the duration of the contract a certain amount normally expressed as a number of cents for each hour worked by each regular employee. The union and management trustees administering the pension fund then fix the details after consulting an independent actuary. This type of plan is commonly called a "money-purchase" type plan because the benefits will be whatever the contributions will buy over a period of years. The most essential element is obviously the investment portfolio of the fund, because no one is standing behind it to make up such deficiencies as might occur from an unfortunate investment performance. The trustees often appoint a bank to act as their agent and investment adviser.

The third type of pension fund, commonly known as a profit-sharing retirement plan, is in effect a money-purchase plan without a fixed rate of contributions. The contribution is whatever the profit-sharing formula provides for a given year. The other striking difference is the fact that the profit-sharing fund is normally fully vested after a fairly short period of years. This means that on the death or separation of a participant the accumulation for his account will be distributed to him or his estate. Provision for withdrawals and continuing valuation is necessary. Whereas in a level-of-benefit plan with the pension trust serving as collateral to a company promise, the fund should not invest heavily in the company's shares, it is quite otherwise in the profit-sharing plan, where the element of incentive is very important. Investment in company stock means that the retirement benefit which may be purchased upon each employee's reaching retirement age will depend largely on the success of the company as measured by the performance of its stock.

Competition for the Pension Trust Business

Banks have secured their large and growing share of the pension business, in competition with life insurance companies offering underwritten contracts, primarily because of their experience and skill in the investment management of long-term funds. Trusteed plans have grown more rapidly than insured plans because of the greater flexibility which they afford and because of the greater scope permitted for investment management, notably in the liberal use of equity securities.

Life insurance companies, faced with a continuing loss in their share of the market, have sought and obtained gradual relief from taxation on the earnings of pension reserves. In several states, they are seeking methods for making large equity investments for individual pension funds. The proposals have included the granting of trustee powers limited to pension plans and the operation of an equity fund apart from other insurance company assets in which a portion of the funds accumulated under individual pension plans might be invested.

Banks have vigorously resisted the granting of even limited trustee powers to nonbank institutions as being inconsistent with the specialized nature and responsibilities of trusteeship. Also, banks have resisted the idea that trust activities should be examined and supervised by agencies other than state and federal banking personnel. Life insurance companies, on the other hand, have sought to avoid supervision by agencies other than state insurance departments. It appears that commercial banks face more intense competition for pension business from the life insurance industry in the years ahead.

The growth of deferred profit-sharing plans has been phenomenal in both large and small companies during the past decade. Trusteeships have been even more widely diffused among banks in all parts of the country than have pension trusts. Closely related to these plans are various savings plans under which the employer makes some form of contribution as a supplement to the employee's systematic savings.

Bank services in these fringe benefit areas are varied and constantly changing. For example, the supplemental unemployment benefit funds were only recently established in a few major industries. Pending in Congress for a number of years has been a proposal to permit self-employed individuals to set aside a limited amount of retirement savings in a restricted annuity policy or trust fund. The contribution would be deductible within the allowable limits for income tax purposes. Banks have already made extensive preparations to handle this service, which is open to persons of modest means, in the event that the legislation is enacted.

During the decade of the 1960's, it seems almost certain that banks will be administering well in excess of $50 billion in various types of employee benefit plans. The range of investments is steadily broadening under the competitive pressures to produce the best possible long-term investment performance. Because of the flexibility possible in a long-lived pension trust, with minimal problems of valuation and liquidity, this growing stream of funds into the capital market can be channeled into different investment areas in response to the most urgent demands. The establishment of commingled funds has made the advantages of broad diversification available to pension and profit-sharing trusts of modest size.

Conditioned by their training in the prudent man tradition, bank trustees have maintained high quality standards in their investment selections. This was shown by a survey by the New York State Banking Department in 1955 of pension funds administered in that state. Also, bank trustees have held consistently to the principle of not permitting the pension trust to become merely another source of long-term funds to the corporate employer.

Despite this record of performance in the close examination and supervision of bank trustees by the banking authorities, state and federal disclosure laws do not consistently treat them differently from individual trustees or others acting in a fiduciary capacity.

State and local government retirement systems, also growing at a rapid pace, have in a number of instances made use of the investment advisory and custody services of commercial banks. Labor union funds and those jointly administered by employer and employee trustees have also made increasing use of bank agency services. As a consequence, bank standards have become increasingly applicable to other funds.

Appraisal of the Trust Function

Economic Significance

Service to the capital market. The trust departments of commercial banks provide many services which are essential in the operation of a free enterprise economy. In an economic system dedicated to private rather than public ownership of industry, large sums have to be raised by corporations through the issuance of equity and debt securities. A commercial bank trust department greatly facilitates this flow of funds, whether as trustee under a bond indenture, as transfer agent or registrar, as fiscal agent for an open-end investment company or as adviser on the planning and timing of security flotations.

Service to the investor. For the individual and institutional investor alike, the work of the corporate trustee does much to minimize his risk in purchasing securities. While the fiduciary, except under an advisory agency arrangement, as executor, or under a personal trust agreement, does not select issues for investors, it does provide considerable assurance for them in other ways. The holder of a corporate bond which is issued under an indenture naming a bank or trust company as trustee knows that his interests will be protected. Moreover, the protection frequently goes beyond the current enforcement of the provisions of an agreement, for many leading corporate fiduciaries play an active role in the preparation of the indenture.

For the stockholder, the trust department's various agency functions speed the transfer of the ownership of shares, which is essential in maintaining a continuous market for an issue. In addition, as registrar the fiduciary guards against the sale of unauthorized stock. Also a subtle but not insignificant contribution to investor confidence is found in the stabilizing effect upon the securities markets which is achieved by the trustee's purchase of equities only after careful analysis rather than by whim or rumor.

Service to the beneficiary. The basic function of a corporate trustee is more than the conservation of wealth. It extends to its productive employment in the economic sense. The corporate trustee must do all that it can within the limitations of the trust instrument and the law to keep the trust property productive. In most states, this implies that the corporate fiduciary must act as a man of prudence, intelligence, and ordinary skill would act in the management of his own affairs.

Only a few decades ago the duties of the trustman primarily involved the management of real property and the supervision of mortgages. Common stocks, preferred stocks and, in some states, industrial bonds were not considered proper investments for trust funds. Today, however, over three-fourths of the states recognize the prudent-man rule in making trust investments, although eight of these apply only a modified rule. Another eight states employ the old-fashioned legal list, and three states do not appear to have any specific legislation or court decisions on the subject to guide the trustee. However, only a very small fraction of all trust funds is, in fact, restricted to "legal" investments.

If the trustee is to provide the maximum economic service for the beneficiary, he must be authorized to manage the trust property effectively under rapidly changing conditions in the economy. In some states, court decisions of the distant past inhibit freedom of action, but more careful drafting of wills and trust agreements can enlarge the scope and flexibility of action.

The data in the 1959 survey of personal trust accounts by The American Bankers Association indicate that trust departments with $10 million of assets and over held approximately 3 percent of the corporate bonds, 12 percent of the state and local government securities, and 8 percent of the corporate stock reported as outstanding.[21] Hence, in its service to individuals through management of personal trust funds, the corporate fiduciary is also one of the most important financial intermediaries. It is essential that trustees of these funds be of demonstrated competence and sound business judgment.

Voting Power

Although corporate trustees provide services which are vital in the American financial system, their sizable holdings of the voting shares of corporations have made some individuals apprehensive of undue concentration of voting power. When one considers that the corporate stock holdings of personal trust accounts represent less than one-tenth of the total dollar volume of shares outstanding, this danger seems remote.[22] Moreover, the trust departments in the ABA survey reported that they had sole investment responsibility for less than 40 percent of the dollar volume of shares in personal trust accounts. In addition, the trust assets reported in the ABA study were distributed among many banks. These factors and the methods trust departments follow in exercising voting power and their fundamental duties to beneficiaries make the threat of undesirable influence in the management of business enterprises appear lacking in substance.

There are four basic types of proxies used by trust institutions when the ballot is not cast in person.[23] These include a special proxy (a person

---

[21] "Flow of Funds/Saving," *Federal Reserve Bulletin* (August 1960).

[22] The holdings of pension and profit-sharing trusts represent an even smaller fraction, about one-fortieth of the shares outstanding.

[23] When a trust department votes shares in trust "in person," a duly authorized director, officer or staff member attends the stockholders' meeting and votes the shares as his judgment dictates. Much of the material in this section and those that

is authorized to attend the meeting and votes as instructed), a limited proxy (the person attending the meeting is not authorized to vote on all matters), a general proxy (a representative other than a director, officer, or staff member of the bank attends the meeting and votes the shares as his judgment dictates), and a mixed proxy (a proxy which involves some combination of the above).

At common law, unless it is otherwise provided by the terms of the trust, the trustee of shares of stock has the power to vote them. This power is confirmed by the statutes of a number of states. Many others follow the outline of Section 8 of the Uniform Trusts Act which reads as follows:

> A trustee owning corporate stock may vote it by proxy, but shall be liable for any loss resulting to the beneficiaries from a failure to use reasonable care in deciding how to vote the stock and in voting it.

According to some trust authorities, the expression "use reasonable care in deciding how to vote the stock and in voting it" covers general as well as special and limited proxies.

Since some measure of uniformity of policies for voting shares in trust was felt to be desirable and practicable, the Trust Division of The American Bankers Association has prepared a suggested *Statement of Policies for Voting Shares of Stock Held in Trust Accounts*. It recommends that the trust institutions in formulating their procedures on voting shares in trust also take care to provide for the exercise of group judgment based upon collective information.

There is no one simple procedure which can be followed by all trust departments to meet all situations. A fiduciary must consider the legal right of a trust institution to vote proxies in a given state. It must adhere to the instructions (if any) regarding voting power in the trust instrument, and it must (within its powers) at all times follow the course of action which will best serve the interests of the beneficiaries.

Generally speaking, it is the duty of a trust institution to vote the shares held in all its trust accounts. Furthermore, it has the potential liability for losses to beneficiaries which result from its voting or not voting the stock. When individual trusts have divergent interests in the situation or contests for control occur, therefore, trustmen cannot follow the easiest road of casting no ballot at all. Trust departments usually follow a policy of reviewing such situations with the trust committee of the board of directors. The decision which is made by this body must be one that these men feel is in the best interests of the particular trusts involved.

---

follow was obtained from Gilbert Stephenson, *Voting Shares of Stock Held in Trust Accounts* (New York: ABA, 1943) and from correspondence with some of the leading banks in the trust field.

Profitability

Determination of the profitability of trust departments is a complex task. Efforts have been made to encourage use of cost accounting systems. The ABA Trust Division Committee on Costs and Charges has issued publications on this subject for nearly thirty years.[24] Considerable experimentation is still in progress in the field, and it will, no doubt, be some time before comparable cost accounting procedures for trust divisions are universally adopted (even among the larger departments) throughout the United States.

New York Study

In 1943 the Superintendent of Banks of New York State prepared a special report on trust department earnings and expenses.[25] This study revealed that in 1939 and 1941 corporate trust accounts of selected New York City and "outside New York City" banks were by far the most profitable. Personal trust and personal agency accounts, on the other hand, showed considerable losses. It was noted in the report that even if the corporate fiduciaries had charged the full statutory fees in force at the time income would still have fallen far short of expenses. The need for an upward revision of fees was plainly indicated.

Federal Reserve Bank Surveys

In 1959, trust department earnings and expense surveys were compiled by four Federal Reserve Banks. Of 133 departments with commissions and fees under $100,000, 50 percent (67) were profitable while the rest were unprofitable. Of 117 corporate fiduciaries with commissions and fees over $100,000, 70 percent reported profits before deposit credits. These credits frequently amount to between 10 and 20 percent of the total trust division commissions and fees reported by banks in the Federal Reserve Bank surveys.

The Federal Reserve surveys showed that both the average small[26] and the average large trust department reported similar expense ratios. About two-thirds of all costs were incurred for salaries, wages, and related expenses; other direct costs amounted to an additional one-fifth of total costs and the balance covered overhead expenses. Although the cost percentages were similar for the large and small banks, the net

---

[24] See, for example, *Recommended Cost Accounting Procedure for Trust Departments* (New York: ABA, 1949).

[25] "Trust Department Earnings and Expenses," Special Report of the Superintendent of Banks of the State of New York, March 5, 1943. During this period studies of trust department costs were made in Ohio and Pennsylvania, among other areas.

[26] "Small" refers to banks with under $100,000 of commissions and fees from fiduciary activities.

earnings figures were higher for large trust departments, which have lower ratios of officers to employees and can use labor-saving machinery more effectively.

All areas of the trust business are not equally profitable as the data in Table 11-2 indicate. Thus, a trust department may be profitable or unprofitable depending upon its product mix.[27]

TABLE 11-2
Distribution of Income and Expense
For Large New York City Bank Trust Departments 1955-1959*
(Expense ratios in percent of total commissions and fees)

| | Personal Trust Divisions | | | | | Corporate Trust Divisions | |
| | | Pension and | | | | | |
Year	Total	Estates	Profit Sharing	Personal Trusts	Personal Agencies	Total	Corporate Trusts	Corporate Agencies
1955	96.0	100.3	110.9	92.8	93.5	82.7	80.3	80.1
1956	91.9	103.2	114.9	81.8	91.3	79.6	81.7	80.2
1957	92.0	107.3	115.2	78.5	93.5	85.6	79.4	81.9
1958	89.6	80.1	112.4	82.3	91.2	88.2	80.8	89.6
1959	85.6	71.5	100.2	81.4	88.4	87.7	84.8	88.2

*Data are before income tax charges or credits and before allowed deposit credits.

Source: Federal Reserve Bank of New York, *Earnings and Expenses of Commercial Banks Surveys*, 1955-1959.

Federal Deposit Insurance Corporation data. For the past fifteen years, trust department gross earnings as reported by the Federal Deposit Insurance Corporation have steadily increased.[28] Only since 1954 have fiduciary earnings advanced at a faster pace than total bank earnings and total bank expenses (Table 11-3).

The growth in trust department gross earnings has not been equally distributed throughout the nation (Table 11-4). Development of new lines of business such as pension trusts, establishment of specialized agency services such as those offered to mutual funds, and increased statutory fees have boosted gross earnings in some sections. In other areas, the advance has stemmed from a general expansion of fiduciary business, sometimes at the expense of banks in other parts of the nation. But, even in those states which have enjoyed a noteworthy expansion of gross trust department earnings, rising costs of trust administration may prevent a comparable growth in net fiduciary income.

It has been the experience of corporate fiduciaries that there is a considerable lag between their increasing costs and changes in statutory or

---

[27] The figures for New York City are not entirely typical because of the large size of the corporate trust divisions in this financial center. Also, personal trust fees are more strictly set by law than in many other states.

[28] The Federal Deposit Insurance Corporation reports gross income from services rendered by the bank in any fiduciary capacity authorized by state law.

TABLE 11-3
Increase in Selected Earnings and Expenses
of Insured Commercial Banks, 1944-1959

(Percent)

	Trust Department Earnings	Total Current Earnings	Operating Expenses
1944 - 1949	43	63	68
1949 - 1954	53	60	59
1954 - 1959	73	67	72
1944 - 1959	279	337	362

Source: FDIC *Annual Reports*.

TABLE 11-4
Growth of Trust Department Earnings and Total
Current Operating Earnings of Insured Commercial
Banks by Geographic Area, 1949-1959

(Percentage increase 1949 to 1959)

	Trust Department Earnings	Total Current Operating Earnings
New England	182	153
Eastern	146	157
Southern	188	182
Midwestern	185	162
Western	263	168
Pacific	193	183
Continental United States	166	167

Source: Compiled from FDIC *Annual Reports*.

negotiated trust fees. Also, fees are frequently based upon the expenses of the larger, more economical trust departments. Moreover, when the expansion of a trust department comes through the introduction of a new service, the costs may be very high in relation to earnings for a considerable period. The earnings of pension trusts cited in Table 11-2 are an excellent example of this. The building up of a staff and equipment in anticipation of a volume of trust business expected to develop in the future can be very expensive and can turn an increase in gross trust department earnings into a temporary loss until the expected business materializes.

If the corporate fiduciaries are to continue to seek new methods of providing better facilities for the customer and to initiate new types of service, a review of the recently prevailing schedules of fees in order to ensure a fair return on investment may be necessary.

Summary Evaluation of Trust Functions

The bulk of the development of the trust business in this country has occurred since the turn of the century. Thus, compared with other primary functions of commercial banks, the trust function is a relative newcomer.

Despite the short period of time the trust business has had in which to develop, a vast number of laws which affect trust operations have been passed. In addition, bank trustees inherited from the past numerous court decisions in the trust area. Unfortunately, many of these statutes and opinions quickly became obsolete in the dynamic American economy. As a result of out-of-date restrictions, the trust department today often finds itself at a distinct competitive disadvantage in investment management. In fact the best available estimates show that the assets of personal trust departments as a percentage of the assets of all leading financial intermediaries have been declining for over two decades.[29] While accurate statistics are not available, it is probable that agency (investment advisory) business has grown more rapidly than personal trust business. One view ascribes the slower rate of growth in trust assets to the failure of the legal framework of the trust business to recognize the major current problems of taxes and inflation in investment management decisions.[30]

The corporate fiduciary faces other obstacles in attempting to serve the beneficiary to the full extent of its abilities. At the federal level, the estate tax and gift tax laws tremendously complicate estate and trust administration. Furthermore, the efforts to close so-called "loopholes" in the income tax laws relating to trusts and estates have made these regulations so complex that some simplification seems essential. The rules covering common trust funds have also posed many problems for the corporate trustee. While these funds are to be used only for proper fiduciary purposes, a case can be made for some change in advertising restrictions. Also, an increase in the $100,000 limit for a single trust might be considered by federal authorities.

To permit the corporate trustee to operate more effectively, a number of state regulations might also be modified. More reciprocal laws among the states would be logical. Broader statutory powers for the fiduciary, similar to those in the Uniform Trust Power Act, to shorten wills and to make the legal instrument creating the fiduciary power less cumbersome, would also be helpful. Of course, the enactment of the full prudent man rule in those states which do not as yet have this legislation would also assist both the trustee and the beneficiary.

---

[29] Raymond W. Goldsmith, *Financial Intermediaries in The American Economy since 1900* (Princeton: Princeton University Press, 1958), p. 76.

[30] For a vigorous expression of this view, see Charles W. Buek, "Prudence Will be Prosecuted," *The Trust Bulletin* (April 1960), p. 6.

Chapter 12

THE EARNING CAPACITY
OF COMMERCIAL BANKS

Bank Earnings and the Bank Capital Problem

Earnings provide the prime inducement to investors to put their funds into business enterprises. This is as true for banks as for any other type of business, and there is always competition between industries and between individual business firms to obtain the equity capital they need. For this reason, earnings on bank stocks must be comparable—in amount or stability, or both—with profits realized in other industries, if banking is to attract and hold sufficient new capital to serve the expanding credit needs of a growing economy.

The capital requirements of banks have a special relation to the protection of the public. Banks need capital for the following purposes:

1) to provide a cushion to absorb possible losses so that depositors will be fully protected at all times;
2) to provide funds for bank buildings, equipment, and other non-earning assets required by the bank for its operations;
3) to conform to requirements of supervisory authorities regarding adequacy of capital in relation to risks incurred;
4) to assure the public, including business enterprises and other banks, of the ability to meet obligations promptly and to continue to serve the community even under conditions which cause losses on loans and sales of investments at a loss.

These purposes indicate why the maintenance of adequate bank capital is important not only to banks as business enterprises, but to those who depend upon banks for financial services as well. Accordingly, this analysis of the earning capacity of commercial banks begins with a discussion of measures of capital adequacy and trends in bank capital accumulation so as to provide a basis for evaluating the extent to which banks have maintained capital strength.

322

Adequacy of Capital Funds

In the past, the adequacy of bank capital was judged by the ratio of capital funds to deposits. This seemed the most direct measure of the margin of assets provided by stockholders of a bank to protect its creditors—the depositors.

However, since losses are incurred not on liabilities but on assets that are acquired with funds entrusted to banks by their depositors, it was recognized that a more logical measure of capital adequacy would be the ratio of capital funds to total assets of a bank. Even this ratio, while indicative of the over-all percentage of loss or depreciation of assets that could be absorbed by capital funds, has been adjudged an inadequate measure, because individual bank assets differ widely in their susceptibility to loss or depreciation.

At one extreme is cash in vault or due from banks, involving no risk. At the other extreme are assets such as long-term corporate bonds, involving both a credit risk and a risk of price depreciation due to a rise in the level of interest rates.

In recognition of such differences in risk exposure on assets, a ratio of "capital funds to risk assets" was devised, and assets other than cash and U.S. Government securities were lumped together as "risk assets." This ratio is still in use, although it is increasingly acknowledged that further refinements are required to make it realistic. Thus assets such as government-underwritten mortgages can logically be shifted to the "non-risk" category. But U.S. Government securities, other than those of short maturity, must be considered to involve some risk, because they are subject to substantial market depreciation in the event of a rise in interest rates. A bank may have to sell such holdings at depreciated prices to meet deposit losses or to obtain funds to satisfy an increased demand for loans from its customers.

It was because of such considerations as these that risk asset ratios, as used heretofore, were deemed insufficiently selective by the Federal Reserve Bank of New York, which has developed a more precise approach to measurement of capital adequacy. This involves the classification of assets according to credit or market risks, and the application of separate minimum capital and liquidity ratios to each class. In this approach assets are classified as (1) primary and secondary reserves; (2) minimum risk assets; (3) intermediate assets; (4) portfolio assets; (5) fixed, classified, and other assets (with separate capital requirements for each of the three in this category). Capital requirements for these several kinds of assets are adjudged to range from 0.0 percent on cash assets, for example, to 100 percent on fixed assets, stocks, and defaulted securities.

This principle, that the quality of bank assets must be taken into consideration in judging capital adequacy, has received growing acceptance. Its usefulness for analysis, however, depends upon the availability of detailed data, such as are obtained only by supervisory authorities, on individual banks. Consequently, in appraising the adequacy of capital funds in the commercial banking system as a whole in this chapter, data which are less selective but which are nevertheless adequate for revealing relevant trends, must necessarily be relied upon.

TABLE 12-1
Capital Funds Ratios of Insured Commercial Banks
1935-1960

Year	Average Capital Accounts (Billions)	Ratio of Capital Accounts to		
		Deposits	Assets	Assets Other than Cash and U.S. Government Securities
1935	$ 6.2	14.71%	12.2%	26.1%
1936	6.3	13.44	11.3	24.6
1937	6.4	13.47	11.8	25.0
1938	6.4	13.19	11.3	25.6
1939	6.5	12.03	10.3	25.4
1940	6.6	10.89	9.4	24.4
1941	6.8	10.22	8.9	22.8
1942	7.0	9.13	8.3	26.0
1943	7.2	7.59	7.0	28.3
1944	7.7	6.73	6.3	27.6
1945	8.3	6.13	5.7	25.2
1946	9.0	6.35	5.9	23.2
1947	9.5	6.93	6.4	20.3
1948	10.0	7.13	6.6	19.3
1949	10.4	7.46	6.9	19.6
1950	11.0	7.52	6.9	17.1
1951	11.6	7.47	6.9	16.8
1952	12.3	7.44	6.8	16.2
1953	12.9	7.61	7.0	15.9
1954	13.8	7.78	7.1	16.0
1955	14.6	7.92	7.2	15.4
1956	15.6	8.16	7.4	14.7
1957	16.6	8.54	7.7	14.6
1958	17.7	8.59	7.8	14.8
1959	18.7	8.78	7.9	14.2
1960	20.0	9.07	8.1	14.4

Source: Federal Deposit Insurance Corporation.

The Decline in Capital Ratios

The ratio of capital funds both to deposits and to assets declined abruptly during World War II, when commercial banks expanded their holdings of U.S. Government securities severalfold (Table 12-1). This did not cause concern, however, both because of the high quality of U.S. Government obligations as investments and because prices of these securities were pegged at or above par by the Federal Reserve banks. In contrast, the ratio of capital funds to assets other than cash and U.S. Government securities held relatively stable during World War II.

Since 1945, however, there has been a persistent and relatively rapid decline in the ratio of capital funds to "risk assets" as banks have liquidated about one-third of the U.S. Government securities they held at the end of 1945. Moreover, the end of the pegging of Government securities prices following the Treasury–Federal Reserve Accord of March 1951 has increased the risk of depreciation and capital losses on Government securities, other than those of very short maturity, which banks now hold.

Table 12-1 indicates that the ratio of risk assets to capital funds declined to 14.2 percent by 1959, the lowest level for the quarter of a century since 1935, despite the growth of capital funds that occurred in the interim. This ratio was 19.7 percent in 1930, at the start of the depression. This trend is significant, for should risk assets and capital funds of insured commercial banks grow at the same rate in the 1960's, the risk asset ratio would sink to 9.5 percent by the end of 1969. Such a decline would be unacceptable to supervisory authorities and to bankers.

It may reasonably be concluded from the foregoing that commercial banks must raise large amounts of additional capital if they are to assure their ability to acquire risk assets and thus keep pace with a future growth in the demand for credit comparable with that of the 1950's. In that decade loans and investments other than U.S. Government obligations increased at an average rate of more than 9 percent per annum. Capital adequacy thus promises to be a major problem for commercial banks, making it all the more essential that earnings be sufficient to enable this industry to attract capital on a larger scale in the future than has been the case in the past. This observation leads to a consideration of the sources from which the requisite capital can be obtained and the factors which will determine the ability of banks to tap these sources.

Sources of Capital Funds

There are two main sources of capital funds for banks, both of which are dependent upon adequate earning capacity. These sources, retained profits and new stock financing, have provided capital in recent years in amounts as shown in Table 12-2.

In the period shown, retained profits provided 82 percent of new capital fund and new stock sales 18 percent. Since this reliance on retained earnings has been accompanied by the persistent decline in the ratio of capital funds to risk assets noted above, this pattern of building up capital funds will not suffice for the future.

TABLE 12-2
Sources of New Capital Funds for Commercial Banks
1947-1959
(Millions)

Year	Increase in Capital Funds of Commercial Banks	New Public Stock Offerings	Retained Profits etc.
Total 1947-1959	$10,123	$1,819	$8,304
1947	482	21	461
1948	421	22	399
1949	487	27	460
1950	623	111	512
1951	626	168	458
1952	672	75	597
1953	671	108	563
1954	1,017	234	783
1955	724	188	536
1956	1,002	326	676
1957	1,066	297	769
1958	1,118	92	1,026
1959	1,214	150	1,064

Source: Securities and Exchange Commission and Board of Governors of the Federal Reserve System.

Superficially, it would seem that the bank capital problem could be solved by increasing the proportion of earnings retained while expanding new stock offerings at the same time. This is impractical, however, because prices of bank stocks are greatly influenced by their dividend yield, and an increase in the proportion of earnings retained at the expense of lower dividends would tend to force sales of new stock at prices that would dilute the equity. In contrast, increased sales of stock at prices above book value would be facilitated, not by reduced dividends, but by liberalization of dividend policy, as the experience of regulated utilities has demonstrated.

Electric and gas utilities and telephone companies, highly successful among the major industries in raising new equity capital through the sale of stock, have accounted for a major proportion of the equity capital raised in the market by established enterprises in recent years. Electric power companies distributed almost 75 percent of their net profits as dividends to stockholders in 1958 according to the Federal Power Commission, and telephone companies distributed more than 73 percent. By contrast, insured commercial banks distributed less than 43 percent of their profits as dividends in that year, and 46 percent of net profits for the five years 1954-58.

The market for bank stocks, as for electric utility and telephone issues, is normally among conservative institutional and individual investors who are interested in the current rate of return provided. A public utility common stock earning something better than 10 percent on its book value, because of the leverage in the capitalization, and paying out 75 percent of profits in dividends would be paying out 7.5 percent or more on the book value. Since this stock would probably sell to yield less than 5 percent, its market price would be upwards of 150 percent of book value.

This means that new stock sales above book value build up the equity of common stockholders, rather than dilute it. This is absolutely essential if an industry is to conduct equity financing on a continuing basis. Each new stock sale will then result in a higher book value for all the shares, facilitating the next offering; whereas the sale of new stock below book value reduces the book value of all shares, and so makes each successive offering of new shares less attractive. Public utility regulatory commissions recognize this, and have generally pursued policies favorable to the sale of new stock as required, at large premiums over book value.

Since adequate bank capital depends basically on earning power, an appraisal of bank earnings experience follows in the next two sections.

Measuring Bank Earning Capacity

A uniform measure of earning capacity, applicable to all types of enterprises, is the ratio of profits to capital funds. This measure is of particular interest to potential investors, since it indicates the rate of return they can expect on new equity capital invested in an industry.

The ratio of net profits to capital funds of all insured commercial banks during the twenty-five years 1935-59, with averages for each five-year period, is shown in Table 12-3.

These net profits reported by banks include realized security profits and losses, charge-offs and recoveries on assets, and transfers to and from valuation reserves.

The extent to which net profits of insured banks have been affected by these debits and credits is shown in Table 12-4.

For the entire twenty-five-year period, these debits and credits reduced net profits before taxes by a little more than 9 percent. While these items may affect the net profits of banks of a particular year to a substantial extent, they have had but limited effect upon the ratio of net profits to capital funds for the whole period. However, net profits on losses on securities merit further comment, particularly with respect to taxation.[1]

Taxation of Capital Gains and Losses

Commercial banks are authorized by the Internal Revenue Code to

---

[1] This subject is discussed in greater detail in Chapter 10.

TABLE 12-3
Net Profits as a Percent of Average Capital Funds
Insured Commercial Banks
1935-1960

Year	Net Profits as Percent of Average Capital Funds	Average for each 5-year period
1935	3.35%	
1936	8.35	
1937	5.97	
1938	4.68	
1939	5.99	5.67%
1940	6.08	
1941	6.72	
1942	6.34	
1943	8.82	
1944	9.78	7.55
1945	10.87	
1946	10.01	
1947	8.20	
1948	7.49	
1949	7.98	8.91
1950	8.51	
1951	7.82	
1952	8.07	
1953	7.93	
1954	9.50	8.37
1955	7.90	
1956	7.82	
1957	8.30	
1958	9.60	
1959	7.94	8.31
1960	10.03	

Source: Federal Deposit Insurance Corporation.

deduct net capital losses in full from taxable income, while net long-term capital gains are taxable, as for other taxpayers, at the alternative rate of 25 percent. This tax provision lessens the threat that bank capital funds could be whittled away by a succession of net capital losses incurred when banks, to obtain funds for loan expansion, liquidate investments in a period of rising interest rates and falling security prices.

Since the restoration of a virtually free market in Treasury obligations in 1951, security losses have substantially exceeded profits on securities sold and redeemed, as Table 12-5 shows.

In seven of the ten years between 1951 and 1960 losses incurred exceeded profits, in some cases by wide margins. In the two recession years 1954 and 1958, large profits were realized on securities sold at the higher prices that prevail when interest rates decline.

Over the long run, commercial banks must expect to incur substantial

TABLE 12-4
Additions To and Deductions From Net Operating
Earnings of Insured Commercial Banks
1935-1960

(Millions)

Year	Transfers from Reserves, Recoveries, and Security Profits	Losses, Charge-offs, and Additions to Reserves	Net Credits (+) or Debits (-)
1935	$432.5	$ 628.1	$ -195.6
1936	585.1	501.7	+ 83.4
1937	308.9	395.1	- 86.2
1938	329.2	454.5	-125.3
1939	381.2	438.2	- 57.0
1940	349.1	386.0	- 36.9
1941	324.5	334.0	- 9.5
1942	222.8	271.1	- 48.3
1943	353.0	290.6	+ 62.4
1944	361.7	265.9	+105.8
1945	509.3	264.1	+245.2
1946	408.6	283.2	+125.4
1947	262.0	294.3	- 32.3
1948	266.4	485.8	-219.4
1949	213.2	379.8	-166.6
1950	245.5	366.9	-121.4
1951	169.2	395.7	-226.5
1952	144.1	362.4	-218.3
1953	152.4	448.3	-295.9
1954	631.5	552.6	+ 78.9
1955	239.6	707.2	-467.6
1956	250.2	993.5	-743.3
1957	198.4	757.4	-559.0
1958	868.1	783.2	+ 84.9
1959	328.9	1,361.5	-1,032.6
1960	574.8	978.4	-403.6

Source: Federal Deposit Insurance Corporation.

net losses on securities as they adapt to the changing needs of the economy. Holdings of securities are necessarily expanded in periods of recession when the demand for loans is at an ebb, but at such times interest rates are low and prices of Government obligations are relatively high. Security holdings are sold when business expands and demands for loans increase, but at such times interest rates rise and prices of Government securities fall. Skillful investment portfolio management may lessen but cannot avoid losses on investments because of these cyclical increases in loan requirements of commercial bank customers.

Further, it is inevitable that banks will experience some losses as they —quite properly—assume the risks inherent in business and other loans.

TABLE 12-5
Security Profits and Losses, All Insured Commercial Banks
1951-1960

(Millions)

Year	Profits on Securities Sold or Redeemed	Losses on Securities Charged against Earnings	Losses on Securities Charged to Reserve Accounts	Net Profits (+) or Losses (-) on Securities
Total 1951-1960	$1,756.7	$2,239.6	$610.2	$-1,093.1
1951	56.6	83.8	17.7	- 44.9
1952	33.8	97.5	25.6	- 89.3
1953	38.9	156.9	38.5	- 156.5
1954	416.5	66.7	15.8	+ 334.0
1955	57.1	221.2	68.1	- 232.2
1956	31.2	317.4	95.5	- 381.7
1957	64.4	237.5	74.5	- 247.6
1958	681.6	93.7	19.7	+ 568.2
1959	47.3	745.1	207.1	- 904.9
1960	329.3	219.8	47.7	+ 61.8

Source: Federal Deposit Insurance Corporation.

This makes the problem of reserves against losses relevant to an analysis of bank earnings.

Reserves Against Losses

Commercial banks, like other businesses, are authorized by the Internal Revenue Code to set aside a reserve against bad debts from earnings.

Under a ruling of the Commissioner of Internal Revenue issued in December 1947,[2] each commercial bank may set aside a reserve for losses on its loans up to a maximum of three times the average annual ratio of losses to loans during any consecutive twenty years in the bank's history. This ratio is applied to the current volume of "eligible" bank loans.

In view of the rapid decline in the ratio of capital to risk assets of commercial banks, this reserve against losses on loans is a very desirable supplementary safeguard for bank depositors. At the end of 1959, reserves against losses on loans aggregated $2.2 billion for all commercial banks. Even inclusive of these valuation reserves against loan losses, however, capital funds and reserves of insured banks were only 16 percent of assets other than cash and U.S. Government obligations.

Basic questions have been raised concerning these reserves against losses on loans. First, the maximum reserve ratio for each bank is deter-

---

[2] Commissioner of Internal Revenue, Commission Mimeograph Collection No. 6209, issued December 8, 1947.

mined as a practical matter by the amount of its losses on loans in the 1930's, the years when such losses were heaviest. The poorer the record of a bank in those years, the higher the maximum amount of its reserve, regardless of changes in loan policy and management that may have taken place since. Hence, a bank that pursued a cautious loan policy in the past but feels justified in expanding loans vigorously under present conditions finds itself limited to an unduly low reserve against loan losses.

With the passage of time, the case becomes ever stronger for setting a uniform maximum ratio for the reserve against loan losses for all banks, regardless of the loss experience of the institution in the distant past when both economic conditions and management policies were often very different from those that prevail today.

A second question is the adequacy of the current maximum reserve based on three times the average annual losses in a period of twenty consecutive years. In the absence of a significant downturn in business, such a reserve has been ample. But adverse economic conditions could cause such reserves to be used up quickly, so that losses would have to be charged against capital on a scale that could cut further into the ratio of capital funds to risk assets. Even in the prosperous years 1956-59, losses charged to loan reserves by insured commercial banks averaged $123 million per annum.

The reserve against loan losses of insured commercial banks amounted to less than 2.0 percent of loans at the end of 1959. The adequacy of such a small reserve is open to serious question. There is need for a reappraisal of bank loss reserves. Such reappraisal would in all probability result in permitting further gradual additions from earnings and thus providing a more adequate cushion against losses.

Commercial Bank Earnings and the Level of Interest Rates

The ratio of net profits to capital funds of commercial banks, contrary to a general assumption, has been highest in years when a low level of money market interest rates has prevailed. Other factors than open-market interest rates have determined the rate of return earned by commercial banks in recent years.

In only three years during the past quarter century did insured commercial banks report net profits of more than 10 percent on capital funds. These were 1945, 1946, and 1960. Short-term interest rates were relatively low in these years; long-term bond yields in 1945 and 1946 were at the lowest level reached in a century.

Conversely, net profits on capital funds averaged 7.8 percent in 1956 and 8.30 percent in 1957, two years of relatively high interest rates. They rose to 9.6 percent in 1958, when interest rates declined, fell back to 7.9

percent in 1959, when interest rates rose sharply, and rose again in 1960 to 10.03 percent with a decline in interest rates.

Two main causes explain this inverse relation between net profits of banks and the trend of interest rates. First, low interest rates reflect easy credit conditions, and banks have expanded earning assets at such times by purchasing Government and other securities in volume. Expansion in the volume of earning assets has offset in part a decline in interest rates received. Secondly, and more important, a decline in interest rates leads to a rise in prices of Government and other securities, and banks have realized large capital gains on securities at such times.

Conversely, when interest rates rise and credit conditions become tight, expansion of earning assets has been slowed and capital losses on bonds have replaced capital gains. Bank profits have tended to be reduced further, when interest rates have risen, by the higher rates of interest that are paid on savings and other time deposits because of intensified competition for these funds at such times. Chart 17 shows that the ratio of net

CHART 17

RATIO OF NET PROFITS TO CAPITAL FUNDS – INSURED COMMERCIAL BANKS AND AVERAGE INTEREST RATES ON SHORT-TERM LOANS TO BUSINESS 1939–1958

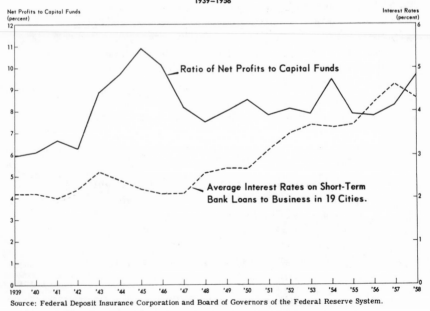

Source: Federal Deposit Insurance Corporation and Board of Governors of the Federal Reserve System.

profits to capital funds of insured commercial banks has been highest in years when the level of interest rates was relatively low, but earning assets were expanded and net profits were realized on securities.

Commercial banks have found that they can increase the rate of return realized on loans apart from any change in the level of interest rates. This is done through increasing the proportion of consumer and other loans on which service considerations determine the rates charged. When the average rate of return from loans is increased by a shift in the character of loans made, rather than because of a general rise of interest rates, there are no accompanying realized capital losses on securities to reduce net profits reported.

By and large, the historical relation between the level of interest rates and bank profits emphasizes the importance of expansion of earning assets if commercial banks are to earn a reasonable rate of return on capital funds.

The Capital Problem in Summary

The preceding review of the major factors which affect bank earnings and capital requirements leads to the general conclusion that commercial banks will have to increase their capital funds at a considerably faster rate in the future than they have in the past, if they are to be in a position to expand loans in the future at the same pace as in the 1950's. Against this background the next section appraises the earning capacity of banks to determine whether it is sufficient to attract the large amounts of capital that will be needed.

Appraisal of Bank Earning Capacity

The only objective yardstick for appraising the earning capacity of banking is a comparison of its rate of return on capital funds with that of other industries.

Every growing industry competes with other growth industries for equity capital. Therefore, banking can expect to attract additional capital only if the rate of return thereon compares favorably with the rates being earned in other growth industries, particularly those that appeal to the same classes of investors in the sale of stock.

Comparison with Manufacturing Corporations

At the outset it should be noted that profit comparisons must take into account differences in methods of accounting for profits.

Manufacturing corporations in the aggregate make very large deductions from earnings for depreciation and for research and development on new products and processes. Depreciation allowances on fixed assets have been greatly expanded in recent years, due both to the adoption of accelerated depreciation schedules and to the acquisition of new fixed assets in record volume.

Capital funds of manufacturing corporations tend to be understated by undervaluation of assets, and overstated, for purpose of comparison with commercial banks, where preferred stock is outstanding in substantial amount. Capital funds of banks tend to be understated to the extent that valuation reserves are excessive and other assets are undervalued on the books.

Taking all these factors into consideration, net profits of manufacturing corporations and the rate of return they earn on stockholders' investment are stated on a considerably more conservative accounting basis than in the case of commercial banks.

The rate of return earned by manufacturing corporations on stockholders' equity has been computed from a large sample by the Federal Trade Commission and the Securities and Exchange Commission. All manufacturing corporations except newspapers have been classified in twenty-three industry groups in this computation. The rate of return is computed on total capital funds, including preferred stock, and so is understated for comparison with commercial banks which have issued preferred stock only in very rare instances. Net profits for both manufacturing corporations and banks include net realized capital gains and losses.

For the five years 1954-58, which included both years of prosperity and the 1958 recession, net profits on stockholders' equity for all manufacturing industries averaged 10.9 percent compared with 8.6 percent for insured commercial banks. The ratios of net profits to stockholders' equity of twenty-three industry groups, in descending order with commercial banks inserted for comparison, are shown in Table 12-6.

The table shows that only five of the twenty-three manufacturing industry groups reported a lower ratio of net profits to stockholders' investment than did insured commercial banks. These included the furniture, leather, apparel, and textile industries, which do not face the need for raising substantial amounts of new capital through equity financing.

Comparison with Service Industries

Since banking is a service industry, profits of banks may be considered comparable to those of other such industries. The First National City Bank compiles data on net profits of leading corporations in a number of service industries. These are compared in Table 12-7.

All insured commercial banks, with net profits averaging 8.6 percent of capital funds, realized a lower rate of return than did the leading corporations in any of these service industry groups, except the amusement industry which was in the throes of a competitive struggle to adjust to the impact of television.

Comparison with Public Utilities

Regulated public utilities and banks have a number of characteristics in

TABLE 12-6
Comparison of Rate of Average Profits on Stockholders'
Equity for Twenty-three Manufacturing Industry Groups and
Commercial Banks, 1954-1958

Industry	Rate of Average Net Profits to Stockholders' Equity
Drugs	18.0%[a]
Aircraft and parts	16.7[a]
Motor vehicles and equipment	14.2
Stone clay and glass products	13.1
Basic chemicals	12.4[a]
Instrument and related products	12.0
Tobacco manufacturers	11.9
Electrical machinery, equipment, and supplies	11.8
Primary nonferrous metals	11.5
Rubber and miscellaneous plastic products	11.3
All manufacturing, except newspaper	10.9
Printing and publishing (except newspapers)	10.7
Primary iron and steel	10.6
Paper and allied products	10.0
Machinery, other than electrical	9.8
Petroleum products and related industries	9.4
Fabricated metal products	9.0
Food and kindred products	8.7
Miscellaneous durable manufacturing and ordnance	8.7
Insured Commercial Banks	8.6
Furniture and fixtures	8.3
Lumber and wood products, except furniture	7.3
Leather and leather products	6.8
Apparel and other finished products	6.0
Textile mill products	4.4

[a]Series started in third quarter, 1956.

Source: Federal Trade Commission, Securities and Exchange Commission, and Quarterly Finance Statements of Manufacturing Companies.

common, from the viewpoint of the equity investor. Both enjoy relative stability of earnings and steady growth. Both appeal to investors as "defensive stocks" that are a good deal less volatile than industrial equities.

Public utilities have two great advantages over banks, however. In the first place, a large part of the funds they require is obtained through the sale of bonds and preferred stock at relatively low cost. Secondly, if earnings do not give what is considered an adequate rate of return on their entire investment, they apply to the regulatory commission having jurisdiction for a rate increase that will lift earnings to the requisite level.

Public utility earnings are compared with those of banks in Table 12-8.

The electric utility and telephone industries have been particularly successful in recent years in attracting capital through the sale of com-

TABLE 12-7
Comparison of Ratio of Profits to Net Assets
of Leading Corporations in Nonmanufacturing
Industries, 1955-1959

Industry	1955	1956	1957	1958	1959	1955-59 Average
Retail and wholesale trade	11.1	11.3	10.9	10.2	11.5	11.0
Air transport	13.9	11.4	5.8	5.9	9.6	9.3
Amusements	8.6	7.8	6.4	4.1	9.5	7.3
Restaurant and hotel	11.5	11.0	9.3	7.3	8.6	9.5
Business services	16.1	20.4	20.4	14.7	10.9	16.5
Construction	12.6	14.3	16.4	14.9	11.8	14.0
Sales finance	16.6	16.2	15.8	14.7	13.7	15.4
Commercial banks[a]	7.9	7.7	8.3	9.7	7.9	8.3
Electric power and gas	9.9	10.0	9.9	10.0	10.2	10.0
Telephone and telegraph	9.5	9.4	8.9	9.6	10.1	9.5

[a]Federal Reserve member banks.

Source: First National City Bank.

TABLE 12-8
Comparison of Ratio of Net Profits to Common Stockholders'
Equity of Public Utilities and Banks
1954-1958

Year	Electric Utilities	Telephone Companies	Insured Commercial Banks
Total			
1954-58	10.6%	7.9%	8.6%
1954	10.5	7.4	9.5
1955	10.8	8.0	7.9
1956	10.8	7.9	7.8
1957	10.6	7.9	8.3
1958	10.3	8.5	9.6

mon stock, despite the tendency of regulatory commissions to hold their rate of return to 6 percent or 7 percent on their total investments. By raising a large part of the capital they require through the sale of bonds and preferred stocks at relatively low average cost, electric utilities have been able to earn a materially higher average rate of return on the equity of their common stockholders than have commercial banks. These higher earnings, in conjunction with a policy of paying out a high proportion of earnings as dividends, have caused electric utility stocks to sell in the market at wide premiums, often of 100 percent or more, over their book value.

Equity financing by the telephone industry was facilitated by the large percentage of earnings paid as dividends to stockholders.

Comparison with Finance Companies

Specialized finance companies have enjoyed spectacular growth in recent years. These specialized lenders both compete with commercial banks and borrow a large part of their funds from banks.

Net profits on stockholders' equity of finance companies have been very high compared with profits of commercial banks, as shown in Table 12-9.

TABLE 12-9
Comparison of Ratio of Net Profits to
Stockholders' Equity of Finance Companies and Banks
1954-1958

Year	Sales Finance Companies	Consumer Finance Companies	Insured Commercial Banks
Total 1954-58	11.66%	12.51%	8.62%
1954	12.33	13.10	9.50
1955	12.17	12.75	7.90
1956	11.50	12.54	7.82
1957	11.48	12.27	8.30
1958	10.84	11.48	9.60

It is evident that specialized finance companies, because of their substantially higher average rate of return on capital funds, are in a far better position to attract additional equity capital for future expansion than are commercial banks.

Conclusion

The ratio of net profits to capital funds of commercial banks indicates that bank earnings have been relatively low as compared with those in industries which represent alternative uses of capital. Consequently, banks will be at some disadvantage in attracting the large amounts of new capital they will require to serve adequately the expanding credit needs of a growing economy.

Obviously banks, unlike public utilities, cannot go to regulatory commissions to ask for "rate" increases when profit levels make the acquisition of new capital difficult. They must improve their situation in a competitive environment through increasing income and control of costs. Bank performance with respect to these vital factors are analyzed in the next section of this chapter.

Factors Limiting Bank Earning Capacity

Relatively low earning capacity in an industry may be caused by an inadequate volume of business, failure to price its products at a level that yields adequate profit margins over expenses, a poor "product mix" or a high cost of capital. Which of these factors is responsible for the earnings record of commercial banks?

The gross operating earnings of commercial banks are derived mainly from interest on loans and investments. In the five years 1954-58, insured commercial banks obtained 84 percent of their current operating earnings from interest and only 13 percent from service charges, commissions, and fees. Much the larger part of interest earnings has been derived from loans since 1947. Hence, the volume of business of commercial banks is best measured by its loans and by total loans and investments, since these assets account for the largest part of their gross receipts.

The rate of growth of loans and investments of insured commercial banks in the period since 1945, has not kept pace with gross national product, the most inclusive measure of growth in the value of the output of the whole economy. Loans alone, however, have registered a more rapid rise than gross national product from the low 1945 level.

In view of the growth in the volume of earning assets, and particularly loans, it is the more significant that commercial banks have realized so low an average rate of return on their capital funds over the past quarter of a century. If the slackening of the rate of growth of assets that has accompanied a restrictive monetary policy should persist or become even more pronounced, the trend of bank operating earnings could prove less favorable in the future than it has been in the past. Even the average rate of return on capital funds of the past decade would not be sustained in that event.

The forces restricting bank deposit growth described in Chapters 2 and 3 of this monograph threaten the ability of commercial banks to increase earning assets sufficiently to improve or even to maintain the rate of return realized on capital funds. The volume of business of commercial banks has not been the cause of inadequate earnings in the past, but it could readily become a cause in the future if the volume of earning assets expands more slowly because of these forces.

The Rise of Operating Expenses

Banks, in common with all enterprise, have been confronted with a rising trend of expenses. Salaries and wages have accounted for nearly 60 percent of current operating expenses other than interest paid on time and savings deposits of commercial banks during the past decade, so that banks have been quite sensitive to the rising trend of salaries and wages.

Bank managements have been successful in keeping total costs under control through increased efficiency of operations. This can be measured by comparative ratio of assets held per employee. Between 1949 and 1959, the proportion of loans to total assets of all insured banks increased from 27 percent to 43 percent while the proportion of securities declined from 48 percent to 34 percent. Since a much larger staff is required to handle a given volume of loans than the same amount of investments, one could expect a sharp decline to have occurred in the volume of assets per officer and employee during this decade, especially because a substantial increase occurred in the volume and character of services provided depositors. But the assets per officer for insured banks actually rose from $2,183,000 to $2,401,000 between 1949 and 1959, and the assets per other employee declined only slightly, from $512,000 to $493,000. Better organization of work, mechanization, and more effective control over expenses have contributed to this result. Thanks to these efforts the ratio of operating expenses other than interest on time and savings deposits to current operating earnings of insured commercial banks has shown a slowly declining trend, as Table 12-10 indicates.

TABLE 12-10
Ratio of Operating Expense, Other Than Interest on Deposits,
to Operating Earnings of Insured Commercial Banks
1949-1960

Year	Ratio
1949	54.2%
1950	53.5
1951	52.7
1952	52.1
1953	51.8
1954	52.3
1955	51.5
1956	50.5
1957	49.4
1958	49.8
1959	48.4
1960	48.0

Source: Federal Deposit Insurance Corporation.

The relatively low ratio of net profits to capital funds of commercial banks is not due to inefficiency or lack of control over costs. The decline in the operating expense ratio, in the face of a strong upward trend in salary and wage levels and a pronounced increase in the proportion of loans in bank assets, points to the conclusion that notable advances have been taking place in efficiency of bank operations.

However, unless gross operating earnings continue to expand, increasing difficulty is bound to be encountered by commercial banks in holding down the ratio of operating expenses to gross earnings. A slowing down of the growth of earning assets would pose a major threat to future profit margins.

Pricing of Bank Services

A growth industry should have no difficulty in pricing its services at a level that will provide an adequate return on the capital employed. Yet this has not been true of commercial banking.

Over the twenty-five years 1934-58, as Chart 18 shows, net profits before taxes of insured commercial banks have increased at a rate to be expected of a growth industry. But net profits after taxes have risen surprisingly little since 1945 and 1946, the only two years in the entire twenty-five-year period in which net profits of commercial banks reached 10 percent of capital funds. In fact, net profits after taxes have risen at a sluggish rate since 1946, the chart shows, while capital funds of commercial banks were doubled, chiefly through retention of profits.

CHART 18

NET PROFITS BEFORE TAXES AND NET PROFITS AFTER TAXES – INSURED COMMERCIAL BANKS
1934–1959

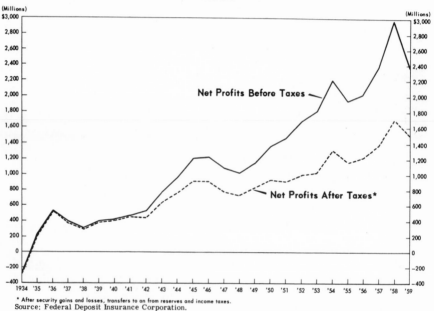

* After security gains and losses, transfers to on from reserves and income taxes.
Source: Federal Deposit Insurance Corporation.

The conclusion indicated by Chart 18 is that a rapid rise in income taxes paid by insured commercial banks—such taxes were four times as large in 1958 as in 1945—was not offset in the prices the banks received for their services so as to maintain an adequate rate of return on the capital employed.

The most inclusive measure of the prices charged by commercial banks for their services is the ratio of gross current operating earnings to total assets. This ratio is determined chiefly by the average rates of interest received on loans and investments. Table 12-11 shows how gross earnings on assets have varied over the twenty-five years 1934-58.

TABLE 12-11
Gross Earnings Ratios
of Insured Commercial Banks, 1934-1958

Year	Operating Earnings per $100 of Assets	Income on Loans per $100 of Loans	Income on Securities per $100 of Securities	
1934	$3.37	$4.63	$3.17	
1935	3.08	4.40	2.87	
1936	2.92	4.34	2.66	
1937	2.97	4.28	2.68	
1938	2.87	4.36	2.56	
1939	2.68	4.46	2.38	
1940	2.45	4.41	2.16	
1941	2.35	4.27	1.95	
1942	2.14	4.08	1.69	
1943	1.90	3.85	1.52	
1944	1.80	3.44	1.49	
1945	1.71	3.09	1.46	
1946	1.88	3.43	1.56	
1947	2.09	3.79	1.60	
			United States Government Securities	Other Securities
1948	2.26	4.04	1.57	2.14
1949	2.38	4.22	1.61	2.15
1950	2.47	4.34	1.59	2.04
1951	2.60	4.45	1.65	1.99
1952	2.74	4.64	1.80	2.04
1953	2.96	4.84	1.98	2.11
1954	2.98	4.79	1.98	2.14
1955	3.15	4.88	2.09	2.15
1956	3.45	5.11	2.31	2.29
1957	3.74	5.42	2.52	2.47
1958	3.72	5.37	2.48	2.61

Source: Federal Deposit Insurance Corporation.

Table 12-11 shows how gross operating earnings per $100 of assets declined sharply during the war period when commercial bank holdings of low-yielding U.S. Government obligations expanded more than fourfold, while interest rates on loans were depressed by the aggressive easy money policy that the Federal Reserve adopted to facilitate Treasury financing of the war. Only in 1955 did the ratio of gross earnings per $100 of assets of insured commercial banks regain the level of 1935, but taxes on bank income had been increased very sharply in the interim.

Factors that have held down operating earnings on bank assets, at times when larger earnings have been required to cope with rising expenses and sharply higher income taxes, include the following:

1) The large proportion of commercial bank assets of a "money market" character, on which interest rates have been influenced over long periods by Federal Reserve credit control and Treasury debt management policies rather than by bank costs. On the other hand, interest rates on consumer and some types of business loans reflect service more than money market influences, and costs of providing the service enter to a much greater extent into the determination of the rates of interest charged.

2) High legal reserve requirements of commercial banks. Cash on hand and due from banks—nonearning assets—have varied from 20 to 36 percent of total assets during the quarter century 1935-59.

3) The emphasis on liquidity of bank portfolios on the part of both supervisory authorities and bank managements. As a result, cash and U.S. Government securities, assets providing a minimum rate of return, have accounted for over one-half of total bank assets even when the demand for loans reached record proportions in the late 1950's.

In the "product mix" of commercial banking, assets yielding rates of interest that reflect money market influences have loomed quite large, whereas assets yielding rates of interest based on service factors have accounted for a limited part of the total. This is the main reason commercial banks have earned a lower rate of return on capital funds than the several classes of finance companies whose assets are virtually all of the second type. Individual banks with a high proportion of loans on which interest rates reflect service rather than money market factors usually earn a larger than average rate of return on capital funds, despite the intense competition that prevails in consumer lending, accounts receivable financing and other specialized lending fields.

Services Charges

Charges for service, fees, and other current earnings other than interest received averaged $1,301 million per annum for insured commercial banks in the five years 1955-59. This total was made up of charges for various types of service as seen in Table 12-12.

To a large extent, increases in bank operating costs have resulted from the rendering of services other than lending. Costs have risen not only because of sharp increases in salary scales, but also because of the expansion in number and extent of the services sought by customers. Businesses have shifted many clerical and accounting functions to the banks in which they maintain deposit accounts and banks, in competing for business, offer to assume such functions. There are reasons to believe that far more effort and ingenuity have gone into the development of new services than in making sure that banks are fully compensated for providing them. The view is widespread among bankers that inadequate pricing of services has been an important factor limiting profits.

TABLE 12-12

| Type of Service | Average Annual Receipts, 1955-1959 | |
	Amount (Millions)	As a Percent of Gross Operating Earnings from Sources Other Than Interest
Total	$1,301	100.0%
Service charges on deposit accounts	437	33.6
Trust department	352	27.0
Service charges and fees on bank loans	87	6.7
Other charges, fees, and commissions	182	14.0
Other current earnings	243	18.7

Source: Federal Deposit Insurance Corporation.

Progress has been made toward basing the pricing of bank services on realistic cost analysis, but much remains to be done in this field. In the past, many banks merely assumed that deposit balances would compensate them for services rendered and yield a profit. This is no longer practical as the volume and variety of services rendered have expanded and the cost of rendering service has risen sharply. Adequate pricing procedure for services requires realistic determination of all costs, direct and overhead, of the services rendered by a bank. Costs as thus determined provide the only reliable guide to the pricing of services, which can then be paid for either on a fee basis, through earnings realized on compensating balances, or a combination of the two.

Realistic costing of services rendered is neither as widespread nor as fully utilized as a basis for pricing in banking as it is in other industries. Tradition, rather than precise cost and profit computation, still plays an important part in determining both the amount and the character of the remuneration received by banks for services rendered their customers.

The Cost of Capital

Commercial banks, in contrast with public utilities and numerous industrial enterprises, are capitalized almost exclusively with common stock. Insured commercial banks had only $76,905,000 of debentures and preferred stock outstanding on December 31, 1958. This was only 0.41 percent of their total capital funds, all the rest being represented by common stock.

By contrast, on that date, 63 percent of the capitalization of electric utilities consisted of long-term debt and preferred stock, while 36 percent of the capitalization of telephone companies and 17 percent of the capitalization of manufacturing corporations consisted of long-term debt.

Because insured commercial banks had $11.70 of deposit liabilities for each dollar of capital funds, the prevailing view among bankers has been that capitalization should not include senior securities.

In some countries abroad, banks have raised capital by selling bonds or preferred stock with limited rates of return, and the leverage thus provided has increased earnings for the common stock when conditions have been favorable. Bonds would provide the lowest cost funds, since interest is deductible from taxable income and lower yields would have to be offered, even though debentures would be subordinated to liabilities of depositors. Preferred stock would be a good deal more costly because dividends would not be a deduction from taxable income. Nevertheless, with average earnings after taxes of 8 percent or more on capital funds, the sale of preferred stock with a dividend of, say, 5 percent would lift the rate of return for the common stock.

However, in the event of a decline in profits, the existence of senior securities would make the drop in earnings per share of common stock much more severe. Also, the sale of new shares of common stock could be more difficult when investors know that their equity is subordinated not only to depositors, but also to debentures or preferred stockholders. Another disadvantage of senior financing for banks is the frequent provision for redemption of bonds or preferred stock out of future profits, which reduces earnings available for dividends and for additions to capital funds to keep pace with growth.

There is no indication that American banks or supervisory authorities will modify the firmly established policy of regarding bank deposit liabilities as ample trading on the equity, and limiting banks' capital structure to common stock. Hence, profits of commercial banks must be large enough to attract and hold the capital funds needed in the form of common stock equity, without the leverage of bond and preferred stock financing which can increase the average earnings realized for common shares.

To this point, the analysis of the earnings experience and potential of commercial banking has dealt with the banking system as a whole. It must be recognized, however, that within banking, as in any given industry, there will be differences in performance, depending upon a myriad of variables such as size of bank, location, and deposit characteristics.

Larger banks, as a class, have reported substantially higher net current operating earnings before taxes than have smaller banks, as a class. This has resulted from a higher ratio of assets to capital funds, a higher ratio of loans to total assets, and a lower ratio of expenses to gross operating earnings of banks.

However, banks in the larger size groups have not carried their higher ratio of net current operating earnings through to net income, chiefly because of higher income taxes and larger allocations to loan reserves.

A comparison of net current operating earnings of central reserve city, reserve city, and country member banks of the Federal Reserve System in the 1954-58 period indicates that city institutions, other than New York City banks, had a higher ratio of net operating earnings to capital funds than country banks. This resulted from a higher loan ratio and a lower expense ratio for city institutions. Likewise, there is considerable variation in the ratio of net operating earnings on capital funds of member banks in the twelve Federal Reserve districts. For example, member banks in the San Francisco district reported the highest ratio of net operating earnings to capital funds, resulting from a higher ratio of assets to capital funds, a larger proportion of loans to total assets, and a relatively high average rate of interest on loans.

Bank earnings are said to be affected, too, by the proportion of time deposits to total deposits, and ratios are presented to indicate that banks with a high proportion of time deposits are relatively unprofitable. Actually, little weight can be given these ratios, because they are arithmetic averages of operating ratios for individual banks rather than overall ratios computed from aggregate dollar figures. Numerous small banks with a high proportion of savings deposits and low ratios of net profits to capital funds reduce the average for banks with a higher ratio of time deposits. Actually, individual banks that have reported the highest ratio of net profits to capital funds year after year include a number that have a high proportion of savings and other time deposits. While it cannot be said that a high proportion of time deposits will assure a more adequate rate of return on capital funds, the evidence clearly indicates that a large proportion of time deposits does not make a bank inherently unprofitable.

The foregoing recognition of variations in the earnings performance of individual banks does not in any way alter the general conclusion that banking as an industry has experienced relatively low earnings. However, the factors which cause variations—higher loan ratios and lower expense ratios, for example—may point to solutions for the over-all problem of earning capacity.

How Bank Earning Capacity Can Be Increased

The ratio of net profits to capital funds of commercial banks can be raised to a level high enough to attract and hold the capital that will be needed to enable these institutions to serve a growing economy. This requires, however, changes in regulatory and management policies to achieve the following results:

1) *A vigorous rate of earning asset growth for the future,* to keep pace with rising costs as well as to assure a more adequate rate of return on capital funds.

2) *More equal opportunity to compete for savings.* Because demand deposit growth has been slowed down by restrictive monetary measures, it is essential that commercial banks be given more equal opportunity to compete for savings deposits to provide funds for expansion of earning

assets. As a minimum, the steps outlined in Chapter 2 are essential if commercial banks are to compete on an equitable basis with thrift institutions for savings. These steps include correction of tax and regulatory inequalities and maintenance of adequate supervisory standards for savings and loan associations.

3) *Increasing the average rate of return on earning assets.* This can be achieved most readily through increasing the proportion of loans on which interest rates reflect service rather than money market influences. However, any shift in loans or investments that increases the average rate of return of a bank on its earning assets would contribute to a more adequate ratio of net profits to capital funds. The extent to which asset shifts to increase the average rate of return are feasible is necessarily affected by quality, liquidity, and capital funds to risk asset ratio considerations. In many cases this could involve changes in the concepts of quality, liquidity, and capital fund adequacy held by regulatory authorities and bank managements.

4) *Lower legal reserve requirements.* Legal reserve requirements of member banks should be reduced to a level that would accomplish the purpose of credit control without immobilizing an unduly high percentage of commercial bank assets. This would permit a substantial increase in earning assets, and thus in the average rate of earning on total assets.

5) *More realistic pricing of bank services.* There is no reason why the major services provided by banks should not each make a full contribution to covering overhead as well as direct costs, and to the net profits of the institution. Adequate cost data are needed to determine the compensatory balances or charges required for services rendered customers.

6) *Reducing expenses.* Major advances in automation and organization of bank operations promise significant further progress toward cost reduction that will help increase net operating earnings.

7) *More equitable taxation.* More uniform and adequate reserves for losses would help commercial banks to achieve an adequate rate of return on capital funds, and would lessen the gross inequality in the allowance for loss reserves that now exists as between commercial banks and competing thrift institutions.

8) *Adoption of more effective profit planning and control techniques.* Marked advances have been made in industry toward effective planning and control of profits that have helped raise the average rate of return on investment. Commercial banks face special problems in planning and controlling profits, such as the impact of frequent changes in the level of interest rates. However similar problems have been solved in other industries, to permit tighter control over profits by management.

These measures, by correcting the causes of inadequate earnings, would assure the ability of commercial banking to make its full contribution to the future growth of the economy. Failure to adopt at least a substantial part of this program could lead to pressure on bank profit margins and an attrition of even the inadequate, relatively low average rate of net profits to capital funds that the banking industry has been able to realize over a period of years.

Appendix A to Chapter 12

Form for Analyzing Bank Capital

FORM FOR ANALYZING BANK CAPITAL

April 1956

Bank: _____

Location: _____

Based on Report of Examination as of _____   District No. _____

	AMOUNT OUTSTANDING	CAPITAL REQUIREMENT Percent	CAPITAL REQUIREMENT Amount	LIQUIDITY CALCULATION
(1) PRIMARY AND SECONDARY RESERVE				
Cash Assets	$	0%		47% of Demand Deposits i.p.c. $
Guar. Portion of CCC or V-loans				36% of Time Deposits i.p.c.
Comm. Paper, Bnk Accept. & Brks' Lns				100% of Deposits of Banks
U.S. Govt. Secs:				100% of Other Deposits
Bills			$	100% of Borrowings
Certificates, etc. (to 1 yr.)		0.5%		Allow. for spec. factors, if info. available (+ or –)
Other (1–5 yrs.) (Incl. Treas Inv. Series A & B)				A. Total Provision for Liquidity
Other Secs. Inv. Rtngs 1 & 2 or Equiv. (to 4 yrs.)		4.0%		B. Liquidity available from Prim. and Secondary Res. ("amt. outstanding" less cap. required thereon)
TOTAL $				
(2) MINIMUM RISK ASSETS				C. Liquidity to be provided from assets in Groups 2, 3 or 4 (zero if B equals or exceeds A, otherwise A less B)
U.S. Govt. Secs. (5–10 yrs.)				
Ins. Portion FHA Rep. & Modr'n Loans				D. Liquidity available from Min. Risk Assets (90% of "amt. outstanding" in line 2)
Loans on Passb'ks, U.S. Secs. or CSV Life ins.				
Short-term Municipal Loans				
TOTAL $		4%		E. Liquidity to be provided from assets in Groups 3 or 4 (zero if D equals or exceeds C, otherwise C less D)
(3) INTERMEDIATE ASSETS				
U.S. Govt. Secs. (Over 10 yrs.)				F. Liquidity available from Intermediate Assets (85% of "amt. outstanding" in line 3)
FHA and VA Loans				
TOTAL $		6%		

(4) PORTFOLIO ASSETS (Gross of Res.)
Investments (not listed elsewhere)
Loans (not listed elsewhere)

TOTAL $ 10%*

*Plus 15% of $100,000 of portfolio, 10% of next $100,000 and 5% of next $300,000.

(5) FIXED, CLASSIFIED & OTHER ASSETS
Bk Prem., Furn. & Fixt., Other Real Est. Stocks & Defaulted Secs.   100%
Assets Classified as "Loss"   50%
Assets Classified as "Doubtful"   20%
Assets Classified as "Substandard"   0%
Accruals, Fed. Res. Bk. Stock, Prep. Expen.

TOTAL ASSETS $

(6) ALLOWANCE FOR TRUST DEPT. (Amt. equal to 300% of annual gross earnings of Department)

(7) EXTRA CAP. REQD. IF ANY ASSETS IN GROUPS 2-4 USED FOR LIQUIDITY (zero if line C in Liquidity Calculation is zero, otherwise Total in line H)

(8) ALLOW. FOR SPEC.; OR ADDIT. FACTORS, IF INFO. AVAILABLE (+ or -) (see notes on reverse side)

(9) TOTAL CAPITAL REQUIREMENT (1 thru 8) $

(10) ACTUAL CAP., ETC. (Sum of Cap. Stock, Surplus, Undiv. Profits, Res. for Conting., Loan Valuation Res., Net unapplied Sec. Valuation Res., Unallocated Charge-offs, and any comparable items) (Exclude Depreciation and Amortization Reserves) $

(11) AMOUNT BY WHICH ACTUAL IS:
MORE than requirement (10 minus 9)   +$
or
LESS than requirement (9 minus 10)   -$

(12) RATIO OF ACTUAL CAPITAL, ETC. TO REQUIREMENT (10 divided by 9)

G. Liquidity to be provided from Portfolio Assets (zero if F equals or exceeds E, otherwise E less F) ....

Extra Capital Required on Any Assets in Groups 2-4 Used for Liquidity

6.5% of line C
4.0% of line E
9.5% of line G

→ H. Total Extra Cap. Reg. $

Appendix B to Chapter 12

The Bank Examinations Department of the Federal Reserve Bank of New York, in its memorandum on "A Measure of Minimum Capital Adequacy," dated December 12, 1952, proposed the following minimum capital requirements for each of six suggested asset groupings.

The first of the six groupings we have made might be called "primary reserve assets." They are the safest and most liquid of bank assets. We include in this category cash on hand and due from banks, and U.S. Government securities maturing in five years. Assets of comparable liquidity, such as prime bankers acceptances and federal funds sold, also belong in this category as do U.S. savings bonds, which are payable on demand regardless of maturity. Against such assets we consider no capital is required. The credit risk in these assets is virtually nil and, while there is some market risk in short-term Governments, it should normally be readily absorbed by current earnings.

The second category might be called "secondary reserve assets" or minimum risk assets. These are assets generally recognized as having less than normal credit risk or as being more readily pledgeable or salable at face value. In this category we would include all Government bonds maturing over five years; Government-guaranteed loans or securities; loans secured by Government bonds, savings passbooks or life insurance; prime commercial paper; brokers loans; etc. We would also include investment grade securities, other than Governments, which mature within five years and other loans or investments of comparable credit risk or liquidity. Against this category of minimum-risk assets we suggest a *minimum capital requirement of 5 percent*. This would seem to be the least amount of capital required to do any kind of banking business that involves any appreciable risk. Banks themselves would not generally lend money on an unsecured basis to any enterprise whose current liabilities exceeded twenty times its net worth no matter how "riskless" the operation might appear to be.

The third category might be called "portfolio assets." They would include all of the remaining loan portfolio, not adversely classified by the bank examiners, and the remaining investment grade securities other than U.S. Governments, i.e., those maturing in over five years. These are in effect the "risk" assets of the bank and to this class we have applied a *capital requirement of 12 percent*. While this requirement is lower than the 6-to-1 ratio that has been generally accepted and is currently used as a test by the Comptroller of the Currency, it is not out of line with his concept of capital adequacy. Our suggested approach requires some capital against all but short-term Government securities, while the risk asset formula used by the Comptroller of the Currency does not, and (as will be discussed below) our approach also requires more capital against classified and fixed assets.

It will, of course, be recognized that the actual degree of risk will vary quite widely among these portfolio assets. The risks may vary for the same type of asset between different banks as well. One bank for instance may confine its mortgage lending to the financing of single-family dwellings on a ten-year pay-out basis while another may finance a sizable amount of industrial or specialty property on a long-term basis. While the latter bank might, upon analysis, need more capital, it is our contention that 12 percent capital protection against these normal risk assets is not too much for the best bank. It is a minimum rather than a maximum requirement.

The fourth category might be called "substandard assets" and includes loans so classified by the examiner plus bonds not in default but not of investment quality. Substandard loans are defined in our examination reports as those "which involve more than a normal risk due to financial condition or unfavorable record of the obligor, insufficiency of security or other factors: noted in the examiner's comments." They do not necessarily contain elements of loss but naturally the possibility of loss is greater. Where a segregation of "other loans specially mentioned" is used by the examiner to point out credit weaknesses (as against technical exceptions), part or all of such loans might also be included in this category. Against substandard assets we suggest a *capital requirement of 20 percent*.

The fifth grouping might be designated as "work-out assets." These will include stocks, defaulted bonds, and other real estate. Such investments are not considered proper banking assets. Banks may not legally acquire them except for debts previously contracted or, as to real estate, when used for or in conjunction with bank premises. Supervisors generally expect that such assets, when acquired for debts, will be disposed of as promptly as possible. With respect to work-out assets *a 50 percent capital requirement* seems not unreasonable.

The final category consists of bank premises and furniture and fixtures. It is not expected that any depositors' money will be invested in such assets. The banking house, furniture, fixtures, and equipment are facilities which the stockholders are expected to provide in order that they may enter into and conduct a banking business. Whether they lease simple and inexpensive quarters or erect a monument in granite and marble is up to them. Costly and elaborate premises may attract business but they afford little or no protection to the depositors. They can generally be disposed of only when the bank goes into liquidation. If this occurs in bad times, it is of course at the very time that real estate will be least salable. From the viewpoint of a bank as a going concern, and as protection to depositors, the bank's supervisor is chiefly concerned with the amount of capital a bank may have over and above the amount invested in premises and fixtures. Therefore, we suggest a full *100 percent capital requirement* against these assets.

Some banks occupy only part of the premises they own, and lease the remainder to others. To the extent that banking houses are not used for banking purposes, they might be considered as other real estate. Arbitrarily, therefore, we suggest capitalizing rents received from others on a reasonable basis (say five times gross rents) and including this capitalized amount as "other real estate" for the purpose of our suggested capital formula. The required capital would consequently be only 50 percent of such amount.

Chapter 13

THE TREASURY AND COMMERCIAL BANKS

The United States Treasury utilizes the commercial banks for a wide variety of functions and services that no other class of financial institution or combination of financial institutions is in a position to provide. The Treasury has a vital interest, therefore, in a vigorous, expanding commercial banking system that will be able to serve its needs, whatever their nature and magnitude, as effectively in the future as it has in the past.

The manifold functions and services performed by commercial banks for the Treasury can be grouped under five major headings.

1) *The commercial banks are by far the largest investors in U.S. Government obligations.* At the end of 1960, commercial banks held almost 30 percent of the public debt of the United States owned outside Federal trust funds and Agencies and the twelve Federal Reserve Banks. All other domestic financial institutions together held only a fraction of the amount of Treasury obligations owned by the commercial banks. In addition, commercial banks are large investors in obligations sold by Federal agencies.

2) *Commercial banks bear the brunt of the task of underwriting and distributing new issues of U.S. Government obligations.* Much the larger part of the new marketable securities sold by the Treasury to the public in the decade 1950-59 was allotted to commercial banks in the first instance. As demand has developed for these issues among other classes of investors, they have been redistributed by the commercial banks.

3) *Commercial banks perform a wide range of banking services required by the Treasury.* Many of these services have been specifically designed or adapted by the banks to handle speedily and efficiently the huge volume of financial transactions of the Treasury.

4) *The officers and employees of commercial banks provide a large pool of highly trained and experienced personnel* that is available to the Treasury at all times for information, advice and assistance.

5) *The commercial banking system constitutes a vast stand-by facility,* flexible and adaptable in character, that the Treasury can call upon whenever the need arises to provide new services and to solve new problems. Experiences in two world wars and other emergencies have dramatically demonstrated the very great value of this facility to the Treasury and to the nation.

While commercial banks thus serve the Treasury in many ways, commercial banking in turn is very much affected by the financial policies of the federal government. Because of the magnitude of federal fiscal and public debt transactions and their special impact upon commercial banks, federal financial policies have a large part in shaping the development of commercial banks. A survey of the relations between the Treasury and the commercial banks logically starts, therefore, with an examination of how fiscal policy and public debt management affect the ability of commercial banking to serve the needs of a growing economy.

Federal Fiscal Policy and the Commercial Banks

Fiscal policy embraces decisions relating to the size and character of expenditures and revenues of the federal government, and hence to the budget deficit or surplus that results for each fiscal period.

The Treasury administers but does not determine the outlays and receipts of the federal government. Congress has the ultimate say in fiscal policy formulation through its powers over appropriations and revenue legislation. Hence, responsibility for adopting fiscal policies that will help attain the nation's economic goals rests with Congress in the last analysis. The Treasury's role is to provide the administrative machinery for carrying out these policies.

The importance of fiscal policy arises from the magnitude of the sums collected and spent by the federal government. Federal tax collections amounted to more than one-fifth of the national income in 1959, and purchases of goods and services by the federal government accounted for some 11 percent of the gross national product. When adapted skillfully and vigorously to furthering the national goals of sustainable economic growth without inflation, fiscal policy not only complements monetary policy but greatly lessens dependence upon monetary measures to attain these goals. Conversely, if fiscal policy is inconsistent with monetary policy, much more drastic monetary measures become necessary to attain economic objectives, and the effectiveness of these measures is lessened.

Commercial banking is affected by the extent to which monetary policy complements fiscal policy far more than is any other segment of the economy. The reason for this is that monetary policy is applied primarily through the commercial banking system. Competing financial institutions,

by contrast, may find that a restrictive monetary policy actually acceler-
ates their growth. As credit restraint compels would-be borrowers to turn
from commercial banks to other sources of funds and to pay higher rates,
nonbank financial institutions are placed in a position to offer higher rates
of interest on savings and so to attract larger amounts of lendable funds.
Hence, while restrictive credit controls curb lending and investing by
commercial banks, they may tend to spur the growth of competing
financial institutions.

It is true that savings institutions tend to be discouraged from selling
Government securities at discounts in periods of credit restriction and
high interest rates, but this factor may be more than offset by the ability
to attract new funds in larger amounts when higher rates can be paid on
savings. In 1959, a year when a restrictive monetary policy was pursued,
savings and loan associations reported an increase in total savings held
of over 13 percent whereas total deposits in all commercial banks increased by less than 2 percent.

In fact, the sharp declines in prices of fixed interest obligations that
accompany credit restraint affect commercial banks considerably more
than other financial institutions. Because they feel the full impact of
restrictive credit measures, and because investment portfolios are in part
designed to provide a reservoir of funds to satisfy increased loan demands, commercial banks have to absorb far larger net security losses at
such times than do other classes of financial institutions.

The specific objective of a restrictive monetary policy is to curtail lending and investing by commercial banks through pressure upon the reserve
positions of member banks. If the federal government is spending more
than it takes in, monetary controls must be all the more severe. And because commercial banking alone feels the full and direct impact of credit
control measures, lack of coordination between monetary restraint and
fiscal policy tends to contract the role of commercial banking in the
nation's financial structure by checking its growth while stimulating the
expansion of such competing institutions as savings and loan associations.

The most extreme example of how a perverse fiscal policy affects
monetary policy was provided by the excess of cash payments over
receipts by the federal government of $13.1 billion in the fiscal year
1959, a period when the Federal Reserve authorities were resorting to an
increasingly restrictive credit policy. This was the largest peacetime
deficit ever incurred by the federal government.

There are elements of "built-in flexibility" in federal income and outgo,
it is true, with income tax receipts particularly sensitive to cyclical fluctuations in the economy. But effective coordination of fiscal with monetary
policy requires much more than deficits in recessions and approximate
balancing of the federal budget when an upsurge in business activity

and inflationary pressures threaten the stability of the economy. In booms, restraint in federal spending and substantial budget surpluses would act as a dampener on the economy and so make drastic monetary action much less necessary. Fiscal policy, like monetary policy, acts as a marginal factor influencing economic conditions. When these two marginal forces complement each other, both are much more effective.

Chart 19 illustrates how little fiscal policy contributed to fostering economic stability and keeping economic growth within sustainable rates during the decade of the 1950's. It will be noted how small surpluses were in boom years as compared with the deficits that accompanied and

CHART 19

FEDERAL BUDGET SURPLUSES (+) AND DEFICITS (-)
FISCAL YEARS 1950–59

(BILLIONS OF DOLLARS)

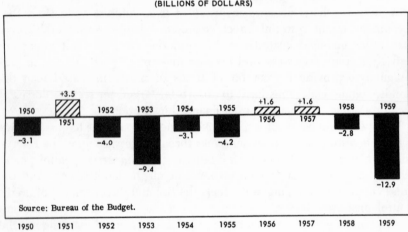

Source: Bureau of the Budget.

followed recessions. Therefore, resort to increasingly restrictive credit measures proved necessary in this period if unstable and inflationary booms, with their aftermaths of depression and widespread unemployment, were to be prevented. Chart 20 shows the rising trend in federal spending other than for security, international affairs, and debt service, which has hampered the use of fiscal policy as a countercyclical force. These charts are taken from the statement of The American Bankers Association before the Joint Economic Committee of Congress at its 1960 hearings on Employment, Growth, and Price Levels.

In recent years, many knowledgeable observers have called for increased use of fiscal policy and less reliance on "tight money" to restrain the economy in periods of excessive ebullience. The banking industry has strongly endorsed such coordination of fiscal with monetary policy, a stand

CHART 20

HOW FEDERAL SPENDING PROGRAMS GROW

EXPENDITURES OTHER THAN NATIONAL SECURITY, INTERNATIONAL
AFFAIRS AND DEBT SERVICE

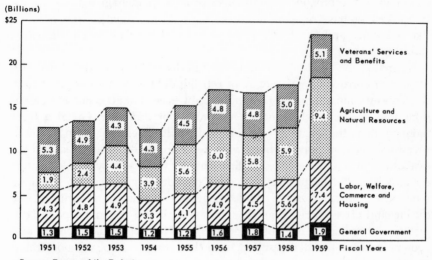

Source: Bureau of the Budget.

that is quite consistent with its unconditional and wholehearted support of the objectives of countercyclical credit policy.

Public Debt Management and the Commercial Banks

The Scope of Debt Management

Public debt management embraces all decisions relating to borrowing by the federal government.

When the public debt was relatively small in size and financing by the Treasury was infrequent, the Treasury could consider only its own convenience and requirements in managing the public debt and had little reason to take broader economic and financial consequences into account. The larger the size of the debt and the more frequent the Treasury's trips to the market, however, the more far-reaching have become the repercussions of debt management decisions upon the economy.

The federal debt today accounts for almost one-third of the gross public and private debt outstanding in the United States. Individual security offerings of the Treasury are frequently so large in size as to have a dominant effect for a time on money and capital markets. Ownership of public debt is widespread among financial institutions, businesses, and individuals. For all these reasons, debt management must now be conducted with constant awareness of its economic and financial repercussions.

Debt management decisions are made by the Treasury. The latter's immediate objective obviously must be to raise the funds required to meet the government's obligations. But the Treasury has become fully conscious of the broader consequences of its debt management decisions. Its spokesmen have repeatedly stated that debt management has become, like monetary and fiscal policy, an instrument for fostering sustainable, stable growth of the economy.

Normally, the Treasury has only limited discretion in its decisions with respect to borrowing new money or retiring debt. Given a budget deficit, the Treasury must increase the public debt even though economic conditions may make a net reduction of such debt desirable. Given a tight money policy, the Treasury will find it difficult to sell long-term bonds to investors because private borrowers tend to outbid the Treasury for available funds. Only when easy financing by the Treasury at a low interest cost is made the primary objective of monetary policy, as was done when the Federal Reserve Banks pegged Government security prices during and after World War II, are monetary and economic policy objectives subordinated to debt management. The large-scale inflation and economic instability that resulted from that episode amply demonstrated the disastrous results of subordinating economic goals to easy debt management.

The discretion of the Treasury in the management of the public debt is further limited by Congressional legislation affecting government borrowing. When interest rates rose in 1959, the Treasury found itself unable to sell long-term bonds because of the statutory 4¼ percent ceiling on interest rates of Treasury obligations with a maturity of five years or more.

Nevertheless, within the frequently rigid framework provided by fiscal and monetary policy and legislation affecting the public debt, the Treasury can, as experience has shown, make significant contributions to the attainment of the nation's economic objectives. By the same token, faulty debt management can have serious adverse consequences for the economy.

The Record of Debt Management, 1947-1959

The ultimate criterion for judging the record of debt management must be the extent to which it has contributed to attaining economic objectives. Yardsticks for applying this criterion are the distribution of the public debt and its maturity structure. The interest cost of the debt is a distinctly subordinate consideration by comparison with the impact of debt management decisions upon the economy.

In evaluating public debt management for the years 1947-59, the most significant development has been the relentless shortening of the maturity of the marketable debt, particularly during the first half of the period. This declined from almost eight years in 1947 to five years and eight months at the end of fiscal 1952 and to four years and seven months at the end of fiscal 1959.

Continued shortening of the marketable debt could greatly impede the contribution of debt management to our economic objectives. For one thing, the shorter the term of the debt, the more like money it is and the greater its inflationary potential. In addition, the larger and more frequent refundings that result from a debt of short maturity can greatly complicate the use of monetary policy in combatting an unsustainable, inflationary expansion. To be sure, however, a growing economy requires a substantial volume of highly liquid credit instruments for businesses, financial institutions, individuals, certain foreign investors, and governmental units. Thus a central problem of debt management is that of providing appropriate amounts of such instruments but avoiding an oversupply.

The contribution of debt management to economic stability during alternating periods of prosperity and recession is not clear. A countercyclical policy would call for sales of long-term securities in booms, in order to exert some restraining effect upon private investment, and sales of short-term obligations in recessions. Actually, until recently the Treasury has marketed a substantial portion of its intermediate- and long-term issues chiefly during recessions, when easy money and reduced loan demands facilitated such sales, and has had to rely almost entirely on short-term issues in periods of tight money and strong loan demand. However, the development of advance refunding as a major debt management technique promises to increase the potential use of countercyclical debt management in the future.

The sale of long-term Treasury issues in periods of tight money and intense competing demands for funds has been made far more difficult by advantages granted to other classes of borrowers. Interest on bonds issued by state and local governments is tax exempt. Corporate borrowers can deduct interest on their debt from taxable income, so that the net after-tax cost of borrowing is usually somewhat less than one-half the interest paid. Numerous borrowers on real estate obtain government insurance or guarantees on their mortgages, so that such loans come to be looked upon as comparable to government obligations by institutional lenders.

The lesson to be drawn from the 1947-59 experience is the need for wide latitude in balancing cyclical with long-run considerations in managing the maturity structure of the public debt. A rigid countercyclical approach has not proved practical.

Basic Principles of Debt Management

Commercial banks are a very important factor in public debt management. As the largest holders and underwriters of Government securities, the position of the banking system must be taken into account by the Treasury in formulating its financing decisions. Treasury financing, in turn, affects bank lending and investing decisions.

Because of their deep and constant involvement with Treasury financing, commercial bankers of necessity have given a great deal of thought and study to debt management problems. Moreover, they have had ample opportunity to observe the consequences of variations in debt management technique and policy as they were tried. In the light of experience over a long period, a large measure of agreement has developed among commercial bankers on basic principles and procedures that should govern debt management in the future. These can be summarized as follows:

1) The overriding objective of debt management must be to contribute to long-term economic growth without inflation, even at the expense of actions that could be called procyclical in the short run. When debt management seeks to attain a different objective, such as maintenance of a fixed level of interest rates for Government securities, it can seriously jeopardize or defeat attainment of these economic goals, as the pegging of Government security prices by the Federal Reserve Banks between 1941 and 1951 and the consequent inflationary push demonstrated. The chief instruments for fostering a sustainable rate of economic growth are monetary and fiscal policy. Debt management can make its greatest contribution to this end when all three policies are coordinated.

2) So far as practicable, the frequency and the size of Treasury financing operations should be minimized. Large-scale Treasury refundings at frequent intervals curtail the freedom of action of the Federal Reserve authorities. When the banking system is heavily involved in aiding Treasury financing operations, the Federal Reserve authorities have to move cautiously to avoid jeopardizing a Treasury refunding or cash offering. This may involve holding off a particular policy action or temporarily supplying more reserves to aid in the flotation of a new issue than would be called for if there were no Treasury financing operation. Subsequent absorption of the added reserves thus supplied may be difficult without producing undesirable repercussions on the money and securities markets, especially if the time period before another Treasury offering is relatively brief.

3) Treasury financing should to a considerable extent be placed on a routine, recurring basis, so that the several classes of investors know what

to expect and can plan their actions in advance with a minimum of uncertainty.

4) The Treasury should not be hampered by artificial and illogical
restrictions, such as the 4¼ percent interest rate ceiling on bond offerings,
which can prevent adaptation of debt management to the attainment of
the nation's economic goals.

5) Because at best the Treasury must repeatedly return to the market
with its security offerings, their terms should be fitted to the requirements
and preferences of the various classes of willing investors. Excessive
reliance on large-scale but short-lived speculative demands for Treasury
issues by those eager to sell for a quick profit results in disruption of the
market for Government securities and consequent difficulties for subsequent offerings.

Commercial Banks as Investors in U.S. Government Obligations

Commercial banks have continuously been the largest holders of
Treasury obligations since the end of World War II.

It is true that commercial bank holdings of U.S. Government securities
reached a peak of over $90 billion at the end of 1945 and were reduced by
over $20 billion in the following two years. But this reflected the fact
that the public debt, having been increased temporarily to $278 billion
by the sale of the Victory Loan in December 1945, was reduced by a
corresponding amount as most of the cash proceeds of that issue, not
required by the Treasury, were used to pay off short-term debt held
largely by commercial banks.

Since 1947, commercial bank holdings of Treasury issues have held
relatively stable, with fluctuations largely cyclical in character, and only
a very slight downward drift apparent. By contrast, life insurance companies and mutual savings banks have been heavy and persistent sellers
of Treasury issues (Chart 21). These sales have been made despite the
fact that assets of such institutions doubled between 1947 and 1959,
whereas commercial bank assets increased by little more than 50 percent.

Savings and loan associations, it may be noted, increased their holdings of Government securities from $1.7 billion to $4.4 billion between
1947 and 1959. But their total funds increased by $44.8 billion during this
period. Government obligations accounted for 7 percent of their assets at
the end of 1959—but 24 percent of the assets of commercial banks.

Role of Government Securities in Bank Portfolios

During the 1950's, the role of Government securities in bank portfolios
underwent a significant change.

In the depressed 1930's and the World War II period, Treasury obligations had a dual role in bank portfolios. First, they were a major source of

CHART 21

COMMERCIAL BANKS, LIFE INSURANCE COMPANIES AND MUTUAL SAVINGS BANKS' OWNERSHIP OF DIRECT AND FULLY GUARANTEED UNITED STATES GOVERNMENT SECURITIES, 1947–1959

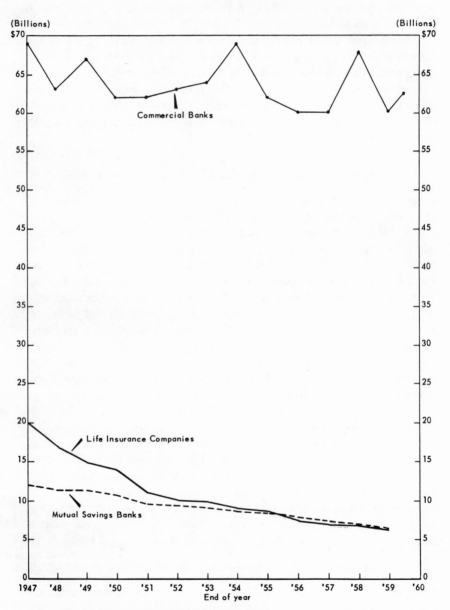

Source: Board of Governors of the Federal Reserve System.

364

liquidity. Secondly, they provided an outlet for surplus funds at a time when loan demand was limited.

As demands for funds from other classes of borrowers expanded in the postwar period, all classes of lenders were under pressure to procure more loanable funds by selling the Government securities they had acquired during the war. Commercial banks, because of the great stress they place on liquidity and because of their close relation with Treasury financing, were slow to sell Governments by comparison with life insurance companies and savings banks.

The easy money policies adopted to combat the recessions of 1949, 1954, and 1958 induced commercial banks to expand their Government security holdings at such times. Conversely, tight money periods like 1956-57 and 1959 witnessed liquidation of Treasury issues by commercial banks to obtain additional funds for loan expansion. Commercial bank holdings of Government securities since 1957 have fluctuated with changes in loan demands and availability of reserves—i.e., with business conditions and credit policies.

Although the provision of liquidity for general and cyclical needs has become the chief function of Government securities in commercial bank portfolios, and their earning asset role has become relatively less important, commercial banks have shown no marked tendency to shorten the average maturity of their portfolios of Treasury obligations. Between 1946 and 1959, the average maturity of the marketable interest-bearing debt of the Treasury declined from nearly eight years to four years and four months. But commercial bank portfolios have shown no corresponding shortening of average maturity. In fact, commercial bank holdings of Government obligations with a maturity of five years or more are about equal to those of a decade ago. Changes in the maturity pattern of commercial bank holdings of U.S. Government issues is compared with that of all holders of these obligations on Chart 22. The desire to maintain income from this large segment of the banks' assets, especially when yields on short-term debt are headed downward, has caused the banks to make strong efforts to keep up the maturity range of their portfolios in the face of the decline in the average maturity of the whole public debt. This attitude of the commercial banks has been and will be of considerable assistance to the Treasury in future efforts to improve the maturity structure of its debt.

The Future Role of Banks As Investors in Treasury Securities

The recent record of commercial bank investing in Government securities reflects a marked preference for retention of their large portfolio of Government securities. However, the combination of a strong loan demand and a credit policy of active restraint does put great pressure on the banks to reduce their holdings, so that U.S. Government obligations

CHART 22

MATURITY DISTRIBUTION OF UNITED STATES GOVERNMENT MARKETABLE AND CONVERTIBLE SECURITIES
HELD BY ALL HOLDERS AND COMMERCIAL BANKS
1953–1959

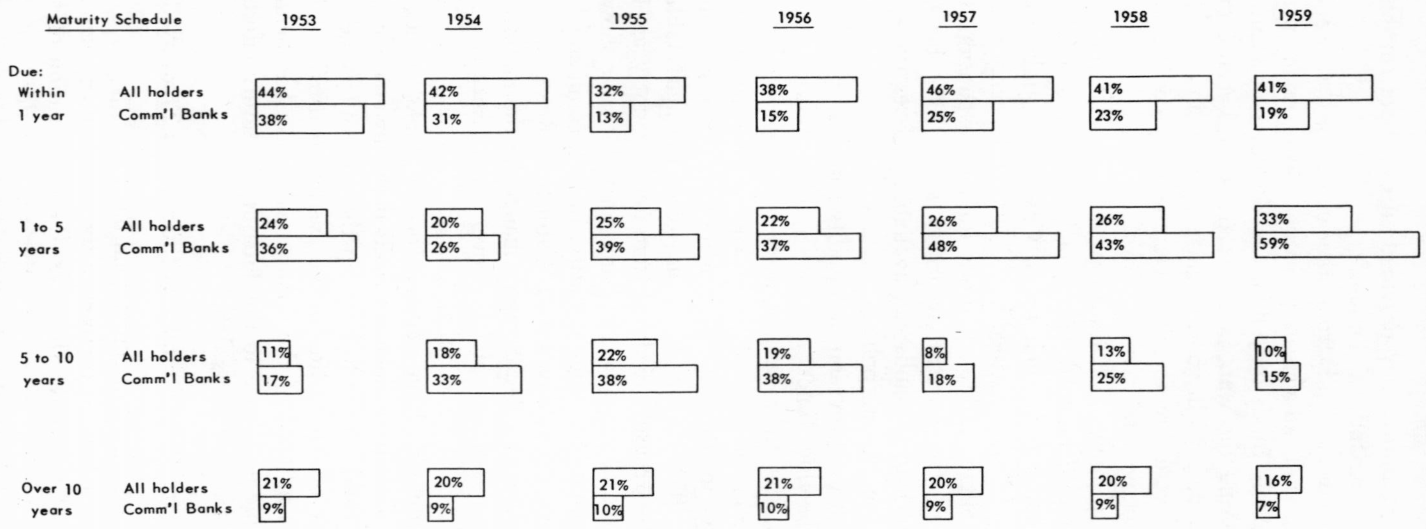

Maturity Schedule		1953	1954	1955	1956	1957	1958	1959
Due:								
Within 1 year	All holders	44%	42%	32%	38%	46%	41%	41%
	Comm'l Banks	38%	31%	13%	15%	25%	23%	19%
1 to 5 years	All holders	24%	20%	25%	22%	26%	26%	33%
	Comm'l Banks	36%	26%	39%	37%	48%	43%	59%
5 to 10 years	All holders	11%	18%	22%	19%	8%	13%	10%
	Comm'l Banks	17%	33%	38%	38%	18%	25%	15%
Over 10 years	All holders	21%	20%	21%	21%	20%	20%	16%
	Comm'l Banks	9%	9%	10%	10%	9%	9%	7%

Source: Board of Governors of the Federal Reserve System and Treasury Department.

held by commercial banks did dip temporarily at the end of June 1960 to about $55 billion, the lowest level reported since the early 1940's.

Two factors are likely to govern the future trend of commercial bank holdings of U.S. Government securities. One will be the degree to which credit restraint is applied by the Federal Reserve authorities. This will reflect chiefly the rate of growth of the economy and the degree to which fiscal and debt management policies are coordinated with monetary policy to lessen the burden upon the latter to keep growth at sustainable levels.

The second factor will be the extent to which equality of opportunity is restored in institutional competition to attract deposit-type savings. If commercial banks are permitted to regain their former share of the increase in such savings, they can be expected to increase their holdings of Government securities, including longer-term issues.

While the degree of credit restraint and the trend of their savings deposits are the chief long-term influences that will affect commercial banks' holdings of Government securities, they will in any case be active net buyers in periods of recession and credit ease such as 1954 and 1958. At such times, Government securities become a readily available outlet for the investment of surplus funds and a store of liquidity for the next cyclical upturn in loan demand, whenever it takes place. In recessions, commercial banks not only provide a needed market for Treasury security offerings to finance the deficits that such periods produce, but also contribute to a countercyclical expansion of the money supply that contributes to the attainment of the national economic goal of maintaining employment opportunities and a high rate of sustainable economic growth.

Commercial banks can be counted upon to add to their holdings of Government securities in recessions as well as other emergencies. They can be expected to expand their Treasury security portfolios over the long run too, unless drastic credit control measures and artificial handicaps on their ability to compete for savings deposits prevent this.

Commercial Bank Underwriting of Treasury Issues

Commercial banks perform a massive underwriting function for the Treasury. The record of changes in commercial bank ownership of U.S. Government securities since World War II does not reflect the magnitude or importance of this function. Even with little change in their total Treasury security holdings, initial purchases of new Treasury issues by commercial banks far exceed the amount of such underwriting done by any other investor group.

During the period from February 15, 1953 to July 15, 1960, when the

Government securities markets were free, over $250 billion of new issues were awarded the public on subscriptions to marketable security issues (other than weekly and some special Treasury bill offerings often largely taken by commercial banks).[1] Commercial banks were allotted over $165 billion of the total amount taken by the public. The ratio allotted commercial banks was almost 90 percent for cash offerings, 53 percent for those issued in exchange for outstanding securities, and more than 65 percent over-all. On special Treasury bill and certificate offerings involving payment by credit to tax and loan accounts, amounts taken by commercial banks are often nearly 100 percent of total awards.

In part, the commercial banks' role as number one underwriter of Treasury issues hinges upon their role as the number one owner of Treasury issues. As outstanding issues which are held in large amounts by banks mature, the need for heavy bank subscriptions to refunding issues is apparent. If the new issues are realistically priced and fall within the desired maturity range for bank ownership, heavy bank purchasing is almost automatic in periods of easy money and is quite substantial during periods of tighter money as well. In tight money periods, in fact, commercial banks will be by far the largest subscribers to some cash offerings where payment through Treasury tax and loan account credits is permitted. Even for cash offerings where payment is not permitted through tax and loan account, commercial banks are large initial subscribers, often for the bulk of the issue.

In sum, the Treasury's chief market for new issues—regardless of ease or tightness of money or the level of interest rates prevailing, regardless of whether the offering has been a refunding or a cash offering, regardless of whether cash payment or payment through tax and loan account has been involved, and almost regardless of whether long-term bonds (even outside the "bank range") or Treasury bills have been offered—has been the commercial banks of the nation.

Nor does this fact, significant as it is, tell the whole story of the commercial banks' part in Treasury financing. While all Treasury issues present problems to the debt managers, from time to time there are offerings that are particularly difficult to consummate. In recent years, these have usually occurred during tight money periods when, because of inadequate adaptation of fiscal policy to prevailing economic conditions or the incidence of debt maturities, the Treasury has had to seek new funds or roll over a large volume of maturity debt in the face of heavy private credit demands. At such times the Treasury has relied heavily on the commercial banks for underwriting support, not only by

---

[1] Excluding securities issued to U.S. Government investment accounts and the Federal Reserve Banks.

offering short-term securities that have particular appeal for the banks but also by specifying that payment for the issues could be made through credit to the Treasury's tax and loan account at the banks.

Role of Tax and Loan Account Credits

The use of the Treasury's tax and loan account to effect payment for its new issues provides an enormous underwriting potential for Treasury offerings, since banks have an added reason to bid for these issues to obtain tax and loan deposits. Payment for such issues purchased by commercial banks involves in the first instance only the amount of fractional reserves required against the increased deposits in the Treasury's tax and loan account. These deposits are then drawn down over a period of time, as needed by the Treasury to replenish its accounts with the Federal Reserve Banks.

This payment procedure is quite advantageous for the conduct of credit policy, since it prevents new Treasury offerings that may reach several billion dollars in size from having a commensurate impact on bank reserve positions, as would occur if payment were made directly to the Treasury's account at the Federal Reserve Banks. The Treasury and the economy thus benefit through the initial distribution of large blocks of Government securities with relatively little impact on the money market and credit conditions. But the Treasury benefits also from the higher prices it obtains and the assurance of large-scale bank subscriptions, because commercial banks actively bid for tax and loan accounts by subscribing to and paying higher prices for new issues in order to obtain the advantages inherent in the tax and loan procedure.

The Federal Reserve Bank of New York in its *Monthly Review* of April 1958 described the role of the Tax and Loan Account in facilitating Treasury financing as follows:

> Payment with credits to the Tax and Loan Accounts results in the subscribing banks serving for a time as "underwriters" and distributors for the Treasury. The banks who calculate correctly are likely to find that they are compensated for their service as "underwriters" of the new issue, while the Treasury is able to keep for itself, by borrowing below the market rate, a considerable portion of the possible earnings value of the Tax and Loan Account credits to the banks.

In its *Report on Treasury Tax and Loan Accounts* issued June 15, 1960, the Treasury stated:

> Experience has clearly shown that, in cases where banks are permitted to make payment in the form of a deposit credit in their Tax and Loan Account for the purchase price of securities sold on a competitive auction basis, the rates of interest paid by the Treasury on such securities are less than otherwise would be paid if the funds did not clear through the account.

The benefit accruing to commercial banks from this payment procedure depends upon the size of the premium over prevailing market prices that banks pay for a new offering because of the value of the privilege of payment by credit to Tax and Loan Accounts, and upon conditions in the secondary market at the time the securities purchased are later redistributed by the banks. Business corporations and other investors benefit to the extent that they are able to purchase the securities from banks at lower prices and higher yields than if they had bid for new issues directly. Commercial banks thus share the value of the tax and loan deposit with the Treasury and with purchasers of the issue in the secondary market. Where the loss incurred by the bank on the resale of the Treasury securities exceeds the value of payment through the tax and loan credits, the bank incurs a net loss on the transaction.

Upon announcement of a Treasury offering with payment permitted through credit to Tax and Loan Accounts, the banks calculate the value of the privilege. This involves estimating the average period of time that is likely to elapse before the newly created Treasury deposits are withdrawn from the commercial banks.

At times in the past, Treasury officials have indicated to the market an estimated average life for tax and loan deposits resulting from a new Treasury offering. These estimates have usually been used by commercial banks in determining the value of the additional tax and loan deposits, and thus in setting the bidding range for the new issue. On occasion, the Treasury has overestimated the length of the tax and loan carry and has been subjected to criticism for this by the market. There are also expert private sources in the Government securities market that make independent estimates of the average life of such accounts, and their estimates receive wide publicity among banks. These estimates often prove precarious, however, since they involve a projection of the Treasury's future cash receipts and expenditures on a daily basis. Although some seasonal and intra-monthly receipts and expenditure patterns are well defined, the sheer size of federal cash transactions and the vast number of accounts involved can result in sizable Treasury cash balance swings that are sufficient to cause substantial variation from the estimates in the average life of tax and loan deposits.

The banks use the estimated average life of the tax and loan deposit as the key to their calculation of the value of the privilege to them. This value will also depend upon the reserve requirement classification of the bank and upon the cost of funds to the bank from other sources—particularly the Federal Reserve discount rate in periods of tight money. Given these factors, it is possible to calculate the dollar value of the privilege, and from that the basis point value per million dollars of participation in the new Treasury offering. This calculation shows the break-even yield point at which banks could sell the issue and still recover cost, after allowing a credit for the tax and loan balance for the period held.

Each bank participating in an auction sale of a Treasury offering in which payment is permitted through tax and loan credits must go through this estimating process, including the estimate of the approximate yield at which it will be possible to sell the issue in the secondary market if it is not held to maturity. Once these estimates have been made, the bank can determine the approximate price at which it will be willing to bid for the new issue.

The privilege of tax and loan payment has also been offered by the Treasury on some coupon issues, thus eliminating the bidding problem but leaving the other calculation problems for banks.

Banks in a tight reserve position are inclined to bid more aggressively for securities available through the tax and loan credits. Securities obtained by such banks tend to be sold promptly after the auction results are made known, with the result that prices decline to such a degree that the value of the privilege is quickly dissipated. In any event, swings in the market for Treasury issues will decide whether the banks realize a profit or loss on their underwriting function after allowing for the value of the privilege of payment through tax and loan deposit accounts.

Commercial bank experience with participations in new Treasury issues over the years has been favorable on balance, considering the value to some banks of expanding lendable funds by this method in periods of tight money. As a result, the procedure has served as a reliable underwriting vehicle for the Treasury. Some secondary market pressure on short-term Treasury securities develops at times when banks attempt to liquidate their purchases of a new issue within a short time. Usually such pressure is well absorbed and market processes remain orderly. In any case, the degree of market pressure is less than it would have been without broad bank participation in the underwriting, since bank selling will tend to taper off as prices in the market decline. This underwriting device has thus proved, under varying conditions, both effective and economical for the Treasury.

The trend toward a shortening of the maturity distribution of the public debt has required more frequent and extensive use by the Treasury of the underwriting assistance provided by commercial banks and so has enhanced the value of the tax and loan account technique as a means of assuring broad bank interest in the underwriting of Government security offerings.

Banking Services for the United States Treasury

Commercial banks perform a number of other essential services for the Treasury. The most important, from the viewpoint of the economy, is to prevent the huge and varying payments to and by the Treasury from causing wide and erratic fluctuations in Treasury deposits in the Federal Reserve Banks, and hence in member bank reserves and credit conditions. "To prevent the irregular ebb and flow of Government funds from interfering with the smooth and effective functioning of the nation's payments mechanism, it has been necessary to develop a set of techniques especially adapted to minimizing the strains and dislocations of drawing money from the commercial banks, in which it is held, into the Federal Reserve Banks, and later disbursing it." [2]

Evolved out of the War Loan Accounts first authorized in 1917, in which payments for Liberty bonds bought by banks and their customers were deposited, the present system of Tax and Loan Accounts was so named in 1950. More than 11,000 commercial banks now act as Special Depositaries holding Tax and Loan Accounts to which proceeds of new security sales, receipts of withheld income taxes, payroll taxes, large income tax payments, and certain excise tax payments are credited. The Treasury is thus in a position to replenish its working balances at the Federal Reserve Banks as frequently as needed, by calling in funds from the Tax and Loan Accounts.

Describing this system, the Treasury has said:

> The Tax and Loan Account System permits the Treasury to leave funds in the banks and in the communities in which they arise until such time as the Treasury needs the funds for its operations. In this way the Treasury achieves a balancing effect not obtainable by any other known device, and thus discharges its primary fiscal responsibility of so handling its money as not to affect the economy unduly.[3]

Added flexibility in the conduct of the Tax and Loan Account System is provided through the Special Depositary banks. Withdrawals usually are made only once or twice a month from the Group A banks that have less than $150,000 in Tax and Loan Accounts. Much more frequent withdrawals are made from Group B banks holding more than $150,000, but such banks with $500 million or more in total deposits (designated as Class C) may be called upon at any time for immediate transfers of funds from Tax and War Loan Accounts to the Treasury's account at the Federal Reserve Banks, or calls on them may be canceled or reduced on short notice.

During 1958, deposits in Treasury Tax and Loan Accounts aggregated $57,177 million, and withdrawals totaled $56,793 million. Daily balances in these accounts for all banks varied from $8,869 million to $1,103 million, and averaged $3,660 million. With withdrawal notices outstand-

---

[2] Federal Reserve Bank of New York, *Monthly Review* (April 1958).

[3] Treasury Department, *Report on Treasury Tax and Loan Accounts, Services Rendered by Banks for the Federal Government and Other Related Matters*, 1960, p. 2.

ing against these accounts deducted, net balances were often less than $1 billion.

Banking Services

There are eight major services rendered the Treasury by the banks. The volume of transactions involved in the rendering of these services for 1958, according to the Treasury Department Report of June 15, 1960, on this subject, can be seen in Table 13-1.

TABLE 13-1
Volume of Transactions Handled by Banking Institutions

Services to Treasury	Number of Items Handled	Amounts (Millions)
Total	311,192,184	- - - -
1. Savings bonds issued	50,174,243	$ 2,619
2. Savings bonds paid	81,257,726	4,328
3. Handling subscriptions to securities	352,860	84,690
4. Handling matured notes, bonds, etc.	800,000	72,000
5. Handling matured coupons	11,774,546	- - - -
6. Cashing Government checks	150,000,000	- - - -
7. Handling depositary receipts	7,822,495	27,617
8. Reporting large or unusual currency transactions	10,314	- - - -

Other services that banks perform for the Treasury listed in the Treasury study are:

1) Promotion of new Treasury offerings and refundings.
2) Submission of information returns to the Internal Revenue Service.
3) Submission of reports relating to liabilities to foreigners, claims on foreigners, and purchase and sale of long-term securities by foreigners.
4) Work involved in processing letters of credit under programs sponsored by ICA, CCC, and other Government agencies, which work is in addition to that normally involved in letter of credit transactions.
5) Furnishing information to agents of the Secret Service, FBI, and other Government agencies.
6) Keeping records and filing reports in connection with Treasury Foreign Funds Control Operations.
7) Acting as agents for the sale of Federal transfer tax stamps.
8) Maintaining lists of "Designated Nations" and related work.
9) Safekeeping of short-term Government securities for purchasers without charge.
10) Forgery losses on savings bonds and government checks cashed.

11) Counseling the general public relative to savings bonds and U.S. marketable securities.

12) Reissuance of savings bonds due to death, change of ownership, etc.

13) Handling transactions through the Treasury Tax and Loan Account.

Bank Expenses and Earnings

The services described above are furnished the Treasury without charge, with minor exceptions, even though part or even all of the time of some bank employees may be required to perform this work. Only for a few services such as redemptions of savings bonds and servicing of Commodity Credit Corporation crop loans, because they involve risk of loss to the banks in addition to expense, are nominal fees charged. The banks must look to earnings on the Tax and Loan Account balances for reimbursement of their costs in rendering these services.

At the suggestion of the Comptroller General of the United States, the Treasury undertook a study in 1959 to determine whether balances in Tax and Loan Accounts produced income to the banks in excess of the cost of the services provided for the federal government. Data from a representative group of banks for the year 1958 indicated that the banks incurred expenses aggregating nearly $58 million in rendering services for the federal government, while estimated earnings on Tax and Loan Account balances totaled over $52.5 million. The study thus indicated an excess of expenses over earnings of $5 million.[4]

The value of the Treasury of the services performed by the banks does not include the higher prices received from banks for new security issues because payment can be made with credits to Tax and Loan Accounts.

The Treasury study demonstrated that the commercial banking system provides the services required by the Treasury at a cost to the banks that exceeds the earnings derived from Tax and Loan Account balances. Any net advantage to the banks must be found in the customer and correspondent relationships that may result from furnishing these services, but mainly in the contribution to the stability of the money markets and credit conditions that benefits banks along with all other segments of the economy.

As the United States Government encounters new needs for services and technical assistance, the commercial banks have proved on repeated occasions that they are ready and able to cooperate actively in solving these problems. The availability of the trained personnel and the specialized facilities of the banks constitute an invaluable asset to the Treas-

---

[4] *Ibid.*, p. 30.

ury in tackling the great tasks which necessarily face the financial arm of the Federal Government. Cooperation between the Treasury and the commercial banks has had very fruitful results for the nation in the past, and there is every reason to expect that the future consequences will be equally constructive for the American economy.

Chapter 14

COMMERCIAL BANKS' RELATIONS
WITH FINANCIAL AUTHORITIES

The Role of Commercial Bankers in Policy Formulation

At least since the time of Robert Morris, whose Bank of North America aided in the financing of the Revolutionary War, bankers have played a major role in counseling, guiding, and influencing the financial affairs of government at all levels. Over the years, banking, currency, and credit reforms—as well as the legislation that provided two Banks of the United States prior to the establishment of the Federal Reserve System in 1913 —have been to a large extent based upon recommendations made by bankers and financiers.

Like his historical counterpart, the modern commercial banker has no formal authority in the formulation of broad national financial policy but, instead, has functioned primarily in an advisory and counseling capacity. Unofficially, bankers have submitted recommendations on proposed legislation and have suggested personnel qualified to administer such laws. Moreover, national, regional, and state banking organizations have often opposed legislation deemed ill-conceived or detrimental. Such proposed legislation has frequently resulted from popular agitation for reform growing out of malfunctioning of the credit system—particularly during money panics—and has sometimes involved repressive features, including hindrances to entry and expansion.

At present, the two most important governmental financial bodies, the Treasury and the Board of Governors of the Federal Reserve System, are advised by groups of bankers—the former by the Government Borrowing Committee of The American Bankers Association and the latter by the Federal Advisory Council. These bodies are discussed in detail below.

In recent years, the great world conferences convened to solve international monetary problems have also been largely manned by bankers, because these men have had the practical experience needed to understand the subtle and complex relationships involved. In addition, bankers have been requested to help solve the difficult economic and financial problems that have confronted many countries in the aftermath of World War II.

In short, bankers have been called upon individually to advise, counsel, and in some instances even to administer agencies at all levels, from the local school board in a rural area to the Treasury of the United States.

Modern banking is a far more complex business than it was thirty or forty years ago. In the not too distant past, most bankers concerned themselves mainly with the affairs of their own communities. They worried about the butcher, the farmer, the local seed merchant, the flow of bullion in and out of their clearing house, and the anticipated volume of exchange items. Modern technology has rendered such intellectual and business isolation an impossibility. If present-day bankers are to be helpful with advice and counsel, they must be well versed in central banking and monetary theory, credit control techniques, taxation, debt management problems, and international gold movements. This responsibility has been and continues to be a stimulating challenge. And yet the vital role of money and banking in the economy is not yet fully understood. One of the nation's critical requirements is the application of its ablest minds to the mastery and institution of sound, creative banking techniques.

Relations with the United States Treasury

Of necessity, the relationship between commercial bankers and the Treasury has been one of mutual consultation. Unlike many European fiscal agencies, the United States Treasury has never completely controlled and operated a commercial bank of its own.[1] Fewer than 10 percent of the secretaries of the Treasury have been commercial bankers. Since 1921, fewer than one-fourth of the undersecretaries of the Treasury have been commercial bankers, and since 1889 fewer than 15 percent of the assistant secretaries of the Treasury had served as commercial bankers prior to their appointment. Because proper execution of federal fiscal responsibilities requires a stable currency, a reliable source of credit in times of emergency, the ready availability of soundly managed depositories to house tax receipts, and conveniently located disbursement agencies—all of which can be provided only through the commercial banking system—Treasury officials have repeatedly sought the advice, counsel, and cooperation of commercial bankers.

---

[1] The two Banks of the United States were primarily privately owned. The Federal Reserve Banks are owned (but not controlled) by their members and do not customarily engage in commercial banking practices.

A review of the financing of the two World Wars and of the assistance provided by the commercial banks, both in actual financing and with advice, will be helpful in understanding the present relationship between the Treasury and the banks.

Financing Two World Wars

When the United States entered World War I, funds were needed for our own war effort and for assisting our allies. Heavy borrowing was necessary in addition to higher taxes. The general public was not familiar with government bonds, and flotation of the Liberty Bonds was accompanied by a vast educational program. Banks and bankers played a vital role in providing the machinery for the distribution of the bonds and the salesmanship to induce investors to acquire and hold them. In addition, the banks provided a continuous source of short-term credit throughout the war period.

A major concern during the war was the rationing of credit to essential industries. In September 1917 a committee of New York bankers developed a voluntary plan to stabilize stock market credit. Early the following year the Federal Reserve Board created a Capital Issues Committee to restrict new security issues to essential uses. This committee, composed of three members of the Board and four commercial bankers, had no official power to prohibit new security issues; but, with the cooperation of the banks, its decisions were effective.

In May 1918 the functions of the Capital Issues Committee of the Federal Reserve Board were taken over by the War Finance Corporation. This agency was created to advance credit to war industries; its membership consisted of the Chairman of the Board of Governors and three others, two of whom were commercial bankers. The War Finance Corporation and the Capital Issues Committee formed the precedent for a comparable advisory body during the Second World War.

The Second World War brought with it financing problems similar to but on a far larger scale than those faced during World War I. Again it was determined that a major portion of the cost of the war should be financed through debt rather than taxes. The commercial banks made a double contribution to the war effort—they increased their own holdings of Government obligations by about $70 billion (325 percent) and they contributed to the successful sale of over $40 billion of savings bonds and other obligations to the public.

In 1942, the Secretary of the Treasury, Henry Morgenthau, suggested the formation of a committee to facilitate the War Loan Drives of the Treasury and to coordinate the participation of the commercial banks. W. L. Hemingway, then President of the Mercantile Commerce Bank and Trust Company of St. Louis and President of The American Bankers Association, appointed twenty bankers to a Committee on Treasury War

Borrowing. The Committee held itself available to the Secretary of the Treasury, whose needs determined the frequency of its meetings. The Secretary, over the years, has solicited the opinions of the Committee about public debt management in general, and in particular about financing operations for raising cash or refunding maturing issues.

The Committee on Government Borrowing

The giant debt resulting primarily from the length and magnitude of the war and the awesome problems of management related to it encouraged the continuation of cooperation between the Treasury and the banks. At the close of the war the Committee was renamed the Committee on Government Borrowing and it now functions in an advisory capacity to the Treasury Department.

Consultation between the Treasury Department and the commercial bankers has contributed significantly to sound, efficient management of the public debt, and thus has aided the Secretary of the Treasury in discharging one of his most important responsibilities. The bankers concerned have provided the Secretary with evaluations of current money market conditions and with informed opinions on rates and maturities. Recommendations of the Committee on Government Borrowing to the Secretary of the Treasury during the period 1952-59 were summarized recently to a Congressional Committee.[2]

The Secretary of the Treasury, as the chief financial officer of the largest fiscal enterprise in the world, must obtain expert evaluation of the money market when he is obliged to seek funds in that market. To do less would be to invite serious criticism of his procedures.

The commercial bankers of the nation are one source of accurate information on market conditions.[3] It was the desire of the Treasury to obtain such information that led to the organization of the Committee on Government Borrowing of The American Bankers Association. The

---

[2] *Employment, Growth, and Price Levels.* Report (No. 1043) of the Joint Economic Committee, Congress of the United States, January 26, 1960.

[3] Other groups which meet with the Treasury from time to time to discuss various debt management problems include:

(a) Investment Bankers Association, Governmental Securities Committee;

(b) National Association of Mutual Savings Banks, Committee on Governmental Securities and the Public Debt;

(c) American Life Convention and Life Insurance Association of America, Joint Committee on Economic Policy;

(d) U.S. Savings and Loan League and National Savings and Loan Association, Joint Committee on Government Securities;

(e) Independent Bankers Association, Government Fiscal Policy Committee.

For a complete description of these advisory groups, see Hearings before the Joint Economic Committee, Congress of the United States, on *Employment, Growth and Price Levels,* Part 6 c, "The Government's Management of its Monetary, Fiscal and Debt Operations," pp. 1746-52.

advisory role of commercial bankers in regard to the Treasury's choice of security issues also creates a sense of responsible loyalty and partnership on the part of bankers towards proposed financing operations.

As noted earlier, some criticism has been leveled against this procedure. It has been charged that the Treasury follows "self-seeking" advice offered by the financial community. The assumption underlying this charge is that the financial community can control conditions in the money market. While commercial bankers in the aggregate have a large investment in U.S. Government obligations, the levels of interest rates and bond prices reflect demand conditions over which bankers have no control and supply conditions in which bankers have only a part—a part which is largely determined by Federal Reserve policy rather than their own discretion. The substantial losses in the bond accounts of most banks in the United States in many recent years hardly suggest that bankers control or greatly influence the bond market. Obviously, control of a market is not implied for one to be able to evaluate the forces in it and to make an accurate appraisal of it. It is this evaluation and appraisal that the Treasury has sought, and that bankers have provided to the best of their ability.

Other committees of The American Bankers Association that cooperate with the Treasury are the Savings Bond Committee and the Committee on Federal Fiscal Procedures.

Summary

Today this nation is confronted with financial problems which may prove even more difficult to resolve than those of the past. The government is currently faced with the management of the largest public debt the world has ever known, and its full implications and consequences may not be wholly comprehended. The problem of maintaining a stable dollar in the world money market is one of great importance. Balance of payments and gold movement problems will have to be solved.

Cooperation between the Treasury and the commercial banks can do much to help evolve constructive solutions to these critical problems.

Relations with the Federal Reserve System

The Federal Reserve System is a central banking authority unlike any other in the world. It is a product of the peculiar historical evolution of banking in the United States and reflects the long-standing traditions of regional representation and freedom from excessive political domination. It constitutes an effective compromise between solicitude for financial and economic stability on the one hand and encouragement of privately formed and managed banks on the other.

About 6,100 commercial banks, or 46 percent of the total in the United

States, are members of the Federal Reserve System. These include all national banks and those state banks which desire to join the System and can meet the membership requirements. Member banks are entitled to certain privileges such as the use of various Federal Reserve facilities, the ability to borrow from the Federal Reserve Banks under certain conditions, the right to participate in the election of two-thirds of the directors of their Federal Reserve Banks, and a 6 percent dividend on their investment in capital stock of the Federal Reserve Banks. In turn, members undertake to abide by the laws and regulations governing the System. Nonmember banks may also be permitted to use certain of the System's facilities.

The commercial banks thus have close relationships with their local Federal Reserve Banks. They also have indirect but nonetheless important relationships with two other agencies of the Federal Reserve System, the Board of Governors, and the Federal Advisory Council.

The Federal Reserve Banks

There are twelve Federal Reserve Banks, of which ten have branches. Although the member commercial banks in the various districts hold stock in their respective Reserve Banks, the member banks do not control the Reserve Banks, which are operated in the public interest. The member bank shareholders receive a fixed 6 percent dividend on the par value of their holdings. Most of the remaining earnings are disbursed to the Treasury, only a small percentage of the earnings since World War II having been retained to build up surplus.

Each Federal Reserve Bank has nine directors. Three, including the chairman of the board, are appointed by the Board of Governors. The remaining six are elected by the member banks of the district. Only three of the nine may be officers, directors, or employees of any bank. Other directors must be actively engaged in commerce, agriculture, or industry. The president of each Federal Reserve Bank is the chief executive officer and is elected by his directors subject to the approval of the Board of Governors.

Unlike central banks in some countries, the Reserve Banks do not conduct a commercial banking business. Although legislation during the 1930's authorized the System to make working capital loans to businesses in exceptional circumstances, this prerogative has seldom been exercised. The decision has been a wise one. The noncompetitive role of regional Reserve Banks enables them to enlist greater cooperation and support in solving the broad credit problems with which they are primarily concerned.

The relations between each Federal Reserve Bank and the commercial banks of its district have proved of very great value in implementing credit policy and banking regulation. There is a two-way flow of information and counsel that has greatly enhanced the ability of both the System and the commercial banks to serve the requirements of business, agriculture, and individuals in each Federal Reserve district.

The Board of Governors

Bank legislation during the 1930's vested control over the credit policies of the Federal Reserve System more completely in the Federal Reserve Board (renamed in 1936 the Board of Governors of the Federal Reserve System).[4] In effect, such legislation increased centralization and, to a degree, moved the locus of power away from the regional Reserve Bank presidents.[5]

Because of the sensitive position which the Board of Governors occupies in the nation's financial system, it is of paramount importance that it be free of political domination and its members be well versed by training or experience in banking and finance. "This does not mean that the Board need be composed solely of men drawn from banking and finance, but rather that its members be persons who understand the problems of money, credit and finance and who, by virtue of such knowledge, are fitted to serve the public interest." [6]

The Federal Advisory Council

The Federal Advisory Council consists of twelve bankers, one from each of the Federal Reserve Districts, who are chosen by the Boards of Directors of the twelve Reserve Banks. The role of the Council is to reflect the views of the banking community and bring them to the attention of the Board of Governors.

Meetings of the Federal Advisory Council, to quote from the Act, "shall be held at Washington, District of Columbia, at least four times a year and oftener if called by the Board of Governors of the Federal Reserve System. The Council may, in addition to the meetings above provided for, hold such other meetings as it may deem necessary." The Council selects its own officers and adopts its own methods of procedure, with a majority of the members of the Council constituting a quorum for the transaction of business.

The Federal Advisory Council is empowered: (1) to confer directly with the Board of Governors on general business conditions; (2) to make oral or written representations concerning matters within the jurisdiction of said Board; and (3) to call for information and to make recommendations in regard to discount rates, rediscount business, note issues, reserve

---

[4] G. L. Bach, *Federal Reserve Policy-Making* (New York: Alfred A. Knopf, Inc., 1950), p. 14.

[5] *Ibid.*, p. 14.

[6] Study by New York Clearing House Association, "The Federal Reserve Re-examined," 1953, p. 138.

conditions in the various districts, the purchase and sale of gold or securities by Reserve Banks, open-market operations, and the general affairs of the reserve banking system.

On occasion in the past, the President of the Federal Advisory Council and various members have testified before Congressional Committees on behalf of the Council. In other situations, the Council has adopted resolutions on current matters and has forwarded them to appropriate persons and/or Congressional Committees.

The work of the Federal Advisory Council, especially during periods of emergency, has been of proven value to the Board of Governors. During World War II, for example, in addition to the scheduled quarterly meetings of the Federal Advisory Council, the Executive Committee of the Council met with the Board at nearly regular monthly intervals.

Both by original intent and design and by virtue of a membership which by and large has been composed of able and experienced bankers, the Federal Advisory Council has been able to furnish the Board with useful suggestions and advice on matters relating to the banking system. The Council channels to the Board an evaluation of regional and national conditions. The individual Council member, in addition to a wide knowledge of businessmen's expectations, has direct personal knowledge of the economic situation in his district that may not yet be reflected in statistics because of the time required to collect, compile, and publish them. In addition, the Council provides the Board with a "sounding board" for its ideas and proposals. At the same time, the Council's recommendations frequently have provided leadership in securing general acceptance by the banking community of Board policies.

Summary

The relationship between the commercial banks and the Federal Reserve System has undergone a great change since 1913. At the time of the passage of the Act, opposition and fears were common. Today, the relationship could best be described as one of friendly cooperation. In view of the fate of early central bank experiments, it is important to the preservation of the present system that this relationship of friendly cooperation be preserved.

Throughout American economic history, there has been a recurring conflict between the general yearning for monetary stability and an overeagerness on the part of many for credit expansion during times of prosperity. Over the past decade, an increasing outcry against "tight money" has been raised by some legislators and by particular segments of the economy. Credit institutions—such as savings and loan associations and credit unions—which are not subject to direct influence by the monetary authorities have expanded very rapidly and so are increasing their relative importance in the financial system. In many quarters, the judgment of the monetary authorities has been attacked. That these trends are fraught with danger is indicated by earlier central banking history in this country. They could lead, in the absence of measures to assure the continued effectiveness of the existing machinery, to developments in our financial system that would undermine and weaken credit control to a point where drastic changes in central banking machinery would be advocated.

Relations with Supervisory Authorities

The banking department of each of the fifty states, as well as the office of the Comptroller of the Currency, the Federal Reserve System, and the Federal Deposit Insurance Corporation, have regulatory authority over the management and operation of commercial banks subject to their jurisdiction. While an individual bank's relationship with its supervisory authorities may vary over a period of time, in the aggregate a satisfactory, cooperative relationship exists. Since regulations and supervisory authorities restrict the freedom of management, bankers naturally find them irksome at times. However, because the state legislatures and the Congress have decided that certain regulations are in the public interest, bankers have governed themselves accordingly, accepting the guideposts and benchmarks established by the regulatory authorities in discharging their official responsibilities. Although some regulations (to be discussed elsewhere in this monograph) appear to be unduly restrictive, regulation and supervision have, by and large, added strength and stability to the banking system.

The First Attempts at Regulation

The evolution of bank supervision has been a slow process, attaining its present status only during the past thirty years. The same pattern has been evident as in regulation of business generally: excesses by the few have resulted in restrictions and regulations for the entire group. Abuses by a minority have often led to over-compensation, and thus to over-regulation of the industry.

The Present System of Supervisory Authority

The office of the Comptroller of the Currency now has general authority over the organization, expansion, operation, and liquidation of national banks, with power to suggest remedial legislation. The Comptroller may also act as referee between conflicting banking interests. All of these functions militate against too close a relationship between supervisor and supervised. On the other hand, frequent consultation between bankers and the Comptroller is necessary in order that he may perform his duties effectively in proposing new legislation and in administrative interpretation of banking law. Such consultation must by its nature be advisory at most, for decisions can be made only by the Comptroller. Although an occasional dispute has risen between the Comptroller and directors of banks, the historic relationship has been cooperative and productive of improving service to the communities in which the banks operate.

State banks are examined and generally supervised by the Federal Reserve Banks (for member banks) or the Federal Deposit Insurance Corporation (for nonmember insured banks), in addition, of course, to the state banking departments.

Deposit insurance had long been discussed and advocated before the Federal Deposit Insurance Corporation was created in 1934. The New York Safety Fund established in the 1850's was the first experiment, and the possibility of such insurance was much discussed at the time of the establishment of the Federal Reserve System. The numerous bank failures of the twenties and early thirties brought these plans and discussions to a climax which led ultimately to the creation of the FDIC.

The American Bankers Association opposed the idea at the time, contending that in effect well-run banks would be taxed to keep inefficient banks solvent, and that this could encourage careless banking practices on the part of those bankers who saw the FDIC as a sure protection against bank runs. It stressed the point that deposit insurance was not a solution to the basic weaknesses in the banking system. The force of these arguments caused the FDIC to insist on certain operational standards for its members and to institute an inspection and reporting system that met a number of these objections to the original proposal.

Summary

Banking is one of the most highly regulated industries in the United States. Some controls have been and are oppressive, usually because they were adopted without a clear understanding of the basic role of commercial banks in the economic development of this country. The most extreme historic example of this was the constitutional prohibition of banks by several Midwestern and Western states until late in the nineteenth century.[7] In these instances, banking was carried on by private individuals, corporations set up in neighboring states, and a few national banks. As knowledge and skill among bankers have developed and as understanding has increased among bankers, bank supervisors, and the public, these repressive measures have tended to be eliminated.

---

[7] Banking was prohibited in Texas from 1845 to 1904, except for the period 1869 to 1876, during which a carpet-bag constitution permitted it. In Iowa it was prohibited from 1846 to 1857 and in Arkansas from 1846 to 1864. In California it was prohibited from 1849 to 1879 and in Oregon from 1857 until about 1880. In Illinois prohibition failed by one vote in the constitutional convention.

A dynamic and growing economy demands a dynamic, growing banking system. To enable the commercial banking system to adjust to new and developing needs and innovations in industry and commerce, the supervisory authorities regulating the banking system must be cognizant of these developments and adjust their regulations and controls accordingly. The present system of three federal and fifty state supervisory authorities is necessarily cumbersome in its attempts to adjust to changing methods of bank operation. However, a remarkable degree of cooperation between the several authorities, arising from their singleness of purpose in maintaining a sound banking system, has reduced overlap and produced a substantial degree of uniformity and effectiveness in supervisory policy.

Other Forms of Assistance in Policy Formulation

Individual Banker Activity

In recent years the United States has witnessed a growing number of privately financed and Congressional inquiries into various aspects of the nation's economy. In almost every case the knowledge and experience of commercial bankers have been tapped. An obvious recent example is the study by the Commission on Money and Credit for which this monograph on commercial banking has been prepared.

An example of Congressional inquiry was the questionnaire on the Financial Condition of the United States submitted early in 1958 by Senator Harry F. Byrd, Chairman of the Senate Committee on Finance, to a number of prominent citizens, including several bankers.[8]

Another was the inquiry conducted in the early fall of 1959 by the Joint Economic Committee, under the Chairmanship of Senator Paul Douglas.[9] Commercial bankers who actively underwrite, trade, and otherwise deal in U.S. Government securities answered questionnaires and The American Bankers Association submitted a statement on behalf of its membership.

Naturally, not every suggestion advanced by bankers has won acceptance—particularly on the state level where local conditions and traditions play a large part—but banker participation in legislative inquiries has often helped to produce sound remedial laws or to prevent short-sighted, punitive measures from being enacted.

Individual bankers also have served the government with distinction in official capacities, as cabinet officers or as members of executive or

---

[8] Committee on Finance, United States Senate, "Investigation of the Financial Condition of the United States," 1958, Chapters 1-6.

[9] Hearings before Joint Economic Committee, Congress of the United States, on *Employment, Growth and Price Levels,* Part 6 c, "The Government's Management of its Monetary, Fiscal and Debt Operations," pp. 1821-1976.

legislative staffs, and as consultants to various committees and/or departments. It goes without saying that these men have not acted as bankers, but as financial specialists, and in many instances were separated from their institutions permanently or for a designated period of time while serving in these capacities.

The Role of Bankers' Associations

The peculiar organization of the commercial banking function in this country, which finds no parallel in any other large industrialized nation, is reflected in the large number of banks—over 13,400, varying greatly in size, character, and service, and divided under our dual banking system into state and national banks. A further peculiar characteristic of our commercial banking system is the large measure of both formal and informal regulation to which it is subject by federal and state laws and by the regulatory and supervisory agencies. These two fundamental factors, the number of separate independent corporations engaged in the banking business and their close regulation, generate—or perhaps, more accurately, require—a high degree of communication within the industry and between the industry and the legislators and administrators engaged in the formulation of financial policies and the development and execution of applicable law and regulation. Without effective and continuing communication between the regulators and the regulated institutions—whether on a formal or informal basis—practical and efficient administration of the law and compliance therewith by the industry would prove difficult indeed.

A substantial percentage of our commercial banking institutions understandably rely on informal advice and guidance from supervisory and regulatory authorities in assuring their compliance with the mass of highly detailed and complex law and regulation. This body of law and regulation is overlaid with exception on exception, and yet may not—indeed often does not—suit the frequently unique local conditions or circumstances of institutions or transactions. Thus practical adaptation and constructive tailoring of law and regulation are constantly required. Even large institutions, having the benefit of internal law departments or the services of retained outside counsel, require a substantial and continuing measure of consultation with the regulatory banking agencies.

There are, of course, occasional instances where limitations of law or the interpretation or application thereof or the attitudes of the supervisory or regulatory authority lead to frictions between regulator and regulated and to conflicts between and among supervisory and regulatory authorities as to the administration or the adequacy of the laws and regulations.

In addition, commercial banking is also subject to much of the body of law which affects business corporations generally, with respect to taxes, competition, labor, hours of work, and a host of other subjects—federal and state—too numerous to list here. Administrative and compliance problems generated by the actual or potential application of these laws similarly necessitate formal or informal interchange of views between the lawmaker and the administrator on the one hand, and the affected institution on the other. These considerations account for the breadth and depth of the relationships between government and banking in the development and administration of statutory and regulatory policy.

This relationship reaches from local to state to federal levels. It is expressed in individual, institutional, and associational terms. Anyone who has served in a bank supervisory agency will have seen supporting evidence in the form of the constant flow of individual, institutional, and associational communications with regard to the purpose and effect of banking law and regulation on the conduct of the banking business. Without such communication, the efficient operation of the machinery of the law in this very complex and technical field would be impeded.

Common difficulties and common objectives, all seeking solution or fulfillment as the case may be, quite naturally lead to the pursuit of common action. This normal instinct has begotten numerous forms of association of bankers organized and operated according to function, geography, or interest, sometimes unifying and sometimes divisive with respect to the industry as a whole.

Communication between such associations and the regulatory or supervisory authorities relates not merely to questions of bank administration, operation and examination as well as technical interpretation and application of the laws, but also to questions of the need for revision of regulation or of statute.

A brief discussion of the purposes and activities of several of these organizations and the relationships which they have with various governmental agencies follows.

The American Bankers Association. The ABA was formed in 1875, both to give broader consideration by banking to the currency problem after the Civil War and to resolve sectional, functional, and other differences which had long plagued the banking industry. The Association soon broadened its sphere of activity to include expressing the viewpoint of bankers before legislative and regulatory bodies. In the first years of its existence, the ABA formed temporary committees to support bills which it favored. By the early 1900's, however, the Association found itself so absorbed in the legislative process that permanent committees were felt necessary to replace the temporary ones.

The Committee on Federal Legislation was established in 1905 to analyze bills affecting banking submitted in the House of Representatives and the Senate. It is the responsibility of this committee to analyze all

Congressional bills as to their effects upon the banking industry, and to support or oppose them accordingly. This is done through appearances as witnesses before the Congressional committees concerned or through special staff assistance to the committees.

One of the ABA's most recent and intensive legislative efforts concerned the proposed Financial Institutions Act in 1957. A special advisory committee composed primarily of bankers was appointed to study this bill and report to the Senate Committee on Banking and Currency. The American Bankers Association and a number of individual bankers and other bank associations and individual bankers testified on this bill.

On a broader front, the Economic Policy Commission of The American Bankers Association has taken every suitable opportunity to urge the adoption of policies and measures to make credit control an effective instrument for fostering sustainable economic growth without inflation. The objective of the Commission has been expressed as follows:

> Bankers are vitally concerned with maintaining and strengthening a flexible monetary policy and helping to preserve the independence of the Federal Reserve System. We are concerned with these problems both from the standpoint of the welfare of banking and also from the standpoint of the welfare of the economy as a whole.[10]

The ABA also has a Committee on State Legislation which reviews the multitude of state laws passed each year which have an effect on banking. This committee has long recognized the fact that each state faces problems peculiar to its own economy. It has concerned itself chiefly with those matters on which uniform banking laws are feasible.

Other committees of The American Bankers Association have standing or sporadic relationships with Federal supervisory or regulatory agencies. The Committee on Government Borrowing has been mentioned previously. The National Bank Division has a continuing relationship with the Comptroller's office relative to problems in their area. The State Bank Division, too, has a relationship with the Comptroller but is more concerned with the Federal Deposit Insurance Corporation, the Federal Reserve System, and the various state banking authorities.

State Bank Associations. The fifty state bank associations have often presented their viewpoints before state legislatures and state supervisory agencies. To present the views of bankers in their states, spokesmen for state bankers associations have often traveled to Washington to testify on Congressional bills which would have repercussions on banking in their states.

The Association of Reserve City Bankers. The Association of Reserve

---

[10] Economic Policy Commission, The American Bankers Association, "An Appraisal of Monetary Policy," report to the 1954 Annual Convention.

City Bankers, as its name indicates, is made up of bankers from the reserve cities across the country. It was organized in 1912 in an attempt to solve some of the problems associated with correspondent banking. As its members are also members of the ABA, the Reserve City Bankers seldom take an active stand on legislative matters. However, when the two groups are at variance on a particular issue the Reserve City Bankers have not hesitated to take a vigorous stand.

During the early 1930's, when Congress was studying banking reform, the Association was often called upon for advice and counsel. Again during the war, Congress and the federal supervisory agencies consulted with the Reserve City Bankers on proposed changes in banking policy.

The National Association of Bank Auditors and Comptrollers. This association is more restricted in its scope than are those previously mentioned, but it has played an important role in increasing the efficiency and strength of the entire banking system by seeking improved methods of accounting, auditing, control and administration. The principal regulatory body with which NABAC has had a relationship is the FDIC, which is understandable considering the community of interest. The FDIC regarded the *NABAC Manual on Bank Accounting, Auditing and Operation* as so valuable from its viewpoint in maintaining a sound banking system that it financed and distributed to all banks the first printing of the manual in 1943. A reprint of this manual was distributed to all banks by the FDIC in 1951. The FDIC will suggest to banks it regards as unsoundly managed that they counsel with NABAC to obtain a knowledge of more proper procedures of bank management.

Other Associations. The Association of Registered Bank Holding Companies was organized after the adoption of the Bank Holding Company Act of 1956, which concluded a struggle of some years' duration over the adoption and character of Federal Bank Holding Company legislation. One of the purposes of this organization is to increase public understanding of holding company banking generally. Another is the consideration of legislative, regulatory and other developments affecting bank holding companies, and the maintenance of a clearing house of information for the benefit of the members.

For many years, too, there has existed in this country an organization known as the Independent Bankers Association, whose primary interest has been to preserve unit banking. Its efforts have therefore been directed toward combatting branch banking and holding company banking throughout the country at any and all levels of government.

In addition, there are other special purpose banking associations which have varying degrees of relationship with authorities formulating financial policies. The National Association of Supervisors of State Banks, and the Robert Morris Associates are two of the more important of these associations.

Cooperation with Legislatures. These organizations on the whole serve a generally common purpose of benefit to their members in assisting in the formulation of financial policies of a legislative, monetary, fiscal, or other character. To this end, these organizations receive constructive cooperation from the state legislatures, Congress, and federal and state bank supervisory and regulatory agencies. Such cooperation is clearly in the public interest.

In the formulation of financial policies, the banking industry has for many decades maintained a close and continuing relationship with state legislatures and Congress. While it would be difficult to discuss this aspect of industry participation in the formulation of statutory financial policy in each of the states because of their number, the relationship between the industry and Congress will be discussed briefly. Through the years, Congress (particularly its committees having primary jurisdiction over banking) has solicited the technical and policy views of the industry in the development of legislation in this field. Participation of the industry in this process is evidenced by the numerous appearances of representatives before committees of Congress on a great variety of matters, both domestic and international. In addition, consultation on an individual basis between industry representatives and members of Congress has long marked a common concern in the enactment of sound banking, fiscal, and monetary laws.

An important recent illustration of such cooperation was the advisory committee of professors, bankers, and representatives of other financial institutions appointed by the Senate Banking and Currency Committee in connection with the proposed broad-scale revision of the Federal laws affecting private financial institutions. This Committee was officially known as "The Advisory Committee for the Study of Federal Statutes Governing Financial Institutions and Credit." Working under the aegis of the Senate Banking and Currency Committee and in close cooperation with Federal bank supervisory authorities, this Committee took a leading role in the development of a proposed general recasting of these laws.

It is a tribute to Congress that such cooperation has been developed. This process provides the best assurance of the continuing development of progressive banking laws based on discussion and understanding of the facts and issues involved.

How Banker Service in Policy Formulation Can Be Improved

Increased understanding is the key to any improvement in relations between bankers and the authorities involved in policy formulation. This would require, among other things, greater knowledge on the part of more bankers of the functions, objectives, and operation of the Treasury Department, the Federal Reserve System, and other agencies of government. Equally important is the need for more understanding on the part of the authorities concerning the functions and responsibilities of commercial banks in our economy.

There are times, such as periods of monetary restraint, when bankers are obliged to reappraise their procedures and the economic climate in which they operate, and then possibly to modify their operations. The more bankers understand monetary policy and the role of the commercial banks in implementing policy and in achieving its objectives, the more intelligent will be the banker's decisions and the more rational his behavior.

Understanding of monetary policy objectives and techniques has been greatly fostered by the several schools of banking that have been established across the nation. A collateral benefit of these schools is the opportunity for bankers to meet officials from policy agencies who teach at the schools. Attendance at these schools of many bank examiners and other representatives of supervisory agencies fosters exchange of ideas and viewpoints between them and commercial bankers.

Research in the area of monetary and banking policies, carried on or sponsored by banking organizations, has provided bankers and the public with deeper insight into trends and issues. Publications such as the six Monetary Studies of The American Bankers Association, published in 1954, make generally available the results of such research.

Leaders in banking recognize that more needs to be done if monetary and fiscal policy, debt management, and economic stabilization are to be fully understood by the whole banking community. This involves knowledge not only of these complex subjects, but of their relation to commercial banking. For the future, bankers will also require greater knowledge of how commercial banking is affected by changes in the United States balance of payments, gold movements, and interest rate changes in the leading commercial nations of the world.

The banker's service of advice and counsel in these critical areas can only be as fruitful as the understanding he has of them. The commercial banking industry strives to spread such understanding among its members through the many agencies it has developed for this purpose.

COMMISSION ON MONEY AND CREDIT

Members

Frazar B. Wilde, CHAIRMAN
Chairman, Connecticut General Life Insurance Company

H. Christian Sonne, VICE CHAIRMAN
New York, New York

Adolf A. Berle, Jr.
New York, New York
(Withdrew to serve as Chairman of the U.S. State Department Latin American Task Force.)

James B. Black
Chairman of the Board, Pacific Gas & Electric Company

Joseph M. Dodge
Chairman of the Board, The Detroit Bank and Trust Company
(Resigned October 7, 1960.)

Marriner S. Eccles
Chairman of the Board, First Security Corporation

Lamar Fleming, Jr.
Chairman of the Board, Anderson, Clayton & Co.

Henry H. Fowler
Fowler, Leva, Hawes & Symington
(Resigned February 3, 1961, on his appointment as Under Secretary of the Treasury.)

Gaylord A. Freeman, Jr.
Vice Chairman, The First National Bank of Chicago
(Appointed April 29, 1960.)

Fred T. Greene
President, Federal Home Loan Bank of Indianapolis
(Died March 17, 1961.)

Philip M. Klutznick
Park Forest, Illinois
(Resigned February 8, 1961, on his appointment as United States Representative to the Economic and Social Council of the United Nations.)

Fred Lazarus, Jr.
Chairman of the Board, Federated Department Stores, Inc.

Isador Lubin
Arthur T. Vanderbilt Professor of Public Affairs, Rutgers University

J. Irwin Miller
Chairman of the Board, Cummins Engine Company

Robert R. Nathan
President, Robert R. Nathan Associates, Inc.

Emil Rieve
President Emeritus, Textile Workers of America, AFL-CIO
(Appointed May 19, 1960.)

David Rockefeller
President, The Chase Manhattan Bank

Beardsley Ruml
New York, New York
(Died April 18, 1960.)

Stanley H. Ruttenberg
Director, Department of Research, AFL-CIO

Charles Sawyer
Taft, Stettinius & Hollister

William F. Schnitzler
Secretary-Treasurer, AFL-CIO
(Resigned April 28, 1960.)

Commission on Money and Credit 395

Earl B. Schwulst
*President and Chairman of the Board,
The Bowery Savings Bank*

Charles B. Shuman
President, American Farm Bureau Federation

Jesse W. Tapp
*Chairman of the Board,
Bank of America, N.T. and S.A.*

J. Cameron Thomson
*Retired Chairman of the Board,
Northwest Bancorporation*

Willard L. Thorp
*Director, Merrill Center for Economics,
Amherst College*

Theodore O. Yntema
*Chairman, Finance Committee,
Ford Motor Company*

Advisory Board

Lester V. Chandler
Professor of Economics, Princeton University

Gerhard Colm
Chief Economist, National Planning Association

Gaylord A. Freeman, Jr.
*Vice Chairman, The First National Bank
of Chicago*
(Resigned April 29, 1960, on his appointment to the Commission.)

Leo Grebler
*Professor of Business Administration,
University of California (Los Angeles)*

Raymond W. Goldsmith
Professor of Economics, Yale University

Neil H. Jacoby
*Dean, School of Business Administration,
University of California (Los Angeles)*

Richard A. Musgrave
*Woodrow Wilson School of Public and
International Affairs, Princeton University*

Richard E. Neustadt
Professor of Public Law and Government, Columbia University

Paul A. Samuelson
*Professor of Economics, Massachusetts
Institute of Technology*

Sumner H. Slichter
*Lamont University Professor, Harvard
University*
(Died September 27, 1959.)

Edward S. Shaw
Professor of Economics, Stanford University

Alan H. Temple
New York, New York

Jacob Viner
Professor of Economics, Emeritus, Princeton University

Staff

Bertrand Fox
Research Director

Eli Shapiro
Deputy Research Director